The Cold War and After

PRINCETON STUDIES IN INTERNATIONAL HISTORY AND POLITICS

Series Editors

G. John Ikenberry, Thomas J. Christensen, and Marc Trachtenberg

Recent Titles

The Cold War and After: History, Theory, and the Logic of International Politics by Marc Trachtenberg

America's Mission: The United States and the Worldwide Struggle for Democracy (Expanded Edition) by Tony Smith

Liberal Leviathan: The Origins, Crisis, and Transformation of the American World Order by G. John Ikenberry

Worse Than a Monolith: Alliance Politics and Problems of Coercive Diplomacy in Asia by Thomas J. Christensen

Politics and Strategy: Partisan Ambition and American Statecraft by Peter Trubowitz

The Clash of Ideas in World Politics: Transnational Networks, States, and Regime Change, 1510–2010 by John M. Owen IV

How Enemies Become Friends: The Sources of Stable Peace by Charles A. Kupchan

1989: The Struggle to Create Post–Cold War Europe by Mary Elise Sarotte

The Struggle for Power in Early Modern Europe: Religious Conflict, Dynastic Empires, and International Change by Daniel H. Nexon

Strong Borders, Secure Nation: Cooperation and Conflict in China's Territorial Disputes by M. Taylor Fravel

The Sino-Soviet Split: Cold War in the Communist World by Lorenz M.Lthi

Nuclear Logics: Contrasting Paths in East Asia and the Middle East by Etel Solingen

Social States: China in International Institutions, 1980–2000 by Alastair Iain Johnston

Appeasing Bankers: Financial Caution on the Road to War by Jonathan Kirshner

The Politics of Secularism in International Relations by Elizabeth Shakman Hurd

Unanswered Threats: Political Constraints on the Balance of Power by Randall L. Schweller

Producing Security: Multinational Corporations, Globalization, and the Changing Calculus of Conflict by Stephen G. Brooks

The Cold War and After

History, Theory, and the Logic of International Politics

Marc Trachtenberg

PRINCETON UNIVERSITY PRESS

PRINCETON AND OXFORD

Published by Princeton University Press, 41 William Street, Princeton, New Jersey 08540
In the United Kingdom: Princeton University Press, 6 Oxford Street, Woodstock,
Oxfordshire OX20 1TW
press.princeton.edu

Library of Congress Cataloging-in-Publication Data

Trachtenberg, Marc, 1946–
  The Cold War and after : history, theory, and the logic of international politics / Marc
Trachtenberg.
    p. cm. — (Princeton studies in international history and politics)
  Includes bibliographical references and index.
    ISBN 978-0-691-15202-8 (hardcover : alk. paper) — ISBN 978-0-691-15203-5
(pbk. : alk. paper) 1. Cold War. 2. World politics—1945–1989. 3. World
politics—1989– 4. World politics—Philosophy. I. Title.
  D840.T73 2012
  327.1—dc23   2011039303

British Library Cataloging-in-Publication Data is available

This book has been composed in Palatino

Printed on acid-free paper. ∞

Printed in the United States of America

10 9 8 7 6 5 4 3 2 1

Contents

Preface   vii

PART I: *Theory*   1

CHAPTER One
The Question of Realism: An Historian's View   3

CHAPTER Two
The Problem of International Order and How to Think about It   44

PART II: *History*   67

CHAPTER Three
The United States and Eastern Europe in 1945: A Reassessment   69

CHAPTER Four
America, Europe, and German Rearmament, August–
September 1950: A Critique of a Myth   110

CHAPTER Five
The Making of the Western Defense System: France, the
United States, and MC 48   142

CHAPTER Six
The Structure of Great Power Politics, 1963–75   154

CHAPTER Seven
The French Factor in U.S. Foreign Policy during the
Nixon-Pompidou Period   183

PART III: *Policy*   245

CHAPTER Eight
Preventive War and U.S. Foreign Policy   247

CHAPTER Nine
The Iraq Crisis and the Future of the Western Alliance   281

Index   313

Preface

I FIRST BECAME interested in international politics almost half a century ago, during my freshman year in college at Berkeley in 1963. From the start I knew that this was the field I wanted to go into, and in fact I have spent practically my whole life working in this area; my particular focus has been the history of great power politics in the twentieth century. One of my main goals at this point in my life is to pass on what I have learned over the years about how historical work in this area can be done, especially to people just starting out in this field. To that end I recently published a book on historical method called *The Craft of International History*. But although I tried there to be as concrete as I could, it seemed to me that I could do more to show how in practice an historian interested in this area of scholarship could proceed.

If I had to sum up in a single sentence what I have learned over the years about how historical work on international politics should be done, it would be this: the key to doing meaningful work in this area is to find some way to get conceptual and empirical issues to link up with each other. I don't think it makes sense to approach the core issues that this field is concerned with—above all, the great problem of war and peace—on a purely abstract level. That sort of theorizing, to my mind, cannot in itself take you very far. On the other hand, a purely empirical approach is also fairly sterile. There is not much point to simply accumulating a lot of facts. You need some way to figure out what they mean, and to do that you need to bring a kind of conceptual framework to bear—if only to generate the questions the empirical evidence can help answer. But general points of this sort are in themselves rather anemic. Their meaning sinks in only when you see how historical work that takes those principles as its point of departure can actually be done.

The basic aim of this book is therefore to show through example how to go about doing that kind of work. Only one of the articles included here (chapter 2) is directly concerned with issues of method, but all the articles, in one way or another, show how that fundamental approach works in practice. The first chapter, for example, on the question of realism, shows how the sort of understanding that takes shape in your mind as you grapple with historical problems can be brought to bear on core theoretical issues—on fundamental questions about what makes for war or for a stable international system. It was written as a kind of reaction to what I had found in the international relations literature. It seemed to me that the claim I found there about how the international system worked—about how the competition for power was the fundamental source of conflict—was simply wrong. Over the years, thinking about particular historical episodes, I had reached very different conclusions about power politics and the causes of war. Those conclusions could be made explicit; there was a certain value, I thought, in showing directly how the historical analysis related to the specific claims that the theorists made.

But it is not just that historical study can have a real impact on your understanding of how international politics works. The connection works the other way as well: grappling with conceptual problems can have an enormous impact on how you do historical work. The goal of historical analysis, after all, is not simply to recount what happened. The aim is to go beneath the surface and try to bring out the logic underlying the course of events. In working out that logic, you have to draw on your whole understanding of why states behave the way they do and why they sometimes go to war with each other. This is not because theory in itself can give you the answers. A theoretical framework can never replace detailed historical analysis. But bringing a theoretical perspective to bear helps you see what is puzzling in the episode you are studying and thus gives you some sense for the specific questions you need to focus on.

The third chapter, on American policy toward eastern Europe in 1945, is a good case in point. This chapter might look like straight history and you might think that theory plays no role there at all. And yet the original article would not have been written if I had not found the coming of the Cold War so puzzling. American power and Soviet power, it seemed, balanced each other so completely that both sides were locked into the status quo; but if that were the case, where was the problem? Why wasn't the status quo of a divided Europe perfectly stable from the very start? That whole way of looking at things was obviously grounded in a certain sense for how international politics works—for how power realities shape policy. That conceptual framework in itself, of course, could not explain the coming of the Cold War. If anything, it "explained" something that did not happen in the immediate postwar period: a U.S.-Soviet accommodation based on a joint acceptance of the status quo.

But this sort of thinking helps you see what the questions are. Were both sides, you wonder, simply incapable of thinking in power political terms? Was it out of the question that they could agree to an arrangement based on a common acceptance of a divided Europe? Were the Americans, in particular, never willing to accept a Soviet-dominated eastern Europe, no matter what the Soviets were willing to give in return? Approaching the problem in this way allows you to see things you might otherwise be unable to see—the importance, for example, of Secretary of State Byrnes's references to the Polish precedent at the September 1945 Council of Foreign Ministers meeting, and of the way eastern Europe and Japan were tied together in the U.S.-Soviet negotiations at the end of the year.

And this kind of approach makes sense not just when you are trying to deal with a relatively narrow historical problem like U.S. policy toward eastern Europe in 1945. It is of even greater value, I think, when you are tackling a much broader subject. In the paper on the 1963–75 period, for example—chapter 6 in this book—my goal was to focus on fundamentals. What did each side want? What were their core interests? What, if anything, were they willing to go to war over? Certain assumptions of a theoretical nature, about what states really do care about, play a key role when you are trying to get a handle on this kind of problem. The western powers, you assume, had to be concerned with the growth of Soviet military power; they had to be concerned with how the USSR could be kept at bay when the American nuclear deterrent was becoming increasingly hollow, and when the most exposed European ally, West Germany, was unable to build a nuclear deterrent of her own. That in turn brings a whole series of questions into focus: how, in the military sphere, did the western powers propose to deal with this problem? How was that situation related to what was going on in the political sphere? Was there a real risk, for example, that western Europe in general, and West Germany in particular, would become "Finlandized"? Is the German Ostpolitik of the Willy Brandt period to be understood essentially in that context—that is, as an example of "Finlandization" in action? And what are we to make of Soviet policy in this period? How is the Soviet military buildup to be explained if the USSR's basic political goal was the stabilization of the status quo in Europe?

The paper itself does not try to answer questions of this sort in any definitive way. It is essentially a rough cut, an attempt not only to sketch out the structure of great power politics during the middle period of the Cold War, but also to give some sense for the structure of the historical problem here—the problem of making sense of what was going on during that period. My aim when I wrote it was to show how a major problem of historical interpretation—whether there was a real risk of war during this period, or whether great power politics was fundamentally stable—could be broken down into its component parts. The way those big issues are dealt with will then depend on how relatively narrow and relatively concrete questions are answered; as you deal with those specific historical problems in this general context, you automatically deepen your understanding of what was happening in the period as a whole.

So a general analysis, like the one included here in chapter 6, can take you only so far. At some point you have to switch gears and do more detailed historical work—never entirely losing sight, of course, of the general historical problem you are concerned with. In the case of the article on the 1963–75 period, the whole question of relations between the United States and its European allies looms large, and you can get some insight into that basic issue by looking at one important bilateral relationship. That is the connection between chapter 6 and chapter 7, the paper on the Franco-American relationship during the Nixon-Pompidou period. A detailed study of this sort can give you a feel for the texture of U.S.-European relations during that period; but it is ultimately just a brushstroke—just one of a whole series of studies you need to do to get to the bottom of this general historical problem.

The main issues I was concerned with in those two papers—U.S.-European relations and military issues, especially issues relating to nuclear weapons—have long been of interest to me, and a number of the other articles in the book deal with those questions: the paper I did with Christopher Gehrz on the German rearmament question in 1950 (chapter 4), the piece on MC 48 (chapter 5), the article on "Preventive War and U.S. Foreign Policy" (chapter 8), and the paper on the Iraq Crisis of 2003 (chapter 9). One of the great questions that anyone interested in the post–1945 period has to be concerned with has to do with how international politics works in a nuclear world, and in particular with how seriously the risk of war in such a world is to be taken, and historical analysis can certainly shed some light on those issues. This implies that the conclusions you reach in studying particular historical episodes can have a certain bearing on how you think about key policy issues today, most notably nuclear proliferation.

History, in fact, can serve as a kind of workshop within which basic views about core policy issues get hammered out. When you are trying to deal with those issues, it helps if you can think about them in concrete historical contexts. It is much easier to wrap your mind around a specific problem than to think about the general issue on a purely abstract level. And indeed when you are doing history, and you are trying to figure out why events took the course they did, you have to put yourself in the shoes of the people you are studying and ask yourself what choices were available to them. When you do that, it is hard not to ask yourself what you would have done if you had to make those choices. As I say in chapter 2 here, there is not much of a jump from thinking about what *could* have been done to what *should* have been done, and that sort of thinking almost automatically produces various general conclusions about how policy ought to be conducted. And conversely, thinking about policy issues helps you see which historical episodes you might want to study and which questions you might want to put at the heart of that historical analysis. Thinking about policy issues, in other words, can help bring historical work into focus—it can help you draw meaning from the work you do.

What all this means is that the three parts of the field—history, policy, and theory—are deeply interconnected, more tightly bound up with each other than I would have been prepared to admit when I was first starting out in this business in the 1960s. If your goal is a peaceful world, you have to concern yourself with fundamental conceptual problems, and above all with the problem of what makes for a stable international order. If your goal is to avoid war, you have to concern yourself with the basic theoretical issue of what makes for war. And there is no way to get at that kind of issue without looking at specific wars, albeit with a mind that has been prepared by grappling with the core conceptual problems that define this field of inquiry.

Years ago I thought that history had to be understood exclusively on its own terms—that the goal of historical research was simply to see the past, to use Ranke's famous phrase, as it really was. At that time, international relations theory was of little interest to me. I could not see how it gave you any insight that you could not get directly from doing ordinary historical work. I thought that an interest in policy issues, even when those concerns were just in the back of your mind and did not show up directly in the historical work you produced, was vaguely improper—that it was somehow illegitimate to make history speak to those issues, that a concern with policy tainted the scholarly enterprise, and that a real scholar should not pay attention to questions of that sort. Today my views on those fundamental questions of method, of how work on international politics ought to be done, are very different. I think that history, policy, and theory can be made to relate to each other in an intellectually respectable way, and indeed the basic rationale for publishing this collection of articles as a book is to show how I think this can be done.

PART I

Theory

CHAPTER ONE

The Question of Realism: An Historian's View

DIFFERENT COUNTRIES WANT different things; sometimes those desires conflict; how then do those conflicts get worked out? The basic insight that lies at the heart of the realist approach to international politics is that the way those conflicts run their course is heavily conditioned by power realities. In a world where war cannot be ruled out if conflicts are not settled peacefully, rational states are bound to be concerned with the structure of power in the sense not just of the distribution of military capabilities both actual and potential, but also of the whole web of relationships that would affect what would happen if war actually broke out. But rational states not only *adjust* their policies to such power realities. If the structure of power is of such fundamental importance, it stands to reason that states might well try to *alter* it to their advantage. That striving for power political advantage in turn might well come to dominate the system. The fact that states live in an anarchic system—that is, a system not governed by supranational authority—can therefore have a profound impact on state behavior, and some of the most central problems of international relations theory thus have to do with the importance of such "systemic" or "structural" effects in international political life.

It is commonly assumed that this concern for power, and especially this striving for power political advantage, puts states at odds with each other—that the struggle for power is a major source of conflict in and of itself. Such arguments are quite familiar. Opponents of realism have always assumed that power politics leads to conflict. Woodrow Wilson's whole approach to international politics was rooted in assumptions of that sort, and even today such attitudes are by no means dead. One leading contemporary theorist, Alexander Wendt, thus takes it for granted that a world in which states behave in accordance with the dictates of Realpolitik is a violence-prone, kill-or-be-killed, Hobbesian world.[1] It is perhaps more surprising to find realists themselves ar-

This is a slightly altered version of an article which originally appeared in *Security Studies* in the fall of 2003. It is reprinted here by permission of the publisher, Taylor and Francis Ltd. Copyright © Security Studies, Taylor and Francis, Oxford, England. Reprinted by permission.

[1] Alexander Wendt, *Social Theory of International Politics* (Cambridge, England, and New York: Cambridge University Press, 1999), pp. 262–66. Hobbes's original argument,

guing along these lines. The prevailing assumption among realists as a whole is that "mutual fear drives the great powers apart," that "international anarchy fosters competition and conflict," and that the "anarchic nature of international politics" encourages "cut-throat behavior among states."[2]

The argument is developed in its purest form by "offensive realists" like John Mearsheimer. "The structure of the international system," Mearsheimer writes, "forces states which seek only to be secure nonetheless to act aggressively toward each other." "Great powers," he says, "that have no reason to fight each other—that are merely concerned with their own survival—nevertheless have little choice but to pursue power and to seek to dominate the other states in the system." They have little choice because they fear other states and they know that they "have to seek more power if they want to maximize their odds of survival." But if states want to "maximize relative power," Mearsheimer argues, they have to "think offensively toward other states, even though their ultimate motive is simply to survive."[3]

The basic argument, however, is by no means limited to people like Mearsheimer. Even the "defensive realists," those scholars of a realist bent who take a relatively moderate position on this whole set of issues, fundamentally agree that a dynamic of this sort plays a central role in international politics. To be sure, their analyses are more guarded, more hedged, more inclined to emphasize the importance of second-order or unit-level considerations—the offense/defense balance, most notably—which in their view determine how strong in practice that dy-

---

an argument that dealt specifically with international politics, was laid out in the *Leviathan*, part 1, chap. 13.

[2] Stephen Van Evera, "The Hard Realities of International Politics," *Boston Review*, 17 (November–December 1992), p. 19; Joseph Grieco, "Anarchy and the Limits of Cooperation: A Realist Critique of the Newest Liberal Institutionalism," *International Organization* 42, no. 3 (Summer 1988): 485; John Mearsheimer, review of Roger Spegele, *Political Realism in International Theory*, in the *International History Review* 20, no. 3 (September 1998): 776. Note also John Mearsheimer, "The False Promise of International Institutions," *International Security* 19, no. 3 (Winter 1994/95): 9; John Mearsheimer, *The Tragedy of Great Power Politics* (New York: Norton, 2001), chap. 2; and Kenneth Waltz, "The Origins of War in Neorealist Theory," in Robert Rotberg and Theodore Rabb, eds., *The Origin and Prevention of Major Wars* (Cambridge, England, and New York: Cambridge University Press, 1989), p. 43. See also the sources cited in n. 7 of this chapter. I say "prevailing assumption" because there are exceptions. See, for example, Charles Glaser, "Realists as Optimists: Cooperation as Self-Help," *International Security* 19, no. 3 (Winter 1994/95); Randall Schweller, "Neorealism's Status-Quo Bias: What Security Dilemma?" *Security Studies*, 5, no. 3 (Spring 1996), reprinted in Benjamin Frankel, ed., *Realism: Restatements and Renewal* (London: Cass, 1996); and Andrew Kydd, "Sheep in Sheep's Clothing: Why Security Seekers Do Not Fight Each Other," *Security Studies* 7, no. 1 (Autumn 1997).

[3] Mearsheimer, *Tragedy of Great Power Politics*, pp. 3, 21, 34.

namic is.[4] And they sometimes write in a way that suggests that security competition need not be a major source of international instability—that states will normally be satisfied with an "appropriate" amount of security, and will show little interest in reaching for more.[5] But the comparatively mild way in which they frame their arguments should not obscure the fact that, whatever qualifications they make, even leading defensive realists believe that in an anarchic system the major powers are pushed into conflict with each other—that anarchy is more than just a permissive cause of war.

Kenneth Waltz, for example, clearly believes that anarchy breeds conflict. Waltz, the most important theorist in the defensive realist camp, developed his argument most explicitly in an important 1988 article called "The Origins of War in Neorealist Theory." "Competition and conflict among states," Waltz wrote, "stem directly from the twin facts of life under conditions of anarchy: States in an anarchic order must provide for their own security, and threats or seeming threats to their security abound. Preoccupation with identifying dangers and counteracting them become a way of life." The measures states take to deal with these problems and make themselves more secure necessarily threaten other powers, who react in kind. "Some states," he says, "may hunger for power for power's sake." But "neorealist theory"—and that means Waltz's own theory—"shows that it is not necessary to assume an innate lust for power in order to account for the sometimes fierce competition that marks the international arena. In an anarchic domain, a state of war exists if all parties lust for power. But so too will a state of war exist if all states seek only to ensure their own safety." This logic does not, of course, explain the origins of particular wars, but it does, he says, "explain war's dismal recurrence through the millennia." The "recurrence of war" is to be understood in structural terms: "The origins of hot wars lie in cold wars, and the origins of cold wars are found in the anarchic ordering of the international arena."[6] Other defensive realists share that basic view. Indeed, as one leading scholar points out,

---

[4] Indeed, the defensive realists have been criticized for placing increasing emphasis on such nonsystemic factors. See especially Jeffrey Legro and Andrew Moravcsik, "Is Anybody Still a Realist?" *International Security* 24, no. 2 (Fall 1999).

[5] Waltz, "Origins of War in Neorealist Theory," p. 40. In context, however, the assumption here was still that rational states would seek to maximize relative power. "Excessive strength" was to be avoided because it might lead "other states to increase their arms and pool their efforts against the dominant state"—that is, because it might actually weaken a state's position in the system. Other defensive realists, however, take a clearer position and say explicitly that states "satisfice"—that they are not necessarily power maximizers but seek only the level of power sufficient for their purposes. See Barry Posen, "The Best Defense," *The National Interest*, no. 67 (Spring 2002): 119.

[6] Waltz, "Origins of War in Neorealist Theory," pp. 43–44.

in the international relations literature more generally nowadays, the anarchic structure of international politics is "routinely cited as a root cause of or explanation for the recurrence of war."[7]

Some traditional realists, however—not every major writer, but people like George Kennan, for example—took a very different view. They took it for granted that stability depended on the ability of states to pursue a policy framed in "realistic" power political terms. Over and over again, they stressed the point that to ignore the importance of power—to allow emotion and ideology and "impractical idealism" to dictate policy—was to court disaster.[8] Implicit in that whole line of argument was the assumption that "realist" foreign policies—that is, policies attuned to power realities—were not the problem. But today most realists seem to assume that they *are* the problem, and that a system of states acting rationally in power political terms—a system of states pursuing "realist" policies, the sorts of policies the system tends to encourage—is a violent, brutal, war-prone system.

For me, this issue was particularly salient because, like those traditional realists, I had come to believe that "power politics" was not the problem—that is, I had come to believe that serious trouble developed only when states *failed* to act in a way that made sense in power political terms. My basic thinking in this area had taken shape as a simple by-product of ordinary historical work; I had never tried to think these issues through on a more theoretical level; and I was puzzled when it

---

[7] James Fearon, "Rationalist Explanations for War," *International Organization* 49, no. 3 (Summer 1995): 384. It is in fact taken for granted in the scholarly literature that this view is held by neorealists of all stripes. Dale Copeland, for example, refers in passing to the "core neorealist premise that anarchy forces states into recurrent security competitions"; the assumption here is that this view is by no means limited to the offensive realists. Stephen Walt says that "the central conclusion of all realist theories—what might be termed the 'realist *problematique*'—is that *the existence of several states in anarchy renders the security of each one problematic and encourages them to compete with each other for power or security.*" Andrew Kydd says that "structural realists"—he has both offensive and defensive realists in mind—"argue that international anarchy renders states insecure, and that the search for security is the main task of states, and the main cause of conflict." And Robert Kaufman notes that "realists of all persuasions agree that the quest for power and the rivalries it engenders offer the most basic explanation for the origins of war." Dale Copeland, "The Constructivist Challenge to Structural Realism," *International Security* 25, no. 2 (Fall 2000): 188; Stephen Walt, "The Enduring Relevance of the Realist Tradition," in *Political Science: The State of the Discipline,* Ira Katznelson and Helen Milner, eds. (New York: Norton, 2002), p. 200 (emphasis in original text); Kydd, "Sheep in Sheep's Clothing," p. 114; and Robert Kaufman, "On the Uses and Abuses of History in International Relations Theory: Dale Copeland's *The Origins of Major War,*" *Security Studies* 10, no. 4 (Summer 2001): 180.

[8] See especially George Kennan, *American Diplomacy, 1900–1950* (Chicago: University of Chicago Press, 1951), chap. 4; the phrase quoted is on p. 69.

became clear to me that the prevailing view among realists today was rather different.

The aim here is thus to bring an historian's perspective to bear on this basic problem. This does not mean that I am going to make the standard "historian's argument" about how political scientists exaggerate the importance of the "system" and about how the problem of war and peace needs to be studied at a much lower level of abstraction. I myself believe that the "system" is enormously important—that a system based on power has a certain logic to it, and that to understand international politics, one has to have some sense for what that logic is. But how exactly does such a system work? Is it really the case that structural imperatives push states into conflict with each other? Or do things work in a very different way?

My basic point in this article is that the argument about the systemic sources of conflict is far more problematic, even in principle, than many people seem prepared to admit. But I want to take things a bit further than that. I want to argue that there are ways in which *systemic* forces can play a *stabilizing* role. And it is that argument, I think, that gives the analysis here its distinct character. The claim that anarchy breeds conflict has of course been challenged before. Scholars have argued that for a variety of reasons the effects of anarchy might be relatively mild. Some scholars have even argued that the system on balance plays a neutral role—that sometimes states find it in their interest to cooperate, and sometimes not. The argument here, however, is that systemic forces can actually play a positive role—and indeed that systemic pressures by and large have a stabilizing effect. [9]

That view might sound somewhat unconventional today, but it is in fact rooted in ideas that have been part of the realist tradition for centuries. Why is it important to resurrect those notions, and why more generally is the argument here worth making? I think there is a gap between the sorts of policies many realists support—moderate, cautious, rooted in a concern with the stability of the system as a whole—and certain important theoretical views those same people hold. On the one hand, you have a theory that suggests at its core that a system in which states act in accordance with the dictates of Realpolitik is a violent, war-prone system. On the other hand, you have people who hold that view calling for "realist" policies—that is, policies based on power and inter-

[9] Terms like *system* and *stability* are not easy to define with any precision. For a discussion, see Robert Jervis, *System Effects: Complexity in Political and Social Life* (Princeton: Princeton University Press, 1997), pp. 5–10 (for *system*) and pp. 94–98, esp. p. 96 (for *stability*). For the purposes of this article, however, precise definitions are not necessary. These terms are used here in a fairly conventional way, and their meaning will be clear enough from context as well as from the examples given.

est, policies that are rational in terms of the imperatives of the system. It is as though you had a group of economists, firmly convinced that the free play of market forces would inevitably lead to economic collapse, nonetheless calling on everyone to act in accordance with market forces. The two levels of argument are just not in harmony with each other. But if we can see why certain basic assumptions about how a power political system works are misleading, we might be able to put those policy arguments on a firmer basis. If we can see how a system based on power has a certain stability, then we might be better able to see why policies that are rational in power political terms might make for a more peaceful world.

So let me begin in the next section by outlining the kind of thinking that lies behind the view that a system based on power is not inherently unstable—or, more precisely, the basis for the view that realist policies, policies that make sense in terms of the basic logic of the system, actually make for a relatively stable international order. In the following section, some key arguments on the other side, especially fundamental arguments about the way an anarchic system is supposed to work, will be examined. In the final section, I want to look at policy arguments, and especially at what they can tell us about the fundamental assumptions that lie at the heart of the realist understanding of international politics.

An Invisible Hand in International Politics?

Adam Smith, in a very famous passage, noted that an individual pursuing his own interest is "led by an invisible hand to promote an end which was no part of his intention." "By pursuing his own interest," Smith wrote, "he frequently promotes that of the society more effectually than when he really intends to promote it."[10] Do we see a mechanism of this sort at work in international life? Can states, in pursuing their own interests, generate a more or less stable international system? What sorts of dynamics come into play in a world of independent powers, and how do those dynamics affect the stability of the system as a whole?

One way to get a handle on such questions is to start with a bit of history and then work back to the theory. And in doing that, it makes sense to begin with one of those periods in history where there was no hegemon, where ideological concerns were of relatively minor importance

---

[10] Adam Smith, *An Inquiry into the Nature and Causes of the Wealth of Nations* (New York: Modern Library, 1937), p. 423.

in shaping foreign policy, and when there were just a handful of major powers relating to each other in a relatively closed system: namely, the classic period of European great power politics, the late nineteenth century. By looking at international politics in that period, one can hope to see far more clearly than in other cases how a system based on power works. Was this a period in which power politics was a source of instability, or did trouble develop only when the major European states put power political considerations aside and allowed other sorts of factors to shape their policy?

To a considerable degree, European statesmen in that period really did think in power political terms. Otto von Bismarck, the German chancellor from 1871 to his fall from power in 1890, is the most obvious example. In a Europe of five great states, Bismarck said, the key thing was to be one of three: "all politics reduce themselves to this formula: try to be *à trois* in a world governed by five Powers."[11] But if being one of three was good, being one of four was even better, since one's own country would be less vulnerable to a partner's threat to defect. In straight power political terms, good relations with other states are a source of strength and bad relations a source of weakness. It thus makes sense to have as many friends and as few enemies as possible.

The great source of weakness in the German position after the unification of Germany in 1871 was the alienation of France that had resulted from the German annexation that year of Alsace-Lorraine. This was an albatross hung around Bismarck's neck. It sharply constrained his freedom of action by ruling out the possibility of a combination that included both Germany and France. Germany's partners could threaten to defect to the side of France, but Germany herself could make no counter-threat to form an alignment of her own with that power. The Franco-German antagonism, moreover, vastly complicated the problem of forming a bloc of powers that would dominate Europe. A bloc of the three eastern empires—Germany, Russia and Austria—was one possibility, but the problem here was that Germany's two partners were themselves at odds over Balkan issues and might expect German support in their conflict with each other, perhaps threatening to go over to the side of France if they did not get it. An alignment with Britain and Austria, based on the containment of Russia, was the other possibility, but here too the drawbacks were obvious: that policy might drive Russia to the side of France; if a continental war did break out, Germany would have to bear the brunt of the fighting, given that Britain was not a land power; and Britain, an island power protected by a strong navy,

[11] Quoted in Raymond Sontag, *European Diplomatic History, 1871-1932* (New York: Appleton-Century-Crofts, 1933), p. 22.

would be relatively free to withdraw from the alignment, especially as new elections brought in new governments free to adopt new policies. The best Bismarck could do was to balance between those two possible alignments—to try to get Britain and Austria to balance Russia more or less on their own, to hold back from supporting that containment policy too openly, and to try to keep the wire to St. Petersburg open and thus head off a Russian alignment with France. This was not an easy policy to pursue, not least because there was no guarantee that either Britain or Russia would cooperate with it, and it was breaking down even before Bismarck fell from power in 1890.

The antagonism with France created by the annexation of Alsace-Lorraine was a source of weakness for Germany. In power political terms, it had not been in Germany's interest to annex those provinces. Yes, adding that territory gave Germany more defensible borders—a real advantage, and something that would have been even more important if Germany had opted for a defensive strategy in the west in the decades to come. And yes, bringing Lorraine with its iron ore into the Reich turned out to be one of the key factors that enabled German steel production—the heart of military power, given the military technology of the period—to rise so dramatically in the period before World War I. In narrow, purely economic terms, it is quite clear that in this case, as in so many others, conquest paid.[12]

But to focus on such points is to miss what was really important about what the new German empire did in 1871. Whatever military and economic advantages Germany got were more than outweighed by the political price that country had to pay, a point that was obvious at the time to clear-sighted observers like Lord Salisbury.[13] The decision to annex Alsace-Lorraine was rooted not in power political thinking but in the belief that France would not accept her defeat by Germany, that a war of revenge was inevitable, and that Germany had to put herself in the best position for fighting it. "The inclination of France to seek revenge," Bismarck wrote, "will remain precisely the same, whether she loses provinces or not."[14] But that kind of belief was not at all in

[12] For a general analysis, see Peter Liberman, *Does Conquest Pay? The Exploitation of Occupied Industrial Societies* (Princeton: Princeton University Press, 1996); for a summary of Liberman's findings, see his article "The Spoils of Conquest," *International Security* 18, no. 2 (Fall 1993), reprinted in Michael Brown, Sean Lynn-Jones, and Steven Miller, eds., *The Perils of Anarchy: Contemporary Realism and International Security* (Cambridge, Mass.: MIT Press, 1995).

[13] [Lord Salisbury], "The Terms of Peace," *Quarterly Review* 129 (1870): 540–56 (originally published anonymously).

[14] Bismarck to his ambassador in Paris, August 15, 1871, cited in Allan Mitchell, *Bismarck and the French Nation, 1848–1890* (New York: Pegasus, 1971), p. 57. Bismarck made this point many times during this period. In September 1870, for example, he told the

keeping with the spirit of the power political approach. A true Realpolitiker would never have taken French hostility as a given, but rather would have assumed that French policy would be governed by interest, and that it was in the interest of both countries to avoid foreclosing a possible alignment. A German policy that was rational in power political terms would thus have sought to keep the door open to reconciliation with France, just as a mild peace with Austria five years earlier had made it possible for Germany to have good relations with that country. Indeed, the basic principle here was recognized by Bismarck himself. "A Great Power," he wrote in his memoirs, "will always have to keep in view not only existing, but future, relations to others, and must, as far as possible, avoid lasting fundamental hostility with any of them." [15]

Given the sort of question we are interested in here, it is important to see this issue in systemic, and not just bilateral, terms. France had a certain interest in a relatively strong Germany as a counterweight to Russia; if Germany had not taken Alsace-Lorraine, that factor might well have played a key role in shaping French policy in the post-1871 period. More generally, the two states had a strong interest in good relations with each other, if only to strengthen their position vis-à-vis third countries, and absent the Alsace-Lorraine problem, that sort of interest could easily have come into play. And a decent Franco-German relationship, a relationship based not on emotion but on cold calculations of interest, might well have affected the ability of third powers (like Russia) to pursue an expansionist policy in Europe. So if both France and Germany had thought in pure power political terms—that is, if they had pursued the sorts of policies the anarchic international system tends to encourage—a more stable international order might well have come into being.

This issue is paradigmatic. Antagonisms of this sort—the kind that the annexation of Alsace-Lorraine had generated—are always a source of weakness, and states therefore have an interest in avoiding these kinds of conflicts. They always have a power political interest in preventing such conflicts from developing and in resolving those that do develop. Any individual state, if it were thinking in power political terms, would thus want to have as many friends and as few enemies as possible. But since that same logic applies to every state in the system, the upshot, in a system where considerations of this sort shape policy,

---

acting French foreign minister, Jules Favre, "I am sure that very soon we will have a new war with you and we want to do so with all the advantages." Cited in Robert Giesberg, *The Treaty of Frankfort: A Study in Diplomatic History* (Philadelphia: University of Pennsylvania Press, 1966), p. 33.

[15] Otto von Bismarck, *Reflections and Reminiscences*, 2 vols. (London: Smith, Elder, 1898), 2:235.

is a general tendency toward stability, in the sense of the ability of the system to avoid war, and above all to avoid major, all-out, system-wide war. Conflicts in such a world would be avoided or resolved, and inter-state relations would be good all around.[16] This effect would be particularly strong since those states that pursue a policy of avoiding antagonisms and improving relations with their rivals are at a competitive advantage, and, for reasons outlined by Waltz, successful policies in such a system tend to be emulated.[17]

This particular dynamic was historically of fundamental importance, and it deserves more attention than it gets: this mechanism is a major force making for international stability. To be sure, it is not the only dynamic that comes into play in a power political system, and in fact in such a system states do sometimes have a certain interest in expanding their power and do for that reason pursue warlike policies. Bismarck's Prussia in the 1860s is perhaps the most important case in point. But even here, a power political frame of mind was in a fundamental sense a source of stability. Bismarck moved ahead only when the power political conjuncture was favorable; his policy was anything but reckless; limits on Prussian (and later on German) power were accepted when other powers threw their weight into the balance and made it clear (in 1875 most notably) that Bismarck could only go so far. The unification of Germany in 1871 brought about a major change in the distribution of power within the European system, but the system itself had not been brought down; the reconfiguration of European politics in the 1862-1871 period did not lead to the sort of war that had ended a half-century earlier or would begin a half-century later.

But if this general idea is correct—if behavior that was rational in power political terms was not the basic problem in pre-1914 Europe, and that if such behavior, the sort of behavior that the system tended to foster, was actually an important source of stability—then it follows that the most serious problems developed because policy in Europe generally during that period was *not* cut from that cloth. And indeed,

---

[16] In trying to explain the limits on human aggressiveness, biologists have sometimes argued along similar lines. As George Williams, one of the great figures in modern evolutionary theory, once pointed out, "an individual who maximizes his friendships and minimizes his antagonisms will have an evolutionary advantage, and selection should favor those characters that promote the optimization of personal relationships." "I imagine that this evolutionary factor," Williams continued, "has increased man's capacity for altruism and compassion and has tempered his ethically less acceptable heritage of sexual and predatory aggressiveness." George Williams, *Adaptation and Natural Selection: A Critique of Some Current Evolutionary Thought* (Princeton: Princeton University Press, 1966), p. 94.

[17] Kenneth Waltz, *Theory of International Politics* (New York: McGraw Hill, 1979), pp. 127–28.

studying the origins of the First World War, one comes away with the strong impression that serious problems developed not because rational power political considerations shaped political behavior, but rather because they *failed* to do so—that is, because other factors come into play. In the case of the German decision to annex Alsace-Lorraine, as Salisbury pointed out at the time, "the fierce passions of war" had come to dominate policy. The Germans wanted to "see the enemy humbled to the earth." "The very consideration," he said, "which makes a cession of territory inadvisable in the judgment of calmer bystanders, makes it desirable in their eyes."[18] Bismarck himself might not have approached the problem in such terms, but, Salisbury argued, he was to a considerable extent a prisoner of the passions he had done so much to unleash.

It is important to bear in mind that the alienation of France was not just a problem for Germany. As Salisbury realized in 1871, the Franco-German antagonism was a serious problem for the system as a whole, and looking back it seems quite clear that that system would have worked much more smoothly if this particular problem had not come into being. The conflict between France and Germany over Alsace-Lorraine in fact turned out to be (along with the Austro-Russian conflict over the Balkans and the Anglo-German conflict over imperial, colonial, and naval issues) one of the three great conflicts whose coming together ultimately led to the First World War.

This, moreover, is not the only example of the instability created by a failure to act in a way that makes sense in power political terms. Germany pursued a policy before 1914 that led to conflict with the three next most powerful nations in Europe, all at the same time, which was hardly the sort of policy a country that thought "security was scarce" would have been inclined to adopt. Britain and France pursued a policy toward Germany, most strikingly at the time of the First Moroccan Crisis in 1905–06, that was rooted more in emotion than in cold power political calculation; that policy, to my mind, clearly had a destabilizing effect, not least because it increased the dependence of the western powers on Russia and thus made it easier for the Russians to pursue a forward policy in the Balkans.[19] And Russia herself, in 1914, went to war even though key officials like the war minister knew that the coun-

---

[18] "The Terms of Peace," p. 553.

[19] See especially George Monger, *The End of Isolation: British Foreign Policy, 1900–1907* (London and New York: T. Nelson, 1963), and Christopher Andrew, *Théophile Delcassé and the Making of the Entente Cordiale: A Reappraisal of French Foreign Policy 1898–1905* (London: Macmillan, 1968). Note also the tone of one very well-known document from this period: Eyre Crowe, "Memorandum on the Present State of British Relations with France and Germany," January 1, 1907, in G. P. Gooch and Harold Temperley, eds., *British Documents on the Origins of the War, 1898–1914*, 11 vols. in 13 (London: HMSO, 1926–38), vol. 6, esp. p. 416.

try was "throwing herself unprepared into a venture beyond her strength."[20] The Russian decision to go to war for the sake of Serbia, a reversal of the original Russian policy during the crisis of advising Serbia not to resist an Austrian invasion and instead to "entrust her fate to the judgment of the Great Powers," was the climax of the "very bold offensive policy" that Russia had been pursuing in the Balkans before 1914, a policy again that was scarcely rational in power political terms.[21]

To understand power—that is, to understand how a system based on power works—is to understand why the most fundamental interests of other major states normally need to be respected, and why it is normally not to one's own interest to allow conflicts to get out of hand. There are times, of course, when more aggressive policies might need to be pursued for the sake of a state's own security—U.S. policy toward Germany in late 1941 is a good case in point—and there are times when states can pursue expansionist policies without running great risks. But moderation is normally a source of stability, above all in a world where the major states all think in power political terms. In a Realpolitik world, the great powers relate to each other on a businesslike basis; power realities are accepted for what they are; compromises can normally be worked out relatively easily because statesmen all speak the same language, the language of power and interest. And "interest" in that kind of world tends to get defined in geostrategic terms: for obvious military reasons, neighboring countries are more important than far-off areas; a region that is important to one great state may well be of secondary importance to another; great nations may therefore find it relatively easy, in such a world, to accept each others' spheres of influence and coexist with each other on that basis.

[20] Luigi Albertini, *The Origins of the War of 1914*, 3 vols. (London: Oxford University Press, 1952–57), 2:546. The Russian interior minister spoke at the time about how war would bring revolution, but "sitting at a table laden with ikons and religious lamps," crossed himself, saying "we cannot escape our fate," and then signed the mobilization decree. D.C.B. Lieven, *Russia and the Origins of the First World War* (New York: St. Martin's, 1983), pp. 108–9, 115.

[21] Special Journal of the Russian Council of Ministers, July 24, 1914, and Sazonov to Strandtmann, July 24, 1914, in Imanuel Geiss, ed., *July 1914: The Outbreak of the First World War: Selected Documents* (New York: Scribner, 1967), pp. 186–88. For this characterization of Russia's Balkan policy, see Paul Schroeder, "Embedded Counterfactuals and World War I as an Unavoidable War," in Paul Schroeder, *Systems, Stability, and Statecraft: Essays on the International History of Modern Europe* (New York: Palgrave Macmillan, 2004), p. 186. Russia's sponsorship of the Balkan League of 1912 is perhaps the most striking case in point. The treaty establishing this alliance, as French Prime Minister Raymond Poincaré noted at the time, "contained the seeds not only of a war against Turkey, but of a war against Austria as well." Quoted in Pierre Renouvin, *La Crise européenne et la première guerre mondiale* (Paris: PUF, 1962), p. 173.

The power political approach, therefore, by defining what needs to be emphasized, by its very nature defines what needs to be played down, and thus tends to rule out other kinds of policy: power, from the Realpolitik point of view, is too precious to squander on moralistic or imperialistic or ideological enterprises. The power political approach thus provides a kind of yardstick for judgments about how power might be intelligently used—and, above all, for judgments about when its use is to be avoided. In this sense also, it is by and large a source of restraint.[22]

Arguments of this sort are by no means new. The eighteenth-century "balance of power" theorists, for example, identified rationality with moderation and restraint. To reach for hegemony, in their view, was both pointless and dangerous: pointless, because other states would probably be able to frustrate an attempt to dominate the whole system, and dangerous, because to attempt to achieve such a position of power was to run great risks. As Fénelon, the most impressive of those theorists, warned, "[S]tates have often perished by these ambitious follies."[23] Traditional realists also often emphasized the importance of keeping goals limited, preventing conflicts from becoming crusades, and making sure the lines of communication remained open with one's adversaries. The very fact (as Henry Kissinger pointed out in a famous passage) that "absolute security for one power means absolute insecurity for all others" and thus "is never obtainable" as part of a settlement whose legitimacy is generally accepted implied that absolute security could not be taken as a serious goal: if the aim was stability, statesmen had to set their sights somewhat lower.[24] Policy from that point of view had to be limited and balanced; the goal was a kind of equilibrium. This was the sort of thinking that inspired the peacemakers at the Congress

[22] For a classic example, see Lord Castlereagh's famous State Paper of 5 May 1820, in Harold Temperley and Lillian Penson, eds., *Foundations of British Foreign Policy: From Pitt (1792) to Salisbury (1902)*, (Cambridge, England: Cambridge University Press, 1938), pp. 48–63.

[23] François de Salignac de la Mothe Fénelon, supplement to his *L'Examen de conscience sur les devoirs de la royauté*, originally written around 1700, and published (under various titles) in many editions of his works—for example, in Fénelon, *Oeuvres* (Paris: Lebel, 1824), vol. 23. An extract from an early English translation can be found in Moorhead Wright, ed., *Theory and Practice of the Balance of Power, 1486–1914* (London: Dent, 1975), pp. 39–45; the passage quoted is on p. 43. Note also the extracts from the writings of Defoe (1706) and Hume (1752), in ibid., pp. 48–49, 64. Rousseau also argued along these lines. See Jean-Jacques Rousseau, "Abstract and Judgement of Saint-Pierre's Project for Perpetual Peace (1756)," in Stanley Hoffmann and David Fidler, eds., *Rousseau on International Relations* (Oxford: Clarendon, 1991), pp. 62–64.

[24] Henry Kissinger, *A World Restored: Metternich, Castlereagh and the Problems of Peace, 1812–22* (New York: Grosset and Dunlap, 1964), pp. 144–45.

of Vienna at the end of the Napoleonic wars. The aim there was balance and equilibrium; the leading statesmen at Vienna, especially the British and Austrian foreign ministers Castlereagh and Metternich, were very much concerned with creating a stable structure of power.[25]

A century later their method was attacked quite sharply by Woodrow Wilson. The peace that would settle the war of 1914, he declared, would not be based on "such covenants of selfishness and compromise as were entered into at the Congress of Vienna." The issues of the war could not be settled by "arrangement or compromise or adjustment of interests"; peace could not be obtained "by any kind of bargain or compromise with the governments of the Central Empires." The aim now that the United States had entered the war was "the overcoming of evil, by the defeat once [and] for all of the sinister forces that interrupt peace and render it impossible." The "old order of international politics" was to be "utterly destroyed." The whole system built on "that unstable thing which we used to call the 'balance of power'" was to be swept away in its entirety.[26] But Wilson's contempt for the method of compromise, accommodation, and the "adjustment of interests" led to disaster. If a compromise peace was out of the question, then Germany had to be crushed. [27] If the rule of law was to be established, the lawbreaker had

[25] See especially Edward Vose Gulick, *Europe's Classical Balance of Power: A Case History of the Theory and Practice of One of the Great Concepts of European Statecraft* (New York: Norton, 1955), esp. part 2; and W. A. Phillips, *The Confederation of Europe: A Study of the European Alliance, 1813–1823, as an Experiment in the International Organization of Peace* (London: Longman's, 1920). Kissinger's arguments, it should be noted, were developed in the context of his analysis in *A World Restored* of the Vienna settlement. Note, however, Paul Schroeder's discussion of the issue in "Did the Vienna Settlement Rest on a Balance of Power?" *American Historical Review* 97, no. 3 (June 1992). Although Schroeder's answer to the question posed in his title is essentially no, a careful reading of that article shows that he agrees that the peacemakers thought in terms of balance and equilibrium; that they, however, defined those concepts rather broadly and not just in narrow balance of power terms; but that this did not mean that balance of power thinking, even in the strict sense, played no role at Vienna. The sort of language that was used at the time, he writes, shows that "checking and balancing power was one element in the process of achieving an overall balance in the system" (p. 695).

[26] Woodrow Wilson, *War and Peace: Presidential Messages, Addresses, and Public Papers*, 2 vols. (New York: Harper, 1927), 1:129, 133, 255, 342–43, 547–48; for another reference to the Congress of Vienna, see p. 179. The passages quoted are from speeches Wilson gave during the war and in 1919. Wilson's contemptuous references here to the peacemakers a century earlier were not mere rhetorical flourishes. His hostility to the method used at Vienna came out even in private. When the New Zealand prime minister alluded to the Vienna Congress at a meeting during the Paris Peace Conference, Wilson exploded with rage. The very subject was taboo: Wilson "hoped that even by reference no odor of Vienna would again be brought into the [Paris] proceedings." *Papers of Woodrow Wilson*, 69 vols. (Princeton: Princeton University Press, 1966–94), 54:314.

[27] See especially Wilson, *War and Peace*, 1:129.

to be punished. In Wilson's view, Germany had committed a great crime, and people had to be shown "that they could not do anything of the sort the Germans attempted without suffering the severest kind of punishment."[28] This was an approach that looked not to the future but to the past; the aim was not stability but justice. And the peace that was imposed, the Versailles settlement of 1919, was very much a Wilsonian peace.[29] It was also an extremely unstable peace: the only major peace settlement to be dictated solely by the great western democracies turned out to be the most unstable peace in the modern history of great power politics. The 1815 settlement, in comparison, looks like a model of what peacemaking should be. The comparison is instructive. The balance of power approach, the approach of Metternich and Castlereagh, an approach very much in the realist tradition, is not to be seen as a source of instability.

What all this suggests is that a power political world, a world of states deeply concerned with the structure of power and behaving rationally in power political terms, is not a "brutal back-alley."[30] In such a world, there are strong forces at play making for stability. But one cannot just leave it at that. To get to the bottom of the issue, it is important to look at the arguments on the other side. Many scholars take a rather

[28] Bernard Baruch diary, entry for June 2, 1919, Baruch Papers, Mudd Library, Princeton University, Princeton, N.J. See also S. G. Millin, *General Smuts,* 2 vols. (Boston: Little, Brown, 1936), 2:232–33. Note also Wilson's defense of the peace treaty in the speeches he gave in late 1919. That treaty, he said on September 4, "seeks to punish one of the greatest wrongs ever done in history, the wrong which Germany sought to do to the world and to civilization; and there ought to be no weak purpose with regard to the application of the punishment. She attempted an intolerable thing, and she must be made to pay for the attempt." The same note was sounded in another speech he gave four days later: "I hear that this treaty is very hard on Germany. When an individual has committed a criminal act, the punishment is hard, but the punishment is not unjust. This nation permitted itself, through unscrupulous governors, to commit a criminal act against mankind, and it is to undergo the punishment." Wilson, *War and Peace,* 1:590–91, and 2:33–34.

[29] The myth persists that Wilson was the champion of a peace of reconciliation with Germany, and that Britain and France insisted on much harsher terms and forced him into disastrous compromises. The terms of the Treaty of Versailles were in fact very much in line with the program Wilson had laid out in his wartime speeches, and the pre-armistice agreement with Germany was based explicitly on that program. The one point where the peacemakers clearly did violate the terms of the pre-armistice agreement had to do with the inclusion of pensions in the reparation bill. The British wanted pensions included, the French would have preferred not to include them, and Wilson sided with the British for moral reasons: he thought it was right that Germany should make amends not just for the material damage her "aggression" had caused, but for the loss of human life as well. On this general issue, see, for example, Marc Trachtenberg, "Versailles after Sixty Years," *Journal of Contemporary History* 17, no. 3 (July 1982).

[30] Van Evera, "Hard Realities," p. 19.

dark view of the international system. What are the arguments that support this view, and what are we to make of them?

THE LOGIC OF ANARCHY

The argument that systemic forces push states into conflict with each other, and indeed that the fundamental structure of international politics "can precipitate open clashes of arms" even among states that "seek only to ensure their own safety," is of central importance in contemporary international relations theory.[31] The idea here is that in a system where no supranational authority can guarantee their security, states have to be very sensitive to power realities. They have to do what they can to make sure that in power political terms they are in as favorable a position as possible. But power, unlike wealth for example, is defined in relative terms. If one state's position improves, another's will inevitably be weakened. Thus states are necessarily at odds with each other. Each is bound to reach for greater power; those efforts are bound to conflict with each other; given what is at stake, no one can be relaxed about the outcome. The competition for power is thus bound to be a major source of international tension.

This is particularly the case, the argument runs, since the growth of another state's power is inevitably seen as threatening—even if that state is acting for defensive reasons, indeed even if it is understood to be acting for defensive reasons. With so much at stake, states cannot afford to remain passive when the balance of power threatens to turn against them; they themselves, regardless of their own fundamental inclinations, are more or less forced by the structure of the system to act energetically and in particular to take advantage of any opportunities to extend their power. The system thus "creates powerful incentives for aggression."[32] It is thus the "anarchic nature of international politics," and not any craving for power or conquest for its own sake, that leads to "cut-throat behavior among states."[33]

Even the defensive realists often, although by no means always, argue along these lines. War, in their view, can in principle come even

[31] Kenneth Waltz, "Origins of War in Neorealist Theory," pp. 43–44 (for the quotations); Mearsheimer, "False Promise," pp. 9–12; John Mearsheimer, "Back to the Future: Instability in Europe after the Cold War," *International Security* 15, no. 1 (Summer 1990): 12; Mearsheimer, *Tragedy of Great Power Politics*, pp. 3, 34; Robert Jervis, "Realism, Neoliberalism, and Cooperation: Understanding the Debate," *International Security* 24, no. 1 (Summer 1999): 49.

[32] Mearsheimer, "Back to the Future," p. 12; Mearsheimer, "False Promise," p. 11.

[33] Mearsheimer review of Spegele, *Political Realism in International Theory*, p. 776.

in a world of simple security-seekers—that is, powers who, if their security were guaranteed, would be happy to live with things as they were—because the policies of such powers are based on fear, and "mutual fear drives the great powers apart."[34] The system at times virtually forces them to play hardball. Indeed, it virtually forces them in certain circumstances to behave like aggressors: given certain conditions, states are led to act aggressively for essentially defensive reasons.[35] And this logic, the logic of the "security dilemma" as it is called, applies to all states in the system. This reaching for power generates suspicion and hostility; states that feel themselves threatened intensify their own efforts, provoking hostile reactions on the part of other powers; tensions spiral upward. These difficulties are all rooted in the basic structure of the system and are hard to overcome in large part because of the familiar problem of collective action. States live so close to the margin that they have little choice but to concentrate on their own narrow security interests. In such a system, "the great powers are seldom able to concert their efforts toward peace, even when they jointly desire it."[36] To be sure, some forms of cooperation—alliances, for example—are possible, but realists tend in general to view even those forms of cooperation as

[34] Van Evera, "Hard Realities," p. 19. Note also Martin Wight, *Power Politics* (New York: Holmes and Meier, 1978), p. 139: fear is "the prime motive of international politics." In this and the following two sentences, I use qualifying phrases—"in principle," "at times," "in certain circumstances"— because the heart of the defensive realist view is its emphasis on the particular conditions, having to do most notably with the offense/defense balance, that determine the extent to which this logic comes into play. Defensive realists like Van Evera—and this is the point on which I part company with them—accept the theoretical proposition that anarchy causes violence, but stress that in practice its importance depends on the setting. The basic theoretical logic, in their view, is not very important in a defense-dominant world, or more precisely in a world where the defense is believed to have the upper hand; in such a world, people can be relatively relaxed. But in a world where the offense is believed to be dominant—where conquest is thought to be easy, where resources are thought to be highly cumulative, and where fears about the shifting military balance run deep—that logic comes into play in a major way. The defensive realists thus do not really challenge the fundamental argument that the anarchic structure of international politics is in principle a source of instability. But since their analysis focuses on a different level—on the conditions that determine in practice just how much instability there is—this argument does not loom as large for them as it does for their offensive realist friends.

[35] Robert Jervis, "Cooperation under the Security Dilemma," *World Politics* 30, no. 2 (January 1978): 187–91. The basic idea here was not unknown to theorists like Fénelon. "We cannot abandon these towers to them without exposing ourselves to their attacks," he has one of his characters say in *Télémaque*, "and they regard them as citadels which we can use to subjugate them." Quoted in Françoise Gallouédec-Genuys, *Le Prince selon Fénelon* (Paris: PUF, 1963), p. 267. But in Fénelon's view this problem was not considered of major importance.

[36] Van Evera, "Hard Realities," p. 19. See also Mearsheimer, *Tragedy of Great Power Politics*, p. 49.

rather tenuous. The offensive realists make the point quite bluntly. Alliances, Mearsheimer writes, are "only temporary marriages of convenience"; in a "brutal" world, where "states look for opportunities to take advantage of each other," they would be foolish to put too much faith in the guarantees offered by others.[37] The general feeling among realists of all stripes is that in the final analysis, states have to rely primarily on their own resources; that fundamental fact, in their view, determines both their behavior and the basic nature of the international system.

The fundamental assumption, in other words, is that fear leads to a hardening of policy and thus to a sharpening of international tension. States fear each other, Mearsheimer argues; they know that the more powerful they are, the more secure they will be; and that is why "the international system forces states which seek only to be secure nonetheless to act aggressively toward each other." "The more profound the fear is," he says, "the more intense is the security competition, and the more likely is war."[38] The problem with that argument is that, as Mearsheimer himself realizes, states will act aggressively only if they calculate that the benefits will outweigh the risks.[39] The fear of what war might bring might well hold a state back, especially if it is weak; the stronger state is better able to behave aggressively, but if it is strong, it has less reason to be afraid. Increased anxiety, in other words, does not necessarily lead to increased aggressiveness. It might in fact lead a state to draw in its horns, pursue more modest policies, and search more actively for political accommodations and for alliances with other powers. Such a state might also try to build up its military power. Those courses of action would not necessarily lead to an increase in tension. A successful alliance policy might have a deterrent effect and thus might actually reduce the level of risk. Even a military buildup, even if it led to an arms race, would not necessarily be a source of instability. A military competition can, in fact, be viewed as a kind of bidding war: it could serve the important political purpose of determining how a conflict would be resolved without recourse to arms, just as an art auction determines who gets which paintings. Thus Britain before 1914 outbuilds Germany in capital ships, and Britain remains the world's premier imperial power. Thus the United States is better able than the Soviet Union to sustain the burden of military spending during the later Cold War, and the Soviets end up adjusting to that basic power reality.[40]

[37] Mearsheimer, "False Promise," pp. 9, 11; Mearsheimer, *Tragedy of Great Power Politics*, p. 33.

[38] Mearsheimer, *Tragedy of Great Power Politics*, pp. 3, 21, 32–33, 42.

[39] Ibid., p. 37.

[40] On this latter point, see Randall Schweller and William Wolforth, "Power Test: Eval-

But are such alternative policies, and especially the policies that aim at interstate cooperation, actually viable? For an historian, one of the most striking features of contemporary American international relations theory, and not just realist theory, is the pervasiveness of the assumption that cooperation is difficult, even when interests overlap.[41] The idea that states are, as a general rule, trapped in suboptimal situations because the "obstacles to cooperation" are so great is often just taken for granted. The well-known prisoner's dilemma game, for example, is widely taken as a kind of metaphor for international politics as a whole.[42] But such notions are quite weak, both empirically and conceptually. It is simply not proven (as leading theorists themselves sometimes point out) that the sort of problem the prisoner's dilemma game illustrates actually does play a fundamental role in international political life.[43] What the empirical record suggests to an historian, moreover, is that cooperation is not particularly difficult when interests overlap: international politics, after all, is an endless series of arrangements and understandings, negotiations and accommodations, alignments and realignments.[44] Power relations are constantly shifting; political adjustments are constantly being made.[45] And the theo-

---

uating Realism in Response to the End of the Cold War," *Security Studies* 9, no. 3 (Spring 2000): 88.

[41] One measure of how common this kind of assumption is is the fact that two leading political scientists consider the point that cooperation is actually possible when interests overlap to be a major finding; see Robert Axelrod and Robert Keohane, "Achieving Cooperation under Anarchy: Strategies and Institutions," originally published in *World Politics* 38, no. 1 (October 1985), and republished first in Kenneth Oye, ed., *Cooperation under Anarchy* (Princeton: Princeton University Press, 1986), and again in David Baldwin, ed., *Neorealism and Neoliberalism: The Contemporary Debate* (New York: Columbia University Press, 1993). The passages in question are on pp. 108 and 113 in the Baldwin book.

[42] See, for example, Robert Axelrod, *The Evolution of Cooperation* (New York: Basic Books, 1984), p. 27. As Charles Lipson notes in his review of the Axelrod book, it is often assumed that there are "powerful analogies between this stylized game and the real world of international affairs." *American Journal of International Law* 81, no. 2 (April 1987): 470. See also Waltz, *Theory of International Politics*, p. 109n., and Jervis, "Realism, Neoliberalism, and Cooperation," p. 49.

[43] See, for example, Robert Jervis, "Realism, Game Theory, and Cooperation," *World Politics* 40, no. 3 (April 1988): 323, 329 (also citing works by Harrison Wagner and by George Downs and his colleagues); and Joanne Gowa, "Anarchy, Egoism, and Third Images: The Evolution of Cooperation and International Relations," *International Organization* 40, no. 1 (Winter 1986): 169, 172 (also citing works by Russell Hardin and Bruce Russett). Note also Mancur Olson's review of Axelrod's *Evolution of Cooperation* in the *American Journal of Sociology* 91, no. 6 (May 1986): 1465–66. Olson argues that one should not expect the prisoner's dilemma logic to apply to great power politics because in the real world the "players" are able to communicate with each other, and since there is a small number of "players," collective action problems are much less likely to arise.

[44] See, for example, William Langer's classic study, *European Alliances and Alignments, 1871–1890* (New York: Knopf, 1931).

[45] Churchill, in his account of the 1911 Agadir crisis, explained how the adjustment

retical arguments that one finds in the literature are not particularly strong. Waltz, for example, argues that in self-help systems in general, fears about survival make cooperation difficult, and to make the point he draws on an example from economics. "Oligopolistic markets," he writes, "limit the cooperation of firms in much the same way that international-political structures limit the cooperation of states."[46] But in industries dominated by a handful of large firms, cooperation (called "collusion" when it is frowned upon) is generally considered so easy and so attractive that antitrust laws have to be passed to prevent firms from engaging in such behavior. In this case it is not anarchy but rather the *absence* of anarchy that makes cooperation difficult. If, as Waltz believes, international politics works the same way, that would imply that international cooperation is not nearly as difficult as he and many other writers seem to think.

The idea that anarchy generates conflict is thus very much open to question. One can get a sense for the basic problem here by going back and looking at the origins of that idea, and by examining the arguments that from the start were used to support it. Rousseau was one of the first thinkers to argue more or less systematically along these lines, and his writings have had a major impact on contemporary international relations theory. The chapter, for example, in Waltz's *Man, the State and War* on the state system as a source of international conflict focuses mainly on Rousseau, and Waltz there treats Rousseau's analysis as definitive. "Rousseau's explanation of the origin of war among states," he writes, "is, in broad outline, the final one so long as we operate within a nation-state system." [47] To understand the problems with this general line of

---

process worked before World War I, and in particular how the sorts of agreements that were reached reflected even subtle shifts in the structure of power—a view at variance with the notion that cooperative outcomes are grossly insensitive to the structure of power and interest. "The great powers marshalled on either side," he wrote, "preceded and protected by an elaborate cushion of diplomatic courtesies and formalities, would display to each other their respective arrays. In the forefront would be the two principal disputants, Germany and France, and echeloned back on either side at varying distances and under veils of reserves and qualifications of different density, would be drawn up the other parties to the Triple Alliance and to what was already now beginning to be called the Triple Entente. At the proper moment these seconds or supporters would utter certain cryptic words indicative of their state of mind, as a consequence of which France or Germany would step back or forward a very small distance or perhaps move slightly to the right or to the left. When these delicate rectifications in the great balance of Europe, and indeed of the world, had been made, the formidable assembly would withdraw to their own apartments with ceremony and salutations and congratulate or condole with each other in whispers on the result." Winston Churchill, *The World Crisis 1911–1914* (New York: Scribner's, 1930), pp. 40–41.

[46] Waltz, *Theory of International Politics*, p. 105.

[47] Kenneth Waltz, *Man, the State and War* (New York: Columbia University Press, 1959);

argument, it thus makes sense to go back to the beginning and take a look at what Rousseau had to say on the subject.

For Rousseau the anarchic structure of international politics was the fundamental source of conflict. "All the horrors of war," he said, "take birth from the precautions [men] have taken in order to prevent them."[48] The strength of a state was "purely relative": "it feels weak so long as there are others stronger than itself." To be secure, it had to "make itself stronger than its neighbors," and it could not increase its own strength "except at their expense." Every state is driven to expand its power, simply for the sake of its security: "even if it has no need to seek for provisions beyond its borders, it searches ceaselessly for new members to give itself a more unshakeable position." States thus try to weaken, perhaps even to destroy, each other. A state of war, he argued, was therefore "natural between the powers."[49]

But Rousseau's thinking did not just stop at that point. He was very much a child of his age, and standard eighteenth-century balance of power arguments played a key role in shaping his thinking.[50] States, he went on to point out, might want to extend their power, but they could not give free rein to those inclinations. The anarchic system might have created the problem, but it also helped to solve it. The system was a source of discipline. It constrained the actual behavior of states. It was more prudent to hold on to what one had than to run substantial risks for the sake of some gain; and, given the tendency of states to balance against those reaching for excessive power, the risks of aggression were substantial indeed.[51] The balance of power mechanism, although not a perfect guarantee of peace, was more effective than many people believed: "the real strength of the existing order is, in truth, to be found

---

the quotation is on p. 231. Jervis, one should note in this context, begins his "Security Dilemma" article by discussing Rousseau's argument about the problem of collective action. And Stanley Hoffmann co-edited a book of Rousseau's writings on international relations, wrote an important article on Rousseau , and called a collection of his writings *The State of War*, which was also the title of one of Rousseau's most interesting pieces on international politics.

[48] Quoted in F. H. Hinsley, *Power and the Pursuit of Peace: Theory and Practice in the History of Relations between States* (Cambridge, England: Cambridge University Press, 1963), p. 51.

[49] Rousseau, "The State of War," in Hoffmann and Fidler, *Rousseau on International Relations*, pp. 38–41; Hinsley, *Power and the Pursuit of Peace*, p. 51. Note the echo in Waltz, "Origins of War in Neorealist Theory," p. 44: "so too will a state of war exist if all states seek only to ensure their own safety."

[50] Rousseau admired Fénelon, the most important and certainly the most widely read of the classical balance of power writers. See Judith Shklar, *Men and Citizens: A Study of Rousseau's Social Theory* (Cambridge, England: Cambridge University Press, 1969), p. 4.

[51] Rousseau, in Hoffmann and Fidler, *Rousseau on International Relations*, pp. 62–64, 77–78.

partly in the play of conflicting policies which, in nine cases out of ten, keep each other mutually in check."[52] It was pointless and therefore foolish to try to reach for hegemony; in the system as it existed at the time, "the aggressor is always bound to find his enemy stronger than himself." War was both costly and risky, and it was wiser to keep what one had than to stake everything on a throw of the dice.[53]

The implication of this analysis, as Rousseau himself realized, was that "peace ought to come of itself." But this was a conclusion that he very much wanted to avoid:

> It may be objected that I prove too much and that, if the matter were as I put it, everyone being manifestly interested in avoiding war and the public interest combining with that of individuals for the preservation of peace, that peace ought to come of itself and last for ever without any need of federation. Given the present state of things, however, that would be to reason very ill. It is quite true that it would be much better for all men to remain always at peace. But so long as there is no security for this, everyone, having no guarantee that he can avoid war, is anxious to begin it at the moment which suits his own interest and so forestall a neighbor, who would not fail to forestall the attack in his turn at any moment favorable to himself, so that many wars, even offensive wars, are rather in the nature of unjust precautions for the protection of the assailant's own possessions than a device for seizing those of others.[54]

So wars are begun simply because there is "no guarantee" that war can be avoided in the future—that the mere possibility of war in the future leads states to start wars when conditions are deemed favorable, without regard to all the risks and problems that Rousseau himself had just spelled out? Those risks and problems, after all, remain the same, whether a state's motivation is defensive or not. The security provided by a system in which the powers "in nine cases out of ten keep each other mutually in check" no longer counts for anything; the fear that war at some point in the future *might* be unavoidable is no longer counterbalanced by the fear of what might happen if one opts for preventive war. The system is thus made to appear as far more war-prone than it actually is.

This in fact is the most basic problem with the whole body of thought that sees war as a product of the anarchic structure of international politics. Far more emphasis is placed on the forces pushing states forward

---

[52] Ibid., pp. 56, 62, 64–65.

[53] Ibid., pp. 62, 77–78.

[54] Ibid., pp. 79–80. The discussion here is based on the analysis in Hinsley, *Power and the Pursuit of Peace*, p. 58.

than on those holding them back; and scant attention is given to the question of why the former can be presumed to prevail over the latter. People thus tend to exaggerate the degree to which the system as such is a source of instability.

Let me give an example that relates to my own main area of interest, the Cold War. Hans Morgenthau, the leading international relations scholar of his generation, argued in 1951 that the Cold War situation was inherently unstable. The "two super-powers and their allies and satellites," he wrote, "face each other like two fighters in a short and narrow lane. They can advance and meet in what is likely to be combat, or they can retreat and allow the other side to advance into what to them is precious ground." The idea that the two fighters could just stay put and block each other's advance—that Soviet power and American power could balance each other so completely that both sides would essentially be locked into the status quo—is not even considered. Instead, according to Morgenthau,

> [T]he international situation is reduced to the primitive spectacle of two giants eying each other with watchful suspicion. They bend every effort to increase their military potential to the utmost, since this is all they have to count on. Both prepare to strike the first decisive blow, for if one does not strike it the other might. Thus, to contain or be contained, to conquer or be conquered, to destroy or be destroyed, become the watch words of the new diplomacy. Total victory, total defeat, total destruction seem to be the alternatives before the two great powers of the world.[55]

"Contain or be contained"? "Conquer or be conquered"? Why not "contain *and* be contained," or "don't conquer, but don't be conquered"? Why this unwillingness to face up to the possibility that the balance of power might be perfectly stable?

Morgenthau's argument was by no means idiosyncratic. Many writers have argued along similar lines. But the common view that the Cold War was "firmly rooted in the [bipolar] structure of international politics" (Waltz), that America and Russia were "enemies by position" (Aron), and that such conflicts are to be understood in terms of the "geometry" of conflict (Butterfield), is to my mind fundamentally mis-

---

[55] Hans Morgenthau, *In Defense of the National Interest: A Critical Examination of American Foreign Policy* (Washington: University Press of America, 1982), pp. 50, 52. This book was originally published in 1951. Even as late as 1979, Morgenthau was still arguing that the world was "moving ineluctably towards a third world war—a strategic nuclear war." See Francis A. Boyle, *World Politics and International Law* (Durham, N.C.: Duke University Press, 1985), p. 73.

taken.[56] The United States and the Soviet Union faced each other in the heart of Europe. Neither could force the other out of the part of the continent it controlled without war, and for each the maintenance of the status quo was vastly preferable to war. Each side had a strong incentive to accommodate to fundamental power realities; Soviet power and American power could balance each other quite effectively; and if that had been the end of it—if no other considerations had come into play—the system from the start would have been quite stable.

Power constrains policy: the key thing to note about the early–Cold War period is that both sides were held back by a sense for power realities. For Stalin in particular, international politics was the politics of power. At the Potsdam Conference in July 1945, he made a remark which one British diplomat considered the "high point" of that meeting. "It was not for him to teach his colleagues in this matter," the Soviet leader told Truman and Churchill, "but in politics one should be guided by the calculation of forces."[57] The Americans were also determined to take what Truman at the time called a "very realistic" line and had little

[56] Waltz, "Origins of War in Neorealist Theory," p. 52, and also his "Structural Realism after the Cold War," *International Security* 25, no. 1 (Summer 2000): 39; Aron cited in Jervis, "Was the Cold War a Security Dilemma?" *Journal of Cold War Studies* 3, no. 1 (Winter 2001): 44; Butterfield cited in Jervis, *Perception and Misperception in International Politics*, p. 66. Note also Raymond Aron's 1951 claim that "the bipolar structure of world politics is, in itself, unfavorable for stability"; earlier published in his *Les Guerres en chaîne* (Paris: Gallimard, 1951), and republished in Raymond Aron, *Une Histoire du vingtième siècle*, ed. Christian Bachelier (Paris: Plon, 1996), p. 255. Actually Aron's views were more subtle than such quotations might suggest. In his interpretation of the Cold War ideological factors loomed large, but he could still see a security dilemma-type dynamic at work. The United States and the Soviet Union, he wrote in 1948, would never accept as final a division of Europe into spheres of influence. "There is no need," he said, "to assume that either contender is striving consciously for hegemony. It is enough to assume that each is suspicious of the other's intentions, that each regards the uncertainties of the future with anxiety, and allows itself to be convinced bit by bit that sooner or later" one side or the other was bound to prevail. Ibid., pp. 229–30; earlier published in Raymond Aron, *Le Grand Schisme* (Paris: Gallimard, 1948). Arthur Schlesinger also interprets the Cold War in ideologically rooted security dilemma terms. See his contribution to Lloyd Gardner, Arthur Schlesinger, and Hans Morgenthau, *The Origins of the Cold War* (Waltham, Mass.: Ginn, 1970), esp. p. 68; this well-known essay was originally published in *Foreign Affairs* in October 1967. For an argument cut from a very different cloth, but bearing on a very different historical period, see Donald Kagan, *The Outbreak of the Peloponnesian War* (Ithaca: Cornell University Press, 1969), esp. chap. 19. Kagan very effectively attacks the view that the bipolar structure of international politics in Greece in the fifth century B.C. was bound to lead to war; see esp. pp. 349–50.

[57] Fourth plenary meeting of Potsdam Conference, July 20, 1945, *Documents on British Policy Overseas*, series I, vol. 1, p. 466. For the British diplomat's comment see Hayter to Howard, July 25, 1945, ibid., p. 903. "One had always known," the diplomat said, that this was Stalin's basic view, "but it was nice to get it from the horse's mouth."

trouble accepting Soviet domination of the part of Europe the Red Army occupied.[58]

Such attitudes are a very important source of stability because they provide an answer to the fundamental problem of how political conflicts can be worked out without a war: when such attitudes prevail, the structure of power roughly determines how those conflicts get resolved. Policies are attuned to the existing structure of power and are thus in harmony with each other. A world in which everyone behaves "realistically," a world in which everyone adjusts to the realities of power—that is, to the *same* realities of power—is thus a stable world. It is in large part for this reason that at least some traditional realists found such policies—those in line with political realities, those that accept the world for what it is—relatively attractive.[59] Even today, in the analysis of war causation, there is an important strand of realist thought that places great emphasis on those factors that prevent states from seeing power realities for what they are and thus from framing policies that are rational in terms of the basic structure of the system; that emphasis reflects the tacit assumption that if people had been able to see things clearly, and if they had been able to act rationally, war could have been avoided.[60]

What all this suggests is that the problem is *not* that states behave rationally in power political terms; the problem is *not* that the system pushes states to pursue aggressive policies. Problems arise when states *fail* to relate to each other on the basis of power realities because other factors come into play. A sensitivity to power realities does not, as a general rule, lead states to opt for aggressive strategies. Aggressive action is risky; the basic idea that states are driven by fear implies that they would be quite sensitive to the risks they would run if they did adopt policies of that sort, and that that sensitivity would be an effective source of restraint.

[58] Forrestal diary entry for July 28, 1945, Forrestal Diaries, vol. 2, Forrestal Papers, Mudd Library, Princeton University, N.J. The result of Hitler's egomania, according to Truman, was that "we shall have a Slav Europe for a long time to come. I don't think it is so bad."

[59] "Realism," as E. H. Carr pointed out (in a passage quoted by Mearsheimer), "tends to emphasize the irresistible strength of existing forces and the inevitable character of existing tendencies, and to insist that the highest wisdom lies in accepting, and adapting oneself to these forces and these tendencies." E. H. Carr, *The Twenty Years' Crisis, 1919–1939*, 2nd ed. (London: Macmillan, 1962), p. 10, quoted in Mearsheimer, *Tragedy of Great Power Politics*, p. 17.

[60] See in particular Geoffrey Blainey, *The Causes of War*, 3rd ed. (New York: Free Press, 1988), esp. pp. 114–24; Fearon, "Rationalist Explanations for War," esp. pp. 380–81, 390–401; Stephen Van Evera, *Causes of War: Power and the Roots of Conflict* (Ithaca: Cornell University Press, 1999), esp. pp. 9, 11, and chap. 2; and, above all, Jervis, *Perception and Misperception in International Politics*.

Politics is in large part about striking balances—about weighing benefits against costs, about assessing risks and dealing with uncertainty, about deciding how much is enough and how much is too much. Political sense is thus a sense for the risks and costs that going too far would entail, a sense therefore for the importance of moderation and balance, compromise and restraint. The fact that warfare is embedded in a political system is therefore of fundamental importance: the use of violence is constrained and limited by the fact that it is subject to political control. This point was one of Clausewitz's most striking insights. In the famous first chapter of *On War*, he explains the tendency of warfare, *in pure theory*, to become absolute, and his argument in that section has a certain security dilemma flavor. Each side in a conflict, he says, is driven by fear: "So long as I have not overthrown my opponent I am bound to fear he may overthrow me." The two sides thus drive each other toward extremes. Each side is driven to "use force without compunction," driven to seize whatever advantage it can get, in the knowledge that if it holds back, its adversary may well get the upper hand.[61] But warfare, Clausewitz insists, is *in reality* not to be understood in that way. "War is only a branch of political activity," he writes; "it is in no sense autonomous….Its grammar, indeed, may be its own, but not its logic": the logic of war can be supplied only from the outside, through political direction and control.[62] If there is a certain tendency for conflict to spiral out of control, there is also a countervailing tendency, rooted in the fact that warfare is a political phenomenon, that works in the opposite direction. For Clausewitz the hallmark of rationality was that the latter tendency would prevail—that in a rational state, the use of force would be governed by political purpose.

But could that purpose be to expand one's own power without limit? Would such behavior be rational in power political terms? The classical eighteenth-century view was that such behavior would be irrational—that states, to preserve their own political freedom, would come together spontaneously to prevent any single power from going too far. Aggressiveness was held in check by the tendency of countervailing power to form. It was thus foolish to reach for too much power or to go too far in reducing the power of one's rivals.[63] The classical balance of

[61] Carl von Clausewitz, *On War*, Michael Howard and Peter Paret, eds. and trans. (Princeton: Princeton University Press, 1976), pp. 75–77.

[62] Ibid., p. 605.

[63] In addition to the passages from Rousseau referred to earlier, note especially the extracts in Wright, *Theory and Practice*, from Fénelon (p. 42), Defoe (pp. 47–48), and Hume (p. 64). For useful discussions of the history of balance of power thinking, see Herbert Butterfield, "The Balance of Power," in Herbert Butterfield and Martin Wight, *Diplomatic Investigations: Essays in the Theory of International Politics* (London: George Allen and Unwin, 1966); Martin Wight, "The Balance of Power and International Order," in Alan

power theorists thus offered counsels of moderation and restraint. They were critical when policies were pushed too far from "obstinacy and passion," as Hume said in his famous essay on the subject.[64] They were particularly critical when statesmen in time of war no longer thought in rational balance of power terms—"when once engaged," to quote Hume again, "we lose all concern for ourselves and our posterity, and consider only how we may best annoy the enemy."[65] From their point of view, power was too precious to be wasted on projects that, when examined closely, made little political sense. The political equilibrium of Europe might be worth fighting for, but even then the goal was to be limited. Enemy aspirations had to be checked, but you had to take care to "not reduce your enemy too low."[66] The system thus served to constrain state behavior. To the extent it was effective, it provided a certain degree of security and created a certain degree of stability.

Indeed, the European state system was seen as "a kind of society," "a sort of republic," whose members were bound together by a common interest in the "maintenance of order and the preservation of liberty."[67] In this system the balance of power principle played a fundamental role. A balanced distribution of power guaranteed the basic political

---

James, ed., *The Bases of International Order* (London: Oxford University Press, 1973); and M. S. Anderson, "Eighteenth-Century Theories of the Balance of Power," in Ragnhild Hatton and M. S. Anderson, eds., *Studies in Diplomatic History* (London: Longman, 1970). For the most thorough account of the early writings on this question, see Ernst Kaeber's dissertation: *Die Idee des europäischen Gleichgewichts in der publizistischen Literatur vom 16. bis zur Mitte des 18. Jahrhunderts* (Berlin: Duncken, 1906). (Only the first part, covering the early period, was ever actually published.) Note also the bibliographical essay in Gulick, *Europe's Classical Balance of Power*, pp. 311–25.

[64] David Hume, "Of the Balance of Power" (1752), in Wright, *Theory and Practice*, p. 64.

[65] Ibid., p. 64.

[66] Fénelon in Wright, *Theory and Practice*, p. 42.

[67] See the well-known extracts from Fénelon (c. 1700) and Vattel (1758) in Wright, *Theory and Practice*, pp. 39, 41, 71–72, and the quotations from Rousseau, Montesquieu and Voltaire in Hinsley, *Power and the Pursuit of Peace*, pp. 57–58, 162, 163. Note also Niklas Vogt, *Über die europäische Republik*, 5 vols. (Frankfurt, 1787–92); Vogt is of particular interest because he was one of Metternich's teachers. This general idea, it should be noted, was not new to the eighteenth century; note, for example, the extract from Botero (1605) in Wright, *Theory and Practice*, p. 21; it in fact has roots in the Middle Ages and indeed in ancient Rome. On the "idea of international society," see Hedley Bull, *The Anarchical Society: A Study of Order in World Politics*, 2nd ed. (New York: Columbia University Press, 1995), pp. 23–38. On the medieval concept of the *res publica Christiana*, a term which by the late Middle Ages had become the "watchword" of the "common interests of the Community of Latin Christendom," see Garrett Mattingly, *Renaissance Diplomacy* (Baltimore: Penguin, 1964), p. 18, and the references Mattingly cites on p. 259 of that book. This concept linked up very naturally with the idea, which in rudimentary form initially took shape in mid-fifteenth-century Italy, that the maintenance of a balance of power was one such common interest. On the emergence of the balance of power idea, see ibid., pp. 67–68, 71, and the sources cited on p. 263 n.2.

rights of the European states, and a general acceptance of the principle that power needed to be balanced and that aims needed to be limited could be an important source of stability. The principle of the balance of power thus became, as Martin Wight remarks, "the first article of the unwritten constitution of the states-system."[68]

Contemporary realist writers still place great emphasis on the balance of power mechanism, and Waltz in particular considers it to be of fundamental importance. But the striking thing here is that in Waltz's theory balancing does not lead to peace: his theory, a theory in which the balance of power plays such a prominent role, he says explains the "dismal recurrence" of war "through the millennia."[69] But shouldn't the balance of power mechanism be a force for peace? The system teaches its lessons; attempts to achieve hegemony have repeatedly been turned back. As Waltz himself points out, what this means is that the problem lies at the unit level. The system may teach its lessons, but ambitious governments refuse to listen. "The leaders of expansionist states," he writes, "have nevertheless been able to persuade themselves that skillful diplomacy and clever strategy would enable them to transcend the normal processes of balance-of-power politics."[70] This, however, simply underscores the point that the problem does not lie at the system level, and indeed that systemic forces have a stabilizing effect.

One of the key arguments made by the eighteenth-century balance of power writers was that the state system could be regarded as a "kind of republic"—that the fundamental, spontaneous balance of power mechanism, plus the political norms that had grown up around it, provided the basis for a kind of political system. States in such a world need not act in a purely selfish way. They might to a certain extent come to identify their interests with the interests of the system as a whole. They might be willing, as Salisbury later put it, to bear some share in the

---

[68] Wight, "The Balance of Power and International Order," p. 102. Friedrich von Gentz, in his *Fragments on the Balance of Power* (1806), in a well-known passage referred explicitly to the balance of power as a constitutional principle. See the extract in Wright, *Theory and Practice*, p. 94. This point has a particular importance, given Gentz's ties to Metternich and the role he played at the Congress of Vienna.

[69] Waltz, "War in Neorealist Theory," p. 44. Randall Schweller makes a similar point. "The notion that states would adopt aggressive policies to acquire security," he writes, "simply does not square with the thrust of Waltz's argument, namely, that expansion is self-defeating because the system induces balancing behavior. In Waltz's scheme, such behavior is irrational." Schweller, "Neorealism's Status-Quo Bias," p. 118. See also Jack Snyder, *Myths of Empire: Domestic Politics and International Ambition* (Ithaca: Cornell University Press, 1991), p. 11.

[70] Waltz, "War in Neorealist Theory," pp. 48–49. The argument about the importance of the lessons the system teaches plays an important role in defensive realist thought. See especially Barry Posen, *The Sources of Military Doctrine: France, Britain, and Germany Between the World Wars* (Ithaca: Cornell University Press, 1984), pp. 68–69.

government of the "great international republic" as the price they would have to pay to enjoy the benefits of such a system.[71] To the extent that anarchy leads to balancing and balancing leads to that kind of behavior, a system without supranational authority might in this way as well have a certain stability.

But older insights of this sort only half-survive in contemporary realist thought. Waltz, for example, argues both sides of the issue. In one passage, he takes it for granted that only selfish behavior is to be expected. Governments, he says, are always being told to "act for the sake of the system and not for their own narrowly defined advantage." But these urgings are pointless; states have to concentrate on their own narrow interests; they "have to do whatever they think necessary for their own preservation." "With each country constrained to take care of itself," he says, "no one can take care of the system."[72] But later on in the same book, he takes exactly the opposite line. "Great power," he points out, "gives its possessors a big stake in their system and the ability to act for its sake. For them management becomes both worthwhile and possible."[73] The issue is easy to resolve historically. As Robert Jervis points out (citing an article by Paul Schroeder), "[I]t is clear that states-

[71] Salisbury, "The Terms of Peace," p. 556. It is important to note that in purely power political terms, Britain would have profited from the development of an antagonism between the two strongest continental powers, who would be prevented from ganging up against their great island neighbor, who would each have an interest in bidding for British support, and who could be threatened with a tilt toward the adversary power if British interests were not adequately accommodated. But Salisbury's interest in the stability of the system was such that he was willing to forgo the advantages that bad Franco-German relations would almost automatically bring Britain: the German annexation of Alsace-Lorraine was opposed in spite of the positive effect it would have had on Britain's power position, narrowly defined.

[72] Waltz, *Theory of International Politics*, p. 109. Note also ibid., p. 91: "no state intends to participate in the formation of a structure by which it and others will be constrained." But in fact states *are* often willing to help build such structures, and indeed it is precisely because they know that in such a system "others will be constrained" that they are normally willing to accept such limits on their own freedom of action. In other words, there is nothing in theory that would prevent them from reaching the conclusion that, given the benefits of such a system, this price might well be worth paying; and if enough states make a judgment of that sort, a constructed system might well come into being. In fact, one can go further still and note that in certain circumstances constraints may make sense even in purely unilateral terms: a strategy of "burning one's bridges" and thus of limiting one's own freedom of action, no matter what other countries do, may well put a state in a stronger position. The delegation to the NATO commander during the Eisenhower period of the authority to begin nuclear operations, a fundamental part of the NATO system in the 1950s, is an important case in point. On this issue, see Marc Trachtenberg, *A Constructed Peace: The Making of the European Settlement, 1945–1963* (Princeton: Princeton University Press, 1999), pp. 163–73. On the political significance of the fact that the U.S. government's hands were somewhat tied by this structure, see chapter 5 below.

[73] Waltz, *Theory of International Politics*, p. 195; also p. 198 and chapter 9 in general.

men often do think in systemic terms, not only in seeking to anticipate how others will respond to their moves, but also in seeing their countries as part of a larger whole."[74] The peacemakers at the Congress of Vienna in 1814–15, especially Metternich and Castlereagh, were very much concerned with the stability of the system as a whole.[75] A policy of this sort, moreover, can make perfect sense in power political terms, above all for status quo powers like Britain and Austria in 1815. The basic point is worth making once again: balance of power thinking, the sort of thinking that inspired statesmen like Metternich and Castlereagh, was very much within the realist tradition; what this example shows is that a world in which power considerations loom large is not necessarily an unstable world and that there are ways in which a deep concern for the structure of power can be a source of stability.

Does this mean therefore that there is nothing to the argument about anarchic structure generating conflict? Is it the case, for example, that a world of simple security-seekers—that is, a world where every state would be happy to live with things as they were, if it could be sure it could keep what it had—would necessarily be perfectly stable? Some scholars do in fact argue along those lines.[76] But to draw that conclusion is, I think, to go too far. It is quite clear that serious problems can have essentially structural causes.

The Cold War is a major case in point. With Europe divided at the end of World War II, one might have thought that each side had little choice but to accept the other side's domination of its half of the continent and that the basic result would be a simple spheres of influence system. In such a system, the fundamental rule would be that each side would have a free hand on its side of the line of demarcation in Europe; if that rule had applied without exception, one would have had a perfectly stable international order right from the start. The problem was that there *was* one great exception to that rule, and that had to do with Germany. This was the one case in which the Soviets could not give the western powers a free hand to do whatever they wanted in their part of Europe. The USSR could not remain passive while West Germany recovered her full independence and with it the freedom to develop her military power. This was a very understandable concern, given the fact that the Soviets were in effective control of half of prewar German territory, and given the sort of military power even West Germany was

---

[74] Jervis, *System Effects*, p. 137.

[75] See, for example, Castlereagh to Liverpool, February 6, 1814, quoted in Phillips, *The Confederation of Europe*, p. 67n., and the quotation from Metternich in Kissinger, *A World Restored*, p. 13. Note also the discussion of the Vienna system in Robert Jervis, "Security Regimes," *International Organization* 36, no. 2 (Spring 1982): 362–68.

[76] See Schweller, "Neorealism's Status-Quo Bias," p. 91.

capable of generating once all the constraints were removed. But the western powers—out of a sense of weakness and vulnerability, and out of the fear that if they did not adopt a liberal policy, all of Germany might be lost—felt they had to make West Germany a kind of partner. They therefore had to restore the Germans' political rights, and they had to build up German power and make it a part of the western defense system—all the more so, since movement along that road had led to a more active and more threatening Soviet policy, which in turn had underscored the importance of building up the military power of the western bloc. Looking at the story, it is hard not to see a security dilemma–type dynamic at play. Both sides were interested in maintaining their positions; the policies of both sides were rooted in fear, not greed; and the interaction of those policies led to a certain spiraling-up of tension.[77]

These points about the Cold War bear directly on the issues we are concerned with here. If Russia and Germany faced a security dilemma in their dealings with each other, then that problem was ultimately essentially solved by the intervention of the western powers and the eventual construction of a "security regime" based largely on the military strength of those outside powers.[78] But to characterize that development in those terms is to cast in the language of contemporary international relations theory the basic insights of classical balance of power theorists like Fénelon: the goal was to avoid engagements which would "prove too beneficial to your ally" and to take care "not to reduce your enemy too low."[79] Thanks to the action of third powers, neither Germany nor Russia would become strong enough to threaten the other, and neither would be too vulnerable to the threat posed by the other. The modern theory thus connects up with a body of thought with deep roots in the past; the modern notion of a "security regime" links up with the classical idea of the world of the great powers as a "sort of republic"; and our ideas today acquire more depth and texture when we

---

[77] This in a nutshell is the basic argument about the origins of the Cold War laid out in Trachtenberg, *Constructed Peace*, esp. chapters 1–3. See also the important book by James McAllister, *No Exit: America and the German Problem, 1943–1954* (Ithaca: Cornell University Press, 2002). Note also the fascinating chapter on the origins of the Cold War (chap. 6) in Dale Copeland's *The Origins of Major War* (Ithaca: Cornell University Press, 2000). Copeland interprets the Cold War in structural terms, but his is what one might call a "first derivative" structural argument—that is, an argument that emphasizes the importance of the way power relations were changing over time.

[78] See Jervis, "Security Regimes," and Marc Trachtenberg, "The Making of a Political System: The German Question in International Politics, 1945–1963," in Paul Kennedy and William Hitchcock, eds., *From War to Peace: Altered Strategic Landscapes in the Twentieth Century* (New Haven: Yale University Press, 2000).

[79] Fénelon in Wright, *Theory and Practice*, p. 42.

see them as new incarnations of important ideas that have been around for centuries.

A second and perhaps more basic point for our present purposes is that the Cold War case in itself shows that fundamental problems *can*, to a certain extent, be structural in nature. A major conflict *can* to a certain degree be rooted in a clash of essentially defensive, status quo-oriented, policies. But if this is a structural interpretation, it is rather different from the sort of structural explanation one finds in the literature. For one thing, it does not view conflict as automatic—that is, as spontaneously generated by the simple bipolar structure of power. It in fact took quite some time for the mechanism to get charged up: it took a good deal of Soviet aggressiveness, vis-à-vis Turkey and Iran in 1945–46, to get the machinery moving. For another thing, the dynamic here is political and not military in nature. The nature of the military system in place at the time—the degree to which it emphasized offense over defense, for example—and the specific character of the weaponry in question—the non-distinguishability of offensive and defensive forces, for instance—were not major factors.[80] The heart of the problem was that those forces might be in German (and not, for example, in American) hands. The problem, in other words, is to be understood not in general terms—that is, as rooted in the "bipolar structure of international politics"—but rather in more historically specific terms, having to do with a particular set of problems relating to Germany and to Germany's place in the international political system.

For our present purposes, however, these are second-order issues. The basic point is that security dilemma-type dynamics certainly do exist and do play a significant role in international politics. The Cold War is an important case in point, but it is not the only one, and other examples could be cited. But if the importance of this kind of mechanism is not to be dismissed out of hand, it is not to be exaggerated either. Systemic forces of this sort play a role, but not as great a role as theorists (and occasionally even historians[81]) sometimes seem to sug-

---

[80] In their analysis of the security dilemma dynamic, political scientists tend to emphasize military factors of the sort alluded to here. See Jervis's pathbreaking article, "Cooperation under the Security Dilemma," esp. pp. 186–214. This type of argument gave rise to an important school of thought, sometimes called "offense/defense theory"; note in particular Van Evera, *Causes of War*, esp. chaps. 6 and 7. It is frequently argued that war is more likely to break out in a world that places a great premium on offensive military strategies, and indeed some scholars claim the effect is so strong that in such a world wars can occur "inadvertently" or "accidentally"; the First World War is generally offered as the main case in point. For an analysis of that particular argument, see my article, "The Coming of the First World War: A Reassessment," in Marc Trachtenberg, *History and Strategy* (Princeton: Princeton University Press, 1991).

[81] Two very important historical works have recently developed interpretations based on this kind of thinking: Melvyn Leffler, *A Preponderance of Power: National Security, the*

gest. States to be sure are sensitive to possible threats to their independence, but they can deal with such problems in various ways. It is a mistake to assume that their only recourse is to adopt policies that their adversary will view as threatening, and that such situations inevitably lead to a constant ratcheting-up of tension. Power can balance power; threats can be checked; accommodations can be worked out; states can be relatively relaxed. Above all, it is a mistake to suppose (as Rousseau did) that states would go to war simply because they thought that an armed conflict *might* break out sometime in the future. It is only when people's sense for the level of risk crosses a certain threshold that preventive war thinking begins to play an important role, and it never dominates policy unless real threats based on an adversary's actual behavior loom large on the horizon. The forces that generate that sense of risk and bring it to the point where preventive war thinking kicks in are the fundamental factors in international political life, and generally speaking they are not systemic in nature.

It is a basic error, therefore, to see conflict as essentially driven by systemic forces—that is, as essentially rooted (in more than a merely permissive sense) in the anarchic structure of international politics. And if the system is not a basic source of instability, then it follows that the real problems are generated by forces welling up at the unit level—forces that give rise to policies that are not rational in power political terms. Problems develop, as a rule, not because the system pushes states into conflict with each other, but because states overreach themselves and pursue policies that make little sense in terms of the incentives the system creates. Such problems can develop in an anarchic world, but this fact does not mean that the system itself is a source of instability, any more than the fact that the market mechanism is imperfect—and that in a market system unemployment, for example, is possible—means that the market mechanism as such plays a destabilizing role in economic life.[82]

The system, as Waltz says, "shapes and shoves," but states often fight back, and it is that resistance, and not the system itself, that lies at the heart of the problem.[83]

Truman Administration, and the Cold War (Stanford: Stanford University Press, 1992), and Paul Schroeder, *The Transformation of European Politics, 1763–1848* (Oxford: Clarendon Press, 1994). For a discussion and a critique, see my review articles in *Orbis*, Summer 1995 (for Leffler) and Winter 1996 (for Schroeder), and also the exchange of correspondence with Schroeder in *Orbis*, Spring 1996.

[82] This is an allusion to the Waltzian argument that "wars occur because there is nothing to prevent them" and that the system—that is, the absence of centralized authority—is a fundamental cause of war. See Waltz, *Man, the State and War*, pp. 182, 188, 232. Note also Waltz, "Structural Realism after the Cold War," p. 8.

[83] Waltz, "Structural Realism after the Cold War," p. 24.

A Theory of War or a Theory of Peace?

Realism, and especially neorealism, according to Paul Schroeder, "is a good theory for explaining war, but not peace."[84] When I first read that comment, I did not quite know what Schroeder had in mind. I was writing a book on how a stable international system had taken shape during the Cold War period, and the interpretation I was developing was very much grounded in what I took to be a realist understanding of international politics. But it gradually became clear to me that Schroeder had been on to something—something important, and something that for some reason had escaped me entirely. Schroeder, it turned out, was simply echoing what realist writers themselves had been saying. A number of leading theorists, Kenneth Waltz and John Mearsheimer, for example, clearly did think of realism as a theory of war. They did take the view that the "anarchic nature of international politics" led to "cutthroat behavior among states."[85] Not only that, but they seemed to take it for granted that this was a reality that simply had to be accepted. "Realism," according to Mearsheimer, "is a pessimistic theory. It depicts a world of stark and harsh competition, and it holds out little promise of making it more benign."[86]

What sort of policy guidance follows from that basic theory? For Mearsheimer, at least, the implications are quite clear. "States *should* behave according to the dictates of offensive realism," he says, "because it outlines the best way to survive in a dangerous world." If great powers "want to survive," they "should always act like good offensive realists"—and given the way he defines offensive realism, what that means is that they should be "primed for offense," that they should "act aggressively toward each other," that they should take advantage of every chance they get to "amass as much power" as they can.[87]

There is no quarreling with Mearsheimer's logic here. If international politics really worked the way he says it does—if one accepts his basic premise about how an anarchic system works, about how anarchy generates conflict, even if states are only interested in making themselves secure—then his conclusions about policy follow as a matter of course. If the rules of the game cannot be changed, one has little choice but to play that game as effectively as possible.

---

[84] Paul Schroeder, Letter to the Editor, *Orbis* (Spring 1996): 308. That letter was a reply to a review I had done of Schroeder's *The Transformation of European Politics*, in which I had criticized him for arguing that balance of power policies were inherently destabilizing (see note 81 in this chapter).

[85] Mearsheimer's paraphrase of a "very important" Waltz argument, in the book review cited in n. 2 of this chapter.

[86] Mearsheimer, "False Promise," p. 48, esp. n. 182.

[87] Mearsheimer, *Tragedy of Great Power Politics*, 3, 11–12, 35. Emphasis his.

But if one accepts that basic premise, how can moderate policies be defended? Many realists, especially the defensive realists, as a general rule favor moderate policies. Is that basic approach to policy consistent with the view that anarchy generates conflict? One can argue that even if that view is correct in principle, in practice the forces pushing states toward aggressive policies are much weaker than that way of looking at the world might at first glance seem to suggest. Aggressive policies might simply not be viable for reasons having to do, for example, with the nature of military technology. The defense might be so strong that aggressive strategies would probably fail. In such circumstances, for very practical reasons, moderate policies would make sense. But those who would argue along these lines would be basing their support for a policy of moderation on what in the final analysis are essentially contingent factors. What if, for example, military technology actually did favor the offense? What if it were fairly easy for one strong country to stamp out potential threats by means of a highly aggressive policy? Would such a policy then be worth adopting for that reason alone?

If the answer is no, then what this suggests is that there should be a more fundamental basis—a political and not just a military basis—for favoring relatively restrained policies. And some leading theorists who support such policies do in fact point to one fundamental political reason why overly ambitious policies are to be avoided—that is, why they are not favored by the system. If a state tries to amass too much power, they say, the other states in the system will feel threatened and will thus come together to oppose that state. The imperative to balance, in their view, is so strong that it makes sense for even strong states to draw in their horns rather provoke the formation of a hostile coalition.

But to place so much emphasis on balancing is to put the political argument for a moderate policy on a relatively weak and vulnerable base. Excessive reliance on the argument about balancing has led to exaggerated claims about the effectiveness and automaticity of the balance of power mechanism. Balancing coalitions do from time to time come into being, but more slowly and with much greater difficulty than people seem to realize. During the period when Napoleon was at the peak of his power, the other continental states tried hard to reach an accommodation with him; balancing was no automatic reflex.[88] In the case of the pre–World War I period, the gradual formation of the Triple Entente is not to be understood as a simple response to the growth of German power. It was not fear of German power—fear that Germany was reaching for hegemony in Europe—that led Russia to form an alliance with France; indeed, the Russians had been more eager to remain

---

[88] For a very persuasive analysis, see Schroeder, *Transformation of European Politics*. Schroeder's conclusions on this point can be found at the end of the chap. 4 of that book.

on good terms with Germany when that country was at the height of its power under Bismarck in the 1880s. As for the British, they turned against Germany only after it had become clear that the Germans had in effect turned against them. They never opted for a policy of balancing German power simply because Germany's war-making potential had grown so dramatically in the late nineteenth century; a strong Germany would have been an attractive partner if her policy had been directed simply toward holding the line against Russia. And finally, with regard to the Hitler period, balancing behavior fell far short of what might have been expected, given the nature of the threat; indeed, Hitler was able to go as far as he did only because the balancing mechanism was so weak. The western powers opted for a policy of appeasement until early 1939. The USSR entered the anti-Nazi coalition only after the Soviet Union was invaded in 1941. As for the United States, that country certainly ended up playing a key role in the anti-German coalition, but President Roosevelt, although he was successful in the end, had tremendous difficulty bringing the United States into the war.

The point here is that the "spontaneous" balance of power mechanism is not particularly strong, and it therefore makes little sense to rest the political argument for moderation and restraint too narrowly on claims about balancing. The argument for a relatively moderate policy (if one accepts it, at least as a general rule) needs to be put on a much broader basis—a basis that can be brought more to the surface in two ways. First, one can try to bring out, drawing on what can be found in traditional realist thought, a whole range of arguments that point toward relatively restrained policies, and this is what I tried to do in the previous sections of this article. But one can also look at what leading realists have to say when they talk about policy issues, and one can then try to draw out the basic theoretical assumptions implicit in those policy arguments. This is what I want to try to do in this section. The assumption here is that the key to understanding the heart of realist thinking is to focus on policy, and especially on the particular policy arguments developed by the leading realist writers. The idea is that arguments about policy are of central importance because it is in this area that theory meets reality: it is the confrontation with reality that draws out what is fundamental in the theory. What then do major theorists have to say about policy issues, and what do their policy arguments reveal about their basic thinking about international politics in general?

Realist writers of course have a good deal to say about contemporary affairs, and their views are naturally rooted in their fundamental understanding of international politics. Those policy arguments tend to have a certain cast. Realists dislike highly ideological policies and prefer policies based on interest and attuned to power realities. Their aim, as a general rule (Mearsheimer is perhaps an exception here), is not to make their own country as strong as possible; the ultimate goal of the American realists is not a world dominated by the United States. Their call for "realist" policies—that is, for policies that are rational in terms of the basic structure of the system as they understand it—is rooted in the assumption that such policies make for a better world, a world in which their own country could achieve its basic goals, and above all provide for its own security, without a war. If they really believe that systemic pressures pushed states into conflict with each other, realist theorists presumably would call upon governments to *resist* those pressures; they would urge governments to use whatever room for maneuver they had to struggle against the basic logic of the system, or perhaps even to try to change the basic nature of the system. But one does not quite find them taking that line.[89] Their real assumption, in fact, is that their policy prescriptions would *not*, if followed, drive states into conflict with each other, for otherwise they would hardly have embraced them so readily. In practice, they take it for granted that "realist" policies do not in themselves lead to war and instability; and they in fact tend to criticize governments for failing to adopt policies of that sort.

The Waltz case is of particular interest in this regard. He looks back on the Cold War with a certain degree of nostalgia. During that period, Waltz says, America and Russia "constrained each other."[90] "So long as the world was bipolar," he says, "the United States and the Soviet Union held each other in check."[91] All this is rather different from the

---

[89] The case of Hans Morgenthau is an exception here, but for that very reason is quite important in the present context. Morgenthau did believe that a system of sovereign states was prone to war. He was therefore an advocate of a world state, whose eventual establishment he considered "indispensable for the survival of the world." He in fact complained in the preface to the third edition of *Politics Among Nations* about "still being told that I believe in the prominence of the international system based upon the nation state, although the obsolescence of the nation state and the need to merge it into supranational organizations of a functional nature was already one of the main points of the first edition of 1948." It is as though an acceptance of the view that a system of sovereign states produces conflict and war had led even the premier realist thinker of his generation to take a view that would now be viewed as very much at variance with the basic tenor of realist thought. Hans Morgenthau, *Politics Among Nations: The Struggle for Power and Peace*, 3rd ed. (New York: Knopf, 1961), p. 539 and preface; see also p. 569 and chap. 29, "The World State," esp. pp. 501 and 509. Morgenthau had in fact come to this conclusion about the need for a world state very early on. See the excellent study by Christoph Frei, *Hans J. Morgenthau: An Intellectual Biography* (Baton Rouge: Louisiana State University Press, 2001), pp. 140–41.

[90] Waltz, "Structural Realism after the Cold War," p. 28.

[91] Kenneth Waltz, "America as a Model for the World? A Foreign Policy Perspective," *PS: Political Science and Politics* 24, no. 4 (December 1991): 669. The assumption that power corrupts and therefore needs to be checked has long been a mainstay of conservative

earlier view that a great conflict like the Cold War was a simple product of the bipolar "structure of international politics."[92] That structure is seen now more as an element of stability than as an engine of conflict. The assumption now is that American power and Soviet power balanced each other quite effectively during the Cold War period, and that that was the bedrock upon which the peace was built. The broader implication is that a system based on power is not inherently unstable. The basic point now is not that power provokes power, but rather that power constrains power, that power accommodates power, and that a system in which power confronts power is therefore to a considerable extent self-stabilizing.

The assumption that the Cold War system was stable because Soviet power and American power balanced each other so effectively implied to leading neorealist theorists that the collapse of that system would be a major source of instability. American power would no longer be balanced by countervailing power. And indeed, as Waltz has pointed out, the United States during the post–Cold War period "has behaved as unchecked powers have usually done. In the absence of counterweights, a country's internal impulses prevail, whether fueled by liberal or by other urges."[93] Yes, he admits, realists like himself had been wrong to think that "the end of the Cold War would mean the end of NATO." But that error "arose not from a failure of realist theory to comprehend international politics, but from an underestimation of America's folly."[94] The expansion of NATO was a particularly foolish policy, and Waltz lists a whole series of reasons why that policy was misguided.[95] History, he says, shows that magnanimity in victory makes sense while the opposite policy generally leads to trouble. But "rather than

thought, and, as Arnold Wolfers pointed out, what this implies is that a "preference for equilibrium" is not necessarily to be understood as a "mere rationalization of national interest." "Men with a conservative bent of mind," Wolfers noted, "need find nothing shocking, therefore, in the suggestion that all nations, including their own, should be restrained by counterpower and thereby be spared temptations as well as prevented from abusing their power." Arnold Wolfers, "The Balance of Power in Theory and Practice," in Wolfers, *Discord and Collaboration: Essays on International Politics* (Baltimore: Johns Hopkins University Press, 1962), p. 121. The point applies both to international and to domestic politics. It was a basis, for example, of the American founding fathers' belief in the importance of a system of checks and balances.

[92] See Waltz, "Origins of War in Neorealist Theory," p. 52, and Waltz, "Structural Realism after the Cold War," p. 39. It is important to note, however, that long before the end of the Cold War, Waltz, as is well known, also argued that bipolarity was a source of stability. See especially Kenneth Waltz, "The Stability of a Bipolar World," *Daedalus* 93, no. 3 (Summer 1964), and Waltz, *Theory of International Politics*, chap. 8, esp. pp. 170–76.

[93] Waltz, "Structural Realism after the Cold War," p. 24.

[94] Ibid.

[95] Ibid., p. 22.

learning from history, the United States is repeating past errors by extending its influence over what used to be the province of the vanquished."[96]

A wise policy, in Waltz's view—and that means, presumably, a policy in line with basic realist principles—would thus have been to avoid kicking Russia while she was down. American behavior—the policy of extending the U.S.-dominated world eastward, indeed the policy of creating a "world order" dominated by American power—was not viewed as only to be expected, given the basic realist understanding of how the world works. But if it was unexpected, this could only be because the most fundamental realist principles suggest that a rational state would behave in a very different way. And Waltz himself makes it quite clear how he thinks America should behave. The United States, he thinks, ought to pursue a more modest policy, a policy that would "give other countries at long last the chance to deal with their own problems and make their own mistakes."[97] But the problem (and he cites Fénelon in this connection) is that countries with a great surplus of power "cannot long be expected to behave with decency and moderation."[98]

When Waltz condemns the extravagance of America's post–Cold War policy and talks in more general terms about how "the selfishness of those who tend to their own narrowly defined interests" is to be preferred to the "arrogance of the global burden-bearers," he is really expressing his appreciation for a system in which policies are constrained—that is, for a system in which competitive pressures limit what states can try to do. "Close competition," he writes, "subordinates ideology to interest; states that enjoy a margin of power over their closest competitors are led to pay undue attention to minor dangers and pursue fancies abroad that reach beyond the fulfillment of interests narrowly defined in terms of security."[99] His basic policy prescription for a country like the United States today is thus that it should act *as though* its power were more narrowly circumscribed—*as though* it were constrained by structural realities to pursue a policy based on a narrower definition of political interest. But that policy prescription reflects a more basic assumption about how a highly competitive system works. It reflects the assumption that in such a system policies are restrained and restraint leads to a kind of stability. If Waltz recommends that states

[96] Ibid., p. 37.
[97] Ibid., p. 30.
[98] Waltz, "America as a Model for the World?" p. 668.
[99] Waltz, *Theory of International Politics*, p. 205. Fénelon (who Waltz admires and sometimes cites) had also talked about how states of limited power, "void of the blind inconsiderate presumption which is incident to the fortunate," were obliged to pursue prudent and relatively moderate policies. Wright, *Theory and Practice*, p. 44.

act as though they lived in such a system, that can only mean that he really believes that such a system is not so bad after all—that is, that a highly competitive anarchic system is not inherently prone to war.

If this is the real thinking of even the most hard-core neorealists—and this type of argument does sometimes come to the surface in their writings[100]—is there any point to *not* making it more explicit? If it were true that a Realpolitik world—a world where state behavior was based on power and interest defined in power political terms—was inherently unstable, if it were true that in a world not governed by supranational authority, states were constantly driven into conflict with each other, then the argument for a very ambitious American policy, a policy whose goal was an American-dominated world order, would be quite strong. But that conclusion is rejected; what is puzzling is that people seem so attached to the premises on which it is based.

To assume that a system of states behaving rationally in power political terms is inherently brutal, violent, and prone to war is to admit that realist principles are not a recipe for stability. To proclaim that the basic structure of international politics leads to "cut-throat behavior among states" and that realism "holds out little promise" of making the world more benign is thus in a sense to hoist the white flag. The effect is to leave the field clear to those calling for a radical transformation of world politics—to those who, like Woodrow Wilson, indulge in "the colossal conceit of thinking that they could suddenly make international life over into what they believed to be their own image," that is, to those advocating the sorts of policies to which the realists are most opposed.[101] If that line of argument is to be answered effectively, the standard way in which realism is presented needs to be recast, and fundamental ideas that have been part of the realist tradition for centuries and are implicit even in certain contemporary realist arguments have to be allowed to rise to the surface once again.

The realists, after all, have little to be ashamed of. Their basic philosophy, from Fénelon through Waltz, has always—or almost always—placed a great premium on moderation and restraint. To be sure, no realist would deny that sometimes a developing threat is so great that a warlike policy might be in order. But the basic thrust of realist thought is to insist on the importance of keeping things under control. If major

---

[100] See esp. the section in Waltz's *Theory of International Politics* called "The Virtues of Anarchy," pp. 111–14. Note in particular the argument on p. 113 that the anarchic international system is a political system *par excellence*. The realm of power, Waltz points out, is the realm of accommodation and mutual adaptation; "the constant possibility that force will be used limits manipulations, moderates demands, and serves as an incentive for the settlement of disputes" (pp. 113–14).

[101] Kennan, *American Diplomacy*, p. 69 (slightly altered).

conflicts have developed, it was not because realist principles have shaped policy, but rather because very different sorts of impulses have come to govern the behavior of great states. Looking back at the history of international politics over the past two hundred years, studying episode after episode, one fundamental conclusion emerges. Power political thinking is not the problem: the problem is that there is not enough of it. Policies that are rational in power political terms are not the fundamental source of international conflict: in themselves, by and large, they help make for a stable international order. To understand why this is the case is to understand why realism is at its heart a theory of peace, and why it ought to be recognized as such.

CHAPTER TWO

The Problem of International Order and How to Think about It

WHAT DO WE mean when we talk about order in international politics? The term might refer to the idea that international political life is not totally chaotic and that there is instead a certain logic to how things work in this area. From that point of view, to grapple with the problem of order is to study how politics works in a world of sovereign states—that is, in what is by convention called an "anarchic" world, a world characterized by the absence of overarching authority. In the international relations literature, the term *order* is in fact sometimes used in this sense. Kenneth Waltz, for example, in his important *Theory of International Politics*, is interested in the question of how there can be "order without an orderer"—of how an anarchic world can have a certain structure, of how a world of sovereign states can be viewed as a system that works in a relatively orderly way.[1]

An *orderly* way, but not necessarily a *peaceful* way: there might be a certain logic to how things work, and certain regularities might be observed, but the world being analyzed might at its heart be highly prone to war. What if systemic forces—pressures generated by the basic structure of the system—push states into conflict with each other? The assumption that the system, if allowed to work in accordance with its own internal logic, might produce unending violence in fact leads many people to approach the issue of international order from a very different perspective. Order, as they see it, has to do with the way those pressures can be brought under control. It does not connote mere "pat-

This article was originally published in a special issue of *The Monist* on the Foundations of International Order, for which the guest editor was Bruce Kuklick, and which came out in April 2006. Copyright © The Monist: An International Quarterly Journal of General Philosophical Inquiry, Open Court Publishing Company, Chicago, Illinois. Reprinted by permission.

[1] Kenneth Waltz, *Theory of International Politics* (New York: McGraw-Hill, 1979), esp. pp. 88–93. For the phrase quoted here, see p. 89; see also p. 77. Note also the title of chapter 6 in this book: "Anarchic Orders and Balances of Power." And indeed the basic notion of the "balance of power" plays a key role in this kind of approach to the question. Note, for example, Robert Osgood and Robert Tucker, *Force, Order, and Justice* (Baltimore: Johns Hopkins University Press, 1967), p. 96: "The prerequisite of order among autonomous states is that force be restrained by countervailing force within a balance (or equilibrium) of power."

tern or regularity"; people who use the term in that sense do not have in mind (as Waltz does) the sort of order that emerges "spontaneously" from the free play of political forces—that is, from the sorts of policies states are led to adopt in an anarchic world.[2] Order instead takes shape only when some limit is placed on how political conflicts run their course—only when interstate relations are "domesticated," when the sharp edge of international politics is blunted, when the free play of political forces is constrained in some way.[3] And the fundamental assumption here is that this happens only when a kind of "international society" develops. Indeed, from this point of view, international order basically means international society. The two notions are essentially conflated. When people talk about "international order" or "international society," they have in mind the whole set of norms, relationships, and institutions—political, economic and cultural, both international and cross-national—which in their view introduces a certain element of stability into what would otherwise be a violent, war-prone world.[4]

[2] For people like Waltz, economic theory was of course the great model here. On the point about *order* not meaning mere "pattern or regularity," see Hedley Bull, *The Anarchical Society: A Study of Order in World Politics*, 2nd ed. (New York: Columbia University Press, 1995), p. 3. On the general idea of order emerging "spontaneously" in social systems without direct state intervention, see also Robert Ellickson, *Order Without Law: How Neighbors Settle Disputes* (Cambridge, Mass.: Harvard University Press, 1991), esp. p. 4, and Robert Axelrod's famous book *The Evolution of Cooperation* (New York: Basic Books, 1984).

[3] Note, for example, Jürgen Habermas's reference to the "civilizing achievement of legally domesticating the state of nature among belligerent nations" in an interview published in *The Nation*, December 16, 2002.

[4] For the basic distinction between the two senses of the term *order*, see Bull, *Anarchical Society*, pp. 3–5, and Dennis H. Wrong, *The Problem of Order: What Unites and Divides Society* (New York: Free Press, 1994), pp. 37–38. Note also the discussion in Oran R. Young, "Regime Dynamics: The Rise and Fall of International Regimes," in *International Regimes*, ed. Stephen D. Krasner (Ithaca: Cornell University Press, 1983), pp. 98–101. Young distinguishes between three "types of order": spontaneous, negotiated, and imposed. For the reference to order emerging "spontaneously" in an anarchic system, see Waltz, *Theory of International Politics*, pp. 90–91. The notion that international order depends on the existence of "international society" is associated with the "English school" of international relations theorists, and especially with Hedley Bull and Martin Wight. Note also Michael Howard, *The Invention of Peace: Reflections on War and International Order* (London: Profile Books, 2000), p. 16: "The history of Europe was henceforward [from the signing of the Peace of Westphalia in 1648 on] to be shaped by the relations between its states, and the international order depended on their ability to create among themselves an effective international society." The basic idea, however, has deep roots, and the notion that the European state system was a "kind of society" or a "sort of republic" played a particularly important role in eighteenth-century balance of power thought. See, for example, the extracts published in Moorhead Wright, ed., *Theory and Practice of the Balance of Power, 1486–1914* (London: Dent, 1975), pp. 39, 41, 71–72, and also F.H. Hinsley, *Power and the Pursuit of Peace: Theory and Practice in the History of Relations between States* (Cambridge,

That whole way of looking at things is thus rooted in a certain set of assumptions about how an anarchic system in its purest form actually works. The basic premise here is that a system in which power is the only thing that matters, a system where no international society can be said to exist, is highly unstable: that in a purely anarchic world, everyone is in a "state of war" with everyone else. It is taken for granted that states, in such a system, are pushed into conflict with each other, no matter how peace-loving they fundamentally are. Peace can therefore not be based on the free play of political forces, not in the way that prosperity, as Adam Smith argued, can be based on the free play of economic forces. If there is an "invisible hand" in international politics, it plays a pernicious role. Order in the international realm thus means constraint; stability is possible only if power is not the only thing that matters.

It follows, therefore, that to get at the issue of international order, you first need to deal with the theoretical question of how politics works in the highly stylized world associated with the term *anarchy*—a world where security and thus power are the only things that matter, a world in which no effective international society can be said to exist. The workings of such an idealized world are worth examining not because the real world necessarily works the same way, but simply because that sort of analysis is a necessary point of departure for thinking about real world problems. Only when one understands how a highly stylized world of this sort works can questions about the role of various factors—international law, for example, or economic interdependence—be posed in any meaningful way. If your goal is to understand what difference those factors make—that is, whether they contribute to order—you need to start with a certain preexisting frame of reference, one that only theoretical analysis can provide.

The two sets of issues—the purely theoretical questions and the questions about how things work in the real world—are thus linked. The way you deal with various specific problems—the question, for example, of international law as a source of order—depends on how you answer basic questions about how a highly stylized anarchic system works. You might conclude that such a system is prone to war for certain particular reasons. You have thus identified various problems that something like international law might conceivably help solve. On the other hand, if you conclude that a system based on power does not in itself generate conflict, and that instead problems develop when states fail to act rationally in power political terms, you will approach questions of this sort in a very different way. Note that I'm not making any

---

England: Cambridge University Press, 1963), pp. 57–58, 162–63, and Bull, *Anarchical Society*, pp. 23–38.

substantive claim here. I'm just making a simple point about method—that to get at the general problem of international order, you first need to deal with the theoretical issue of how things work in a purely anarchic world, and that only after you've reached certain conclusions at this level will you be in a position to deal meaningfully with questions about the role of specific real world factors—questions about democratic institutions, international organizations, economic interdependence, international law, and so on.

That might be the way the question of international order ought to be handled, but how well has it actually been dealt with? What, in fact, are we to make of the way international politics as a whole has been studied? My own view is that there are real problems with this whole area of thought, but I should note that that's not a totally idiosyncratic judgment. For some time now, many people who work in the field have had the sense that something is amiss. If asked to assess this field of scholarship, they would certainly say that a lot of very interesting work has been, and is being, produced. But when they look at the larger picture, they are not particularly happy with what they see.

Martin Wight, a very eminent British international relations scholar, seemed to put his finger on the problem forty years ago in a widely cited article called "Why Is There No International Theory?"[5] By *international theory* he meant "a tradition of speculation about relations between states, a tradition imagined as the twin of speculation about the state to which the name 'political theory' is appropriated," and he thought that international theory in that sense could scarcely be said to exist.[6] There were great works of political philosophy—Plato and Aristotle, Hobbes and Locke and Rousseau. But "the only acknowledged counterpart in the study of international relations is Thucydides," and Thucydides was an historian, not a philosopher.[7] What international theory there was, if you could even call it that, was "scattered, unsystematic, and mostly inaccessible to the layman. Moreover, it [was] largely repellent and intractable in form."[8] It was marked "not only by paucity but also by intellectual and moral poverty."[9] People who studied political issues, in Wight's view, were obsessed with the state, and insofar as they were concerned with international issues at all, they focused on problems of foreign policy—that is, on a particular state's foreign policy. "Few political thinkers," he pointed out, "have made it

[5] Martin Wight, "Why Is There No International Theory?" in Herbert Butterfield and Martin Wight, eds., *Diplomatic Investigations: Essays in the Theory of International Politics* (London: George Allen and Unwin, 1966), pp. 17–34.

[6] Ibid., p. 17.

[7] Ibid., p. 32.

[8] Ibid., p. 20.

[9] Ibid.

their business to study the states-system, the diplomatic community *itself.*"[10]

Wight was not the only leading scholar in the field to express this sort of view. "Is theory in the field of international politics," Kenneth Waltz asked a decade later, "thriving or moribund?" His answer was blunt: "Almost everyone who knows the field tends toward the latter view."[11] Do scholars now take a fundamentally different view? People today would probably not be quite so negative, but still, looking around, you do detect a certain sense of unease, a sense that on core issues people often seem to be talking past each other. What passes for debate often comes across as an intellectually sterile "war of the isms" that never seems to get anywhere.

If there is a problem, maybe it has to do with the way the core issues—the issues that define the field—have been approached. I spoke before about the need, for analytical purposes, to separate the theoretical problem of how a highly stylized anarchic system works from questions relating to how things work in the real world. But this is something many people in the field find hard to do. They find it hard, that is, deal with the theoretical issue on its own terms—to understand that a theory is not *supposed* to be an exact mirror of reality. Over and over again, those who have some sense for what a theory is supposed to be—Kenneth Waltz, most notably—are criticized for not taking this or that factor sufficiently into account, as though a theory should take account of every factor that comes into play in the real world. And over and over again Waltz has to explain that it is a mistake to think that the best model "is the one that reflects reality most accurately"—that explanatory power "is gained by moving away from 'reality,' not by staying close to it."[12] Over and over again he has to point out that "to say that a 'theory should be just as complicated as all our evidence suggests' amounts to a renunciation of science from Galileo onward." But to Waltz's considerable frustration the point just never seems to register.[13]

[10] Ibid., pp. 21–22. Emphasis in original text.

[11] Kenneth Waltz, "Theory of International Relations," in *Handbook of Political Science*, vol. 8, *International Politics,* ed. Fred Greenstein and Nelson Polsby (Reading, Mass.: Addison-Wesley, 1975), p. 1.

[12] Waltz, *Theory of International Politics*, p. 7.

[13] Kenneth Waltz, "Evaluating Theories," *American Political Science Review* 91, no. 4 (December 1997): 914; the internal quotation is from a well-known book on method, Gary King, Robert Keohane and Sidney Verba, *Designing Social Inquiry: Scientific Inference in Qualitative Research* (Princeton: Princeton University Press, 1994), p. 20. Note also the tone of Waltz's comments in a 1993 interview: "I am tired of people who say, 'You've got a theory of international politics; you need to include domestic politics.' Well, don't these people understand anything about what a theory is? A theory has to be *about* something.

The basic problem here has to do with what might be called the philosophy of the field, and above all with the fundamental assumption that the facts have a kind of elemental quality and that theories can be tested (and indeed built up) in a very straightforward way by looking at the empirical evidence. Philosophers of science, from Pierre Duhem to N. R. Hanson, Imre Lakatos, and beyond, might have shown how problematic such assumptions are. But their arguments have not had much of an impact on how the field deals with issues of this sort.

The prevailing set of epistemological assumptions, assumptions above all about the relationship between fact and theory, has a very strong hold on the field. It is hard to escape its grip. Just how hard it is is perhaps best illustrated by the case of Waltz himself, probably the most prominent international relations theorist in the United States today. Waltz's approach to these issues nowadays is quite sophisticated. He recently explained, for example, why he assigns Lakatos in his seminar on international political theory. Students of politics, he wrote, should pay attention to Lakatos "for one big reason: Lakatos's assaults crush the crassly positivist ideas about how to evaluate theories that are accepted by most political scientists. He demolishes the notion that one can accept theories by pitting them against facts."[14] But Waltz did not reach that position overnight. In his most famous book, *Theory of International Politics*, he certainly had intelligent things to say about what a theory was, things based on what the philosophers of science had been saying. But in spite of that, he talked about theory testing as though that basic notion were in no way problematic, so much so that he later practically apologized for having sounded there "like a 'naïve falsificationist.'"[15] The point here is simply that if it took even someone as sophisticated and intelligent as Waltz so long to develop his current views, it should not be surprising that most political scientists still approach this question of the relationship between theory and reality in a relatively naïve way.

So what is the solution? A first step would be to recognize the impor-

---

It can't be about everything. So you have to figure out what it is you're trying to explain, what is this domain you're trying to deal with." "Interview with Ken Waltz," conducted by Fred Halliday and Justin Rosenberg, May 7, 1993, *Review of International Studies* 24 (1998): 379.

[14] Kenneth Waltz, "Thoughts about Assaying Theories," in *Progress in International Relations Theory: Appraising the Field*, ed. Colin Elman and Miriam Fenius Elman (Cambridge: MIT Press, 2003), p. xii. See also Waltz, "Evaluating Theories," pp. 913–917.

[15] Waltz, *Theory of International Politics*, pp. 13–16. Note also his use of terms like "falsification" in a piece he had published a few years earlier, a sort of forerunner to that book. Waltz, "Theory of International Relations," p. 42. For the later view, see Kenneth Waltz, "Reflections on *Theory of International Politics*: A Response to My Critics," in *Neorealism and Its Critics*, ed. Robert Keohane (New York: Columbia University Press, 1986), p. 334.

tance of these meta-issues. People in the field need to think more deeply about what understanding is and how it can be developed, about what theory is and what role it plays in that process, about what "systemic" or "structural" explanations are and how they relate to other kinds of explanations—and in fact some serious thought has been given to issues of this sort.[16] Just not enough: international relations scholars need to pay a lot more attention to the philosophy of science literature—and not so much to works like Lakatos's famous but very hard-to-read article on "Falsification and the Methodology of Scientific Research Programs," but instead works like that same scholar's wonderfully clear and lively "Lectures on Scientific Method."[17] And Hanson's ideas, also very engagingly presented, should get a lot more attention than they do.[18]

But these philosophical issues, as important as they are, do not really lie at the heart of the problem. An even more serious problem has to do with the way the purely theoretical side of the question is handled— that is, with the way the workings of the highly stylized anarchic system are analyzed. The (to me surprisingly widespread) assumption here is that disorder, in the sense of a basic tendency toward conflict and interstate violence, is built into the fundamental structure of the system—that the "structure of the system" (as one leading contemporary theorist puts it) "forces states which seek only to be secure nonetheless to act aggressively toward each other."[19] With no higher authority to provide for their security, the argument runs, states have to do whatever they can to provide it for themselves. They thus all try to make themselves more powerful—more powerful, that is, vis-à-vis each other. They thus are forced into competition with each other, and international politics—international conflict—is rooted in that struggle for power. States (in Robert Jervis's phrase) are trapped by the logic of the system in which they find themselves; they are unable to cooperate, even when all would benefit from cooperation; they get involved in

---

[16] See, for example, James D. Fearon, "Domestic Politics, Foreign Policy, and Theories of International Relations," *Annual Review of Political Science* 1 (1998): 289–313.

[17] Imre Lakatos, "Falsification and the Methodology of Scientific Research Programmes," in *Criticism and the Growth of Knowledge*, ed. Imre Lakatos and Alan Musgrave (Cambridge: Cambridge University Press, 1970); Imre Lakatos, "Lectures on Scientific Method," in Imre Lakatos and Paul Feyerabend, *For and Against Method: Including Lakatos's Lectures on Scientific Method and the Lakatos-Feyerabend Correspondence*, ed. Matteo Motterlini (Chicago: University of Chicago Press, 1999).

[18] See especially N.R. Hanson, *Patterns of Discovery: An Inquiry into the Conceptual Foundations of Science* (Cambridge: Cambridge University Press, 1958), and N.R. Hanson, *Perception and Discovery: An Introduction to Scientific Inquiry* (San Francisco: Freeman, Cooper, 1969).

[19] John Mearsheimer, *The Tragedy of Great Power Politics* (New York: Norton, 2001), p. 3.

wars even when they would all prefer to avoid them. If wars break out, it's the system, and not the individual states, that is fundamentally to blame.

It is hard to exaggerate the importance of this way of looking at things. It has a very long pedigree, going back to Hobbes and Rousseau, if not to Thucydides. Today it is accepted by all sorts of international relations scholars—not just by realists of various kinds (and in this field a "realist" is simply someone who emphasizes the importance of power in international politics), but also by those deeply critical of the basic realist approach to international politics. I don't mean to say that no one ever sees any of the ways in which an anarchic system can be self-stabilizing. Arguments that point in that direction are in fact made from time to time. I'm just talking about what I see as the prevailing view, a view which, moreover, does have a rather broad appeal, in large part, I think, because it has a certain counter-intuitive edge. It purports to explain something real, "war's dismal recurrence through the millennia." And it explains war not just by discussing conflict in terms of the specific policies pursued by particular states at a given time, but by looking below the surface of events and pointing to the basic anarchic structure of international politics.[20]

I also do not mean to imply that realists and their critics see completely eye-to-eye on this issue. They differ most notably on the question of the real world importance and intractability of this sort of problem. But the fact that they differ in that area should not be allowed to obscure the fact that they agree this is a core problem—that they agree that the anarchic structure of international politics is "a root cause of or explanation for the recurrence of war."[21] In other words, they answer the basic theoretical question the same way: in the highly stylized anarchic world, states are pushed into conflict with each other. And that basic theoretical framework serves as a point of departure for the analysis of real world problems. When problems of that sort are discussed, it is by and large simply assumed that order (in the sense of the ability of the system to avoid war) can come only if that core dynamic is brought under some kind of external control. It is simply taken for granted that order, in that sense, is not a product of the "system"—that it does not emerge spontaneously, à la Adam Smith, from the pursuit of power

---

[20] For the quotation: Kenneth Waltz, "The Origins of War in Neorealist Theory," in *The Origin and Prevention of Major Wars*, ed. Robert Rotberg and Theodore Rabb (Cambridge, England, and New York: Cambridge University Press, 1989), pp. 43–44. On these points in general, see chapter 1 above, pp. 3–6, 18–20, 22–24.

[21] James Fearon, "Rationalist Explanations for War," *International Organization* 49, no. 3 (Summer 1995): 384.

political interest, and in fact can come only if those drives are constrained in some way.

But if the theoretical issue is of such fundamental importance, then the question has to be whether the common assumption that anarchy breeds conflict is in fact correct—or, more precisely in the present context, how well that absolutely central issue has been studied. And my basic point here—my basic point in this chapter as a whole—is that it has not been studied nearly as well as it ought to be, especially given the real world importance of this issue.

Is there any reason, however, to study that issue in any depth—any reason, that is, to question that basic assumption? I tried to deal with the issue in a recent article and there is no point in repeating in detail here what I said there.[22] But let me sum up the argument very briefly. The fundamental claim there was that a whole series of considerations point to the conclusion that a purely anarchic system is not inherently unstable. The basic idea was that policies that are rational in power political terms—the policies that states would adopt if their power political positions were all that they cared about, the very policies states would be led to adopt in a purely anarchic world—were policies "in harmony with the existing structure of power" and were thus "in harmony with each other." In a power political world, the world posited by the pure theory, everyone would adjust to the same core political realities; those realities would constrain everyone's political behavior. In such a world, states would profit in power political terms from good relations with other states; they would be hurt when relations with other states deteriorate. A rational state would therefore want to have as many friends and as few enemies as possible, and since that logic applies to all states in the system, the upshot in a world where power political considerations are decisive is a general tendency toward stability. To understand power, moreover, is to understand why other states' interests normally need to be respected. The power political approach is thus a source of moderation, and moderation is in turn normally a source of stability. The power political approach implies that goals need to be limited, and in particular that states cannot allow themselves to get carried away pursuing policies—especially ideologically based policies—that make little sense in power political terms. Instead states in such a world relate to each other on a more mundane level, accepting power realities for what they are, dealing with each other on a businesslike basis, reaching agreements relatively easily because they all speak the same language, the language of power and interest. And that basic argument was supported by a number of histori-

[22] This is the article on the "Question of Realism" in chapter 1 of this book.

cal examples, which taken as a whole pointed to the conclusion that problems developed over the past couple of centuries not because states pursued policies that were rational in power political terms, but rather because their policies were not cut from that cloth.

The problem with the prevailing view that anarchy breeds war, moreover, is not just that it fails to recognize dynamics of the sort I just mentioned—that is, that it fails to understand the ways in which an anarchic system is self-stabilizing. An even more basic problem has to do with the quality of the argument that is used to support those standard views. The argument one finds in this area is relatively superficial. One comes away from the discussion with a certain sense of incompleteness—with the feeling that key issues had not been thought through nearly as well as they might have been.

Consider, for example, Hobbes's famous argument about how politics works in the absence of overarching authority, an argument that is in a sense the wellspring of this whole body of thought. "For want of a common power to keep them all in awe," Hobbes wrote, every man is an enemy to every man.[23] No purely voluntary agreement, in such circumstances, can make for a peaceful society: "covenants, without the sword, are but words."[24] In such a world, men, and indeed states, are pushed into conflict with each other. They become enemies, he says, principally because they all have to do whatever is necessary to provide for their own security, even if that means taking anticipatory action. They are in effect led to adopt aggressive policies for purely defensive purposes.[25] A world where there was "no common power to fear"

[23] Thomas Hobbes, *Leviathan, or the Matter, Forme and Power of a Commonwealth Ecclesiasticall and Civil* (Oxford: Blackwell, 1955), p. 95 (chap. 15). See also pp. 82–83, 110, 112 (chaps. 13 and 17).

[24] Ibid., pp. 109 (for the quotation), 111–12 (chap. 17).

[25] Ibid., p. 81 (chap. 13): "And from this diffidence of one another, there is no way for any man to secure himself, so reasonable, as anticipation; that is, by force, or wiles, to master the persons of all men he can, so long, till he see no other power great enough to endanger him: and this is no more than his own conservation requireth, and is generally allowed. Also because there be some, that taking pleasure in contemplating their own power in the acts of conquest, which they pursue farther than their security requires; if others, that otherwise would be glad to be at ease within modest bounds, should not by invasion increase their power, they would not be able, long time, by standing only on their defence, to subsist. And by consequence, such augmentation of dominion over men being necessary to a man's conservation, it ought to be allowed him." One is amazed, the archaic language notwithstanding, by how modern-sounding this whole line of argument is. Hobbes applies this sort of argument explicitly to interstate relations in chapter 17 (p. 110). "For their own security," he writes, cities and kingdoms "enlarge their dominions, upon all pretences of danger, and fear of invasion, or assistance that may be given to invaders, and endeavour as much as they can, to subdue, or weaken their neighbours, by open force, and secret arts, for want of other caution, justly; and are remembered for it in after ages with honour."

was, in Hobbes's view, a lawless world, a world prone to war, a world in which every man was at war with every other man. The world of international politics was a world of this sort: states, "because of their independency," were "in continual jealousies," and in the "posture of gladiators; having their weapons pointing, and their eyes fixed on one another."[26] It was not that the inhabitants of such a world were always actually fighting with each other. It was just that the system bred conflict and violence was never far from the surface.[27]

What is to be made of the basic Hobbesian notion of the "war of every man against every man"?[28] What is to be made of the idea that in an anarchic realm, where there is "no visible power to keep them in awe," men, or sovereigns, are in a constant state of war with their peers?[29] When you think about that whole basic concept of the "war of every man against every man," it is hard to avoid saying to yourself: *it just can't be*, it just doesn't make sense, even in purely theoretical terms. To take the simplest case: it makes no sense for one person to be in a state of war with two other individuals, each of whom is at war with the other. "The enemy of my enemy is my friend"—doesn't the sort of behavior based on that kind of calculation introduce a certain degree of order into the system? Doesn't the fact that actors can be presumed in an anarchic world to make that kind of calculation mean that something other than pure violence, something other than brute force, comes into play in a major way? Doesn't all this necessarily introduce a certain *political* element into the equation, an element that perhaps introduces a measure of order into the system?

So the question then is: how would *politics* work in such a world? Would you, for example, find actors coming together, for purely predatory purposes, in simple, temporary, alliances of convenience? Even in a world of three actors, why would any two of them (call them A and B) gang up to destroy a third actor C? Why would the weaker member of that putative coalition (say B) agree to such a course of action? After the common enemy had been destroyed, that actor would be at the mercy of its partner. Wouldn't it be to B's interest, therefore, to keep C's power intact as a counterweight to the power of B's present ally? In such a world, as Fénelon said three hundred years ago, the rational course of action might be to avoid arrangements that would "prove too beneficial to your ally" and to take care "not to reduce your enemy too low."[30] And if that policy became known, wouldn't B be supported by which-

[26] Ibid., p. 83.
[27] Ibid., chapter 13, and esp. p. 82.
[28] Ibid., pp. 82–83.
[29] Ibid., p. 109.
[30] François de Salignac de la Mothe Fénelon, supplement to his *L'Examen de conscience*

ever of the two remaining units would find its own security diminished by B's destruction? Conceivably that could mean both of them. And wouldn't this sort of thing—the sort of behavior that might emerge spontaneously in a purely anarchic world—automatically introduce a certain element of stability, of order, into the system?[31]

That's how things might work in a simple three-actor system. Adding more actors would obviously increase the level of complexity. But the basic point here applies to more complex systems as well: there is a lot more to political life in an anarchic system than the simple Hobbesian view might lead you to expect. Politics is not a mere congeries of isolated one-on-one relationships, where everyone is in a state of war with everyone else. All relationships are interconnected, and even in a purely anarchic world things will sort themselves out in some way or other. Political calculations will be made. States, for example, will come to realize they cannot be enemies with each other if they are each threatened by a third party. That will lead to a kind of balancing and balancing leads to a sort of order. So you can't just talk about the "war of every man against every man" and simply leave it at that, as though those notions about the instability of an anarchic system were in no way problematic. You really need to consider how stability—how order in the second sense of the term—might emerge spontaneously in a purely anarchic world. And to do that, you need to put the kinds of calculations I've been talking about—that is, you need to put the political element—at the heart of the analysis.

Let me try to make the basic point here in a somewhat different and rather unconventional way—namely, by approaching the issue from the point of view of evolutionary biology. The key ideas here are quite familiar. Individuals within a species vary in terms of their genetic endowment; the genetic material best suited to produce traits that promote reproductive success in the organisms in which they reside will, practically by definition, spread throughout the species. Natural selection is a harsh process; reproductive success is the only thing that matters; any form of behavior that serves that goal will be favored, no matter how violent or distasteful it is. And even human evolution—and here I'm paraphrasing an argument a number of biologists have made— is to be understood in these terms. As humans became increasingly able to protect themselves from predators like leopards and lions, their

---

sur les devoirs de la royauté, originally written around 1700, and published in many editions of Fénelon's work. For this extract, see Wright, *Theory and Practice,* p. 43.

[31] For a similar argument, see Richard Dawkins, *The Selfish Gene,* 2nd ed. (New York: Oxford University Press, 1989), p. 68. Note also the analysis in Jervis, *System Effects,* pp. 133–34, and in Timothy Crawford, *Pivotal Deterrence: Third-Party Statecraft and the Pursuit of Peace* (Ithaca: Cornell University Press, 2003).

numbers expanded; given that resources were limited, they were thus forced to compete directly with each other. Darwin's "hostile forces of nature"—climate, predators, parasites, and so on—were no longer the fundamental forces driving evolution. A far more powerful force had come into play. Humans had "become so ecologically dominant that they in effect became their own hostile force of nature." Human beings were thus selected out for their ability to compete—and indeed to compete violently—with other human beings.[32]

This picture so far corresponds to the Hobbesian vision of the "war of every man against every man." So it is important to note, given the issue we are interested in here, that this line of argument does not just stop at that point. The scholars who argue in this vein go on to point out that the ability of human beings to form increasingly large groups and to cooperate with each other more effectively within those groups was a major factor promoting reproductive success. The problems of social life, and especially the problems of cooperating as a group in order to prevail over other groups, are more complex and more difficult than the problems of dealing with the natural environment. The process thus generated a strong selective pressure favoring the growth of mental ability; and only this, it is argued, explains the extraordinary growth in the size of the human brain during a mere two- or three-million-year period. This body of thought, in other words, portrays a world within which recognizably *political* behavior—indeed, conscious, deliberate, political calculation—had become adaptive. Political maneuvering—the formation of friendships and coalitions, the development of relations of trust, the counteractions taken against those who seem to be exploiting the cooperative system, the countermeasures taken by the putative exploiters to avoid punishment—all this would come alive in such a world. And those political abilities are to be understood not just in intra-group terms. This whole line of thought would seem to imply

---

[32] Richard Dawkins's *Selfish Gene* is still the best introduction to this body of thought. For the theory of human evolution sketched out here, see especially R.D. Alexander, *How Did Humans Evolve? Reflections on the Uniquely Unique Species* (Ann Arbor: University of Michigan Museum of Zoology, Special Publication No. 1, 1990) (the quotation is on p. 4). Note also Alexander's *Darwinism and Human Affairs* (Seattle: University of Washington Press, 1979), pp. 222–33. Given W. D. Hamilton's importance in the field, two articles of his are worth noting in this context: "Innate Social Aptitudes of Man: An Approach from Evolutionary Genetics," in Robin Fox, ed., *Biosocial Anthropology* (New York: Wiley, 1975); and "Selection of Selfish and Altruistic Behaviour in Some Extreme Models," originally published in *Man and Beast: Comparative Social Behavior*, ed. J. F. Eisenberg and Wilton S. Dillon (Washington, D.C.: Smithsonian Institution Press, 1971), pp. 57–91, and republished, with a long introduction, in W.D. Hamilton, *Narrow Roads of Gene Land: The Collected Papers of W.D. Hamilton*, vol. 1: *Evolution of Social Behaviour* (Oxford: Freeman, 1996), pp. 198–227.

that those abilities would also be of value in terms of a group's relations with other groups.[33]

Again, the point here is that these *political* dynamics are of fundamental importance, and that it is thanks to them that a certain structure—a certain order—can emerge spontaneously even in an anarchic world. To ignore those dynamics—to assume that in the absence of overarching authority every group is at war with every other group—is thus (to use a phrase Waltz uses in a very different context) to take "the politics out of international politics."[34] The anarchic realm, as Waltz himself points out, is a political realm *par excellence*.[35] It is the realm neither of pure violence, where every actor fights a war to the death against every other actor, nor of pure harmony, like a bee hive or an ant colony.[36] It is instead something in between, a realm where interests overlap, but not totally, an area where relations are normally characterized by some mix of conflict and cooperation. That point is very basic, and many writers have made it. But the aim is to understand how such a world works; and to achieve that goal you cannot simply assume that the fundamental structure of the system makes for conflict, pure and simple. You need to take account of the ways in which an anarchic system might be self-stabilizing—the ways in which a degree of order might emerge spontaneously from the free play of political forces.

How then can this be done? This is essentially a theoretical issue, but you can get only so far by approaching the problem on a purely abstract level. You also need to study certain types of empirical problems. If your goal, for example, is to understand how an element of order can emerge in an anarchic world, you might want to study triangular conflicts—like Britain, France, and Germany around 1900; or America, China, and Russia in the 1960s; or Iran, Iraq, and the United States more recently—and see how they sort themselves out. Indeed, you might want to study what political life is like in areas where for one reason or another the writ of civil authority does not run, like the Old West or

---

[33] See especially Robert Trivers, "The Evolution of Reciprocal Altruism," *Quarterly Review of Biology* 46, no. 1 (March 1971), 35–57, and especially the final part of that paper, dealing with the "psychological system underlying human reciprocal altruism," and above all the section (pp. 52–53) on multiparty interactions. Note also Nicholas Humphrey's seminal article, "The Social Function of Intellect," in *Growing Points in Ethology*, ed. P.P.G. Bateson and R. A. Hinde (New York: Cambridge University Press, 1976). For the relevance of the Humphrey approach to the body of thought we are concerned with here, see the discussion of his ideas in Alexander, *How Did Humans Evolve?*, pp. 4–6, and in Dawkins, *Selfish Gene*, pp. 280–81.

[34] Kenneth Waltz, "Structural Realism after the Cold War," *International Security* 25, no. 1 (Summer 2000), 8.

[35] Waltz, *Theory of International Politics*, p. 113.

[36] See Hobbes, *Leviathan*, p. 111 (chap. 17).

even the Walled City of Kowloon.[37] The goal, in such exercises, is not to test any particular theory. You're just looking for some insight into the central theoretical issue. As Thomas Kuhn once put it, you're searching in the empirical evidence for "clues" that might help you understand how things work at a more general level.[38]

Let me again stress the fact that I haven't spent all this time talking about the theoretical issue—the question of how a purely anarchic world works—because I think the fundamental goal of the field is to develop a theory of international politics as an end in itself. Theory-building has to be understood as a means to an end. The real aim is to understand how international politics works. The theoretical analysis provides us with a kind of springboard—a framework for thinking about real world issues, a way of getting a handle on them, a way of bringing them into focus so that they become intellectually manageable. If you assume that anarchy breeds war—that a world in which power political considerations shape policy is inherently unstable—then you are going to approach the problem of international order in a particular way. You are going to be looking for things that might introduce some element of order into what you assume would otherwise be an inherently war-prone system. If the free play of political—meaning power political—forces is the problem, then stability would depend on whether those forces can be brought under control—on whether the harshness of international politics in its pure form can be softened in some way. Order, in that case, would be identified with constraint. The presumption, in this case, is that things that limit the free play of political forces play a positive role—that things like the development of international law, the spread of democratic or free market institutions, or the establishment of organizations like the United Nations, provide the basis for

---

[37] A number of scholars who studied the Old West were surprised to discover, given its reputation, how little crime and violence there was. Crimes against women, for example, were generally unheard of, and even theft and burglary were rare. The explanation often given, both by residents of those areas at the time and by later scholars, is that retaliation was swift and severe. "Crime was of rare occurrence," according to one miner, "because punishment, like an avenging nemesis, was sure to follow." See Roger McGrath, *Gunfighters, Highwaymen and Vigilantes: Violence on the Frontier* (Berkeley: University of California Press, 1984), pp. 157, 181, 190, 261–70 (reviewing some of the work done in this area); Mary Ellen Jones, *Daily Life on the Nineteenth Century American Frontier* (Westport, Conn.: Greenwood, 1998), pp. 145–46; Thomas Stone, *Miners' Justice: Migration, Law and Order on the Alaska-Yukon Frontier, 1873–1902* (New York: Peter Lang, 1988), pp. 58, 142–43. For a survey of the literature on the subject, see Richard M. Brown, "Historiography of Violence in the American West," in Michael P. Malone, ed., *Historians and the American West* (Lincoln: University of Nebraska Press, 1983), pp. 234–69 (p. 267 for the quotation given above).

[38] Thomas Kuhn, *The Trouble with the Historical Philosophy of Science* (Cambridge, Mass.: Harvard History of Science Department, 1991), p. 6.

whatever international order there is. This way of approaching the problem in effect loads the analytical dice. Because of the way the questions are framed, the answers are in effect virtually predetermined.

On the other hand, if you think the anarchic system is at its heart self-stabilizing and that problems develop only when its workings are thwarted in some way—that is, only when policies are *not* based on cool, power political calculation—then those questions will be viewed in a very different light. The "intrusion" of ideology, even democratic ideology—the "intrusion" of values, even liberal values—might then be seen as sources of disorder and instability in what would otherwise be a relatively stable system.

Note that this is not a right-versus-left issue. The left, of course, certainly does tend to assume, without giving the matter all that much thought, that power politics is bad and that the institutions and values that tend to keep it within bounds play a positive role. But on the right, the reaching for empire or its equivalent—the talk, for example, about the need for American "leadership" or for an American-led "world order"—is also rooted in the assumption that stability is not natural and that without a hegemon there is no order. And the idea that order depends on the existence of a hegemonic power is by no means the exclusive property of the right. E. H. Carr, for example, was one of the first major writers to argue along these lines, and Carr was certainly no conservative.[39]

This is basically an intellectual and not a political problem, and the key point here is that unless the analysis is framed the right way, these issues will not be brought into focus the way they need to be. If we think we know the answers in advance, in large part because we have reached overly simple or perhaps even fundamentally wrong conclusions on the core theoretical issue, we are not going to approach the real world questions the way they need to be approached. The issue will be,

---

[39] See E. H. Carr, *The Twenty Years' Crisis, 1919-1939: An Introduction to the Study of International Relations,* 2nd edition, esp. pp. 107, 232–35. For the role that Carr's book (and in particular this argument) played in the development of the so-called "hegemonic stability" theory, note what Robert Gilpin, one of the main architects of that theory, recently wrote about that book. "My interest in the relationship between the structure of the international political system and the nature of the international economy was first aroused," he remembered, by his reading of Carr's book. "In this classic study of the collapse of the open world economy at the outbreak of World War I and the subsequent inability of a weakened Great Britain to re-create a liberal international economy after the war, Carr demonstrated that a liberal world economy must rest on a dominant liberal power." Robert Gilpin, *Global Political Economy: Understanding the International Economic Order* (Princeton: Princeton University Press, 2001), pp. 100–101 n. 52. As a characterization of Carr's argument, this leaves much to be desired, but it does throw some light on the question of the origins of the "hegemonic stability" argument. On Carr in general, see Jonathan Haslam, *The Vices of Integrity: E. H. Carr 1892–1982* (London: Verso, 1999).

for example, "how does international law make for a more orderly world?" and not "what impact, whether positive or negative or even both, does international law have on international political life?" For it is by no means inconceivable that legal constraints, to the extent that they influence political behavior, can play a negative role, shackling the law-abiding power and thus empowering would-be aggressors, as in the 1930s.[40] The point here is not, of course, that international law is essentially a source of disorder in international affairs. It is simply that if you are serious about dealing with these issues of international order, the questions have to be framed in such a way that answers turn on what the evidence shows— that is, in a way that might allow you to see beyond your own preconceptions.

The goal, in other words, is to do the kind of empirical work that will enable you to deepen your understanding of what makes for order in international political life. In doing that work, you'll be looking for "clues," in Kuhn's sense. Your aim is to see things—important things— you might not otherwise have seen. You might, for example, be interested in the role the United Nations played during the Cuban Missile Crisis. What difference did it make, you wonder, in terms of the way the crisis ran its course, that the U.N. organization existed? Studying the crisis with that question in mind, you might notice things that most scholars who have examined the crisis (or, indeed, who have studied the U.N.) haven't noticed. President John F. Kennedy, it turns out, wanted to settle the crisis by entering into a negotiation with the Soviets; the settlement he had in mind involved a withdrawal of the American Jupiter missiles from Turkey. But while these negotiations were going on, in Kennedy's view, work on the missile sites in Cuba was to be suspended. That proposal for negotiations *cum* standstill, however, was not actually presented to the Soviets. As a result, there were no real negotiations, and the Soviets instead gave way in the end to what amounted to a kind of ultimatum—which, arguably, from the point of view of international order, was not the best way of settling the crisis. And it wasn't presented to them because the U.S. government, instead of approaching them directly, chose to go through U.N. Secretary General U Thant, who basically bungled the job. Instead of bringing the matter up with the Soviets, as the Americans wanted, he brought it up with the Cuban leader Fidel Castro, who rejected it out of hand.[41] But it was no accident that the Secretary General, coming from a relatively

---

[40] See chapter 9 below, pp. 302–304.

[41] The evidence (some of which was from the U.N. archives) can be found in a little piece I wrote included in the *Proceedings of the Hawk's Cay Conference on the Cuban Missile Crisis, March 5–8, 1987*, ed. David Welch (Cambridge, Mass.: Belfer Center for Science and International Affairs, John F. Kennedy School of Government, Harvard University, 1989),

weak Third World country (Burma, as it was then called), would behave in this way, and it was no accident that the Secretary General would come from such a country. What you see going on in this particular episode is the sort of thing you would want to take into account when thinking about the role institutions like the U.N. actually play in international political life, and it might not have occurred to you that the U.N. could have this kind of effect if you had not done this sort of empirical work—that is, if you had not taken the time to study this particular issue with a more or less open mind.

Why are such issues worth studying? Why, more generally, does it make sense to invest intellectual resources in this area of study? It is not just that we want to understand the world we live in as a kind of end in itself. We are also interested in these issues in large part because they relate directly to questions of policy, questions above all about the kind of international system we would want to live in. Questions of this sort are never far below the surface when we deal with these matters.

But should international relations scholars concern themselves directly with policy issues? It is sometimes argued that not only is it legitimate for scholars in this field to be concerned with such matters, but that questions about policy should lie at the intellectual heart of the discipline. Bernard Brodie, for example, a giant in the area of strategic studies, could not understand how theorizing could be cut off from real world problems. "Strategic thinking," he argued, "or 'theory' if one prefers, is nothing if not pragmatic. Strategy is a 'how to do it' study, a guide for accomplishing something and doing it efficiently."[42] But that sort of attitude makes many people uneasy. They doubt whether the "science of international relations" can ever become "operational." "If we expect a theory of international relations to provide the equivalent of what a knowledge of construction materials provides the builder of bridges," Raymond Aron wrote, "then there is no theory and never will be."[43] Many scholars, moreover, take it for granted that getting too involved with policy issues might do more harm than good in analytical terms—that identifying with the powerful and cozying up to them might affect the kind of work that is done, and not in a very positive way.

My own feeling, however, is that it makes sense for people in the field to be concerned with policy issues, provided they do not overdo it.

---

and is also available online (http://www.polisci.ucla.edu/faculty/trachtenberg/cv/cmc.1.pdf).

[42] Bernard Brodie, "Why Were We So (Strategically) Wrong?" *Foreign Policy*, no. 5 (Winter 1971–72): 151.

[43] Raymond Aron, "What is a Theory of International Relations?" *Journal of International Affairs* 21, no. 2 (1967): 201, 204.

Such concerns can play an important role, even for those who, like myself, rarely write on such issues. The international relations field can, in fact, be viewed as a kind of triad. Theory, history, and policy are its three component parts, and they are more tightly connected to each other intellectually than you might think. Historical analysis and policy analysis, for example, are quite similar in some ways. The historian makes claims about cause and effect: a particular course of action is chosen, and the claim is that it had certain consequences. Implicit in that claim is the notion that if different choices had been made, the effect would have been different. But to make assumptions about what would have happened if different policies had been adopted, you have to draw on a kind of theory, a certain sense (in the present case) for how international politics works. A policy analyst has to do much the same thing—namely, speculate about what would happen if various alternative policies were adopted by drawing on a kind of theory—by drawing, that is, on a certain general sense for how things work. And thinking about concrete issues, both historical issues and policy issues, helps bring the theoretical questions into focus. It is much easier to get a handle on those questions when you are dealing with them in some concrete empirical context than when you are approaching them on a purely abstract level.

When you study historical problems, moreover, you in fact often end up thinking not just about theoretical questions but also about policy issues of a certain sort. To analyze what was done at a given point in the past, you need to consider what, even in theory, the alternatives to a particular course of action were. And to think about what else *could* have been done often spills over into thinking about what *should* have done. That type of thinking might have both a certain theoretical taproot and a certain general policy relevance.

Consider, for example, the case of British policy during the July Crisis in 1914, the crisis that led to the outbreak of the First World War. Many people say that Britain should have made it very clear to Germany from the start of that crisis that if war broke out Britain would come in on the side of France and Russia. That point of view is linked to a certain general approach to strategic issues, an approach that makes deterrence the be-all and end-all of strategy. My own view, however, is that if the goal was to avoid war—and for a country like Britain in 1914 that goal would certainly have made sense—a strategy of siding very clearly with France and Russia and against Germany would not have been optimal. It would have been better, I think, not just to warn Germany that if she went to war prematurely—that is, say, before Russia had ordered general mobilization—Britain would almost certainly come into the conflict on the side of France and Russia, but at the same time also to warn Russia that if she took the decisive step of ordering general mobilization without first getting British consent, Britain might very well stay out of the war. The aim would have been to avoid war by holding both sides back. Such a policy, a policy of balancing between Russia and Germany, would have been based on the idea that Britain could not profit from the destruction of either of those powers, each of whom served as a kind of counterweight to the other. An analysis of that sort, one should note, is rooted in the classical balance of power tradition—a tradition that leads you to be almost reflexively critical of the idea that strategy should be based essentially on simple deterrent threats.

But one could push this type of thinking a bit further. For such a balancing policy to be viable, Britain and France together would have had to free themselves from dependence on Russia—that is, from the implicit Russian threat that if the western powers did not give Russia a blank check, the Russians might work out an accommodation with Germany, and the western powers would then have to deal with Germany all by themselves. The threat could carry weight only because the western powers, mainly because of Britain's unwillingness to deploy large forces in northern France, were not in a particularly good position militarily vis-à-vis Germany. It would have made sense, therefore, for them to build up their defensive military power to the point where they could withstand a German onslaught without help from Russia—not just because that effort would be of direct value in military terms, but even more because that effort would increase their political freedom of action by making them less dependent on Russia and thus better able to balance between Germany and Russia. This is somewhat at variance with the way military issues are normally analyzed, but it is typical of the kind of insight you get by thinking about historical issues of this sort. The insights you get from grappling with the historical issue have a certain theoretical resonance—in this case, the historical analysis both draws on and gives you a sense for the value of the kind of classical balance of power thinking you associate with Fénelon. But these historical ruminations also have a certain policy relevance—a certain bearing, in this case, on the way issues of both military and foreign policy ought to be approached, and indeed on the way military and foreign policy need to be related to each other.

Let me give a second example, this one relating to U.S. policy during the Vietnam War. Both right and left tended at the time to approach the subject in moral terms, but in fact the policy issue could have been approached in a very different way. You could have looked at how an American victory would have affected the global structure of power— of how in that case the Chinese heartland would have been largely surrounded by an arc of American power, from South Korea and Japan down through Taiwan and the Philippines, and reconnecting with the Asian mainland in South Vietnam. In that event, the Chinese would probably have felt more inclined to mend fences with the Soviets, and a Sino-Soviet rapprochement would have weakened America's position in the world. On the other hand, a U.S. withdrawal from Vietnam and a reunification of that country under Communist auspices would probably have had the opposite effect. A unified Vietnam would be less dependent on China for support and more inclined to look to the Soviet Union as a counterweight to the great power to its north. As the unified Vietnam moved closer to the USSR, China would feel surrounded not by American but by Soviet power, and would in fact have an incentive to look to the United States as a counterweight to Russia. Such a turn of events would have been in America's interest. Wouldn't it have made sense to approach the issue, at least in large part, from that point of view? And yet you wouldn't even think of analyzing the problem in that context unless you had come to think about international politics in general in a certain way. Grappling with those theoretical issues can thus enable you to see things you otherwise would not have seen. It can give you a framework—a very valuable framework—for thinking about these issues of policy. And, conversely, grappling with policy problems can help you develop that framework. When you try to come to grips with a certain policy issue, you're virtually forced to think about which general principles apply. And in the process you're able to take your measure of those principles—that is, you're able to see how much real world resonance they have.

So all three areas of international relations scholarship—theory, history, and policy—are quite closely interrelated. It thus makes sense for people doing work in each of these three areas to interact with each other, to engage each other intellectually, and to draw on and react to what people in other parts of the field have to say about the problems they're concerned with. That's one of the ways people can develop a certain sense for what the core questions are, for whether they are being dealt with in the right way, and for whether the whole enterprise is in any sense more than just the sum of its parts.

All of which brings me to the question of what this area of scholarship can reasonably hope to achieve. I referred before to Martin Wight's well-known article, "Why Is There No International Theory?" But I didn't tell you then how he answered the question posed in the title. His answer, in fact, was a little bizarre. He thought the problem had to do with a "kind of recalcitrance of international politics to being theorized about." And the reason for that, in his view, was "that the theorizing has to be done in the language of political theory and law."[44] But

---

[44] Wight, "Why Is There No International Theory?" p. 33.

theorizing can obviously be done in whatever language is appropriate to the subject at hand or in new language developed for that purpose. So the answer Wight gave is not particularly strong.

But couldn't it be, you might wonder, that his question has a very simple answer? Maybe there is just not much to philosophize about. Maybe the issues here are just not intellectually challenging enough to produce high-level work of the sort Wight would have called "international theory." It might make sense to study individual conflicts, but maybe there is simply not much of a general nature to be said about the larger issue of how international politics works.

I think, however, that there are serious issues here, intellectually demanding issues, issues which we haven't yet been able to deal with entirely adequately. Brodie once said that the nuclear revolution had posed problems of "great intellectual difficulty, as well as other kinds of difficulty," and my sense is that most scholars who have tried to grapple with those problems would say "amen" to that point. I think, however, that what Brodie said about the nuclear revolution applies also to international politics as a whole. Many of the issues we deal with here are profoundly puzzling, and sometimes you realize how difficult they are only when you go into them in some depth. But that does not mean that the issues that lie at the heart of this field of inquiry are essentially unanswerable. There are points of a general nature that can be made—points that go well beyond, and in some respects even run counter to, what people tend to believe before they study the subject seriously. You can, in fact, identify a whole series of such points; you can see a whole variety of dynamics at work in the international sphere. The problem is seeing how they all fit together, seeing how much weight each of them carries in the real world, and seeing how to reconcile those points when they are in some ways at odds with each other. Dealing with that problem is not in principle an impossible task. But to deal with it effectively, we have to think more deeply than we have about how the larger problem needs to be tackled—about what the larger intellectual enterprise we are engaged in is, about how it needs to be organized, about how we should go about studying the fundamental problem of war and peace.

PART II

History

CHAPTER THREE

The United States and Eastern Europe in 1945: A Reassessment

THERE WAS A time when it all seemed so simple. The Soviet Union, it was said, sought to communize eastern Europe at the end of World War II; the western powers, and especially the United States, were deeply opposed to that policy; and the clash that developed played the key role in triggering the Cold War. But historians in recent years have been moving away from that sort of interpretation. It is not that there has been a fundamental shift in our understanding of Soviet policy. Some scholars, to be sure, claim that the USSR, even in the latter part of the war, did not plan to communize any of the countries in that region— that "nowhere beyond what Moscow considered the Soviet borders did its policies foresee the establishment of communist regimes."[1] But the prevailing view today is rather different. Soviet leaders might not have had a "master plan" or a "detailed blueprint" for the communization of eastern Europe, but by the end of the war, it is now commonly argued, they did have certain general goals and a certain general strategy for achieving those goals. The USSR, according to that view, would initially take a relatively moderate line and Sovietization would not be on the agenda. But the Communists would "proceed step by step" and would gradually tighten their grip on power. Eventually the "appropriate moment" would come; at that point, as the Soviet leader Josif Stalin himself put it, the "mask" would come off and the "maximal program" would be put into effect.[2]

A slightly different version of this article originally appeared in the fall 2008 issue of the *Journal of Cold War Studies*. Copyright © Journal of Cold War Studies, MIT Press, Cambridge, Massachusetts. Reprinted by permission. Documents marked with an asterisk in the footnotes are available on an Internet supplement: http://www.sscnet.ucla.edu/polisci/faculty/trachtenberg/usee/usee.html.

[1] Vojtech Mastny, *The Cold War and Soviet Insecurity: The Stalin Years* (New York: Oxford University Press, 1996), p. 21. See also Geoffrey Roberts, "Ideology, Calculation, and Improvisation: Spheres of Influence and Soviet Foreign Policy, 1939–1945," *Review of International Studies* 25 (1999): 671–73, and Geoffrey Roberts, *Stalin's Wars: From World War to Cold War, 1939–1953* (New Haven: Yale University Press, 2006), pp. 245–53. For a more moderate version of this argument, see Melvyn Leffler, "Inside Enemy Archives: The Cold War Reopened," *Foreign Affairs* 75, no. 4 (1996): 122–24, and Melvyn Leffler, *For the Soul of Mankind: The United States, the Soviet Union, and the Cold War* (New York: Hill and Wang, 2007), p. 29.

[2] For the comments about "proceeding step by step," the "appropriate moment," and

That view is by no means universally shared, but it does seem that most major scholars have come to interpret Soviet policy in those terms. Vladislav Zubok, for example, argues in his most recent book that Stalin was determined by early 1945 "to keep Eastern Europe in the Soviet Union's grip at any cost"; that point, he says, "has now been established beyond a doubt." The Soviet leader, according to Zubok, "assumed that the Soviet sphere of influence must and would be secured in the countries of Eastern Europe by imposing on them new political and social orders, modeled after the Soviet Union."[3] And Odd Arne Westad seems to agree. "As we learn more about Stalin's post-war foreign policy," he writes, "it seems unlikely that the Soviets would have

---

Sovietization not being on the agenda at that point, see Georgi Dimitrov's instructions to the Czechoslovak Communist leaders in December 1944, quoted in Elena Aga-Rossi and Victor Zaslavsky, "The Soviet Union and the Italian Communist Party, 1944–8," in Francesca Gori and Silvio Pons, eds., *The Soviet Union and Europe in the Cold War, 1943–53* (New York: St. Martin's, 1996), p. 180 (originally quoted in an unpublished paper by the Russian scholar V. Mariina). For Stalin's reference to a broadly based "people's party" being "a convenient mask for the present period," and his comment about how "later there will be time for the maximal program," see the widely cited entry in the Dimitrov diary for September 2, 1946, *The Diary of Georgi Dimitrov, 1933–1949*, ed. Ivo Banac (New Haven: Yale University Press, 2003), pp. 413–14. For the idea that the Soviets had "a remarkably uniform and to all appearances well considered strategy to gain control of Eastern Europe while minimizing and deferring conflict with the United States," see especially Eduard Mark, "Revolution by Degrees: Stalin's National-Front Strategy for Europe, 1941–1947," Cold War International History Program Working Paper No. 31 (February 2001), esp. pp. 6–7, 22, 30–33; the quotation is from Mark's contribution to the H-Diplo roundtable on Arnold Offner's *Another Such Victory* in December 2002. (A link to the text can be found at http://www.h-net.msu.edu/~diplo/roundtables/index.html). A number of other writers see things much the same way. See, for example, the articles by Gerhard Wettig and Donal O'Sullivan and the synthesis by the editors in the important collection of articles on the subject, Stefan Creuzberger and Manfred Görtemaker, eds., *Gleichschaltung unter Stalin? Die Entwicklung der Parteien in östlichen Europa 1944–1949* (Paderborn: Ferdinand Schöningh, 2002), esp. pp. 15 (Wettig), 50, 80, 83 (O'Sullivan), 421–22, 429, 431, 434 (Creuzberger and Görtemaker). Note, finally, Norman Naimark's comment in his review of the Creuzberger-Görtemaker book that the contributors "demonstrate"—not just "argue"—that the Soviet-backed "national front" policy in eastern Europe "was no more than an effort to grind down political opposition and boost the fortunes of the Communists." *Journal of Cold War Studies* 6, no. 4 (Fall 2004): 171.

[3] Vladislav Zubok, *A Failed Empire: The Soviet Union in the Cold War from Stalin to Gorbachev* (Chapel Hill: University of North Carolina Press, 2007), p. 21. See also Vladislav Zubok, "Stalin's Plans and Russian Archives," *Diplomatic History* 21, no. 2 (Spring 1997): 296, 299–300, 305. In 1996, in a book he wrote with Constantine Pleshakov, Zubok had taken a much milder view: Stalin, he and his co-author wrote, "was prepared to keep in power 'transitional' regimes that would be acceptable to the West"; his "postwar foreign policy was more defensive, reactive, and prudent than it was the fulfillment of a master plan." Vladislav Zubok and Constantine Pleshakov, *Inside the Kremlin's Cold War: From Stalin to Khrushchev* (Cambridge, Mass.: Harvard University Press, 1996), pp. 276–77. The change in perspective is quite striking.

tolerated even restricted participatory political systems in any of the countries their armies controlled in Eastern Europe."[4] This of course is not a new interpretation. Years ago, traditionalist scholars like Hugh Seton-Watson and Zbigniew Brzezinski had argued that the "Communist 'takeover' in Eastern Europe was ultimately designed and executed by Moscow for the purpose of extending its sphere of influence in Europe and the world."[5] But what is striking today is that most scholars seem to have come to the conclusion that this interpretation was essentially correct. As Norman Naimark and Leonid Gibianskii put it in their introduction to an important collection of articles on the subject, "Brzezinski and Seton-Watson had it right the first time."[6]

It is *American* policy that is now seen in a new light, at least by many historians. Increasingly the argument seems to be that U.S. leaders in 1945 did not really care much about eastern Europe—that their commitment to representative government in that region was surprisingly thin and that by the end of 1945 they had more or less come to the conclusion that the sort of political system the Soviets were setting up in that part of the world was something the United States could live with. The president and his top advisors, the argument runs, were not deeply concerned with east European issues; insofar as they had any policy at all, their basic goal was to maintain a certain cooperative relationship with the Soviets as a kind of end in itself. [7] But again that view is by no

[4] Odd Arne Westad, introduction to Odd Arne Westad, Sven Holtsmark, and Iver Neumann, eds., *The Soviet Union in Eastern Europe, 1945–89* (New York: St. Martin's, 1994), p. 3. Leffler, incidentally, has also argued that Stalin was not willing to tolerate governments based on free elections in countries like Poland. See Leffler, *For the Soul of Mankind*, p. 33. This has been his view for quite some time. In 1992, for example, he said that the idea that "Soviet security interests" could be reconciled with "popular elections" was "naïve." See Melvyn Leffler, *A Preponderance of Power: National Security, the Truman Administration, and the Cold War* (Stanford: Stanford University Press, 1992), p. 49. And in an article published in 1986 he had quoted Stalin as saying at Potsdam, "A freely elected government in any of these countries would be anti-Soviet, and that we cannot allow." Melvyn Leffler, "Adherence to Agreements: Yalta and the Experiences of the Early Cold War," *International Security* 11, no. 1 (Summer 1986): 102.

[5] Hugh Seton-Watson, *The East European Revolution* (London: Methuen, 1950); Zbigniew Brzezinski, *The Soviet Bloc: Unity and Conflict* (Cambridge, Mass.: Harvard University Press, 1960). The quotation is from a passage in Norman Naimark and Leonid Gibianskii, eds., *Establishment of Communist Regimes in Eastern Europe, 1944–1949* (Boulder, Colo: Westview, 1997), p. 7, summarizing the sort of interpretation developed by Seton-Watson and Brzezinski.

[6] Naimark and Gibianskii, *Establishment of Communist Regimes*, p. 8.

[7] See, for example, Leffler, "Inside Enemy Archives," p. 134, and Leffler, *For the Soul of Mankind*, pp. 42–44. Note also the reference in passing to the "relative indifference of the West to the fate of Eastern Europe" in Naimark and Gibianskii, *Establishment of Communist Regimes*, p. 7. See also Fraser Harbutt, *The Iron Curtain: Churchill, America, and the Origins of the Cold War* (New York: Oxford University Press, 1986), pp. 104–5, 109, 111, 115,

means universally shared, and even today some scholars find it virtually inconceivable that the U.S. government could have "written off" eastern Europe in that way.[8] Students of Soviet foreign policy, in particular, commonly take it for granted that the western powers were bound to oppose the communization of eastern Europe, and indeed often criticize Stalin for provoking a hostile western response by pursuing a "unilateralist" rather than a "cooperative" policy in this area.[9]

So what policy did the American government pursue in this area in 1945? Had it in fact "written off" eastern Europe by the end of the year? Did it even have a policy in any real sense of the term, or was what passed for policy little more than a series of ad hoc responses to the problems that presented themselves? I want to get at these questions by looking at how the U.S. government dealt with this issue in the course of the year, from the Yalta Conference in February through the Potsdam Conference in July to the Moscow Conference in December. This discussion will set the stage for the analysis in the final section. That part of the chapter will deal with some basic questions about how American policy in 1945 is to be understood, and in particular with the question of whether American leaders knew what they were doing. Was there a guiding philosophy, an overarching strategic concept, at work here?

FROM YALTA TO POTSDAM

How then did the American government deal with the problem of eastern Europe in early 1945, say from January through April of that year—that is, through the first month of the new administration of President Harry S Truman? The basic story here is quite familiar and can be reviewed quickly. The fate of Poland was the key issue in relations between the Soviet Union and the western powers at this time. Together with the British, the Americans did make a certain effort to establish a representative government in Poland in the early part of the year. This was one of the main reasons why President Franklin D. Roosevelt went to Yalta in February. And U.S. and British leaders were quite pleased, even in private, with the Yalta agreement.[10] According to that agree-

---

123, 132, 133, and Wilson Miscamble, *From Roosevelt to Truman: Potsdam, Hiroshima and the Cold War* (Cambridge, England: Cambridge University Press, 2007), pp. 212, 216, 325–26.

[8] See Eduard Mark's contribution to the H-Diplo roundtable on Miscamble's *From Truman to Roosevelt*, September 10, 2007 (http://www.h-net.msu.edu/~diplo/roundtables/PDF/FromTrumantoRoosevelt-Mark.pdf), pp. 8–9.

[9] See, for example, Aleksei Filitov, "The Soviet Union and the Grand Alliance: The Internal Dimension of Foreign Policy," in Gabriel Gorodetsky, ed., *Soviet Foreign Policy 1917–1991: A Retrospective* (London: Frank Cass, 1994), p. 100.

[10] See the evidence cited in Marc Trachtenberg, *A Constructed Peace: The Making of the European Settlement, 1945–1963* (Princeton: Princeton University Press, 1999), p. 9.

ment, the government the Soviets had installed in Poland would be "reorganized on a broader democratic basis with the inclusion of democratic leaders from Poland itself and from Poles abroad," and the new provisional government would hold "free and unfettered elections as soon as possible on the basis of universal suffrage and secret ballot." But the negotiations in Moscow on the reorganization of the Polish government did not go well. The western powers blamed the Soviets for the deadlock, and on April 1 Roosevelt sent Stalin a letter complaining about what had happened: "I must make it quite plain to you that any such solution which would result in a thinly disguised continuance of the present Warsaw regime would be unacceptable and would cause the people of the United States to regard the Yalta agreement as having failed."[11] And Truman, as is well known, took an even tougher line in a famous meeting with Soviet Foreign Minister Vyacheslav Molotov three weeks later. A shaken Molotov, evidently afraid that Stalin would hold him responsible for Truman's behavior, could not even bring himself to send his master in the Kremlin an honest account of his encounter with the president.[12]

But Truman's truculent mood soon passed. He by no means wanted to break with the Soviets and in May sent Roosevelt's old advisor Harry Hopkins to Moscow to try to resolve the problem. And Hopkins did work out a deal with Stalin: some non-Communist Poles, including Stanislaw Mikolajczyk, the Polish leader the British and American governments were pinning their hopes on, would be brought into the Communist-dominated government, albeit in nonessential positions. On that basis a more detailed agreement was worked out, and in early July the reconstituted government was recognized by the United States and Britain.

It is often assumed in the historical literature that the Hopkins mission represented something of a turning point. Eduard Mark's view is typical of the way most scholars have come to interpret this episode. "For all the brave rhetoric" Truman permitted himself in his first weeks in office, Mark says, "virtually his first act in relation to Eastern Europe was to accept what Roosevelt had vowed he would not: in return for Stalin's renewed promise to permit free elections, the United States recognized a 'thinly disguised continuance' of the Lublin regime as the interim government of Poland."[13] Other scholars go a bit further and

---

[11] Roosevelt to Stalin, April 1, 1945, U.S. Department of State, *Foreign Relations of the United States, 1945*, vol. 5, p. 195; henceforth cited in this form: FRUS 1945, 5:195.

[12] See Zubok, *Failed Empire*, pp. 14–15. Note also the careful analysis of this episode in Miscamble, *From Roosevelt to Truman*, pp. 114–23.

[13] Eduard Mark, "American Policy toward Eastern Europe and the Origins of the Cold War, 1941–1946: An Alternative Interpretation," *Journal of American History*, Vol. 68, No. 2 (September 1981), p. 327.

suggest that America was basically writing off Poland—that the Americans were accepting the fact that a Communist-dominated regime was being imposed on the country, that the broadening of the government was just "temporary window-dressing," that the "concessions" Stalin had made were merely "cosmetic" in nature, that Truman was not particularly concerned with the fate of Poland as such, and that the overriding U.S. goal at this point was just to settle the dispute.[14]

But this general argument cannot rest solely on evidence from the period of the Hopkins mission itself. To be sure, there is some evidence from that period that points in this direction—for example, Truman's reference to the importance of "Uncle Joe" making "some sort of gesture—whether he means it or not," or Hopkins's remark in one of his meetings with Stalin that Poland as such was "not so important" and that the United States had "no special desire to see any particular kind of government" in that country.[15] But the argument that a fundamental shift in American policy on Poland took place at this time—that from May 1945 on the United States essentially gave the Soviets a free hand in Poland—rests not so much on evidence of this sort as on a study of how the U.S. government dealt with this issue in the latter half of 1945. For it is important to note that the U.S. government at the time did not see the deal Hopkins worked out with Stalin as a capitulation. Key State Department officials, for example, still thought there was a certain chance that Poland would not become a Communist police state and that the country might instead end up with a good deal of internal autonomy and political freedom.[16] The real test of American policy came only later, when it gradually became clear that this was not to be—that in all probability there were not going to be any "free and unfettered

---

[14] See Miscamble, *From Roosevelt to Truman*, pp. 156–58; Harbutt, *Iron Curtain*, pp. 105–7; James McAllister, *No Exit: America and the German Problem, 1943–1954* (Ithaca: Cornell University Press, 2002), p. 63–67; William Taubman, *Stalin's American Policy: From Entente to Détente to Cold War* (New York: Norton, 1982), p. 107; A. W. DePorte, *Europe between the Super-Powers: The Enduring Balance* (New Haven: Yale University Press, 1979), p. 97; John Lewis Gaddis, *The United States and the Origins of the Cold War, 1941–1947* (New York: Columbia University Press, 1972), p. 235; Lisle Rose, *After Yalta* (New York: Scribner's, 1973), p. 43.

[15] See McAllister, *No Exit*, p. 64; Miscamble, *From Roosevelt to Truman*, p. 145n.; Harbutt, *Iron Curtain*, p. 106.

[16] Note, for example, Joseph Grew's comment at the time, quoted in Miscamble, *From Roosevelt to Truman*, p. 160. Grew, as Miscamble notes, generally took a "tough line on the Soviet Union." See also Harriman to Acting Secretary, June 28, 1945, *Foreign Relations of the United States: The Conference of Berlin (The Potsdam Conference)*, Vol. 1 (Washington, D.C.: GPO, 1960), p. 728, henceforth cited in this form: FRUS: Potsdam, 1:728. The British attitude was more guarded. See Churchill to Halifax, July 6, 1945, and Anderson to Hankey, July 16, 1945, *Documents on British Policy Overseas*, Series I, Vol. 1 (London: HMSO, 1984), pp. 5–6, 318–19, henceforth cited in this form: DBPO I:1:5–6, 318–19.

elections" in Poland and that the Communists were determined to hold on to power there no matter what.

So when exactly did the Americans begin to understand what was going on in that country? To answer that question we first need to answer a more basic question: what exactly *was* going on there? On the surface the answer is simple: well before the war in Europe had ended the Soviets had begun to build a Communist police state in Poland. But the story behind that development is not as simple as one might think, since it is by no means clear that Stalin intended from the start to communize Poland, and it is by no means inconceivable that in 1942 or even 1943 some sort of accommodation between the Soviet Union and the Polish exile government in London could have been worked out. To be sure, that government would have had to accept the Curzon line as Poland's new eastern border—that is, it would have had to accept the loss of half of Poland's prewar territory, an area, however, in which only a minority (albeit a large minority) of the population was ethnically Polish. And even if it had accepted that condition, there was no guarantee that Poland would not have ended up as a Communist state. But whatever hope there was that Poland's fate would be different depended on the Polish government's acceptance of the USSR's demand for recognition of what the Soviets viewed as their new border.

The London Poles, however, would not accept that demand, and that either led Stalin to view the Polish government as "unfriendly" (and the forces loyal to it as hostile) or gave him an excuse for doing so. And indeed key leaders of the exile government and of the Home Army, the military organization within Poland loyal to that government, from the start viewed the USSR (after Nazi Germany) as "enemy number two"; Home Army leaders, in fact, created an organization that was intended to serve as the nucleus of an "anti-Soviet resistance movement."[17] In such circumstances, it is scarcely surprising that by

---

[17] See especially Jan M. Ciechanowski, *The Warsaw Rising of 1944* (Cambridge, England: Cambridge University Press, 1974), chapter 1. On the "doctrine of two enemies," see ibid., pp. 137, 278, 312; for the document referring to Russia as "enemy number two," see p. 144. On the "anti-Soviet resistance movement," see ibid., p. 194; see also John Coutouvidis and Jaime Reynolds, *Poland 1939–1947* (Leicester: Leicester University Press, 1986), pp. 149–51, and Krystyna Kersten, *The Establishment of Communist Rule in Poland, 1943–1948* (Berkeley: University of California Press, 1991), p. 96. Note also the report from Ukrainian Minister of State Security Savchenko dated March 28, 1944, and sent to Stalin on April 10 by Nikita Khrushchev, then head of the Ukrainian Communist Party, quoted in its entirety in Jeffrey Burds, "The Early Cold War in Soviet West Ukraine, 1944–1948," *Carl Beck Papers in Russian and East European Studies*, No. 1505 (Pittsburgh: University of Pittsburgh Center for Russian and East European Studies, 2001), pp. 19–20. According to that report, an armed resistance movement linked to the London government was being organized in what Soviet officials considered the "western *oblasts* of Ukraine and Belorussia."

mid-1944 at the latest Soviet policy on the Polish question was no longer based on the idea that an accommodation could be reached with the Polish authorities in London—if indeed the Soviets had ever honestly wanted to reach a genuine understanding with the London Poles. Soviet policy now became increasingly clear: the exile government would be replaced by a new Communist-dominated government, which the Soviets would set up in the country, and the forces loyal to the government in London would be disbanded or otherwise liquidated soon after the Red Army moved in. By this point, there was little reason for Stalin to hold back. He certainly did not feel, given the attitude of the western powers, that in moving ahead with that kind of policy he would be running much of a risk in geopolitical terms. He was convinced, as he told the Polish Communist leaders in October 1944, that the alliance with Britain and the United States would "not break up over Poland."[18]

So as Soviet troops in 1944 moved into territory that had been part of Poland before the war, one of their main goals was to disarm the Home Army units they found there. There was some resistance and Soviet policy hardened.[19] "At the end of September," according to the Polish scholar Krystyna Kersten, "Stalin, who had been briefed by the Polish Communists as well as by the Soviet ambassador, the NKVD, and military counterintelligence, acknowledged that it was necessary to strike in a sufficiently powerful fashion to liquidate all opposition and subdue society."[20] The result was a "turn to intense political repression in October," a development referred to in the literature as the "October turn."[21] The goal was "the annihilation of active opposition"—or, in the words of one of the Polish Communist leaders, "the neutralization of those who oppose the program of the PKWN," the Communist-dominated proto-government.[22] But the new policy was

[18] Meeting of the PKWN [Polish Committee of National Liberation] with Comrade Stalin, October 9, 1944, in Antony Polonsky and Boleslaw Drukier, *The Beginnings of Communist Rule in Poland* (London: Routledge and Kegan Paul, 1980), p. 298. For perhaps the best overview of developments in Poland in general during the 1944–45 period, see Coutouvidis and Reynolds, *Poland*, pp. 137–97. On the timing of preparations for the establishment of a Communist-dominated regime in Poland, see Leonid Gibianskij, "Osteuropa: Sicherheitszone der UdSSR, sowjetisiertes Protektorat des Kreml oder Sozialismus 'ohne Diktatur des Proletariats'?" *Forum für osteuropäische Ideen- und Zeitgeschichte* 8, no. 2 (2004): 125, and esp. the Polish and Russian sources cited there in n. 27.

[19] See Coutouvidis and Reynolds, *Poland*, pp. 150–61, and Kersten, *Establishment of Communist Rule*, pp. 93–97.

[20] Kersten, *Establishment of Communist Rule*, pp. 98–99.

[21] Ibid., p. 102.

[22] Ibid., p. 103. See also Polonsky and Drukier, *Beginnings of Communist Rule in Poland*, pp. 108–9; Coutouvidis and Reynolds, *Poland*, p. 172; John Micgiel, "'Bandits and Reactionaries': The Suppression of the Opposition in Poland, 1944–1946," in Naimark and

not a success; there was an "upsurge in guerrilla activity" in the spring of 1945; society as a whole had been alienated and the Communists had been unable to establish a real political base in the country.[23] As a result the Communists adopted a new and somewhat softer policy—a shift scholars refer to as the "May turn"—and were ready in fact to accept a certain broadening of the government.[24] The Hopkins mission and its aftermath—the inclusion of some non-Communist Poles, especially Mikolajczyk, in a reconstituted "national unity" government—is to be understood in this context.

But these changes were made for essentially tactical purposes. The Communists were not seeking a real accommodation with the rest of society; they were not interested in any genuine form of power-sharing. They were determined, as they themselves said at the time, to hold on to their "hegemony" within Poland by whatever means turned out to be necessary. As the Communist leader Wladyslaw Gomulka told Mikolajczyk in Moscow in June, "[W]e shall never hand over power." The non-Communist parties were in effect told they would be tolerated only if they did not seriously contest Communist hegemony in the country. Otherwise they would be "ruthlessly destroyed."[25]

The Polish Communists could pursue this sort of policy only because they had the Soviet Union behind them. As Stalin himself reminded them "on at least several occasions," their whole political system rested on Soviet military power.[26] And the Soviet leader was not seriously interested in getting the Polish Communists to settle for less than total control. The fate of Poland, in his view, would not be decided by "free and unfettered elections." The will of the majority would not be the controlling factor. A relatively small but highly disciplined party was all that was needed. "A membership of 200,000," he told Gomulka in late 1945, "is a force which can overturn a whole country if it is well

---

Gibianskii, *Establishment of Communist Regimes*, p. 93; Andrzej Paczkowski, "Poland, the 'Enemy Nation,'" in Stéphane Courtois et al., *The Black Book of Communism: Crimes, Terror, Repression* (Cambridge, Mass.: Harvard University Press, 1999), esp. pp. 372–76.

[23] Coutouvidis and Reynolds, *Poland*, p. 174.

[24] See Coutouvidis and Reynolds, *Poland*, chapter 7, esp. pp. 188–97.

[25] See Coutouvidis and Reynolds, *Poland*, p. 196, 201–2; Kersten, *Establishment of Communist Rule*, p. 193; Polonsky and Drukier, *Beginnings of Communist Rule*, pp. 49, 126; and Andrzej Paczkowski, *The Spring Will Be Ours: Poland and the Poles from Occupation to Freedom* (University Park: Pennsylvania State University Press, 2003), p. 144.

[26] Andrzej Paczkowski, "Polish-Soviet Relations 1944–1989: The Limits of Autonomy," *Russian History/Histoire Russe* 29, nos. 2-4 (Summer–Fall–Winter 2002): 283–84. One such comment is quoted in Donal O'Sullivan, *Stalins 'Cordon sanitaire': Die sowjetische Osteuropapolitik und die Reaktionen des Westens 1939-1949* (Paderborn, Germany: Ferdinand Schöningh, 2003), pp. 243–44: "If it weren't for the Red Army" Stalin told the Polish Communists in the fall of 1944, "you wouldn't last a week."

organized, well managed and controlled, and if it has instructions as to what to say and how to say it."[27]

The goal was "hegemony." This implied that sooner or later all possible sources of opposition to Communist rule would have to be tamed or destroyed. For the time being, however, for both domestic and foreign policy reasons, it made sense to take a relatively soft line—to ease up on the repression and pretend that the party was truly interested in reconciliation and national unity. To be sure, the apparatus of the police state continued to grow; the press was by no means free; and opponents of the regime were sometimes arrested or beaten up. But the level of repression in mid-1945 was not nearly as great as it might have been. The Communists did not monopolize Polish political life, and other parties, especially Mikolajczyk's, were more or less tolerated. Mikolajczyk himself was relatively optimistic. He knew his party could not operate with total freedom, but even so the Communists were so deeply unpopular in the country that he thought he and his allies should be able to win even minimally free elections. There was no guarantee, of course, that such elections would ever actually be held. The Soviets would have the final say in the matter, but, as Mikolajczyk saw it, the USSR might be willing to tolerate a non-Communist but "friendly" Poland on its border. This turned out to be an illusion, but it was not preposterous in June 1945 to think, given the political situation both within Poland and in the wider world, that Stalin might be willing to settle for an arrangement of this sort.[28]

How did the western powers react to what was going on in Poland at the time? As noted above, the prevailing view in late June, when the new Polish "national unity" government was set up, was that the situation was not hopeless. It was by no means certain that things would not turn out satisfactorily. To be sure, the whole affair of the sixteen Polish resistance leaders, arrested after having been invited in for talks and then put on trial in Moscow even as the negotiations for the establishment of a "national unity" government were going on elsewhere in that city, was not a good sign. But even people like Averell Harriman, the U.S. ambassador in Moscow—the man who had warned Truman in April about a new "barbarian invasion of Europe"—thought there was a "fair chance" that Poland might end up as a relatively free coun-

---

[27] Notes of Gomulka-Stalin meeting, November 14, 1945, *Cold War International History Project Bulletin*, no. 11 (Winter 1998): 135.

[28] On the political situation in Poland at the time, see Paczkowski, *Spring Will Be Ours*, pp. 154–59, 161–62, 169, and Kersten, *Establishment of Communist Rule*, p. 193. On Mikolajczyk, see Coutouvidis and Reynolds, *Poland*, pp. 202–8; Kersten, *Establishment of Communist Rule*, pp. 186–90; and also Harriman to Secretary of State, June 28, 1945, FRUS Potsdam, 1:728. For Mikolajczyk's "cautious optimism" in mid-July, see Clark Kerr to Eden, July 16, 1945, DBPO I:1, microfiche supplement, calendar 319i.

try.[29] After all, hadn't Stalin told Hopkins that Poland would become a western-style democracy like Holland?[30]

It was hard at that time to know what would happen in Poland. Things, it seemed, could go either way. But it was not long before the western governments began to get some information about how the situation was developing in that country, and the news was not good. On July 25, while he was at Potsdam, Secretary of State James Byrnes was told about some "disquieting reports" that had come in from Poland via the British Foreign Office. One of the non-Communist Polish leaders had reported that the "Polish people enjoy practically no civil liberties, that Soviet officials are behind each local government, and that secret service under Soviet direction is making many arrests."[31] The British were in fact receiving a good deal of negative information and often shared what they learned with the Americans. Some of that information came from Mikolajczyk, who was also at Potsdam and met with high British officials a number of times. On July 25, he told the Foreign Secretary, Anthony Eden, that things had taken a turn for the worse in Poland; the head of the Communist-dominated government there, he said, was trying to set up a one-party system.[32] There were many arrests, he told another key British official. The Soviet army and the secret police, the NKVD, "exercised a general terror" in the country.[33] Mikolajczyk, another British official noted, was "far from cheerful about the present trend of events in Poland"; he felt "that the battle for Poland's independence was now joined."[34] The outcome of that struggle was still in doubt; things still turn might turn out satisfactorily, but only if the Red Army and the NKVD left the country first.[35]

The western governments were now in direct contact with the Soviet leadership at Potsdam. How did they deal with this issue? "Of Stalin's purposes" with respect to Poland, George Kennan wrote, there was at this point "no longer any excuse for ignorance or doubt"—and that assessment, while perhaps a bit too strong, was essentially correct.[36] But the Americans did not seem overly concerned with what was going on

---

[29] Truman meeting with top officials, April 20, 1945 (for Harriman's remark about a "barbarian invasion"), FRUS 1945, 5:232, and Harriman to Secretary of State, June 28, 1945, FRUS Potsdam, 1:728.

[30] Hopkins-Stalin meeting, May 27, 1945, FRUS Potsdam, 1:38–39.

[31] Grew to Byrnes, July 25, 1945, FRUS: Potsdam, 2:647. For the original British report, see Hankey to Eden, July 19, 1945, DBPO I:1:765.

[32] Eden-Mikolajczyk meeting, July 25, 1945, DBPO I:1:681–82.

[33] Clark Kerr-Mikolajczyk meeting, July 25, 1945, ibid., pp. 683–84

[34] Allen to Warner, July 25, 1945, ibid., pp. 903–4.

[35] Bevin-Mikolajczyk meeting, July 31, 1945, and annex, ibid., pp. 1058–60, and Sargent to Cadogan, July 30, 1945, ibid., pp. 1039–40.

[36] George Kennan, "An Historian of Potsdam and his Readers," *American Slavic and East European Review* 20 (April 1961): 289.

in that country. The British were somewhat more active, but even they did not press the Soviets very hard on the core issue. The three powers discussed certain Polish questions at Potsdam, most notably the question of Poland's western border. But the key question of whether a Communist police state was going to be imposed on that country was not dealt with in any serious way. The Polish problem, in Truman's view, had been "settled" by the agreements worked out during and immediately after the Hopkins mission, and U.S. leaders in general very much wanted to put that whole issue behind them.[37]

FROM POTSDAM TO MOSCOW

So the Potsdam evidence strongly suggests that by July at the latest the Americans had decided to acquiesce in what the Soviets were doing in Poland, and that general point is confirmed by what we know about U.S. policy on this issue in the post–Potsdam period in late 1945.[38] That conclusion is important in its own right, but it also bears directly on the question of how U.S. policy on eastern Europe in 1945 more generally is to be interpreted. For if the American government was willing to accept what was going on in Poland, does it really make sense to think that it would make a serious effort to prevent the communization of countries like Romania and Bulgaria?

But there is a puzzle here. The Americans at Potsdam and after might have been relatively passive on the Polish question, but they seemed to take a strong stand at Potsdam on Romania and Bulgaria, and they pursued a vigorous policy in those countries in mid-August, soon after the conference adjourned. At Potsdam, for example, the U.S. government proposed that the control commissions in those countries "henceforth operate on a tri-partite basis" and that elections there be conducted under three-power "supervision."[39] U.S. leaders, moreover, repeatedly

[37] Note especially Truman's reaction to the news from Moscow that Hopkins had worked out an arrangement with Stalin, in Robert H. Ferrell, ed., *Truman in the White House: The Diary of Eben A. Ayers* (Columbia: University of Missouri Press, 1991), entry for June 1, 1945, p. 39. Churchill's attitude at the time was very different. See Churchill to Truman, June 4, 1945, FRUS 1945, 5:324.

[38] See, for example, Geir Lundestad, *The American Non-Policy Towards Eastern Europe, 1943–1947* (Oslo: Universitetsforlaget, 1978), pp. 209, 211.

[39] Foreign Ministers meeting, July 20, 1945, and U.S. Proposal on the Implementation of the Yalta Declaration on Liberated Europe, July 21, 1945, in FRUS Potsdam, 2:152, 155, 647. The word *supervision* was too strong for Churchill and even Truman, so Byrnes proposed softening it to *observation* . The next day, however, he was again talking about "supervision of elections." Truman-Churchill-Stalin meeting, July 20, 1945, and Foreign Ministers meeting, July 22, 1945, ibid., pp. 166, 229.

made it quite clear the United States would not recognize the governments of Bulgaria and Romania until they were "set up on a satisfactory basis," and at the first plenary meeting at Potsdam they submitted a proposal for the "immediate reorganization of the present governments in Rumania and Bulgaria."[40] So it seemed that the Americans were taking a tough line on the issue.

But the Soviets came away from Potsdam with the sense (as Molotov put it) that the decisions made at the conference relating to "Bulgaria and the Balkans" were "to our advantage" and that "in effect, this sphere of influence has been recognized as ours."[41] What had led them to draw that conclusion? The Americans, to be sure, had dropped the proposal for the "supervision of elections" and had opted for compromise language on the question of diplomatic recognition.[42] But that really did not mean much: the proposals had been dropped because the Soviets would not agree to them, not because the U.S. government had changed its position. So what then was the basis for the Soviet view that the Americans had written off the Balkans?[43]

Perhaps something was said, something that did not find its way into the documents, that led the Soviets to conclude that the Americans' tough talk was once again not to be taken too seriously. There are certainly many indications that U.S. leaders were not deeply concerned with the fate of eastern Europe. Truman was not outraged by what the Soviets were doing in the areas they occupied. At Potsdam, as he later noted, he had been a Russophile "as most of us were." He actually liked Stalin and enjoyed doing business with him.[44] The Soviet leader, he

[40] Foreign Ministers meetings, July 20, 22 and 24, 1945, Truman-Churchill-Stalin meetings, July 21 and 24, 1945, and U.S. Proposal on the Implementation of the Yalta Declaration on Liberated Europe, July 17, 1945, in FRUS Potsdam, 2:151, 207, 231, 326, 371, and, for the two documents quoted, pp. 216 and 644.

[41] *Diary of Georgi Dimitrov*, entry for August 6, 1945, p. 377. Similar comments were reported at the time by the Yugoslav ambassador in Moscow. See Mastny, *Cold War and Soviet Insecurity*, p. 22, and Roberts, *Stalin's Wars*, p. 279. This evidence was originally presented in a 1994 article by the Russian historian Leonid Gibianskii, which both Mastny and Roberts cite.

[42] For Byrnes's reference to a "compromise," see Byrnes-Molotov meeting, July 30, 1945, FRUS Potsdam, 2:480. For the new language, compare a U.S. proposal of July 30 with a corresponding proposal of July 26, ibid., pp. 628, 630.

[43] In this paragraph, and indeed in the article as a whole, I use the term *the Balkans* to refer essentially to Romania and Bulgaria, since that term was commonly used this way at the time.

[44] See Leffler, *Soul of Mankind*, pp. 42–44, and Trachtenberg, *Constructed Peace*, pp. 37–38. Indeed, as late as October he still thought Stalin was "a fine man who wanted to do the right thing." John Morton Blum, ed., *The Price of Vision: The Diary of Henry A. Wallace, 1942–1946* (Boston : Houghton Mifflin, 1973), p. 490.

thought, was "honest—but smart as hell."[45] Yes, of course, the Soviets were out to dominate the area their armies now occupied, but that was something America could live with. Hitler, in Truman's view, had opened the floodgates. The result, he said, was that "we shall have a Slav Europe for a long time to come." He then added his own personal gloss: "I don't think it is so bad."[46] It is thus by no means out of the question that the Soviets somehow sensed that the U.S. government was not deeply concerned with eastern Europe, and in particular with Bulgaria and Romania, and that Molotov's remarks about the West at Potsdam accepting the Balkans as a Soviet sphere of influence are to be understood in that context.

But if the Soviets really did come away from Potsdam with that impression, they were in for a bit of a shock. American officials in both Romania and Bulgaria had for some time felt that U.S. policy in those countries had been too passive, but now that the president had said that the United States would not recognize the Communist-dominated governments there, they felt they could play a more active role. In Romania especially they now encouraged the Communists' opponents to take action. The non-Communist Romanians were in fact anxious to act before it was too late and the Communist grip on power became irreversible. But they would not move unless they were assured of western, and especially American, support. On August 11, Byrnes seemed to give them the signal they were waiting for. U.S. representatives in the country were told that if asked they could tell the opposition leaders that the United States hoped to see "a more representative regime" established in Romania.[47] And that was precisely what they did: U.S. officials were in "virtual daily contact" with opposition leaders, and the king, encouraged by all this, on August 19 "demanded the resignation of the Roumanian government."[48] The British were amazed by what American diplomats were doing: "The Americans are intervening vigorously in Roumanian internal affairs," one British official wrote. "In fact they have begun a full-scale plot against one of the Russians' favorite puppets."[49]

[45] Truman diary entry, July 17, 1945, in Eduard Mark, "'Today Has Been a Historical One': Harry S Truman's Diary of the Potsdam Conference," *Diplomatic History* 4, no. 3 (July 1980): 322.

[46] James Forrestal Diary, entry for July 28, 1945, Forrestal Diaries, vol. 2, Forrestal Papers, Mudd Library, Princeton University, Princeton, N.J.; extract available online (http://www.sscnet.ucla.edu/polisci/faculty/trachtenberg/documents/forrestal.html).

[47] Byrnes to Melbourne, August 11, 1945, FRUS 1945, 5:565–66.

[48] Melbourne to Byrnes, August 14, 1945, ibid., p. 567, and Elizabeth Hazard, *Cold War Crucible: United States Foreign Policy and the Conflict in Rumania* (Boulder, Colo.: East European Monographs, 1996), p. 124.

[49] Foreign Office minute, August 16, 1945, quoted in Paul Quinlan, *Clash Over Romania:*

The Soviets were angered by what Stalin called his allies' "machinations" in Romania, and especially by the role the Americans had played in provoking the crisis.[50] The Soviet leader was certainly not prepared to accept a change in government. The Americans, for their part, did not want an armed confrontation. Indeed, U.S. officials on the scene probably went much further in encouraging the Romanian opposition than Byrnes had intended.[51] With the war with Japan nearly over, Byrnes at this point obviously had much more important things to worry about. All sorts of issues had to be dealt with. In such circumstances, he could scarcely exercise close day-to-day control over the situation in Romania. But when he did realize what was going on, he pulled in the reins. U.S. representatives in the country were instructed on August 25 to avoid contact with the opposition for the time being. The king was to be advised that "measures which might further provoke Soviet officials" should be avoided.[52] As the Norwegian historian Geir Lundestad notes, the active American policy had lasted a mere two weeks.[53]

In Bulgaria the story was very similar, although perhaps not quite so

---

British and American Policies towards Romania, 1938–1947 (Los Angeles: American Romanian Academy of Arts and Sciences, 1977), p. 141; see also p. 143. For the story of this mini-crisis, see Quinlan, *Clash over Romania*, pp. 140–45; Lundestad, *American Non-Policy*, pp. 237–42; and Hazard, *Cold War Crucible*, pp. 121–26.

[50] Stalin to Molotov, September 12, 1945, quoted in Vladimir Pechatnov, "'The Allies Are Pressing on You to Break Your Will,': Foreign Policy Correspondence between Stalin and Molotov and Other Politburo Members, September 1945–December 1946," trans. Vladislav Zubok, Cold War International History Project Working Paper No. 26 (September 1999), p. 2.

[51] Did Byrnes understand that his August 11 dispatch would "greatly stimulate local demands to overthrow the [Communist-dominated] Groza government"? Lundestad says that he did (*American Non-Policy*, p. 240), and in his n. 105 on p. 550 he cites three documents to back up that contention: two telegrams from Melbourne, the U.S. representative in Bucharest, and Byrnes's own August 11 dispatch. But that evidence scarcely proves the point. The plan, as Melbourne reported it in one of those documents, was that the king would dismiss the government only after all three allies had authorized him to do so; he would not proceed without first getting the Soviets' okay. In such circumstances, Byrnes might well have felt that there was little harm in authorizing U.S. officials in Romania to simply reiterate existing American policy. Indeed, he warned U.S. officials in Bucharest not to get too deeply involved in what the Romanian opposition was doing—to not comment on any "particular plan of action," and to speak only "in general terms." It is hard to avoid the conclusion that officials on the scene got more deeply involved in the opposition plot than Byrnes would have liked. Two of the documents that Lundestad cites are readily available in FRUS, and the third, *Melbourne's August 9, 1945, telegram to Byrnes, is available on microfilm in *Records of the U.S. Department of State Relating to the Internal Affairs of Romania, 1945–1949* (Wilmington, Del.: Scholarly Resources, 1987), reel 2.

[52] Byrnes to Melbourne, August 25, 1945, FRUS 1945, 5:594.

[53] Lundestad, *American Non-Policy*, pp. 241–42.

dramatic. U.S. officials on the scene thought that American policy toward that country had been much too passive, but were encouraged by the line their government took on the issue at Potsdam. Byrnes, again on August 11, instructed the U.S. representative in Sofia to make a tough declaration to the Bulgarian government: "[W]e cannot overlook the preponderance of current evidence that a minority element in power in the country is at present endeavoring by the use of force and intimidation to prevent the effective participation in the scheduled elections of a large democratic section of the electorate"; the implication was that a government that resulted from that sort of electoral process would not be recognized by the United States.[54] The policy itself was not new. "What *was* new," as Lundestad notes, "was that the Bulgarian government was directly informed about this attitude and, equally important, this was done at a time when the Bulgarian Opposition was becoming more restive than before."[55]

The U.S. representative in Sofia, Maynard Barnes, was pleased by this new turn in American policy, but he himself took a tougher line than Byrnes had intended.[56] The Secretary of State, upset by what his representative in Bulgaria had been doing, rebuked Barnes on August 24.[57] Again, Byrnes was pulling in the reins; again, the tough policy, such as it was, had lasted a mere two weeks—indeed, for the same two weeks in both cases.

But these events were enough to anger the Soviets, and they took a very hard line on these Balkan issues at the London Council of Foreign Ministers meeting in September. Stalin was personally calling the shots at this point, and he made sure that Molotov, the Soviet representative at the meeting, was utterly intransigent.[58] As for the Americans, some historians argue that Byrnes (in an attempt to practice "atomic diplomacy") also took a tough line at the start of that conference; when that proved unproductive, the argument runs, Byrnes wanted to compromise, but was prevented from doing so by John Foster Dulles, the Republican in the U.S. delegation, who threatened to resign and have Byrnes denounced as an appeaser if he gave way in this area. Other historians say that Byrnes was initially inclined to compromise, but provoked by Molotov's attacks on American policy, hardened his posi-

[54] Byrnes to Barnes, August 11, 1945, FRUS 1945, 4:283.

[55] Lundestad, *American Non-Policy*, p. 268.

[56] Michael Boll, *Cold War in the Balkans: American Foreign Policy and the Emergence of Communist Bulgaria, 1943-1947* (Lexington: University Press of Kentucky, 1984), pp. 136–50. See also Lundestad, *American Non-Policy*, pp. 257–71, and Vesselin Dimitrov, *Stalin's Cold War: Soviet Foreign Policy, Democracy and Communism in Bulgaria, 1941–48* (New York: Palgrave Macmillan, 2008), pp. 117–27.

[57] Boll, *Cold War in the Balkans*, p. 150, and Lundestad, *American Non-Policy*, pp. 269.

[58] Pechatnov, "'The Allies Are Pressing on You,'" esp. pp. 1–2, 6.

tion early on and took a tough line for the rest of the conference. The interpretations differ, but the bottom line is the same: the U.S. government, in the final analysis, was uncompromising on Romania and Bulgaria at London.[59]

The evidence, however, points in a very different direction: Byrnes made it quite clear at the London meeting that the U.S. government was willing to live with the Communist-dominated regimes in those two Balkan countries. The point is important because of the light it sheds on American policy as a whole during this period. It means that the policy Byrnes was to pursue at the Moscow Conference in December—a policy based on America's willingness essentially to accept Soviet control of eastern Europe—had been in place for months. That in turn means that what happened at Moscow was no flash in the pan—that the policy Byrnes pursued at Moscow had a deeper base. It also implies that the Potsdam policy—America's refusal to recognize the Bulgarian and Romanian governments so long as they were not truly democratic—was not rooted in a strong commitment to representative government in eastern Europe on America's part. The Potsdam meeting ended in early August and by September Byrnes was already taking an accommodationist line on this issue: the rapid change in the U.S. line shows how shallow the commitment was.

What is the proof for these claims? They rest essentially on one key point: namely, that Byrnes at London repeatedly suggested that the arrangement that had been worked out for Poland following the Hopkins mission could serve as a model for settling the Romanian and Bulgarian problems. He first proposed a solution along these lines at a private meeting with Molotov on September 16, a few days after the conference

[59] See (for the first sort of interpretation) Robert Messer, *The End of an Alliance: James F. Byrnes, Roosevelt, Truman, and the Origins of the Cold War* (Chapel Hill: University of North Carolina Press, 1982), pp. 132–33; Daniel Yergin, *Shattered Peace: The Origins of the Cold War and the National Security State* (Boston: Houghton Mifflin, 1977), pp. 122–30, esp. p. 124; and Arnold Offner, "'Another Such Victory': President Truman, American Foreign Policy, and the Cold War," *Diplomatic History* 23, no. 2 (April 1999): 136. (Copies of two documents that Offner cites to support his argument in that passage—*messages that Truman sent Byrnes during the conference—can be found in the internet supplement.) For the second type of interpretation, see Mark, "American Policy toward Eastern Europe," pp. 327–28, and James Gormly, *The Collapse of the Grand Alliance, 1945–1948* (Baton Rouge: Louisiana State University Press, 1987), pp. 65–69, 85. With regard to the claims that are commonly made about Dulles's behavior at the London meeting, it is important to take account of the evidence presented in Ronald Pruessen's careful study, *John Foster Dulles: The Road to Power* (New York: Free Press, 1982), pp. 281 and 318–19. In late 1945 Dulles was already inclined to accept eastern Europe as a Soviet sphere of influence, and on the Romanian question specifically, Pruessen shows, Dulles actually took a relatively soft line at London: he viewed the policy of nonrecognition as likely to prove "barren" in the long run.

convened. He began by praising the arrangement Hopkins had worked out with Stalin in the spring. "Everyone," he said, "was satisfied with the compromise" that had been reached on that issue. He thought the Romanian problem could be dealt with the same way: in dealing with Romania, he "inquired whether it would not be possible to proceed as we had in the case of Poland." His Soviet counterpart said no and repeatedly suggested that the United States wanted to see a government in Romania that was hostile to the USSR—complaints that obviously have to be understood in the context of what had happened in that country in August. Byrnes was offended by those charges, but Molotov's attacks on American policy did not lead Byrnes to drop his plan: he simply "repeated his suggestion that some solution along the lines of that adopted in Poland would be the best." Later in that meeting he again suggested that the Polish arrangement could be taken as a model, noting that "once the agreement with Poland had been reached it had worked out very satisfactorily."[60]

He returned to the charge in another private meeting with Molotov three days later. Molotov again claimed that America had in the past supported a Romanian government hostile to the USSR, but was unwilling to support the present "friendly" government. Byrnes said there was not a "grain of truth" in that accusation, but although obviously angry did not drop his idea of using the Polish settlement as a model: "He recalled that for weeks and weeks after Yalta we had discussed Poland and had eventually reached a solution which gave various parties in Poland adequate representation. He said no one would be happier than he if some such solution would be found in this connection"—that is, on the Romanian question.[61]

But then Byrnes made another move. Angered by Molotov's accusations, and against the advice of his advisors (including Dulles), he submitted a document calling for a sweeping reorganization of the Romanian government to the full Council of Foreign Ministers.[62] That document seemed to support the idea that Byrnes was now taking a very tough line, but in reality this move is to be understood in bargaining terms. It was just a shot across the bow. In submitting it Byrnes was in effect warning the Soviets what lay in store for them if they remained intransigent. In substantive terms, U.S. policy had not actually hardened.

The proof is that just two days after that document was written, at the very meeting of the full Council at which it was discussed, Byrnes

---

[60] Byrnes-Molotov meeting, September 16, 1945, FRUS 1945, 2:195–97, 200.

[61] Molotov-Byrnes meeting, September 19, 1945, FRUS 1945, 2:243–47.

[62] Gormly, *Collapse of the Grand Alliance*, pp. 68–69. For the document itself, see U.S. Suggested Directive, September 19, 1945, FRUS 1945, 2:266.

again made it clear that the arrangement Hopkins had worked out with Stalin on Poland was basically quite satisfactory from the U.S. point of view; the clear implication was that this arrangement could serve as a model for dealing with the Romanian problem. "After Yalta," he said, "when the situation in regard to the Provisional Government in Poland was improved the United States was very happy about this and its relations with the Polish Government were excellent, although we knew of things about which we were surprised and which we hoped would be remedied."[63] And toward the end of the conference, in another small meeting with Molotov (the British Foreign Secretary, Ernest Bevin, was also present this time), Byrnes again suggested that the Polish settlement could serve as a basis for dealing with the Balkan problems. He was convinced, he said, that by the time the peace treaties with countries like Romania and Bulgaria were ready to be signed, the three main allied governments "would have found some way out of the difficulty. After all, they had been confronted with an equally difficult problem in Poland, although he realized the circumstances were different, yet they had found a solution."[64] Nor was that the last time his remarks pointed in that direction. On September 30, as the conference was winding down, in yet another private meeting with Molotov, he made it clear that sweeping reorganizations would not be necessary and that only relatively minor changes would be required: his government "wished to find some means of justifying such a step as recognition," and "if some change could be made in the governments of these countries [Bulgaria and Romania], it might be a way out."[65]

How is all this to be interpreted? It is simply a question of putting two and two together. On the one hand, Byrnes was proposing that the Balkan issues be settled the same way the Polish problem had been settled. On the other hand, the western governments were now under no illusions about what was going on in Poland. That country, a British representative in Warsaw reported on August 17, was a police state; "the so-called security police control everything" and "people disappear (in driblets not masses) all the time."[66] On September 7, the British ambassador sent in a report summarizing the situation in Poland: the press was not free; "political arrests continue"; the promises about free

---

[63] Fifteenth meeting of the Council of Foreign Ministers, September 21, 1945, FRUS 1945, 2:293.

[64] Byrnes-Molotov-Bevin meeting, September 28, 1945, ibid., p. 437.

[65] Byrnes-Molotov meeting, September 30, 1945, ibid., p. 489. Byrnes even held up the Polish settlement as an example of the not very "exacting" standard the U.S. government was applying in its negotiations with the Soviets on eastern Europe more generally. Byrnes's radio report to the nation on the London Council of Foreign Ministers meeting, October 5, 1945, in the *Department of State Bulletin* 13, no. 328 (October 7, 1945): 509.

[66] Hankey to Warner, August 17, 1945, DBPO I:6:15–16.

elections and so on "have not been carried out."[67] The American ambassador in Warsaw, Arthur Bliss Lane, was even more pessimistic.[68] To make sure Byrnes understood the situation, Lane flew to London just as the conference was about to convene to report to the secretary in person.[69] The Office of Strategic Services, the U.S. intelligence agency at the time, told the president on September 5 that the Communists were in the process of creating a "virtual one-party system."[70] By October the situation in Poland had become clear to the whole world.[71] But the western governments certainly knew what was going on in that country well before journalists were able to publish their findings. Indeed, the way top officials referred to the situation at that time suggested that the press reports came as no surprise—that it had been known for some time that "Soviet policies and actions" in the countries the Red Army was occupying were "directed towards the establishment of complete Soviet domination and control over all phases of the external and internal life of those countries."[72]

So Byrnes certainly knew what he was calling for when he proposed that the Polish settlement be taken as a model for dealing with the Romanian and Bulgarian problems. If those Balkan problems were not settled at London, this was not because Byrnes had taken an intransigent line. It was because Molotov, on Stalin's orders, had been absolutely uncompromising in this area. Stalin was willing to allow the

[67] Cavendish Bentinck to Foreign Office, September 7, 1945, copy in 860C.00/9-1945, U.S. State Department Central Files, Record Group 59, U.S. National Archives, College Park, Maryland. This is also available on microfilm in *Confidential U.S. State Department Central Files: Poland, 1945–1949* (Frederick, Md.: University Publications of America, 1986), reel 1.

[68] Warner memo of meeting with Arthur Bliss Lane, September 14, 1945, DBPO I:6, microfiche supplement, calendar 21i.

[69] Arthur Bliss Lane, *I Saw Poland Betrayed* (Indianapolis: Bobbs Merrill, 1948), pp. 173, 175.

[70] *Donovan Memorandum for the President, September 5, 1945, Truman Papers, Rose A. Conway Files, Box 10, Harry S Truman Library, Independence, Mo. Also in Records of the Office of Strategic Services: Washington Director's Office Administrative Files, 1941–1945, U.S. National Archives microfilm publication M1642, roll 25, frames 627–28.

[71] Note especially a series of articles that Gladwin Hill published in the *New York Times* in October 1945: "Poles Found Cowed by Fear Into Submission to Regime" (October 22); "Polish Reds Rule by Ersatz Parties" (October 24); "Freedom of Speech and the Press Found to Be Only Myth in Poland" (October 26). This marked quite a change in that newspaper's reporting of the Polish affair. The main article the *Times* had published prior to that point on the political situation after the Moscow accord, Sydney Gruson's "Polish Freedom Reported Growing: Observers Say Independence is Far Greater Than Had Been Expected Abroad" (July 19), had given a rather different impression.

[72] Bohlen memorandum of October 18, 1945, quoted in Eduard Mark, "Charles E. Bohlen and the Acceptable Limits of Soviet Hegemony in Eastern Europe: A Memorandum of 18 October 1945," *Diplomatic History* 3, no. 2 (April 1979): 207.

conference to end without an agreement, but that did not mean he wanted to break with the western powers. His tough line—his "policy of tenacity," he called it—was also a kind of shot across the bow. The London meeting was for Stalin a kind of "combat reconnaissance" operation; as Vladimir Pechatnov says, he "wanted to continue bargaining, albeit in a highly harsh manner, on the terms as close as possible to Soviet ones."[73]

How did the president react to all this? The British ambassador, Lord Halifax, saw him on September 25. Truman, Halifax reported, was "frankly fogged as to what had apparently so soon and so darkly clouded the atmosphere of Potsdam." This implied that his tough stand at Potsdam on Romania and Bulgaria is not to be taken too seriously; if he had been serious about this issue, he would scarcely have been surprised by the deadlock at London. In any event, he thought he might be able to deal with the problem the same way the Polish problem had been dealt with in the spring. "He was thinking very hard," Halifax wrote, "about sending another special emissary to Marshal Stalin. I said another Harry Hopkins? To which he replied, 'or possibly Hopkins himself.' But he was still thinking hard about it."[74] The events in Poland had obviously not discredited the policy associated with the Hopkins mission in his mind. Indeed, it seemed that Truman agreed with Byrnes that the sort of arrangement Hopkins had worked out with Stalin in May for Poland could serve as a model for resolving the Balkan problems.

The dying Hopkins was in no condition to go to Russia a second time, and it was Byrnes who went to Moscow that December. A deal was worked out quickly: there would be minor changes in the composition of the Communist-dominated governments in Bulgaria and Romania; the usual promises about free elections would again be made; and the United States would recognize the new governments. It was the Hopkins mission all over again, but this time it was even clearer than it had been in May that the Communists' promises would not be honored. The United States was in effect accepting the fact that the Soviets would have a free hand in Romania and Bulgaria.

Few historians would perhaps put it so bluntly, but this essentially is the way the Moscow agreement is usually interpreted. Stalin himself viewed it as a Soviet victory, and the American mission in Bucharest, according to one scholar, "regarded the agreement as a 'sell-out' and threatened to resign en masse."[75] But not everyone thinks the Moscow agreement is to be interpreted in those terms. The decision to recognize

[73] Pechatnov, "'The Allies Are Pressing on You,'" pp. 8, 14.

[74] Halifax to Bevin, September 25, 1945, DBPO I:2:367.

[75] Zubok, *Failed Empire*, p. 34; Quinlan, *Clash over Romania*, p. 151.

the Communist regimes in the Balkans, it is sometimes argued, is to be understood as a tactical move: the Moscow agreement did not really mean the United States was writing off Romania and Bulgaria. Byrnes, the argument runs, now calculated that if peace treaties were signed, the Soviets might well withdraw their troops from those countries; he hoped that with the Red Army gone, the Communists would not be able to hold on to power there. But if peace treaties were to be signed, the United States would first have to recognize the "still-unrepresentative governments of Bulgaria and Romania, as otherwise the United States could hardly conclude treaties with them."[76]

What is to be made of this interpretation? The idea that it would make sense for the West to go this route—to negotiate peace treaties in the hope that this would lead to the withdrawal of Soviet troops and thus to dramatic political changes in the countries in question—was certainly in the air at the time. The British, for example, often made this kind of argument, even in mid-1945.[77] But there is not much evidence to show that Byrnes was actually thinking along these lines at the end of the year. The strongest piece of evidence cited in support of this thesis is from a volume of memoirs Byrnes published in 1958, in which the former Secretary of State explained that until peace treaties were signed, "the Soviets would have an excuse to keep large military forces in the Balkans and in Austria," and that, protected by those forces, "their agents could work to take control of, or strengthen the Russian hold on, occupied countries."[78] But it is hard to believe that for Byrnes in late 1945 such legalistic arguments carried much weight—that he actually thought that if peace treaties could be signed, the Soviets, deprived of an excuse, would pull their forces out and allow the Communist regimes in the area to collapse. In any event, the way Byrnes used the Polish precedent at London—the way he held up the earlier arrangements that had been worked out for Poland as a model for how the Balkan countries should be dealt with—shows quite clearly what the real policy was. The Soviets were in effect told that what had happened in Poland was acceptable—that the United States could live with the situation that was developing there. Why would Byrnes have given

[76] Mark contribution to H-Diplo Miscamble Roundtable, p. 8 (http://www.h-net.msu .edu/~diplo/roundtables/PDF/FromTrumantoRoosevelt-Mark.pdf), and Mark, "American Policy toward Eastern Europe," p. 330.

[77] Brief for the U.K. Delegation to the Conference at Potsdam, c. July 10, 1945, DBPO I:1:152.

[78] James F. Byrnes, *All in One Lifetime* (New York: Harper, 1958), pp. 318–19. *Other evidence cited by Mark in his 1981 article and elsewhere does not strike me as very strong. I posted it in the Internet supplement so that interested readers can draw their own conclusions.

them that message if his goal was to save some hope for representative government in eastern Europe as a whole?

Understanding the Byrnes Policy

Byrnes has not fared well in the hands of the historians. He is often viewed as someone for whom politics boiled down to deal-making—as someone who was therefore too prone to compromise, too prone to think he could deal with Stalin the same way he had dealt with his colleagues in the Senate, as someone who had no real strategic concept, no overarching sense of political purpose. But Byrnes was no appeaser. In 1945 he took a harder line on some key issues than some of the most prominent Cold Warriors of the 1950s took at the time: a harder line than Dean Acheson on the question of sharing America's nuclear secrets with the Soviets, and a harder line than Dulles on the defense of the Turkish Straits.[79] On some issues—questions, for example, relating to the occupation of Japan—he was from the start as hard as nails. Indeed, he refused point blank to even discuss the Japan question in any serious way when Molotov brought it up at London.[80]

Byrnes clearly wanted to reach certain understandings with Stalin, but that does not necessarily mean that for him deal-making was a kind of end in itself. The real question has to do with what if anything he was trying to accomplish—with whether the deal-making was directed toward some larger end, with whether the different aspects of his policy had some sort of common taproot, with whether they were rooted in a certain vision of the kind of world he wanted to see take shape.

Byrnes, although he was not very open about it, did, I think, have a vision of this sort. The basic problem he faced was obvious. The United States and the Soviet Union would be by far the two most powerful countries in the postwar world. How should they relate to each other? Questions relating to eastern Europe had a certain importance in that context. The Soviets were tightening their grip on countries like Poland, Romania, and Bulgaria. Should the United States try to prevent them from doing so? Given that America was not going to go to war over the issue, there was a limit to how much the U.S. government could hope to accomplish. In all probability, Europe was going to be

[79] See (for Acheson) Forrestal diary entries for September 21 and October 16, 1945, Forrestal Diaries, Vol. 3, Forrestal Papers, Mudd Library, Princeton University, Princeton N.J.; and (for Dulles) Byrnes to Truman, October 19, 1945, FRUS 1945, 8:1256. On Dulles, see also Pruessen, *Dulles*, pp. 318–19.

[80] Council of Foreign Ministers meetings, September 11, 24 and 25, 1945, FRUS 1945, 2:118n, 339, 365–66.

divided anyway. In such circumstances, wouldn't it make sense to reach some sort of understanding with the Soviets? The United States would make it clear that it was willing to live with a Soviet-dominated eastern Europe—that it would be willing to live with the Communist regimes that were the instruments of Soviet control there—and the Soviets, for their part, would respect American interests on the western side of the line of demarcation in Europe, and in certain other key areas (like Japan) as well. The two sides could get along not by trying to "cooperate," Roosevelt-style—that is, by trying to work hand-in-hand with each other on whatever problems turned up. They could instead get along by pulling apart.

But the policy aimed at something more than just a *de facto* separation between east and west. The goal was to create an agreed framework—to make sure that the separation was based on a genuine understanding, and that it had a certain official sanction. That was why diplomatic recognition mattered so much; that was why it was so important for the Soviets to take part in the various advisory bodies being set up for Japan. The United States, in recognizing the proto-Communist regimes in eastern Europe, would not exactly be giving its seal of approval to what the Soviets were doing in that part of the world. But the policy would be more than just one of passive acquiescence. Byrnes was willing to go a bit further than that. He was willing to give the message that the United States accepted the new status quo in eastern Europe—that America was willing to live with the new political system the Soviets were setting up in that region—and this was something that the U.S. government by no means had to do.

Recognition, the critics charged, meant that the U.S. government would be "lending respectability" to the "stooge governments" the Soviets had set up in the region.[81] There is certainly something to that charge; indeed, recognition had political value for that very reason. But recognition was not a gift. It was part of a more far-reaching policy. Byrnes's goal, I think, was to put U.S.-Soviet relations on a relatively solid basis without sacrificing any of America's core interests. And the sort of arrangement he had in mind would on balance be quite satisfactory from America's point of view. Western Europe, after all, was more valuable than eastern Europe; Italy, Greece, and Japan counted for more than Poland, Bulgaria, and Romania. But if the arrangement he was reaching for could be worked out, America's interests would not have to be defended simply by raw military power. An agreement, even a tacit understanding, would introduce a certain element of stability into the system that would otherwise be lacking.

[81] George Kennan, *Memoirs, 1925–1950* (Boston: Little Brown, 1967), p. 255.

How solid is this interpretation? Did Byrnes actually pursue this sort of policy—that is, a policy rooted in the idea that an understanding had to be reached with the Soviets and that at the heart of that understanding would be a common acceptance of the notion that Europe would be divided between east and west? The answer, of course, turns on what the evidence shows. When you look closely at what was going on, do you see this kind of philosophy at work? When you look, for example, at Potsdam, do you get the sense that U.S. policy there was rooted in a strategic concept of this sort?

The German question was the main issue at Potsdam, and Byrnes's policy in this area was quite striking. Basically it was a policy built on the premise that Germany was going to be divided between east and west. The argument supporting that conclusion is a little complicated, but since James McAllister and I have both developed it in some detail elsewhere, only the bare bones of that argument will be presented here.[82] The heart of Byrnes's policy on this issue was his plan for dealing with the reparation question. His basic idea here was that each side would take what it wanted from its zone of occupation in Germany. But that plan implied that Germany could not be run as a unit from the point of view of foreign trade. For if Germany were treated as a unit, any deficit that country would run would have to be financed by the allies as a whole, so the bigger the deficit, the greater the burden on the American taxpayer. What that meant was that the more the Soviets took from their part of Germany, the bigger the overall deficit would be; the upshot would be that the Americans would end up in effect financing part of Germany's reparation deliveries to Russia, and this the U.S. government would simply not countenance. Hence exports and imports would also have to be managed on a zonal basis and any deficit would be the responsibility of the power in charge of that particular zone. But the management of foreign trade was the key to the overall economic treatment of Germany: if there were no common regime for exports and imports, the two parts of Germany would have to relate to each other economically as though they were foreign countries. And the management of the economy, in turn, had major political implica-

---

[82] See Trachtenberg, *Constructed Peace*, pp. 15–33, and McAllister, *No Exit*, pp. 84–98. See also Laure Castin-Chaparro, *Puissance de l'URSS, misères de l'Allemagne: Staline et la question allemande, 1941–1955* (Paris: Publications de la Sorbonne, 2002), p. 145. Note also the comment by the editors (Jochen Laufer and Georgij Kynin) of *Die UdSSR und die deutsche Frage: Dokumente aus dem Archiv für Aussenpolitik der Russischen Föderation*, Vol. 2: *9. Mai 1945 bis 3. Oktober 1946* (Berlin: Duncker and Humblot, 2004) that the Potsdam reparation settlement "amounted to the recognition of two spheres of influence in Europe" (p. lxxii) and their reference (p. cvii) to the "only partially formally agreed upon peace settlement."

tions: the economic division of the country would mean that it was probably going to be divided politically as well.

Was any of this understood at the time? Byrnes and the other American and allied officials involved with these questions at Potsdam knew perfectly well what the implications of the reparation plan were, and the secretary and his main collaborators accepted that plan because it was in line with a more far-reaching political concept. The thinking was that the two sides could get along best by pulling apart. Over and over again Byrnes argued that trying to run Germany on a unitary basis would lead to unending conflicts; he therefore thought each power should have a "free hand" in its own zone.[83] And the assumption was that this would lead to a division of Germany between east and west. Byrnes and other key U.S. officials at Potsdam took it for granted that the western powers (including the French, who were not even present at the conference) would be able to pull together and run western Germany as a unit. Byrnes himself usually referred at Potsdam to the "western zone" in the singular. The Soviets would control eastern Germany, but they had to be kept out of the western part of the country; it was for that reason that he totally rejected the whole notion of an internationalization of the Ruhr.[84] Germany, he told the French in late August 1945, would be a country of 45 million—and that meant a country composed of the three western zones, that being almost exactly the population of the western part of the country at the time. He took it for granted that the old Germany of 65 million would cease to exist—that the eastern zone would not be part of the Germany that he assumed would come into being.[85]

But this was not a situation that Byrnes proposed to bring about by fiat: he did not propose to just present the Soviets with a simple fait accompli. On the reparation issue, he knew that the West had the power to impose the solution he had in mind. As one of the American delegates at Potsdam put it, the Soviets would have to "bow" to whatever America and her friends decided they would allow the USSR to get from western Germany, and, as Molotov himself pointed out in reacting to the original Byrnes concept, according to which each power would simply take whatever it wanted from its zone, "[I]f they failed to

[83] See Trachtenberg, *Constructed Peace*, pp. 26–27.

[84] See, for example, Byrnes-Bidault meeting, August 25, 1945; Note de la Direction d'Amérique, "Conversations à Washington et à New York sur certains problèmes européens," August 31, 1945; and especially Chauvel to Massigli, September 2, 1945; in *Documents diplomatiques français 1945*, vol. 2, pp. 345, 382–83, 407. See also McAllister, *No Exit*, p. 86.

[85] Byrnes-Bidault meeting, August 23, 1945, FRUS 1945, 4:720. For the original French text, see *Documents diplomatiques français 1945*, 2:333.

agree on reparations, the result would be the same as under Mr. Byrnes' plan."[86] This was absolutely true, but Byrnes did not want to just slam the door in the Soviets' face. He put a high premium on getting the Soviets to accept this sort of arrangement voluntarily. He was therefore willing, in the final analysis, to sweeten the pot for them, and in particular was willing to give them a major share of the plant and equipment in western Germany considered unnecessary for that country's peacetime economy. This again shows a certain general concept at work: it was important not just that each side have full freedom of action in its part of Germany but that the arrangement be sanctioned by an understanding that the two sides had entered into voluntarily.

How did the Soviets react to all this? Stalin was delighted to see Byrnes pursuing this kind of policy. The Soviet leader was also inclined to think that there would be "two Germanies"—he had in fact predicted as much in a meeting with German Communist leaders a month before Potsdam—and he was not deeply opposed to that sort of arrangement.[87] At the conference itself, he was happy to go along with a plan—the Byrnes reparation plan—that took as its premise the idea that each

---

[86] See Trachtenberg, *Constructed Peace*, pp. 28, 29.

[87] The notes of this June 4, 1945, meeting between Stalin and German Communist leaders were first published in 1991. A facsimile and transcription can be found in Rolf Badstübner and Wilfried Loth, eds., *Wilhelm Pieck: Aufzeichnungen zur Deutschlandpolitik 1945–1953* (Berlin: Akademie Verlag, 1994), pp. 48–52. A number of scholars (including Loth and Badstübner) do not think that Stalin's comment about how there would be two Germanies should be taken at face value. Indeed (since Stalin goes on to talk about "securing the unity of Germany through a unified KPD [German Communist Party], a unified ZK [Central Committee], a unified workers' party") it is sometimes argued that this document actually supports the view that the Soviet leader favored a unified Germany. But those interpretations strike me as rather forced. My own feeling is that Stalin's talk there about German unity is to be understood in light of the fact that the German Communists were in Moscow to discuss the manifesto that would soon be issued to launch their new party: Stalin was apparently just laying out the official line the KPD was to take. The Soviet leader, after all, was scarcely outlining a workable political strategy: it is hard to imagine that he actually thought that having a "unified KPD," a "unified ZK," and so on, would really "secure the unity of Germany." Given what we know about Stalin's general strategy at this time in the part of Europe he controlled, my guess is that his thinking ran as follows: Germany would be divided, but for the time being the Communists would have to play a certain game and take a moderate line on major political issues; that meant in particular that they should come across as supporters of German unity. For the text of the KPD's June 11 *Aufruf*, see Peter Erler, Horst Laude and Manfred Wilke, eds., *Nach Hitler kommen wir: Dokumente zur Programmatik der Moskauer KPD-Führung 1944/45 für Nachkriegsdeutschland* (Berlin: Akademie Verlag, 1994), pp. 390–97; the penultimate paragraph on p. 396 is of particular interest in this context. For the debate on the interpretation of this document, see the eight references cited in Jochen Laufer, " 'Genossen, wie is das Gesamtbild?': Ackermann, Ulbricht und Sobotka in Moskau im Juni 1945," *Deutschland Archiv* 29 (May–June 1996): 356 notes 10–17.

side would have a free hand in the area it occupied.[88] He was so taken with that basic idea that he even proposed that another major issue, the distribution of Germany's foreign assets, be dealt with in much the same way—that everything west of the "line running from the Baltic to the Adriatic" would go to America and her friends, and everything east of that line would go to Russia.[89]

Soviet policy in the eastern zone is another important indicator: it also suggests that Stalin was already thinking in terms of a divided Germany, with the eastern zone under Communist control. In that zone, behind a façade of moderation, the rudiments of a police state were gradually being put in place: as Walter Ulbricht, one of the top Communist leaders, said at the very start of the occupation: "It's quite clear—it's got to look democratic, but we must have everything in our control."[90] But that policy could scarcely go unnoticed for long; people in the western zones were bound to react; and the western powers would feel freer to create their own political system in the part of Germany they controlled. The more forcefully the Soviets moved ahead in the east, the less chance there was that Germany could be run as a unit; one can therefore infer from what was going on in the eastern zone that a unified Germany was not a major Soviet goal.

The evidence from the diplomatic sources for the post–Potsdam period points in the same general direction. Contrary to what some scholars have argued, the Soviets were not particularly interested at this time

---

[88] See Trachtenberg, *Constructed Peace*, pp. 31–32. Note also a widely cited passage from the memoirs of Soviet defector Gregory Klimov: "It was often said in the economic spheres of the [Soviet Military Administration in Germany] headquarters that the Kremlin regarded the decisions of the Potsdam Conference as a great victory for Soviet diplomacy. The Moscow instructions emphasized this aspect at every opportunity." Gregory Klimov [in Russian Grigorii Klimov; in German: Gregory Klimow], *Berliner Kreml* (Cologne: Kiepenheuer und Witsch, 1951), pp. 158–59. For the English translation, see Gregory Klimov, *The Terror Machine: The Inside Story of the Soviet Administration in Germany* (London: Faber and Faber, 1953), p. 147. Note finally Molotov's comment on Potsdam many years later: "The main question at Potsdam was about reparations, but the Polish question was also of great importance. The Americans offered us a way out of the situation that reduced friction between us and our Western allies." Albert Resis, ed., *Molotov Remembers: Inside Kremlin Politics: Conversations with Felix Chuev* (Chicago: Ivan Dee, 1993), p. 53.

[89] Notes of plenary session, August 1, 1945, FRUS: Potsdam, 2:566–569.

[90] Quoted in Wolfgang Leonhard, *Child of the Revolution* (Chicago: Henry Regnery, 1958), p. 303. That comment of Ulbricht's is often taken as a good indicator of what Communist policy in eastern Germany boiled down to at that point. The phrase itself, for example, is used in the title of Monika Kaiser's article on eastern Germany in the 1944–49 period in Creuzberger and Görtemaker, *Gleichschaltung unter Stalin?*, and is also used in the title of the first chapter in Dirk Spilker, *The East German Leadership and the Division of Germany: Patriotism and Propaganda, 1945–1953* (Oxford: Oxford University Press, 2006).

in setting up central administrations under four-power control.[91] They were against working out a "common import-export program" for all of Germany—something which would have had to be done if that country was to be run as an economic unit.[92] And they had little interest in working out a plan for the German economy as a whole. The four occupying powers were supposed to come up with such a plan—the "level of industry" plan—but the Soviets made it abundantly clear to their western partners that they did not take that effort very seriously.[93]

That policy on Germany has to be seen in a somewhat broader context. Stalin tended to think in spheres of influence terms. He wanted a free hand in his own sphere in the east and was willing to accept the fact that the western powers would dominate the part of Europe that lay on their side of the line of demarcation in Europe.[94] Everyone who

[91] For the argument that the Soviets sought to set up central administrations that would allow them to extend their influence over Germany as a whole, see, for example, Gerhard Wettig, *Bereitschaft zu Einheit in Freiheit? Die sowjetische Deutschlandpolitik 1945–1955* (Munich: Olzog, 1999), p. 81. See also Mastny, *Cold War and Soviet Insecurity*, p. 24. But the USSR, in fact, did not make much of an effort in this area. See Laufer and Kynin, introduction to *Die UdSSR und die deutsche Frage*, 2:lvi and lxiv, and, in the volume itself, Semenov to Sobolev, October 16, 1945 (p. 148), and Smirnov memorandum, December 3, 1945 (pp. 187–88). Note also the discussion of the issue in Castin-Chaparro, *Puissance de l'URSS*, pp. 155–63. As is well known, the French vetoed the establishment of the central administrations in the Allied Control Council. The Soviets, however, were not particularly upset by that French action; France, it was felt, was to be treated rather gently in this area. See Gunther Mai, *Der Alliierte Kontrollrat in Deutschland 1945–1948: Alliierte Einheit, deutsche Teilung?* (Munich: Oldenbourg, 1995), pp. 91 and 91n; note also Maiski to Molotov, November 19, 1945, in *Die UdSSR und die deutsche Frage*, 2:182. The Soviets also declined to go along with General Clay's proposal to circumvent the French veto by setting up the central administrations only in the U.S., Soviet, and British zones. See *UdSSR und die deutsche Frage*, 2:694 n. 214; Trachtenberg, *Constructed Peace*, p. 44 n. 39; and Castin-Chaparro, *Puissance de l'URSS*, pp. 153–54. For the most detailed study of this issue, see Elisabeth Kraus, *Ministerien für das ganze Deutschland? Der Alliierte Kontrollrat und die Frage gesamtdeutscher Zentralverwaltungen* (Munich: Oldenbourg, 1990). Kraus also argues that the Soviets were not seriously interested in setting up central administrations in this period; see esp. pp. 118, 349–50. There is a related argument to the effect that by allowing all-German political parties to begin operations in Berlin—parties the USSR would have some control over—the Soviets hoped to be able to influence developments in Germany as a whole. For an analysis of that argument, see Dietrich Staritz, "Parteien für ganz Deutschland? Zu den Kontroversen über ein Parteiengesetz im Alliierten Kontrollrat 1946/47," *Vierteljahrshefte für Zeitgeschichte* 32, no. 2 (April 1984): esp. 241–45, 255–56.

[92] See Trachtenberg, *Constructed Peace*, pp. 30, 45.

[93] See especially the account of the negotiations in G.D.A. MacDougall, "Some Random Notes on the Reparation Discussions in Berlin, September-November 1945," DBPO I:5:527.

[94] Note especially in this connection the very moderate line the Soviets took at the time in matters relating to countries on the western powers' side of the line of demarcation in Europe. On France, for example, see Georgette Elgey, *La République des illusions, 1945–1951*, rev. ed. (Paris: Fayard, 1993), pp. 50–54, and Irwin Wall, *French Communism in the Era*

has any familiarity with this subject knows about his comment to the Yugoslav Communists in April 1945: "Whoever occupies a territory also imposes on it his own social system. Everyone imposes his own social system as far as his army can reach. It cannot be otherwise."[95] This is evidence not just of Stalin's intention to communize eastern Europe, but also of his willingness to accept western Europe as a western sphere of influence.

This basic philosophy about how things should be organized was also reflected in the kinds of arguments Stalin and Molotov made in dealing with the western powers, and especially in how they defended themselves when U.S. or British officials complained about what was going on in eastern Europe. They often responded by pointing to how the USSR was excluded from having any say over what was being done in the areas the western powers controlled. The Soviets, Stalin wrote Truman on April 24, 1945, were not interfering with what the western powers were doing in Greece or Belgium. Why then were the Americans making such a big fuss about Poland?[96] The West was applying a double standard, and they genuinely resented it. One is struck, for example, by Molotov's comment on a memorandum by another high Soviet official on the Polish question during the Yalta period: "Poland—a big deal! But how governments are being organized in Belgium, France, Greece, etc., we do not know."[97]

And the western powers, it is important to note, did not dismiss this sort of argument out of hand. From the start it was understood that what was done in the areas the western armies occupied could serve as a precedent for what the Soviets would do in eastern Europe. As American and British forces moved into Italy in 1943, the U.S. government, invoking the "doctrine of the supremacy of the Theatre Commander," made it clear that the Soviets would have little say as to how that country would be run.[98] The implications were hard to miss. As General Dwight Eisenhower, then allied commander in the Mediterranean the-

---

of Stalin (Westport, Conn.: Greenwood, 1983), pp. 30–31. On Italy, see Silvio Pons, "Stalin, Togliatti, and the Origins of the Cold War in Europe," *Journal of Cold War Studies* 3, no. 2 (Spring 2001): 3, 5, 14–15, 20–22, 25–26. On Greece, see John Iatrides, "Revolution or Self-Defense? Communist Goals, Strategy and Tactics in the Greek Civil War," *Journal of Cold War Studies* 7, no. 3 (Summer 2005): esp. 17–18.

[95] Milovan Djilas, *Conversations with Stalin* (New York: Harcourt Brace, 1962), p. 114.

[96] Stalin to Truman, April 24, 1945, FRUS 1945, 5:263–64. See also Stalin-Churchill meeting, July 18, 1945, DBPO I:1:389.

[97] Quoted in Vladimir Pechatnov, "The Big Three after World War II: New Documents on Soviet Thinking about Post War Relations with the United States and Great Britain," Cold War International History Project Working Paper No. 13 (May 1995), p. 23.

[98] See Bruno Arcidiacono, *Le "Precédent italien" et les origines de la Guerre Froide: Les Alliés et l'occupation de l'Italie 1943–1944* (Brussels: Bruyant, 1984), and Bruno Arcidiacono, "The 'Dress Rehearsal': The Foreign Office and the Control of Italy, 1943–1944," *The His-*

ater of operations, pointed out at the time, the choices the western allies now had to make would "establish precedents far-reaching in scope."[99] The British in particular saw quite clearly that the kind of arrangement the Americans had in mind "might become a precedent for excluding Anglo-American participation in any Armistice Commission set up in a predominantly Russian theatre."[100] The American approach, in their view, meant that they would probably find themselves "completely in the cold when it comes to winding up hostilities with Finland, Hungary and Rumania."[101] The Foreign Secretary, Anthony Eden, referred specifically to Poland in this context.[102] Giving the Soviets more of a say in Italy, he said, "was the only way to avoid 'the creation of a situation in which Russia would organise an independent system of her own in Eastern Europe.'"[103] The implication here was that it was only natural, if the western powers insisted on a free hand in Italy and other areas they controlled, for the Soviets to have a free hand in the part of Europe the Red Army occupied.

The same kind of point applies to policy on Germany. The American government wanted to make sure that the U.S. commander there would have the final say in the American zone.[104] But it was taken for granted that the other zonal commanders, including the Soviet commander, would have the same kind of authority in their zones. The Americans were not asking for any special treatment for themselves; the basic principle they insisted on would apply across the board.

And the Soviets, in both cases, had little trouble accommodating to that basic philosophy. They recognized Anglo-American predominance in Italy.[105] In Germany, they, like the Americans (but unlike the British or even the French), took an "anticentralist" view. The USSR, as one scholar writes, "made no secret of its determination to retain maximum autonomy in its zone."[106] This was in line with what Vladimir Pechat-

---

torical Journal, 28, no. 2 (June 1985): esp. 423, 425. The quotation is from a memorandum written by a Foreign Office official in September 1943, quoted on p. 419 of that article.

[99] Quoted in Arcidiacono, "The 'Dress Rehearsal,'" p. 418. President Roosevelt also understood that the arrangements worked out for Italy would "set the precedent for all such future activities in the war." Roosevelt to Churchill, October 4, 1943, FRUS 1943, 2:382–83.

[100] Minutes of a meeting of high-level British officials, June 30, 1943, quoted ibid., p. 422.

[101] Gladwyn Jebb note, July 6, 1943, quoted ibid., p. 423.

[102] Arcidiacono, *"Précédent italien,"* p. 380.

[103] Arcidiacono, "The 'Dress Rehearsal,'" p. 421.

[104] See the evidence cited in Trachtenberg, *Constructed Peace,* p. 22 n. 62.

[105] See Arcidiacono, *"Précédent italien,"* esp. pp. 441, 443. Note also the first two sentences in Pons, "Stalin, Togliatti, and the Origins of the Cold War in Europe": "After World War II Italy was included in the Western 'sphere of influence.' There is no evidence that the Soviet Union tried to forestall this outcome."

[106] Gunther Mai, "The United States in the Allied Control Council," in Detlef Junker

nov referred to as Stalin's and Molotov's "unwritten operational presumption" that there should be "full freedom of action" within their
respective "spheres [of influence] for the great powers."[107]

It was clear to both sides that there could be no double standard—not
if they were to put their relations with each other on a workable basis,
not if the two sides were to reach an understanding about how they
could live with each other in the postwar world. The western governments, in particular, could obviously not have it both ways. If they
wanted full control of the areas on their side of the line of demarcation,
wouldn't Soviet control of eastern Europe also have to be accepted?
And if the Soviets were going to dominate their sphere anyway, why
not accept that fact, if, by so doing, you could get them to accept the
status quo on the western side of the line? And the Soviets were bound
to make the same kind of calculation in reverse. It was as though the
basic realities of the system were asserting themselves, drawing both
sides into an arrangement based on a mutual acceptance of the postwar
status quo—on mutual acceptance of a divided Europe and indeed of a
divided Germany.[108]

Or to put the matter another way: by constantly drawing parallels
between eastern Europe and the areas the western allies controlled, the
Soviets were in effect proposing a deal: each side would give the other
a free hand on its side of the line of demarcation. The sort of argument
Stalin made in his April 24 letter to Truman can thus be viewed as a bid
in a bargaining process. The Soviets were making an offer, and in the
background was a kind of threat: if the deal was turned down, and if
the West refused to accept the sort of system they were setting up in
eastern Europe, they, for their part, would not accept the political system the western powers were setting up in their part of the continent—
and with large Communist parties in countries like Italy and France, it
was clear they could make a lot of trouble if they wanted to.

As it turned out, the two sides did reach a certain understanding at
Moscow in December 1945: the western governments would recognize

---

et al., eds., *The United States and Germany in the Era of the Cold War, 1945–1990*, Vol. 1,
1945–1968 (Cambridge, England: Cambridge University Press, 2004), pp. 50–51. See also
Mai, *Alliierte Kontrollrat*, pp. 82, 106–8, 218–19. Note also the evidence cited in Castin-
Chaparro, *Puissance de l'URSS*, p. 131.

[107] Pechatnov, "Big Three after World War II," p. 22.

[108] As Robert Jervis pointed out to me, this point has a certain resonance in the context
of international relations theory. It relates directly to the argument, associated above all
with James Fearon, about how both parties to a dispute have a strong interest in avoiding
the costs of conflict and thus in agreeing to a settlement that reflects their joint sense for
how things would turn out anyway. It also brings to mind the well-known German concept of the "normative Kraft des Faktischen"—of the "normative force of the factual"; the
term itself was coined by Georg Jellinek over a hundred years ago.

the Communist-dominated regimes in Romania and Bulgaria, and the Soviets would accept the fact that the United States would have the final say in Japan. Many historians, of course, have noted that there was some connection between the Japan and Balkan issues.[109] But the point is generally just made in passing, as though Byrnes, eager for agreement and reversing what American policy had been up to that point, decided more or less on his own to work out an arrangement of this sort while he was in Moscow. But what happened at that conference was the climax of a process, and by looking at that process a bit more closely we can get a clearer sense for what was going on between the United States and the Soviet Union in late 1945, and a clearer sense especially for whether a real strategic concept was at work on the American side.

What was the story here? Soon after Potsdam the war with Japan came to an end, but how was the occupation of that country to be run? The Americans wanted to have the final say over how it was to be managed. The Soviets wanted to set up an allied control regime in which they would play a role. The Americans understood from the outset that they could use the east European precedents as a way of fending off the Soviet challenge to their Japan policy. As early as August 23, Harriman urged Byrnes to "stand firm" in resisting the Soviet proposals on Japan, pointing out that the "Russian pattern set in Hungary, Bulgaria and Rumania" was a "good precedent" in this case.[110] The mere fact that this point was made suggests that the Americans were beginning to think in terms of a deal: if they were going to rely on the Balkan precedents to support their Japan policy, they could scarcely at the same time claim

---

[109] See, for example, Robert Messer, " 'Et Tu Brute!' James Byrnes, Harry Truman and the Origins of the Cold War," in Kendrick Clements, ed., *James F. Byrnes and the Origins of the Cold War* (Durham, N.C.: Carolina Academic Press, 1982), p. 38; Lundestad, *American Non-Policy*, p. 101; Caroline Kennedy-Pipe, *Stalin's Cold War: Soviet Strategies in Europe, 1943 to 1956* (Manchester, England: Manchester University Press, 1995), pp. 88–89; Harbutt, *Iron Curtain*, p. 139; and Miscamble, *From Roosevelt to Truman*, pp. 270–71. It is interesting to note that Herbert Feis, in his *Contest over Japan* (New York: Norton, 1967), without having seen much hard evidence, simply assumed that U.S. officials were unwilling to admit that the situations were analogous. According to Feis, the Soviets wanted a deal whereby the USSR would "yield primacy to the United States in Japan" in exchange for an American recognition of Soviet primacy in "Eastern and Southeastern Europe," but the Americans, he says, "did not think these situations were related" (pp. 56–57). As will be seen, the Americans *did* think the situations were related, but it is not hard to imagine why someone like Feis would have argued along those lines. Given that the Americans were insisting on having the final say in Japan, to admit that U.S. officials recognized that the situations were analogous would be tantamount to admitting that they were willing to accept the fact that the Soviets would have the final word in eastern Europe. But for a traditionalist like Feis it was practically inconceivable that the U.S. government was willing to write off eastern Europe in that way.

[110] Harriman to Byrnes, August 23, 1945, FRUS 1945, 6:689.

that those Balkan precedents were not valid—that is, that the Soviets did not have the right to set policy in Romania and Bulgaria. They could accept Soviet preeminence in the Balkans if the Soviets would accept American preeminence in Japan.

And the Soviets, for their part, were also coming to think in terms of a deal. The Americans were intransigent on Japan. At the London Council of Foreign Ministers meeting in September, Byrnes had refused to even discuss the matter. So faced with that American attitude, Molotov on October 21 proposed that the "Allied Control Commission for Japan should operate on [a] basis analogous to [the] Allied Control Commission, for example, in Rumania." The control commission in Japan, he took care to point out, would "operate under [the] direction of [the] US representative."[111] And Stalin expanded on the point in a meeting with Harriman three days later. The Soviets were not proposing a "Control Council" of the sort that existed in Germany, he said, but merely a control commission of the kind that existed in Hungary and Romania where "the final word rested with the Soviet commander." "It went without saying," he added, "that the United States representative, General MacArthur, should be the permanent Chairman of the Control Commission and should have the final voice."[112]

The Americans were delighted. It seemed that the Soviets had decided to accept the American plan for Japan. Molotov was now "climbing down"—that was Harriman's comment on the Soviet foreign minister's October 21 letter.[113] Byrnes was also encouraged by the fact that Stalin had told "Harriman that he would be willing to approve something for Japan on [the] lines of [the] Balkan Control Commissions," and other top State Department officials—people like Under Secretary Acheson—very much liked the idea of a Japan arrangement based quite explicitly on the Balkan precedents. Indeed, the U.S. government as a whole had no problem accepting the idea that the same principles applied in both cases. The War Department in particular wanted it to be very clear that "any Control Council" scheme for Japan would be "patterned on the Balkan model."[114]

To invoke the Balkan precedents was thus to accept the notion that

[111] Molotov communication of October 21, 1945, quoted in Harriman to Byrnes, October 22, 1945, ibid., p. 768.

[112] Stalin-Harriman meeting, October 24, 1945, ibid., p. 785.

[113] Harriman to Byrnes, October 22, 1945, ibid., p. 768.

[114] See Halifax to Bevin, October 29, 1945 (for Byrnes), DBPO I:2:510; Trans-Pacific Teletype Conversation, October 22, 1945 (for Acheson), FRUS 1945, 6:771; *meeting of State-War-Navy Coordinating Committee, October 22, 1945 (for views of official State Department and War Department representatives), *Minutes of Meetings of the State-War-Navy Coordinating Committee, 1944–1947*, U.S. National Archives microfilm publication T-1194 (Washington, D.C.: National Archives, 1945) (single reel), p. 5.

the two situations—Japan on the one hand and Bulgaria and Romania on the other—were analogous. And that meant that if the U.S. government proposed to have the final say in Japan, it would have to accept the fact that the Soviets would have the final say in countries like Romania and Bulgaria. American policy was thus being pulled toward the idea of a kind of spheres of influence deal with the USSR. Byrnes was certainly open to this sort of arrangement; he in fact preferred a cleaner separation than other high U.S. officials wanted at that point. The military authorities, for example, wanted to include Soviet troops in the occupation of Japan.[115] But Stalin did not like that idea. If countries other than America sent troops to Japan, he told Harriman, "the effect would be to restrict the rights of General MacArthur. This was not desirable. In order to preserve the freedom of action of MacArthur it, perhaps, might not be advisable to send other troops to Japan."[116] And Byrnes, much to the irritation of the War Department, agreed not with the U.S. military chiefs but with Stalin. He felt that "Stalin's position was sound and that the presence of other Allied forces could only be a source of considerable irritation."[117] The Potsdam philosophy was at work again: the basic idea was that a clean separation was the best solution.

Given the fact that both Byrnes and Stalin accepted that general approach, one might have thought that a straight spheres of influence deal would have been worked out very quickly in late October. But this was not to be. After getting the Americans' hopes up, Stalin unexpectedly changed course. It was all sweetness and light when he met with Harriman on October 24, but when the two men saw each other the next day the Soviet leader was in a very different mood. He was now bristling with resentment at the way the Soviets were being treated in Japan. The Soviet government was not being treated with respect; "it had never been informed or consulted on Japanese matters"; "Soviet views on Japan were completely disregarded." It could not be responsible for what the Americans were doing there; it would not allow itself to be treated as a "piece of furniture." Maybe it would be better for the Soviets to just wash their hands of this matter entirely—to not participate in the charade of an advisory commission, to just "step aside and let the Americans act as they wished in Japan."[118]

[115] See Joint Staff memo for State-War-Navy Coordinating Committee, October 11, 1945; War Department memo, enclosed in Marshall to Byrnes, October 19, 1945; and Byrnes to Harriman, October 20, 1945; in FRUS 1945, 6:744–45, 763, 766–67.

[116] Stalin-Harriman meeting, October 24, 1945, ibid., p. 785.

[117] Byrnes-Patterson-Forrestal meeting, November 6, 1945, ibid., p. 833. See also Byrnes to Harriman, November 2, 1945, ibid., p. 819. For the reaction of the War Department, see McCloy to Acheson, November 15, 1945, ibid., pp. 853–54.

[118] Stalin-Harriman meeting, October 25, 1945, ibid., pp. 789–92.

How is this sudden shift in the Soviet attitude to be understood? Well, what exactly *was* Stalin now objecting to? Not to the fact of American control in Japan, but just to the idea that the USSR should make it clear that it accepted the U.S.-dominated regime there by participating in the advisory commission for Japan which the Americans wanted to set up. Maybe Stalin really did resent the fact that the USSR would just be part of the "furniture"—furniture, however, which might help give the U.S. regime there a certain legitimacy. On the other hand, he certainly knew that the Americans felt the same way about the role they played in the control commissions in eastern Europe—and if he didn't, Harriman was quick to point it out to him.[119] In any event, Stalin clearly understood that window-dressing of this sort had a certain political function: taking part in allied bodies of this sort, like sending ambassadors to a country, would not change the fundamentals—real control would remain in the hands of the country whose armies occupied the area—but it would be a symbol of acceptance. The Soviets in Japan, like the Americans in eastern Europe, would not exactly be giving their blessing to the regime dominated by the occupying power. But having a representative on an advisory commission, or sending an ambassador to a new government, gave a certain message. It suggested that a government was not just grudgingly acquiescing in what another power was doing in the area in question. It implied that that government was willing to live with the system the other side was setting up in the area it controlled.

So Stalin said he might not take part in the advisory commission. He knew that this option provided him with a certain amount of leverage. His goal clearly was to reach a deal. Each side would give the other a free hand in the area it controlled. Each side would also make it clear that it accepted the new status quo by providing the new arrangements with a certain formal sanction: diplomatic recognition in the case of eastern Europe and participation in the advisory commissions in the case of Japan. And indeed the sudden shift in Stalin's line is probably to be understood in bargaining terms. First he dangled the carrot, then he yanked it away: first he showed the Americans what he was prepared to accept, but then he made it clear that to close the deal they would have to make corresponding concessions of their own, on eastern Europe.

That bargaining process culminated in the arrangements worked out at the Moscow Conference in December, but how exactly did it work? It was not overt. Even Stalin, with all his cynicism, never actually said, in effect, "we'll accept your domination of Japan if you accept the system

---

[119] Ibid., p. 792

we've set up in eastern Europe—can we make a deal on that basis?" The sort of direct bargaining that is par for the course, for example, when a house is being sold is rarely seen in international politics. The process is different in certain fundamental ways. When a house is on the market, the bargaining focuses on the bottom line: what price is the property to be sold for? The terms of the agreement of sale, the document that actually gets signed, are what matter. But in international bargaining, negotiations have a rather different function. People think that the main purpose is to reach agreement on a set of texts, but in major negotiations the formal texts that are agreed to are often of relatively minor importance. They are often just the tip of the iceberg, and what really matters is the 90 percent of the iceberg that lies below the surface, the whole web of interlocking understandings that takes shape in the course of the talks.

How did the negotiation process work in this particular case? Stalin and Harriman had met in late October. Two months of negotiations in Moscow followed.[120] Various American texts—plans for what would eventually become the Allied Council for Japan and the Far Eastern Commission—were the focus of these discussions.[121] The Soviets would comment, either verbally or in writing, on those American plans. The Americans would then submit new drafts that took those comments into account. This drafting process had a certain importance (if only because it gave the message that Soviet views were taken seriously and the U.S. government wanted to accommodate the USSR within certain limits), but what really mattered were the positions each side took in these talks. Byrnes, for example, was very tough on the Japan question. The Americans clearly wanted to have the final say in that area. But in defending their position they often pointed to the Balkan precedents. Indeed, they stressed the point that Stalin himself had accepted the

[120] At the Moscow conference, Molotov in fact repeatedly referred to the talks as "negotiations," and not just as "conversations" or "discussions." See, for example, Moscow Conference, Third Formal Session, December 18, 1945, FRUS 1945, 2:658–59. By using that term, he was emphasizing the seriousness of what had been going on. He had no qualms, moreover, about using that language in front of Bevin. The message was that in the Soviet view (and in effect in America's view as well), the United States and the USSR were the only two states that really mattered in the world and that they felt they could settle the world's problems à deux. This was certainly a source of irritation for countries like Britain and France, but it was also an element of bonding between America and Russia.

[121] The Allied Council for Japan was the more important of the two. For the texts of the main proposals, see FRUS 1945, 6:797–98 (October 27) and 874 (December 1); FRUS 1945, 2:626–27 (December 16), 661–62 (Soviet counterproposal of December 18), and 679–80 (December 19). For the main U.S. concession, compare the second paragraph in the fourth point of the December 19 proposal (ibid., pp. 679–80) with the corresponding point in the December 16 proposal (ibid., p. 626), noting how the point the Soviets made in their December 18 counterproposal was in some measure accommodated (ibid., pp. 661–62).

principle that the local commander would have the "last voice" in countries like Romania and were quite irritated when the Soviets seemed to be drawing back from the idea that the occupying power's hands should not in the final analysis be tied in any way.[122]

And the Americans, in fact, made it clear in these talks not just that they accepted the general principle that each power would have "final say" in the area it occupied. They also accepted the particular situation that had developed in the Balkans. This was quite clear, for example, from a comment that Harriman made in his October 25 meeting with Stalin. The Americans in the past, the ambassador pointed out, had gotten upset about the way their representatives in the Balkans had been treated—at the fact that they were essentially powerless—but this, he said, was now "past history."[123] Harriman was in effect saying that in the past the Americans had been disturbed by the fact that they had little influence in Romania and Bulgaria, but that they were now willing to live with that fact. And Byrnes wrote (in his November 7 instructions to Harriman, a very important document) that "in view of the fact that the occupying forces were Soviet, the United States accepted the ultimate right of the commander-in-chief of those forces, acting on the instructions of his government, to have final decision in matters pertaining to the occupation of those countries."[124]

So the hardening of the Soviet position had served a certain purpose. The Americans had been drawn out: they were very tough on the core issue in Japan, somewhat flexible on the secondary issues relating to the control regime there, but quite accommodating on Romania and Bulgaria. The Soviets for their part had also made it fairly clear what their real feelings were; sometimes this was simply a question of the fervor—or lack of it—with which they pressed their case.[125] But what this meant was that there was no need for any serious horse-trading at the Moscow Conference. The real feelings of each side had already been revealed, and the elements of an agreement now easily fell into place, like ripe fruit falling from a tree.

All this is important because it gives us some insight into the question of what Byrnes was up to. In Kennan's view, there was something

[122] See especially Harriman to Byrnes, November 4, 6 and 12, 1945, and Byrnes to Harriman, November 7 and 17, 1945, FRUS 1945, 6:821, 831, 835, 847–48, 858. It should be noted, given his reputation as a hard-liner, that Harriman himself was very eager to conclude an agreement on this basis. He thought an "impasse would have serious repercussions not only in the Far East but in Europe and on world collaboration generally" (ibid., p. 831; see also ibid., p. 851).

[123] Stalin-Harriman meeting, October 25, 1945, ibid., pp. 792–93.

[124] Byrnes to Harriman, November 7, 1945, ibid., p. 835.

[125] Note, for example, Harriman's comment at one point that Molotov was not defending his position "aggressively." Harriman to Byrnes, November 24, 1945, ibid., p. 868.

frivolous about the way Byrnes conducted the negotiations at Moscow. "He plays his negotiations by ear," Kennan wrote at the time, "going into them with no clear or fixed plan, with no definite set [of] objectives or limitations"; "his main purpose is to achieve some sort of agreement, he doesn't much care what."[126] Insofar as Byrnes had a goal, Kennan later wrote, it was "to rescue something of the wreckage of the Yalta Declaration on Liberated Europe, to preserve, that is, some fig leaves of democratic procedure to hide the nakedness of Stalinist dictatorship in the respective Eastern European countries."[127] But Byrnes was under no illusions at this time about the fate of eastern Europe.[128] And he was not just playing by ear: the Moscow agreement was not simply improvised by a Secretary of State who had no clear sense for what he wanted to accomplish and was interested only in cutting a deal, more or less as an end in itself. The policy he pursued at that conference had taken shape months earlier. It was rooted in a certain set of principles—in the idea that the two sides could live with each other if they pulled apart, and in the idea that the two sides could reach an understanding based on that notion. A genuine understanding was of fundamental importance. Peace, in Byrnes's view, depended on agreement, on compromise, on deal-making, at least in areas where core political interests did not have to be sacrificed.[129] If an agreement of the sort Byrnes had in mind were reached, the peace could be based on something a bit more solid than the raw balance of power.

So the Byrnes strategy was quite extraordinary. There *was* a guiding philosophy here. The U.S. government was trying to reach a real understanding with the USSR on the very fundamental issue of how the postwar world was to be organized. The basic idea here was that those two

[126] Kennan diary notes, December 19, 1945, Kennan, *Memoirs*, p. 287.

[127] Ibid., p. 284.

[128] One has the sense that Byrnes understood what Soviet policy was relatively early on. That impression is based on certain straws in the wind—for example, a memo a *New York Times* reporter wrote in late February summarizing the information he had gathered from "certain people in Washington" about the Yalta Conference. One of those informants—almost certainly Byrnes, who was the "main contact"—was struck by a comment Stalin had made at Yalta, supposedly as a joke: the Soviet leader had said he was "perfectly willing to agree to the proposal for an election as raised by Roosevelt, but [had] added facetiously that under the circumstances of Poland's occupation, he didn't have much doubt as to the election's outcome." *Catledge to Krock, February 26, 1945, p. 3, Krock Papers, box 1, Mudd Library, Princeton University, Princeton, N.J.

[129] Note in this context the comment he made at the beginning of his radio report to the nation on the London Council of Foreign Ministers meeting, October 5, 1945, in the *Department of State Bulletin*, 13, no. 328 (October 7, 1945): 507: "In the past I have been both criticized and commended for being a compromiser. I confess that I do believe that peace and political progress in international affairs as in domestic affairs depend upon intelligent compromise."

great states would respect each others' most basic political interests—that they would respect the status quo that had come into being at the end of World War II. This involved an American acceptance of the new political order the Soviets had set up in eastern Europe. But in choosing to go that route, the U.S. government was by no means opting for a policy of appeasement. It would, after all, be getting something in return: the Soviets, for their part, would essentially be accepting the political system the Americans and their friends were setting up in western Europe, and in Japan as well.

This was a serious policy, but Byrnes could not be open about what he was doing. As far as the public was concerned, the policy, if Byrnes had been honest about it, would probably have come across as callous. So in a sense the wool had to be pulled over people's eyes at the time, and it is perhaps not too surprising that historians should have been taken in as well. That is why, incidentally, it is so important in this case to examine the evidence closely. A superficial analysis is bound to give a very misleading impression.

But when one does that analysis a certain picture emerges: Byrnes knew what he was doing. He thought essentially in political and not moral terms. He accepted fundamental political realities for what they were, and he wanted the other side to relate to the world in that same businesslike way. On that basis, he thought, the two sides could reach a certain understanding. A genuine accommodation was possible if each side made it clear that it was willing to live with the sort of system that was clearly coming into being in 1945.

Stalin's views were not that different. He too was willing to accept a division of Europe into spheres of influence, at least for the time being and probably for some time to come. He wanted a free hand on his side of the line of demarcation and in return was willing to give America and her friends a relatively free hand on their side of the line in Europe, and in Japan as well. This was perhaps not a policy of "cooperation" in the normal dictionary sense of the term. But what Stalin had in mind *was* cooperation of a sort. The U.S.-Soviet relationship could be based on a genuine political understanding, and if both sides accepted this sort of relationship they could get along with each other reasonably well.

So the picture that emerges is quite striking. Here you had two very great powers, the United States and the Soviet Union, both with strong political ideologies. Given, however, the sort of world each found itself in—a world in which another very powerful country was playing an active role—there was a limit to how much of an ideological edge their foreign policies could have. At the point where their desires came up against the other state's core strategic interests, they had to draw in their horns. They were both under enormous pressure to adjust to basic political realities, and the real point of the story here is that they did accommodate to those realities more quickly and more easily than one might have thought possible. Their policies were in line with the same political realities; they were therefore in harmony with each other. It thus seemed that a genuine political accommodation was in the cards in December 1945—that the foundation for a relatively stable great power political system was being put in place at that time.

This is what makes the Cold War so puzzling. If both America and Russia were willing to live with things as they were—if each accepted, and made it clear to the other that it accepted, a divided world—where was the problem? Why couldn't the two sides just go their separate ways in peace? Those questions provide a focal point for the analysis of what happened in 1946 and 1947: why exactly did things move off the track so dramatically and so quickly? A sense for what the puzzle is thus serves as a kind of springboard for the historical analysis.[130] But that puzzle comes into focus only when you understand what the Americans, and the Soviets as well, were actually trying to do in late 1945.

---

[130] It in fact serves as the springboard for the analysis of the coming of the Cold War in the second chapter of *A Constructed Peace*.

CHAPTER FOUR

America, Europe, and German Rearmament, August–September 1950: A Critique of a Myth

In September 1950 U.S. Secretary of State Dean Acheson met in New York with the British foreign secretary, Ernest Bevin, and the French foreign minister, Robert Schuman. Acheson had an important announcement to make. The United States, he declared, was prepared to "take a step never before taken in history." The American government was willing to send "substantial forces" to Europe. The American combat force would be part of a collective force with a unified command structure, a force that would ultimately be capable of defending western Europe on the ground. But the Americans were willing to take that step only if the European allies, for their part, were prepared to do what was necessary to "make this defense of Europe a success." And his government, he said, had come to the conclusion that the whole effort could not succeed without a German military contribution. So if the NATO allies wanted the American troops, they would have to accept the idea of German rearmament—and they would have to accept it right away. The U.S. government, he insisted, needed to "have an answer now on the possible use of German forces" in the defense of western Europe.[1]

The position Acheson took at the New York Conference was of quite extraordinary historical importance. The American government was finally committing itself to building an effective defense of western Europe and to playing a central role in the military system that was to be set up. But the Americans were also trying to lay down the law to their

---

This article, co-authored with Christopher Gehrz, was originally written for a special issue of the *Journal of European Integration History* on U.S.-European relations, vol. 6, no. 2 (December 2000). A slightly revised version was published in Marc Trachtenberg, ed., *Between Empire and Alliance: America and Europe during the Cold War* (Lanham, Md.: Rowman and Littlefield, 2003). Copies of some important unpublished documents cited here are available online at http://www.polisci.ucla.edu/faculty/trachtenberg/1950.html; those documents are marked in the notes with an asterisk.

[1] Minutes of foreign ministers' meetings, September 12–13, 1950, U.S. Department of State, *Foreign Relations of the United States 1950*, vol. 3 (Washington, D.C.: GPO, 1977), pp. 1192, 1208; henceforth references to this source will be cited in the following form: FRUS 1950, 3:1192, 1208.

European allies: the U.S. government wanted to force them to go along with a policy that made them very uneasy.

It was not, of course, that the Europeans disliked the whole package Acheson was now proposing. They knew that an effective defense of western Europe would have to be based on American power and therefore welcomed much of the American plan. The offer of a major American troop presence in Europe, the proposal to set up a strong NATO military system, the suggestion that an American general would be sent over as NATO commander—all this was in itself music to their ears. The problem lay with the final part of Acheson's proposal, the part relating to German rearmament, and even here the issue had more to do with timing than with ultimate objectives.

The allied governments were not against the very idea of German rearmament. Of all the NATO allies, the French were the most reluctant at this point to accede to Acheson's demands. But Schuman was not dead set against German rearmament as a matter of principle.[2] He in fact now admitted that it was "illogical for us to defend Western Europe, including Germany, without contributions from Germany."[3] The French government, he told Acheson, was "not irrevocably opposed to German participation" in the NATO army. Indeed, he thought it was likely that "some day" Germany would join the western defense force.[4]

The problem from Schuman's point of view was that Acheson wanted to move too quickly. The Americans were insisting on immediate and open acceptance of the principle of German rearmament. But Schuman could go along with the U.S. plan, he said, only if this were kept secret. It was politically impossible for him to accept the plan publicly at that point.[5] Only a minority in France, he pointed out, appreciated "the importance of Germany in Western defense."[6] The French public could probably be brought along and would ultimately accept the idea of a German defense contribution, but only if the West moved ahead more

[2] This claim is somewhat at variance with the conventional wisdom on this point. See, for example, Laurence Martin, "The American Decision to Rearm Germany," in Harold Stein, ed., *American Civil-Military Decisions: A Book of Case Studies* (Birmingham: University of Alabama Press, 1963), p. 658: "To the end of the New York meetings, however, the French representative refused to accept even the principle of German rearmament." But the real story is not nearly that simple.

[3] Foreign ministers' private meeting, September 12, 1950, FRUS 1950, 3:1200.

[4] Acheson to Truman and Acting Secretary, September 16, 1950, ibid., pp. 312–13.

[5] Acheson-Schuman meeting, September 12, 1950, and meeting of British, French, and American foreign ministers and high commissioners, September 14, 1950, ibid., pp. 287, 299–300.

[6] Acheson-Schuman meeting, September 12, 1950, ibid., pp. 287–88.

cautiously—only if a strong European defense system had been built up first.

Domestic politics was not the only reason why Schuman took this line. The east-west military balance was perhaps an even more fundamental factor. In late 1950 the western powers were just beginning to rearm. In military terms, they felt they could scarcely hold their own in a war with Russia. General Omar Bradley, the Chairman of the U.S. Joint Chiefs of Staff (JCS), for example, thought in November 1950 that if war broke out, the United States might well lose. The Soviets, on the other hand, seemed to be getting ready for a war: the sense was that they were poised on the brink and might be tempted to strike before the West built up its power. In such circumstances, people like Schuman asked, was it wise to move ahead with the rearmament of Germany, something the Russians were bound to find highly provocative? Rather than risk war now, at a time of western weakness, didn't it make sense to put off the decision until after the West had rearmed itself and would thus be better able to withstand the shock?[7]

These were perfectly reasonable arguments, and were in fact supported by the U.S. government's own assessments of the risk of war with Russia at the time. The U.S. High Commissioner in Germany, John McCloy, thought, for example, in June 1950 that "the rearmament of Germany would undoubtedly speed up any Soviet schedule for any possible future action in Germany and would, no doubt, be regarded by [the Soviets] as sufficiently provocative to warrant extreme countermeasures."[8] In December, the CIA concluded that the USSR

---

[7] Schuman and Bevin in meeting of British, French, and American foreign ministers and high commissioners, September 14, 1950, ibid., pp. 296–97. This fear of provoking a Soviet attack had been an important element in French policy since early 1948. The concern at that time was that the Russians would interpret movement toward the establishment of a West German state as a major step toward German rearmament, which, it was felt, might provoke preventive military action. See, for example, Chauvel to Bonnet, March 18 and May 19, 1948, Bonnet Papers, vol. 1, and Massigli to Foreign Ministry, May 3, 1948, Massigli Papers, vol. 67, both French Foreign Ministry Archives [FFMA], Paris. In 1950 this factor continued to play a fundamental role in French policy on the issue, even before the German rearmament question was pushed to the top of the agenda by the events in Korea in June. See, for example, a Quai d'Orsay memorandum from April 1950, published in Horst Möller and Klaus Hildebrand, eds., *Die Bundesrepublik Deutschland und Frankreich: Dokumente 1949–1963* (Munich: K.G. Saur, 1997), 1:376: "We can expect the Americans to bring up the question of an eventual German contribution to the rearmament of the western powers. A program of that sort is acceptable to us only to the extent that it would not constitute a provocation vis-à-vis the USSR." On these issues in general, and for the Bradley quotation in particular, see the discussion in Marc Trachtenberg, *A Constructed Peace: The Making of the European Settlement, 1945–1963* (Princeton: Princeton University Press, 1999), pp. 96–100, 111–12; and in Marc Trachtenberg, *History and Strategy* (Princeton: Princeton University Press, 1991), pp. 118–27, 130–31.

[8] McCloy to Acheson, June 13, 1950, President's Secretary's Files [PSF], box 178, Germany, folder 2, Harry S Truman Library [HSTL], Independence, Mo.

would "seriously consider going to war whenever it becomes convinced that progress toward complete Western German rearmament," along with the rearmament of NATO as a whole, had reached the point where it could not be "arrested by other methods."[9] It was of course possible that the Soviets might choose to live with a rearmed Germany, especially if there continued to be major limits on German power, but certain groups within the U.S. government—Army Intelligence for example—believed that if the West moved ahead in this area, it was more likely "that the Soviets would decide on resort to military action rather than make the required adjustment."[10]

So if even American officials were worried about what a decision to rearm Germany might lead to, it is not hard to understand why the Europeans, and especially the French, were so disturbed by the U.S. proposal. The NATO allies would have to accept the whole package, Acheson told them. They would have to agree, publicly and immediately, to the rearmament of Germany. They would have to go along with what they honestly viewed as a very provocative policy vis-à-vis Russia and risk war at a time when no effective defense was in place—either that, Acheson said, or the Americans would simply not defend them.

The fact that the U.S. government had chosen to deal so roughly with its allies had one very important effect: it helped bring France and Germany together. It helped bring about a certain change in perspective—a change in the way the Europeans viewed America and thus in the way they viewed each other. Up to this point, the French, for example, had tended to think of the policy of "building Europe" in essentially manipulative and instrumental terms. It was, to use Raymond Poidevin's phrase, a way "to seduce and to control" Germany.[11] But now the idea was beginning to take hold that the Europeans—that is, the continental west Europeans—were all in the same boat in strategic terms. The Europeans had interests of their own—interests that overlapped with, but which were in important ways distinct from, those of the United States. The fact that the Americans could adopt a highly provocative policy toward Russia, with scant regard for European interests, meant that the Europeans could not afford to be too dependent on the United States. Yes, there had to be a strong counterweight to Soviet power in Europe, and yes, that counterweight had to rest largely on American power. The American presence in Europe was obviously essential, and an Ameri-

[9] "Probable Soviet Reactions to a Remilitarization of Western Germany," National Intelligence Estimate [NIE] 17, December 27, 1950, both in PSF/253/HSTL.

[10] "Soviet Courses of Action with Respect to Germany," NIE 4, January 29, 1951, PSF/253/HSTL. The views of Army Intelligence are laid out in a long footnote on p. 3 of this document.

[11] Raymond Poidevin, *Robert Schuman, homme d'état: 1886–1963* (Paris: Imprimerie Nationale, 1986), p. 220.

can combat force would have to be the heart of an effective NATO defense system. But there needed to be some counterweight to American
power within the Atlantic alliance. And given that Britain held herself
aloof from Europe, the counterweight had to be built on a real understanding between France and Germany.

We do not want to overstate the argument here. This sort of thinking
was just beginning to take shape in 1950 and things obviously had a
long way to go.[12] But the importance of what was going on at the time
should not be underestimated either. The line Acheson took at the New
York Conference was quite extraordinary, and what was at stake was of
enormous importance. The events of late 1950 were therefore bound to
make a profound impression. They were bound to lead many Europeans to begin thinking more seriously about the importance of coming
together as a unit in order to give Europe more of a voice in setting the
policy of the West as a whole.

Consider, for example, the reaction of the German chancellor, Konrad
Adenauer, to the American plan. Shortly after the New York Conference, Adenauer had his top advisor, Herbert Blankenhorn, tell Armand
Bérard, the French deputy high commissioner in Germany, that he did
not want Germany to simply provide forces for an American army—
that is, an army in which the Americans would have all the power. The
two men soon met again, and Blankenhorn returned to the charge.
"With great emphasis," Bérard wrote, Blankenhorn "repeated what he
had already told me a couple of weeks ago, namely, how desirable it
was that an initiative come from the French side. Germany did not
want to take her place in an American army." "If France," Blankenhorn
continued, "proposed the creation of a European army under allied
command, an army whose supreme commander might even be a
Frenchman," his government "would support that solution."[13]

Bérard's comment on this is worth quoting at length:

> The chancellor is being honest when he says he is worried that what
> the German [military] contribution will boil down to is simply Ger-
> man forces in an American army. He is afraid that his country will
> end up providing the foot soldiers and shock troops for an anti-
> Communist offensive force that the United States might build in Eu-
> rope. People in our own country are worried about the same sort of
> thing. Adenauer is asking for a French initiative that would head off

[12] For the best study of the subject, see Georges-Henri Soutou, *L'Alliance incertaine: Les
rapports politico-stratégiques franco-allemands, 1954–1996* (Paris: Fayard, 1996). Soutou begins his story in 1954, which, as he points out (for example, on p. 22), is when a real bilateral Franco-German strategic relationship began. This is true enough; the point here is
simply that the thinking had begun to take shape a number of years earlier.

[13] *Bérard to Foreign Ministry, mid-October 1950, series "Europe 1949–55," subseries
"Allemagne," volume 187 (formerly vol. 70), folio 7, FFMA.

this American solution, which he fears. I think he is sincere in all this, just as sincere as he was, and still is, in his support for the Schuman Plan [for a coal and steel community in western Europe]. He believes that the problems of western Europe have to resolved on a Franco-German basis, the military problem as well as the economic problems.[14]

The important point here was that France and Germany had major interests in common, not just vis-à-vis Russia, but vis-à-vis America as well. There was, Bérard noted, "a certain parallelism between the position of France and that of West Germany with regard to the defense of the West. Both of them are concerned above all with making sure that they are not invaded and that their territory does not serve as a battleground; they both feel very strongly that the West should hold back from provoking the Soviets, before a western force, worthy of the name, has been set up."[15] To go from that point to the conclusion that the Europeans had to act more as a strategic unit—that European integration had to be real, and not just a device to keep Germany from becoming a problem—did not require any great leap of the imagination.

Reading these and related documents, one thus has the sense of a new way of thinking beginning to take shape—of French leaders rubbing their eyes and waking up to the fact that they and the Germans had more in common than they had perhaps realized, of an important threshold being crossed, of France and Germany just starting to think of themselves as a strategic unit. And if this kind of thinking was beginning to emerge, it was in large part in reaction to the heavy-handed way in which the U.S. government had chosen to deal with its European allies in September 1950.

But had the American government, in any real sense, actually *chosen*

---

[14] Bérard's next sentence is also worth noting, because it shows how French officials were already thinking in terms of balancing between Germany and America within the western alliance: "This is not to say that one has to think in terms of a western army from which the Americans would be excluded, and within which the French and the Germans would provide the main forces. Such a solution might some day force us to fight, if not 'for the king of Prussia' ['pour le roi de Prusse']—a French expression implying that one is not getting anything for oneself in return, then at least for the reconquest of Prussia." *Bérard to Foreign Ministry, October 17, 1950, Europe 1949–55, Allemagne, vol. 187 (formerly vol. 70), ff. 16–17, FFMA. These documents shed light not only on the beginnings of European integration (and on the origins of the European Defense Community project in particular), but also on the evolution of Franco-German relations. Adenauer, for example, is often portrayed as pursuing a very pro-American policy at this point; the standard view is that his attitude toward France at this time was relatively cool. Note the tone, for example, of the discussion in Hans-Peter Schwarz, *Adenauer: Der Aufstieg, 1876–1952*, 3rd ed. (Stuttgart: Deutsche Verlags-Anstalt, 1986), p. 836. But it is clear from these French sources that the roots of his later policy were already in place in 1950.

[15] *Bérard to Foreign Ministry, October 17, 1950 (as in n. 14).

to deal with the allies in that way? It is commonly argued that the policy that Acheson pursued in September 1950 is not to be understood as a choice freely made at the top political level, but is rather to be seen as the outcome of a bureaucratic dispute in which Acheson ultimately had to give way to pressure from the Pentagon.[16] The State Department, according to this argument, understood the need for an effective defense of western Europe; now, following the outbreak of the Korean War in June, the need for action was obvious. It therefore wanted to begin building an effective defense by sending an American combat force over to Europe. But this gave the military authorities the leverage they needed to achieve their "long-standing objective of German rearmament."[17] They were willing, they now said, to go along with the plan to send over the U.S. combat divisions, but only as part of a "package": the JCS "wanted categorical assurances that they could count on German assistance in the shape they desired and that they would be able to make an immediate start on raising and equipping the German units"; they insisted that the offer to deploy the U.S. force "be made strictly conditional upon iron-clad commitments by the Europeans to their own contributions, and in particular, upon unequivocal acceptance of an immediate start on German rearmament in a form technically acceptable to American strategists."[18]

The State Department, the argument runs, resisted the Pentagon's efforts to bring the German rearmament question to a head in such a blunt and high-handed way. The two sides debated the issue for about two weeks in late August, but the "Pentagon stood united and unmovable." Acheson, according to his own widely accepted account, "agreed with their strategic purpose," but "thought their tactics murderous."[19] At the end of August, however, Acheson had reluctantly decided that he had to give way. He had earlier felt that insisting on the inclusion of Germany at the outset "would delay and complicate the whole enter-

---

[16] See, for example, Martin, "Decision to Rearm Germany," pp. 656–57; Robert McGeehan, *The German Rearmament Question: American Diplomacy and European Defense after World War II* (Urbana: University of Illinois Press, 1971), pp. 41, 47; David McLellan, *Dean Acheson: The State Department Years* (New York: Dodd, Mead, 1976), pp. 328–29; James Chace, *Acheson: The Secretary of State Who Created the American World* (New York: Simon and Schuster, 1998), p. 324; David Clay Large, *Germans to the Front: West German Rearmament in the Adenauer Era* (Chapel Hill: University of North Carolina Press, 1996), pp. 84–85; Saki Dockrill, *Britain's Policy for West German Rearmament, 1950–1955* (Cambridge, England: Cambridge University Press, 1991), 32–33.

[17] McLellan, *Acheson*, 328.

[18] Martin, "American Decision to Rearm Germany," 656.

[19] Dean Acheson, *Present at the Creation: My Years in the State Department* (New York: Norton, 1969), p. 438; McLellan, *Acheson*, p. 329; McGeehan, *German Rearmament Question*, p. 41.

prise," and that a more flexible approach made more sense, but, by his own account, he was almost totally isolated within the government and therefore had no choice but to back off from that position. "I was right," he said, "but I was nearly alone."[20] Most of the State Department, and even the president himself, seemed to be on the other side. So somewhat against his better judgment, he accepted what he later recognized as a mistaken policy.[21] He accepted not only the "package" approach— that is, as one scholar put it, a formula that "tied German rearmament to the State Department package much more rigidly than the State Department had intended"[22]—but a plan that would allow Germany to rearm on a national basis, which was also very much at variance with what the State Department had originally wanted.[23] But this was the only way he could get the Pentagon to accept the rest of the plan.

If all this is true—if the American government just stumbled into the policy it pursued in September 1950, if the policy, that is, is to be understood essentially as the outcome of a bureaucratic process—then the episode might not tell us much about how the American government, at the top political level, dealt with its European allies. But if that standard interpretation is not accurate, then the story might tell us something fundamental about the nature of America's European policy, and indeed about the nature of U.S.-European relations in general.

The goal here, therefore, is to examine this interpretation of what happened in August and September 1950 in light of the evidence. But is there any point, one might wonder, to conducting an analysis of this sort? If so many scholars who looked into the issue all reached essentially the same conclusion, that conclusion, one might reasonably assume, is probably correct. There is, however, a basic problem with this assumption: the standard interpretation rests on a very narrow evidentiary base. It rests, to a quite extraordinary extent, on Acheson's own account and on scholarly accounts that depend heavily on Acheson's story.[24] A self-serving account, however, should never be taken at face

[20] Acheson, *Present at the Creation*, p. 438.

[21] Ibid., 440; Dean Acheson, *Sketches from Life of Men I Have Known* (New York: Harper, 1961), pp. 26, 41; McGeehan, *German Rearmament Question*, p. 41.

[22] Martin, "American Decision to Rearm Germany," p. 657.

[23] McGeehan, *German Rearmament Question*, p. 41. This aspect of the argument is emphasized in Thomas Schwartz, *America's Germany: John J. McCloy and the Federal Republic of Germany* (Cambridge, Mass.: Harvard University Press, 1991), p. 134.

[24] The two published accounts that Acheson gave—*Present at the Creation*, pp. 437–40, and *Sketches from Life*, pp. 25–27, 41–43—are cited frequently in the historical literature relating to this issue. Scholars sometimes also relied on information Acheson provided in personal interviews. See Martin, "Decision to Rearm Germany," p. 665, and McLellan, *Acheson*, p. viii. Other sources are sometimes cited, but this additional evidence turns out upon examination to be quite weak. McLellan, for example, cites a memorandum of a

value; given the importance of the issue, the standard interpretation really needs to be tested against the evidence. And a good deal of archival evidence has become available since the publication of Acheson's memoirs and the first scholarly accounts. But what light does this new material throw on the issue?

GERMAN REARMAMENT: ON WHAT BASIS?

The State and Defense departments did not see eye-to-eye on the German rearmament question in mid-1950. On that point, the standard interpretation is indeed correct. But the differences between the two departments were not nearly as great as they sometimes seemed, and the area of disagreement had virtually disappeared by the time the New York Conference met in early September.

The military authorities had favored German rearmament since 1947. On May 2, 1950, they had officially called for the "early rearming of Western Germany," and had formally reiterated this call on June 8. But the State Department had taken a very different line and on July 3 had flatly rejected the idea that the time had come to press for German rearmament.[25] It was not that top State Department officials felt that Germany could never be rearmed. Acheson himself had noted, even in 1949, that one could not "have any sort of security in western Europe without using German power."[26] But until mid-1950, it was thought for a variety of reasons that it would be unwise to press the issue.

In July 1950, however, a major shift took place in State Department thinking. Acheson told President Truman at the end of that month that

conversation between Acheson and JCS Chairman Bradley on August 30 from the Acheson Papers at the Truman Library as supporting his contention that Acheson had at this point "given in to the military point of view" (p. 329). But according to the archivists at the Truman Library, no such document exists in that collection. The press accounts cited in n. 41 in the Martin article also do not prove the point they are meant to support. They are cited to back up the claim that the JCS was insisting on including German rearmament in the package, but the picture the press accounts give is that the German rearmament issue was a relatively minor issue ("only an incidental part of a much larger American program") and that the U.S. government had not embraced the package concept ("Acheson has not definitely made it a condition without which the United States would refuse to send troops to Europe"). "Western Europe" (editorial), *Washington Post*, August 31, 1950, p.8, and "Schuman Got Little Warning on U.S. Plans," *Washington Post*, September 17, 1950, p. 10.

[25] "Extracts of Views of the Joint Chiefs of Staff with Respect to Western Policy toward Germany," NSC 71, June 8, 1950, and "Views of the Department of State on the Rearmament of Western Germany," NSC 71/1, July 3, 1950, in FRUS 1950, 4:686–87, 691–95.

[26] Policy Planning Staff meeting, October 18, 1949, Records of the Policy Planning Staff, 1947–53, box 32, RG 59, U.S. National Archives [USNA], College Park, Md.

the issue now was not whether Germany should be "brought into the general defensive plan," but rather how this could be done without undermining America's other basic policy goals in Europe. He pointed out that the State Department was thinking in terms of a "European army or a North Atlantic army"; that force would include German troops, but the German units "would not be subject to the orders of Bonn."[27] A whole series of key State Department officials, both in Washington and in the major embassies abroad, had, in fact, come to the conclusion at about this time that some kind of international army that included German troops would have to be created, and Acheson's own thinking was fully in line with this emerging consensus.[28]

This shift in State Department thinking is not to be viewed in bureaucratic politics terms as an attempt by the State Department to reach some kind of compromise with the JCS on the German rearmament issue. It was instead a quite straightforward consequence of the outbreak of the Korean War in June. As Acheson later noted, after the North Korean attack,

> [W]e and everybody else in Europe and the United States took a new look at the German problem. It seemed to us that it was now clear that Germany had to take a part in the defense of Europe; it seemed clear that the idea that we had had before that this would work out through a process of evolution wasn't adequate—there wasn't time, the evolution had to be helped along by action. It was quite clear by this time, as a result of the staff talks in NATO, that the Western Union idea of defense on the Rhine was quite impractical and foolish, and that if you were going to have any defense at all, it had to be in the realm of forward strategy, which was as far east in Germany as possible. This made it absolutely clear that Germany had to be connected with defense, not merely through military formations, but emotionally and politically, because if the battle was going to be fought in Germany it meant that the German people had to be on our side, and enthusiastically so.

The U.S. government "immediately went to work" on "this German matter"—at least as soon as it could, given the need to deal, in July especially, with even more urgent problems relating to the Korean War.[29]

---

[27] Acheson memo of meeting with Truman, July 31, 1950, FRUS 1950, 4:702–3. President Truman had earlier opposed the JCS call for German rearmament. See Truman to Acheson, June 16, 1950, ibid., pp. 688–89.

[28] Bruce to Acheson, July 28, 1950; Acheson-Truman meeting, July 31, 1950; McCloy to Acheson, August 3, 1950; Douglas to Acheson, August 8, 1950; Kirk to Acheson, August 9, 1950; in FRUS 1950, 3:157, 167–68, 181–82, 190–93.

[29] Princeton Seminar, pp. 910–11, 921, Acheson Papers, HSTL. Soon after he left office,

So there was now a certain sense of urgency: an effective defense of western Europe had to be put in place and, indeed, put in place rather quickly. It was obvious from the start that this would "require real contributions of German resources and men." But the German contribution could not take the form of a German national army; the Germans could not be allowed to build a military force able to operate independently. The only way the Germans could make their defense contribution was thus to create some kind of international army that included German forces—but forces not able to conduct military operations on their own.[30]

A plan based on this fundamental concept was worked out by a key State Department official, Henry Byroade, at the beginning of August. Byroade, the Director of the State Department's Bureau of German Affairs, discussed his ideas with the Army staff officers most directly concerned with these issues on August 3. (The Army, for obvious reasons, took the lead in setting policy on this issue for the military establishment as a whole.) Those officers were pleased by the fact that the State Department now appeared "to be looking with favor toward the controlled rearmament of Western Germany"; they "felt that great progress had been achieved on the question of German rearmament, since both the State Department and the Department of Defense are now attempting to work out a suitable plan which would make possible a German contribution to the defense of Western Europe." These Army officers had in fact just come up with their own plan for a "controlled rearmament of Germany."[31]

There were, however, major differences between the two plans, or so

---

Acheson and some of his former collaborators got together at Princeton to discuss what had happened during the Truman administration; tapes were made of those discussions and a transcript was prepared. Microfilm copies of the transcript of this "Princeton Seminar," as it was called, are available at a number of university libraries in the United States. But the microfilm is often illegible, and the best source is the original transcript at the Truman Library. All the references from this source cited here come from the transcript of October 11, 1953, discussion.

[30] See the sources cited in n. 28 of this chapter, esp. pp. 157, 181 (for the quotation), 190, 193.

[31] The Byroade Plan, "An Approach to the Formation of a 'European Army,'" was drafted on August 3; the text is included in *Byroade to McCloy, August 3, 1950, 740.5/8-350, Department of State Central Files [DOSCF], RG 59, USNA. For the record of Byroade's talks with the Army officers on August 3, see *Memorandum for General Schuyler, August 5, 1950, Army Operations General Decimal File 1950–51, box 21, file G-3 091 Germany TS, sec 1c, case 12, book II, RG 319, USNA; henceforth cited in this form: AOGDF 1950–51/21/G-3/091/1c/12/II/RG 319/USNA. For the Army plan, see *"Staff Study: Rearmament of Western Germany," August 2, 1950, and *Bolté Memorandum for General Gruenther on Rearmament of Germany, August 10, 1950 (containing a systematic comparison of the State and Army plans), both in same file in RG 319.

it seemed to both sides at the time. The Byroade plan called for the establishment of a highly integrated "European Army"; that army would include practically all the western military forces—American and German as well as west European—stationed in Europe; it would have a "General Staff of truly international character," and a single commander, an American general, with "complete jurisdiction" over the whole army. The force would have as much of an international flavor as possible. The goal, Byroade said, was to apply the Schuman Plan concept to the military field; the aim was to enable the Germans to contribute to the defense of the West, without at the same time becoming too independent—that is, without getting a national army of their own.[32]

The U.S. Army, on the other hand, was not in favor of setting up a highly integrated "European army." The Army staff did not call explicitly for a "German national army," but key officers did seem to feel that any plan the U.S. government came up with would need to "appeal to the nationalistic tendencies of the German people." The Army plan, moreover, called for "controlled rearmament," but the officers who drafted it were reluctant to state formally what the "nature of the controls" would be. In short, the State Department called for a truly international force, while the military authorities, it seemed, wanted a less highly integrated force composed of national armies. The two plans, in Byroade's view, were "miles apart." Or as the Army staff put it, the State Department proposal would reduce the "military sovereignty status" of the European countries down "to the level of Germany in order to secure her contribution," while the Army proposed "to raise Germany's status" to the level of the NATO allies.[33]

So there was clearly a major difference of opinion on this issue at this point—at least at the level of rhetoric. But in practical terms were the two sides really so far apart? The great goal of the State Department was to make sure that there was no new German national army—that is, an army capable of independent action, and thus able to support an independent foreign policy. The military authorities understood the point, and it was for this reason that they, from the start, favored the "controlled" rearmament of Germany. And when one examines the sorts of controls they had in mind, and when one notes that certain key

[32] Byroade meeting with Army staff officers, August 3, 1950, in *Memorandum for General Schuyler, August 5, 1950, and *Army "Staff Study: Rearmament of Western Germany," August 2, 1950, both in AOGDF 1950–51/21/G-3/091/1c/12/II/RG 319/USNA. *"An Approach to the Formation of a 'European Army,'" in Byroade to McCloy, August 3, 1950, 740.5/8-350, DOSCF, RG 59, USNA.

[33] *Army "Staff Study: Rearmament of Western Germany," August 2, 1950; *Byroade meeting with Army staff officers, August 3, 1950 (document dated August 5); *Bolté to Gruenther, August 10, 1950 (with attached "Comparison of Plans"); all in AOGDF 1950–51/21/G-3/091/1c/12/II/RG 319/USNA.

military controls in their plan would apply to Germany alone, it becomes obvious—the rhetoric notwithstanding—that military leaders had no intention of giving the Federal Republic the same "military sovereignty status" as the NATO allies. In the Byroade plan, not just allied headquarters but also field army and corps headquarters were to be "international"; in the plan worked out by the officers in the Pentagon, "Army and Corps should be national," except that the Germans would be "allowed none." In both plans, the Germans would contribute only ground forces, and not air or naval forces; in both plans there would be German divisions, but no larger purely German units; in both plans, the German forces would be under allied control; in both plans, the Germans would not be allowed to manufacture certain kinds of weapons ("heavy ordnance, etc."); and both plans implied German participation in NATO.[34]

The real difference thus had to do not with Germany but with how the NATO forces were to be treated. Byroade was not too explicit about this part of the proposal, but his plan called for virtually all the allied forces in Europe to be integrated into the proposed "European Defense Force" (EDF). There would be no distinct British, French, or even American army on the continent, only an international army with a single commander served by an integrated international staff. The U.S. military authorities did not like this proposal at all, even though the whole force would have an American general as its commander. Byroade, it seemed to them, wanted to go too far in pushing the allies down to the German level; the Chiefs also felt that something this radical was not essential, and that instead of creating an entirely new institution, the EDF, it made more sense to build on the one basic institution that had already been created: the North Atlantic Treaty Organization. Both NATO and the Western Union military organization set up by the Brussels Treaty of 1948, were already in existence; to create a new international force would "tend to complicate an already confusing structure."[35] And there was no point in doing so, because NATO itself could provide the necessary degree of integration; a German force integrated into the NATO system—especially a strengthened NATO system—would be incapable of independent action.

---

[34] *Bolté to Gruenther, August 10, 1950 (with attached "Comparison of Plans"), AOGDF 1950–51/21/G-3/091/1c/12/II/RG 319/USNA. See also Byroade meeting with Army staff officers, *August 3, 1950, Memorandum for General Schuyler, August 5, same file in RG 319, and, for the Byroade plan, see *Byroade to McCloy, August 3, 1950, 740.5/8 -350, DOSCF, RG 59, USNA.

[35] Byroade meeting with Army staff officers, August 3, 1950, in *Memorandum for General Schuyler, August 5, 1950, and *Army "Staff Study: Rearmament of Western Germany," August 2, 1950, both in AOGDF 1950–51/21/G-3/091/1c/12/II/RG 319/USNA.

This logic was quite compelling. It did not matter if the international force was called EDF or NATO. The name was not important. What really mattered was whether you had an international structure within which the Germans could make their contribution, but which at the same time would prevent them from becoming too independent. And if an institution that had already been created—that is, NATO—could achieve that result, then so much the better.[36]

Even Byroade himself, who by his own account was quite conservative on these issues in comparison with other State Department officials, was quick to see the point. His original plan, in any event, had not really been put forward as a practical proposal; his aim there had been to sketch out a "theoretical solution from which one could work backwards" with an eye to working out a "compromise between the theoretical and what is already in existence." So when a top Army officer explained to him on August 10 how NATO could do the trick, he at least temporarily dropped his objections and basically accepted the military's approach: he agreed that "German divisions, organized as such, might well be integrated into the NATO forces as now planned, provided only an American commander for these forces were set up in the near future." The differences between the two departments were clearly narrowing. Indeed, it turned out that Byroade's earlier objection to the Army plan had "stemmed entirely from a misunderstanding of terms." Byroade had thought that when Army officers referred to "controlled rearmament," they had in mind only a "limitation on numbers and types of divisions." When he was told that the Army "also contemplated as part of the control a very definite limit as to the types and quantities of materiel and equipment which Germany should manufacture, Byroade said he was in complete accord."[37]

By the end of the month, it seemed that a full consensus had been reached. For Acheson, far more than for Byroade, only the core issue was really important. For him, it was not a problem that the Germans

---

[36] The idea that NATO could do it—that one did not need to create a new institution but could rely on a strong NATO structure to solve this whole complex of problems—reemerged in 1954 as the European Defense Community project was collapsing and people were looking for alternatives. The military authorities, especially the NATO commander, General Alfred Gruenther, played a key role at that point in pushing for the NATO solution; see Trachtenberg, *Constructed Peace*, p. 127. But they were drawing on basic thinking that had taken shape in 1950. At that time, both Gruenther—then Deputy Army Chief of Staff for Plans—and General Schuyler, another top Army officer who would end up as Gruenther's Chief of Staff in 1954, were already pressing for the NATO solution.

[37] Byroade to McCloy, August 4, 1950, FRUS 1950, 3:183–84; *Bolté to Gruenther, July 25, 1950 (account of Byroade's meeting with Schuyler the previous day), and *memorandum of Byroade-Schuyler-Gerhardt meeting, August 10, 1950, in AOGDF 1950–51/21/G-3/091/1c/12/I,II/RG 319/USNA.

would have a national army in an administrative sense—that is, that they would recruit their own troops, pay them, provide them with uniforms, and so on. The only important thing was to make sure that things did not go too far—that the "old German power," as Acheson put it, was not resurrected.[38] If an arrangement could guarantee that, he was prepared to be quite flexible on the secondary issues. Acheson was certainly not going to go to the wall to defend those parts of the Byroade concept that would tend to strip the NATO forces, including the American force in Europe, of their national character.

Acheson had an important meeting with JCS Chairman Bradley on August 30 to work things out, and he discussed that meeting with his principal advisors later that morning. He did not complain that the military wanted to go too far toward creating a German national army; his real complaint was that the JCS was "confused" and had somehow gotten the idea that the State Department position was more extreme than it really was. The Pentagon's own position, Acheson thought, was just not clear enough: "he did not know what was meant by 'national basis' and 'controlled status.'"[39]

But the military authorities were now willing to be more accommodating on this point and were prepared to state more explicitly what they meant by those terms. This represented a certain shift from the line they had taken at the beginning of the month. In early August, they had preferred not to outline formally the sorts of controls they had in mind.[40] But by the end of the month, the Army leadership had concluded that it needed to be more forthcoming.

This was because President Truman had intervened in these discussions on August 26. On that day, he had asked the two departments to come up with a common policy on the whole complex of issues relating to European defense and West German rearmament. Given the president's action, a simple rejection of the Byroade plan was no longer a viable option. Leading military officers now felt that they needed to come up with a more "positive approach" to the problem. A "Plan for the Development of West German Security Forces" was quickly worked out and approved by the Army leadership at the beginning of September. That plan spelled out the controls the military had long favored:

[38] *Acheson-Nitze-Byroade-Perkins meeting, August 30, 1950, *Official Conversations and Meetings of Dean Acheson (1949-1953)* (University Publications of America microfilm), reel 3.

[39] *Ibid. The references are probably to various JCS documents from this period that contained these terms. See, for example, JCS 2124/18 of September 1, 1950, p. 162, in CCS 092 Germany (5-4-49), JCS Geographic File for 1948–50, RG 218, USNA.

[40] See the *Army "Staff Study: Rearmament of Western Germany," August 2, 1950, paragraph 8, AOGDF 1950–51/21/G-3/091/1c/12/II/RG 319/USNA.

the NATO organization would be strengthened; Germany would not be allowed to have an air force or a navy; the largest German unit would be the division; there would be no German general staff; German industry would be permitted to provide only light weapons and equipment. The military authorities were thus not pressing for the creation of a German national force that would have the same status as the British, French, or American armies. Indeed, by the beginning of September, there was no fundamental difference between their position and that of Acheson on this issue.[41]

THE ORIGINS OF THE PACKAGE PLAN

So the State Department and the Pentagon had clashed in August 1950 on the question of German rearmament. That conflict had focused on the question of the extent to which the German force would be organized on a "national" basis—or, to look at the issue from the other side, the degree of military integration needed to keep Germany from having a capability for independent action. But by the end of the month that conflict had essentially been resolved. Misunderstandings had been cleared up and differences had been ironed out. There would be a German military contribution, both departments agreed, but no German national army. The German force would be fully integrated into the NATO force; the German force would not be able to operate independently. This was all Acheson really required, and the JCS had never really asked for anything more by way of a German national force.

But even if the conflict had been sharper, even if the Pentagon had been intransigent on this issue, and even if the State Department had capitulated to the JCS, all this would in itself tell us very little about the

---

[41] *Gruenther to Davis, Duncan and Edwards, September 1, 1950, enclosing the "Plan for the Development of West German Security Forces." The plan had been worked out "pursuant to verbal instructions" that Gruenther had given General Schuyler on August 31; the feeling in military circles was that after the president's letter, the JCS needed to take a more accommodating line in their discussions with the State Department than they had taken thus far. Gruenther, Bolté and Army Chief of Staff Collins were briefed on the plan on September 1, Collins approved it, and it was officially presented to the JCS that same day. *Miller memorandum for record, September 1, 1950, *Bolté to Collins on Rearmament of Western Germany, August 31, 1950, and *Ware to JCS Secretary, September 1, 1950. All in AOGDF 1950–51/21/G-3/091/1c/12/II/RG 319/USNA. The old conventional argument—laid out, for example, in McGeehan, German Rearmament Question, p. 41—was that the U.S. government, by early September, had decided to press for a German national army "with no particular control arrangement other than that which would have resulted simply by virtue of the German troops being under NATO command and without their own general staff." But this, it turns out, was incorrect: the controls the U.S. Army was now calling for were quite far-reaching.

most important issue we are concerned with here: the question of the origins of the "package plan." This was essentially a separate issue. The American government, at the New York Conference in mid-September, demanded that the NATO allies agree, immediately and publicly, to the rearmament of West Germany; if they refused to accept that demand, the Americans would not send over the combat divisions and would not send over an American general as NATO commander. Everything was tied together into a single package, and it was presented to the allies on a "take it or leave it" basis. It was this policy, this tactic, that created the whole problem in September 1950.

How exactly did the issue of German rearmament get tied to the question of sending over American combat divisions and to appointing an American general as NATO commander? The standard view is that the JCS was responsible for the package plan. The military authorities, it is commonly argued, simply refused to accept the deployment of the American combat force unless the Europeans, for their part, agreed to the rearmament of West Germany. Acheson supposedly thought these tactics "murderous" and tried hard to get the Pentagon to change its mind. But the JCS was intransigent, this argument runs, and to get the troops sent, Acheson gave way in the end and reluctantly accepted the tactic the military leadership had insisted on.[42] But does this basic interpretation hold up in the light of the archival evidence now available?

First of all, did the military push throughout August for the package approach? The military leaders certainly felt that a German military contribution was essential. The west European NATO allies, in their view, could not generate enough military force by themselves to provide for an effective defense; German troops were obviously necessary for that purpose; German rearmament was therefore seen as a "vital element" of an effective defense policy.[43] The military authorities also supported the idea of beefing up the U.S. military presence in Europe and of sending over an American general as NATO commander.[44] But the key point to note here is that these were treated as essentially separate issues. Military leaders did not say (at least not in any of the docu-

[42] See especially McLellan, *Acheson*, pp. 328–30; Martin, "Decision to Rearm Germany," pp. 656–57; and Acheson, *Present at the Creation*, pp. 437–38, 440.

[43] See, for example, Joint Strategic Survey Committee report on Rearmament of Western Germany, July 27, 1950, JCS 2124/11, JCS Geographic File for 1948–50, 092 Germany (5-4-49), RG 218, USNA.

[44] *Bolté to Collins, August 28, 1950, AOGDF 1950–51/20/G-3/091/1/RG 319/USNA. Note also the initial draft that the military had prepared of a joint reply to the president's "Eight Questions" letter, given in JCS 2116/28 of September 6, 1950. The original draft, according to another document, was given to the State Department on September 1. See Bolté to Collins, September 2, 1950. Both documents are in AOGDF 1950–51/21/ G-3/091/1c/12/II,III and (for September 6 document)/RG 319/USNA.

ments that we have seen) that U.S. troops should be sent only if the allies accepted German rearmament. They did not say that the way to press for German rearmament was to tell the allies that unless they went along with the American plan, the U.S. combat divisions would be kept at home.

Indeed, in the formal policy documents on the defense of Europe, the JCS did not make the German rearmament issue its top priority. The Chiefs instead tended to play it down. The basic JCS view in those documents was that NATO Europe—the "European signatories" of the North Atlantic Treaty—needed to "provide the balance of the forces required for the initial defense" over and above what the United States was prepared to supply.[45] West Germany, which at this time, of course, was not a member of NATO, was not even mentioned in this context. What this suggests is that the military leadership was not pounding its fist on the table on the German rearmament question. The German issue was important, of course, but the choice of this kind of phrasing suggests that the Chiefs were prepared to deal with it in a relatively reasonable, gradual, businesslike way.

What about the State Department? How did it feel about the package approach? Did it agree to the inclusion of German rearmament in the package because this was the only way to get the Pentagon to go along with its plan to send additional troops to Europe? Some scholars suggest that this was the case, but the real picture is rather different.[46]

The outbreak of the Korean War was the key development here, and State Department officials understood from the start that if Europe was to be defended, a German force of some sort would be required. As McCloy wrote to Acheson on August 3, "[T]o defend Western Europe effectively will obviously require real contributions of German resources and men."[47] This was simply the conventional wisdom at the time: neither McCloy nor anyone else in the State Department needed the JCS to remind them that an effective defense meant a German military contribution. But they were also dead set against the idea of allowing the Germans to build up an army of their own—a national army, able to operate independently and thus capable of supporting an independent foreign policy. It followed that some kind of international force would

[45] This key phrase found its way into a whole series of major documents in early September. See appendix to memorandum for the Secretary of Defense, "United States Views on Measures for the Defense of Western Europe," JCS 2073/61, September 3, 1950, JCS Geographic File for 1948–50, box 25, RG 218, USNA. The same document, after being approved by the Secretary of Defense, was forwarded to the State Department on September 12 and appears in FRUS 1950, 3:291–93. A very similar phrase was included in NSC 82; see FRUS 1950, 3:274.

[46] See, for example, McLellan, *Acheson*, p. 328.

[47] McCloy to Acheson, August 3, 1950, FRUS 1950, 3:181.

have to be created: the Germans could make their contribution, an effective force could be built up, but there would be no risk of a German national army. The whole concept of a multinational force—of military integration, of a unified command structure, of a single supreme commander supported by an international staff—was thus rooted in an attempt to deal with the question of German rearmament. It was not as though the thinking about the defense of western Europe and the shape of the NATO military system had developed on its own, and that it was only later that the German rearmament issue had been linked to it by the JCS for bargaining purposes.

The fundamental idea that the different elements in the equation— the U.S. divisions, the unified command structure, the forces provided by NATO Europe, and the German contribution—were all closely interrelated and needed to be dealt with as parts of a unified policy thus developed naturally and organically as the basic thinking about the defense of Europe took shape in mid-1950. This idea—in a sense, the basic idea behind the package concept—took hold quite early in August 1950, and it was the State Department that took the lead in pressing for this kind of approach. The Byroade plan, for example, explicitly tied all these different elements together: in this plan, which in mid-August became a kind of official State Department plan, German units could be created if and only if they were integrated into an allied force with an American commander.[48]

The State Department was thus the driving force behind this kind of approach. For the entire month of August, its officials pressed for a unified policy. But the military authorities, because of their dislike for the Byroade plan, tended to drag their feet in this area.[49] The State Department, in frustration and aware that a policy needed to be worked out before the NATO ministers met in mid-September, then got the president to intervene. On August 26 (as noted earlier), Truman asked the two departments, State and Defense, to come up with a common policy. He laid out a series of eight questions that the two departments were to answer by September 1, a deadline that was later extended to September 6.[50] The "Eight Questions" document was actually drafted in the

[48] *Byroade-Schuyler-Gerhardt meeting, August 10, 1950, AOGDF 1950–51/21/G-3/091/ 1c/12/II/RG 319/USNA. For the final Byroade plan, and for its adoption as the official State Department position, see Matthews to Burns, August 16, 1950, with enclosure, FRUS 1950, 3:211–219.

[49] See, for example, Paul Nitze, with Ann Smith and Steven Rearden, *From Hiroshima to Glasnost: At the Center of Decision* (New York: Grove Weidenfeld, 1989), p. 123; and Princeton Seminar, p. 914. Note also the tone of Secretary of Defense Johnson's initial reply to State Department letter asking for comments on the August 16 Byroade plan: Johnson to Acheson, August 17, 1950, FRUS 1950, 3:226–27.

[50] Truman to Acheson and Johnson, August 26, 1950, FRUS 1950, 3:250–51.

State Department by two of Acheson's closest advisors. The State Department goal, in getting Truman to sign it, was to prod the Pentagon into accepting a common plan.[51]

The tactic worked. Military leaders understood that the Eight Questions document was based on the State Department plan.[52] Given the president's intervention (again, as already noted), they now felt they could no longer simply "disregard" that plan, but instead needed to take a more accommodating and "positive" line.[53]

The military authorities now drafted a document which, they felt, might serve as a basis for a joint reply to the president. That draft was given to the State Department on September 1; Acheson had been shown a preliminary version a couple of days earlier.[54] Events now moved quickly. In a few days of intensive talks, a joint reply acceptable to both departments was worked out. The final document was approved by the president and circulated to top officials as NSC 82 on September 11, a day before the New York Conference was due to begin.[55]

---

[51] Draft memo by Nitze and Byroade, August 25, 1950, Records of the Policy Planning Staff, Country and Area file, box 28, RG 59, USNA. Some scholars—Martin, for example, in "The Decision to Rearm Germany," p. 659—portray the JCS as "prodding" the State Department to take "prompt diplomatic action." And Acheson, in *Present at the Creation* (p. 428), also portrays himself as having been pushed forward, especially by pressure from the president, and actually cites the "Eight Questions" document in this context. But in reality—and not just at this point, but throughout this episode—it was the State Department that was pushing things forward, and it was Truman who followed Acheson's lead. The president, for example, had been against German rearmament when the JCS had pressed for it in June. But when Acheson told him on July 31 that it no longer was a question of whether Germany should be rearmed, that the real issue now was how it was to be done, and that the State Department was thinking in terms of creating "a European army or a North Atlantic army," Truman immediately "expressed his strong approval" of this whole line of thought. Truman to Acheson, June 16, 1950 (two documents), and Acheson-Truman meeting, July 31, 1950, FRUS 1950, 4:688, 702.

[52] *Bolté to Collins, August 28, 1950: "The questions listed in the President's letter are apparently based upon the State Department's proposal for the establishment of a European defense force." AOGDF 1950–51/20/G-3/091/1/RG 319/USNA. The point was clear from the text of the letter. The two departments were not simply asked, for example, to consider what, if anything, should be done on the German rearmament question; they were asked instead to consider whether the U.S. government was prepared to support "the concept of a European defense force, including German participation on other than a national basis"—which was not exactly a neutral way of putting the issue. Truman to Acheson and Johnson, August 26, 1950, FRUS 1950, 3:250.

[53] Bolté to Collins, August 31, 1950, and *Gruenther to Davis, Duncan and Edwards, September 1, 1950, enclosing the "Plan for the Development of West German Security Forces," both in AOGDF 1950–51/21/G-3/091/1c/12/II/RG 319/USNA.

[54] Bolté to Collins, September 2, 1950, AOGDF 1950–51/21/G-3/091/1c/12/II/RG 319/USNA; *Acheson-Nitze-Byroade-Perkins meeting, August 30, 1950, cited in n. 38 in this chapter.

[55] Acheson and Johnson to Truman, September 8, 1950, FRUS 1950, 3:273–78.

This period from August 26 through September 8—from the Eight Questions letter to the joint reply—is thus the most important phase of this whole episode, and the evidence relating to this period needs to be examined with particular care. Does it support the view that the military insisted on the package approach and that the State Department opposed it, but gave in reluctantly at the end?

By far the most important document bearing on these issues is the record of a meeting Acheson had on August 30 with his three top advisors in this area, the three officials who, in fact, were conducting the negotiations with the Defense Department: Byroade, Assistant Secretary for European Affairs George Perkins, and Paul Nitze, head of the State Department's Policy Planning Staff. Acheson (as noted in the previous section) had just met with JCS Chairman Bradley earlier that morning. He had also just seen the draft reply that the JCS had prepared to the president's Eight Questions letter. At the meeting with his advisors, Acheson discussed the JCS draft section by section and found most of it acceptable. The few small problems he had with it did not involve any issue of principle. At no point did Acheson complain about, or even comment on, any insistence on the part of the military that all the elements in the program were to be tied together in a single package. The conclusion to be drawn from this is absolutely fundamental for the purposes of the analysis here: if the JCS had been insisting on the package concept and if Acheson and the State Department had been opposed to that concept, it is scarcely conceivable that the issue would not have come up at this meeting.

Nor is it very likely that a conflict over the package issue developed suddenly over the next few days. Nitze's recollection (in 1953) was that following the Acheson-Bradley meeting things moved very quickly.[56] He says nothing about a dispute over the package question suddenly emerging at that point, and it is in fact highly unlikely that things could have moved so quickly if a serious dispute had developed. Indeed, Perkins and Nitze spoke in those 1953 discussions of the common policy document—the document that later became NSC 82—as though it essentially reflected their views, and which, through great efforts on their part, they had finally managed to get the military authorities to accept. "We had great difficulty," Perkins recalled, "in finally getting the Pentagon" to sign on to the common policy.[57] Nitze agreed: he remembered going over to the Pentagon after Acheson had worked "this thing" out with General Bradley on August 30, and "we trotted out the specific piece of paper which spelled out the package proposal with the Penta-

---

[56] Princeton Seminar, pp. 920–21.
[57] Princeton Seminar, p. 914.

gon people and got their agreement to this document."[58] It was scarcely as though the State Department was going along with the package plan reluctantly or against its better judgment.

An analysis of the drafting history points to the same general conclusion. The passage in NSC 82 that served as the basis for the package policy—indeed, the only passage in the document that called for such a policy—was part of the answer to the sixth question: "We recommend that an American national be appointed now as Chief of Staff and eventually as a Supreme Commander for the European defense force but only upon the request of the European nations and upon their assurance that they will provide sufficient forces, including adequate German units, to constitute a command reasonably capable of fulfilling its responsibilities."[59] That final document was based on the draft the JCS had turned over on September 1; the key phrase "including adequate German units" did not appear in the original JCS draft.[60] It scarcely stands to reason that the military authorities, having decided to be cooperative, would harden their position in the course of their talks with State Department representatives, above all if State Department officials had argued strongly against an intransigent policy.

None of this means, of course, that the JCS was opposed to including a call for German rearmament in the package. This was in their view a goal that the U.S. government obviously had to pursue. But this does not mean that the Chiefs were going to try to dictate negotiating tactics to the State Department—that they were going to insist on a diplomatic strategy that Acheson and his top advisors rejected.

State Department officials, in fact, did not really blame the JCS for what had happened at the New York Conference. Nitze, for example, although he said in 1953 that the Chiefs would not agree to send additional forces until they got assurances from the British and the French about a German military contribution, did not actually hold them primarily responsible for the confrontation with the Europeans in mid-September.[61] He pointed out at that time that the German rearmament issue could have been dealt with very differently. The issue, he said, could have been presented "to the British and French in a way which emphasized the supreme commander and the American commitment";

[58] Princeton Seminar, p. 914.

[59] NSC 82, FRUS 1950, 3:276.

[60] See JCS 2116/28, September 6, 1950, which gives the final draft and shows changes from the earlier draft; AOGDF 1950–51/21/G-3/091/1c/12/III/RG 319/USNA. For another copy, see JCS to Johnson, September 5, 1950, Records of the Administrative Secretary, Correspondence Control Section Decimal File: July to Dec 1950, CD 091.7 (Europe), box 175, RG 330, USNA.

[61] Princeton Seminar, p. 915.

the "question of German participation" could have been "put in a lower category and kind of weaved in gradually."[62] Nitze did not blame the JCS for vetoing that approach. In his view, the real responsibility lay elsewhere. "We were fouled up on this," he said, by press leaks primarily coming from McCloy, "who agreed entirely with the tactical importance of doing it the other way"—that is, of dealing with the German rearmament issue head on.[63]

But Acheson was not fundamentally opposed to the blunt approach, and (contrary to his later disclaimers) he himself, on balance, thought that the U.S. government had chosen the right course of action at the time. Would it have been better, he asked in that same discussion, to have opted for quiet talks with the British and the French, when a plan had just been worked out, when a NATO foreign ministers' meeting was about to be held, and when the issue was being "talked about everywhere"? "It seemed to me then," he said, "and it seems to me now, that we did the right thing."[64]

And indeed, in his reports to Truman from the New York Conference, Acheson gave no sign that he was pursuing the package plan strategy reluctantly or against his better judgment. He gave no sign that he was looking for a way to soften the general line and deal with the allies in a more conciliatory manner. He explained to the president on September 15 how he had laid out the American demands, how he had discussed the issue "with the gloves off," how he had "blown" some of the allies' objections to the American plan "out of the water," and how it might well be a question of "whose nerve lasts longer." He was clearly pleased with his own performance and was not at all unhappy about the line he had taken.[65]

As one of its top officials pointed out at the time, the State Depart-

[62] Princeton Seminar, p. 916.

[63] Princeton Seminar, p. 916; see also p. 912. The archival evidence confirms the point that McCloy favored a very tough line at this time. See especially the handwritten letter from McCloy to Acheson, September 20, 1950, in the Acheson Papers, Memoranda of Conversations, September 1950, HSTL. A high-level French official, McCloy reported, had just "referred again to the delicacy of French opinion" on the German rearmament issue. "I think the time has come," he wrote, "to tell these people that there is other opinion to deal with and that U.S. opinion is getting damn delicate itself. If there should be an incursion in January and U.S. troops should get pushed around without German troops to help them because of a French reluctance to face facts, I shudder to think how indelicate U.S. opinion would suddenly become."

[64] Princeton Seminar, p. 913.

[65] Acheson to Truman, September 15, 1950, FRUS 1950, 3:1229–31. For more information relating to the part of the story from the New York Conference on, see Christopher Gehrz, "Dean Acheson, the JCS and the 'Single Package': American Policy on German Rearmament, 1950," *Diplomacy and Statecraft* 12 (March 2001): 135–60.

ment was conducting a "hard-hitting kind of operation" in this area—and was proud of it.[66]

DEAN ACHESON: THE MAN AND THE STATESMAN

There is one final set of considerations that needs to be taken into account in an assessment of U.S. policy in September 1950, and this has to do with what we know about Acheson in general—about the sort of person he was and the kind of policy he favored throughout his career. Was he the type of leader who believed in compromise, especially with America's most important allies, and was inclined to take a relatively moderate and cautious line? Or was he, as General Bradley later called him, an "uncompromising hawk," aggressive in terms of both his goals and his tactics?[67]

The great bulk of the evidence points in the latter direction.[68] In 1950 in particular, Acheson tended to take a very hard line. He was in favor of a rollback policy at that time. This was the real meaning of NSC 68, an important policy document with which Acheson was closely associated.[69] American scholars generally tend to portray U.S. policy as essentially defensive and status quo–oriented, and NSC 68 is commonly interpreted as simply a "strategy of containment."[70] But the aggressive thrust of this document is clear from its own text: NSC 68 called explicitly for a "policy of calculated and gradual coercion"; the aim of that policy was to "check and roll back the Kremlin's drive for world domi-

[66] Under Secretary Webb, in telephone conversation with Acheson, September 27, 1950, Acheson Papers (Lot File 53D 444), box 13, RG 59, USNA. Webb was comparing the State Department "operation" with the way the Defense Department under Marshall was handling the issue.

[67] Omar Bradley and Clay Blair, *A General's Life* (New York: Simon & Schuster, 1983), p. 519.

[68] The idea that Acheson was an exceptionally aggressive statesman is scarcely the consensus view. American writers tend to treat Acheson rather gently, but this, we think, is to be understood in essentially political terms. Acheson's reputation profited enormously from the fact that during his period in office he had been the target of a great deal of ill-informed criticism from right-wing Republicans; Richard Nixon's famous reference at the time to the "Acheson College of Cowardly Communist Containment" is a good case in point. And with enemies like that, it was not hard to find friends—among liberal academics, at any rate.

[69] Trachtenberg, *History and Strategy*, pp. 109–10.

[70] See, for example, Ernest May, ed., *American Cold War Strategy: Interpreting NSC 68* (New York: St. Martin's, 1993), and John Lewis Gaddis, *Strategies of Containment: A Critical Appraisal of Postwar American National Security Policy* (Oxford and New York: Oxford University Press, 1982), chap. 4.

nation." The whole goal at that time, as Nitze recalled in 1954, was to "lay the basis," through massive rearmament, for a policy of "taking increased risks of general war" in order to achieve "a satisfactory solution" of America's problems with Russia while the Soviet nuclear stockpile "was still small."[71]

This extraordinary aggressiveness was not out of character for Acheson, and its wellspring was not simply anticommunism or extreme distrust of the Soviet Union. His general hawkishness can in fact be traced back to the summer of 1941, when, as a mid-level State Department official, he played a major role in shaping the policy that put the United States on a collision course with Japan. Acheson was one of a handful of officials who helped engineer the oil embargo in mid-1941—a development that led directly to a sharp crisis in U.S.-Japanese relations and ultimately to the attack on Pearl Harbor in December.[72]

His aggressiveness was also apparent in the early 1960s. During the Berlin and Cuban missile crises especially, he pushed for very tough policies. In 1963, he even called (in a talk to the Institute for Strategic Studies) for what amounted to a policy of armed intervention in East Germany.[73] When he was attacked for taking this line, he lashed out at his critics: "Call me anything you like, but don't call me a fool; everybody knows I'm not a fool." "I will not say that Mr. Acheson is a fool," one of his critics replied. "I will only say that he is completely and utterly reckless."[74]

Acheson often sneered at those he viewed as soft and indecisive. After Eisenhower took office in 1953, Acheson complained repeatedly

[71] NSC 68, April 7, 1950, FRUS 1950, 1:253, 255, 284; Nitze quoted in Trachtenberg, *History and Strategy*, 112n. Nitze, the principal author of NSC 68, was quite close to Acheson throughout this period. See, for example, David Callahan, *Dangerous Capabilities: Paul Nitze and the Cold War* (New York: HarperCollins, 1990), pp. 95–96, 155; and Strobe Talbott, *The Master of the Game: Paul Nitze and the Nuclear Peace* (New York: Knopf, 1988), p. 51.

[72] See Jonathan Utley, "Upstairs, Downstairs at Foggy Bottom: Oil Exports and Japan, 1940–41," *Prologue* 8 (Spring 1976): 17–28; Jonathan Utley, *Going to War with Japan* (Knoxville: University of Tennessee Press, 1985), pp. 153–56, 180; Irvine Anderson, "The 1941 *de facto* Embargo on Oil to Japan: A Bureaucratic Reflex," *Pacific Historical Review* 44 (1975): 201–31; and Irvine Anderson, *The Standard Vacuum Oil Company and United States East Asian Policy, 1933–1941* (Princeton: Princeton University Press, 1975).

[73] Acheson speech at annual meeting of the Institute of Strategic Studies, September 1963, in Adelphi Paper No. 5, *The Evolution of NATO*. See also Douglas Brinkley, *Dean Acheson: The Cold War Years, 1953–71* (New Haven: Yale University Press), p. 153. Note also Acheson's comment in 1961 about the need for the sort of forces which would enable the western powers to intervene in the event, for example, of a new uprising in Hungary: Acheson-de Gaulle meeting, April 20, 1961, *Documents diplomatiques français* 1961, 1:494.

[74] Bernard Brodie, *War and Politics* (New York: Macmillan, 1973), p. 402. The critic in question was the former British Defence Minister Harold Watkinson.

to Truman about the "weakness" of the new administration.[75] After the Democrats returned to power in 1961, President John F. Kennedy allowed Acheson to play a major role in the making of American policy, but Acheson viewed the young president with barely concealed contempt. The Kennedy administration, in his view, was weak, indecisive, and obsessed with appearances.[76] He even criticized the administration in public, going so far at one point that he was virtually forced to apologize.[77]

At another point, he practically told the president to his face that he was indecisive. Kennedy had asked Acheson to look into the balance of payments problem, and in early 1963 he presented his report to the president. It was a "very strong, vivid, Achesonian presentation. And the President thanked him and said, 'Well, we have to think about that.' Acheson said, 'There's nothing to think about, Mr. President. All you have to do is decide. Here it is, and why don't you decide?'" Kennedy turned red, and then broke up the meeting. He was furious. "It's a long time before Dean Acheson's going to be here again," he remarked to an aide.[78] As for Acheson, he continued to criticize Kennedy as weak and indecisive, even after Kennedy's death.[79]

Acheson treated President Johnson the same way he had treated President Kennedy. When he met with Johnson in 1965, he was so irritated by the president's whining and indecisiveness that he "blew [his] top" and told him to his face that all the trouble America was having in Europe "came about because under him and Kennedy there had been no American leadership at all. The idea that the Europeans could come to their own conclusion had led to an unchallenged de Gaulle."[80]

[75] See, for example, Acheson to Truman, May 28, 1953, box 30, folder 391, and Acheson memorandum of conversation, June 23, 1953, box 68, folder 172, in Acheson Papers, Sterling Library, Yale University, New Haven, Conn. Note also Nitze's complaint at the very end of the Truman period that the U.S. government had opted for a purely defensive policy. America, he was afraid, was in danger of becoming "a sort of hedge-hog, unattractive to attack, but basically not very worrisome over a period of time beyond our immediate position." Nitze to Acheson, January 12, 1953, FRUS 1952–54, 2:59.

[76] See especially Acheson to Truman, June 24, July 14, August 4, and September 21, 1961, Acheson Papers, box 166, Acheson-Truman Correspondence, 1961, Sterling Library, Yale University; some extracts are quoted in Trachtenberg, History and Strategy, p. 230. See also Michael Beschloss, The Crisis Years: Kennedy and Khrushchev, 1960–1963 (New York: Edward Burlingame, 1991), p. 410; and Honoré Catudal, Kennedy and the Berlin Wall Crisis: A Study in U.S. Decision-Making (Berlin: Berlin-Verlag, 1980), 182n.

[77] Walter Isaacson and Evan Thomas, The Wise Men: Six Friends and the World They Made (New York: Simon & Schuster, 1986), pp. 612–13; see also Brinkley, Acheson, p. 138.

[78] Carl Kaysen oral history interview, July 11, 1966, p. 85, John F. Kennedy Library, Boston. We are grateful to Frank Gavin for providing this reference.

[79] See, for example, Brinkley, Acheson, pp. 174, 202.

[80] Acheson to Truman, July 10, 1965, in Dean Acheson, Among Friends: Personal Letters

These stories reveal a lot about Acheson. A man who could deal with presidents that way was not the type of person who would allow himself to be pushed around by mere military officers on a issue of central political importance—above all at a time when he was at the height of his power and had the full confidence of President Truman. Nor was he the type who would be understanding if he thought allied leaders were reluctant to face up to fundamental problems and make the really tough decisions.

Acheson, in fact, did not believe in taking a soft line with the allies or in treating them as full partners. In 1961 he played the key role in shaping the new Kennedy administration's policy on NATO issues; the goal of that policy was to get the Europeans "out of the nuclear business" (as people said at the time)—that is, to concentrate power, and especially nuclear power, in American hands.[81]

Acheson, moreover, was not the sort of statesman who viewed consultation and compromise as ends in themselves. At one point during the Berlin crisis in 1961, he complained that the United States had been trying too hard to reach agreement with the Europeans. The U.S. government did not need to coordinate policy with the allies, he said, "*we need to tell them.*"[82] "We must not be too delicate," he said at another point, "about being vigorous in our leadership." It was America's job, practically America's duty, to lay down the law to the allies. The United States—and he actually used this phrase—was "the greatest imperial power the world has ever seen."[83] "In the final analysis," he told McGeorge Bundy, "the United States [is] the locomotive at the head of mankind, and the rest of the world is the caboose."[84]

American interests were fundamental; European concerns were of purely secondary importance. Paul Nitze, who was very close to Acheson throughout this period, made the point quite explicitly in 1954. The

---

of Dean Acheson, ed. David McLellan and David Acheson (New York: Dodd, Mead, 1980), p. 273.

[81] See Trachtenberg, *Constructed Peace,* pp. 304–11. Acheson, however, deliberately gave the Europeans a very different impression. Note especially his discussion of the issue in an April 20, 1961, meeting with Charles de Gaulle, and especially his reference to a system that "would permit Europe to make its own decision on the nuclear matter." *Documents diplomatiques français* 1961, 1:495.

[82] White House meeting, October 20, 1961, FRUS 1961–63, 14:518–19. Emphasis in original.

[83] Quoted in Frank Costigliola, "LBJ, Germany and the 'End of the Cold War,'" in Warren Cohen and Nancy Tucker, eds., *Lyndon Johnson Confronts the World: American Foreign Policy, 1963–1968* (New York: Cambridge University Press, 1994), p. 195. Acheson was complaining about what he viewed as Johnson's weak response to de Gaulle's decision in 1966 to take France out of the NATO military organization.

[84] Brinkley, *Acheson,* p. 133.

"primary goal," he said, was the "preservation of the United States and the continuation of a 'salutary' world environment"; the "avoidance of war" was of secondary importance. "Even if war were to destroy the world as we know it today, still the US must win that war decisively." He then again stressed the point that "the preservation of the US" was "the overriding goal, not the fate of our allies."[85]

People like Nitze and Acheson were thus not inclined to take European interests too seriously or to deal with the Europeans on a basis of mutual respect. And Acheson himself was clearly not the kind of person who would have found it difficult to deal roughly with the allies in September 1950.

THE MEANING OF THE STORY

The goal here was to test a particular interpretation of what happened in the late summer of 1950. According to that interpretation, the military authorities had essentially forced the package plan on Acheson, who had accepted it reluctantly, and only after a struggle. The basic conclusion here is that that interpretation simply does not stand up in the light of the evidence from late 1950 and in the light of what we know about Acheson in general. The policy the U.S. government pursued at the New York Conference is not to be understood as a more or less accidental by-product of a bureaucratic dispute in Washington. The way Acheson dealt with the allies at the New York conference—the bare-knuckled tactics he pursued, the way he tried to lay down the law to the Europeans, the way he dismissed their most fundamental concerns out of hand—has to be seen as deliberate: he knew what he was doing, and he had not been forced by the Pentagon to proceed in that way. There is certainly no evidence that he thought those tactics were "murderous": he did not give way on this point after a long battle; he never complained at the time about the military's (alleged) insistence on this strategy; he never raised the issue with Truman or expressed misgivings about the policy as he was carrying it out.

Does this mean that the Acheson interpretation was a complete fabrication? The truth is probably not quite that simple. For Acheson, as for many people in public life, honesty was not the top priority, and he was fully capable of deliberately misleading the public on these issues.[86] But

[85] *Notes of Council on Foreign Relations Study Group on Nuclear Weapons and U.S. Foreign Policy, November 8, 1954, meeting, p. 12, Hanson Baldwin Papers, box 125, folder 23, Yale University Library.

[86] An account Acheson gave in 1952, implying that the issue emerged only in the

that in itself does not mean that the Acheson story about the package plan was manufactured out of whole cloth.

Indeed—in a certain sense at least—there was probably some basis to the story. After all, the military authorities were willing to send over the American troops only if the European allies agreed to provide the balance of the forces needed to make an effective defense possible, and the JCS did believe that German forces would be needed for that purpose. So in that sense, from the military point of view, German rearmament was certainly a vital part of the package. But this was at the level of fundamental objectives, not at the level of tactics, and the basic JCS view was consistent with a relatively soft negotiating strategy: if the State Department (to paraphrase Nitze) had called for emphasizing the U.S. troop commitment and only then gradually "weaving in" the question of a German defense contribution, it is hard to believe that the JCS would have objected. But an agreement on the part of the JCS that all the elements of the problem were interconnected could be interpreted as a call for presenting the allies with a single package: the basic policy could be interpreted as translating directly into a particular negotiating strategy. The basic military point of view, in other words, could serve as cover—that is, as a kind of license for pursuing the sort of negotiating policy State Department officials considered essential at this point.[87] The fact that the military view could be interpreted (or misinterpreted) in this way—whether deliberately or not is not the issue here—made it easier for Acheson and his advisors to do what they probably really wanted to do in any case.

This is all quite speculative, of course, and there is really not enough evidence to get to the bottom of this particular issue. But these uncertainties should not be allowed to obscure the facts that the documents are able to establish. And one thing, at least, is very clear: the State Department did not fight the military over the package plan. If Acheson actually thought the tactics the U.S. government adopted were "murderous," he certainly had a very odd way of showing it.

---

course of the New York meeting, was particularly misleading. For the quotation and a discussion pointing out how inaccurate that account was, see McGeehan, *German Rearmament Question*, pp. 48–49.

[87] This point is suggested by the structure of the discussion of this issue in the Princeton Seminar: after establishing the basic point that the Pentagon had insisted on the package plan and was thus responsible for what happened in September (pp. 911, 915), Acheson and Nitze then felt free to ease up and talk about how the real reason why the German rearmament issue could not have been played down and "kind of weaved in gradually" had to do not with the JCS but rather with what McCloy was doing (p. 916). They then went on to say that McCloy, in fact, probably performed a service in forcing people to face the issue then and there (pp. 922–25).

Why is this story important? Partly because it shows how easy it is for scholars to get taken in by self-serving memoir accounts, and thus how crucial it is to test claims against the archival evidence; partly because of what it tells us about civil-military relations in the United States, about the willingness and ability of the military leadership to impose its views on issues of great political importance, and about the validity of the bureaucratic politics theory of policy-making in general; but mainly because of the light it throws on the political meaning of what happened in September 1950. The American government did not just stumble along and adopt a policy against its better judgment because of pressure from the military; the package policy was adopted quite deliberately; and that fact has a certain bearing on how American policy toward Europe during the early–Cold War period is to be interpreted.

There has been a certain tendency in recent years to idealize U.S.-European relations during the Cold War period. The argument is that the NATO system worked because, no matter how lopsided power relations were, the Americans did not simply insist on running the show. Instinctively the democratic countries dealt with the problems that arose in their relations with each other the same way they dealt with domestic issues: not through coercion, but through persuasion and compromise, "by cutting deals instead of imposing wills."[88] The democratic habit of compromise, of give and take, was the bedrock upon which the Atlantic Alliance was built. The Americans treated their allies with respect, and this, it is said, was one major reason why the Europeans were able to live with a system that rested so heavily on American power.[89]

The story of how the U.S. government managed the German rearmament issue in late 1950 suggests that things were not quite so simple. The Americans were capable of dealing rather roughly with their European allies, even on issues of absolutely central political importance. If the "package plan" story tells us nothing else, it certainly tells us that. And the fact that the Americans were capable of treating their allies that way had a certain bearing on how many people, especially in Europe, thought about core political issues.

In 1880, after a remarkable electoral campaign, William Gladstone was swept back into office as prime minister of Great Britain. Glad-

[88] John Lewis Gaddis, *We Now Know: Rethinking Cold War History* (Oxford: Clarendon, 1997), p. 201.

[89] Gaddis, *We Now Know*, 199–203, 288–89. The idea here of internal political norms projected outward was also a theme in the "democratic peace" literature of the 1990s. See for example Bruce Russett, *Grasping the Democratic Peace: Principles for a Post–Cold War World* (Princeton: Princeton University Press, 1993), p. 119.

stone, in that campaign, had laid out a series of principles on which British foreign policy was to be based; one fundamental aim was "to cultivate to the utmost the concert of Europe." Five years later, Gladstone's policy lay in ruins. He had managed to alienate every other major power in Europe—even France and Germany had come together in 1884 in a short-lived anti-British entente—and in 1885 his government fell from power. The Gladstone government had achieved its "long desired 'Concert of Europe'" all right, Lord Salisbury noted bitterly at the time. It had succeeded in "uniting the continent of Europe—against England."[90]

The parallel with American policy during the early–Cold War period is striking. The U.S. government very much wanted the European countries to come together as a political unit, and support for European unification was one of the basic tenets of American foreign policy in this period.[91] But it was not American preaching that led the Europeans to cooperate with each other and begin to form themselves into a bloc. The United States played an important role in the European integration process, but America had an impact mainly because of the kind of policy she pursued—a policy which, on occasion, did not pay due regard to the most basic interests of the European allies.

Acheson's policy in late 1950 is perhaps the most important case in point. Acheson was pressing for a course of action that would have greatly increased the risk of war at a time when western Europe was particularly vulnerable. The U.S. government could treat its allies like that—it could pursue a policy that might well have led to total disaster for Europe—only because the United States was so much stronger than any single European country. It followed that there had to be a counterweight to American power within the western alliance, a counterweight based on the sense that the Europeans had major strategic interests in

[90] R. W. Seton-Watson, *Britain in Europe, 1789–1914* (Cambridge, England: Cambridge University Press, 1938), 547; Lady Gwendolen Cecil, *Life of Robert Marquis of Salisbury,* vol. 3 (London: Hodder and Stoughton, 1931), p. 136.

[91] See especially Geir Lundestad, *"Empire" by Integration: The United States and European Integration, 1945–1997* (Oxford: Oxford University Press, 1998) and Pierre Mélandri, *Les États-Unis face à l'unification de l'Europe, 1945–1954* (Paris: A. Pedone, 1980). Note also an important series of interpretative articles on the subject by Klaus Schwabe: "Die Vereinigten Staaten und die Europäischen Integration: Alternativen der amerikanischen Außenpolitik," in Gilbert Trausch, ed., *Die Europäischen Integration vom Schuman-Plan bis zu den Verträgen von Rom* (Baden-Baden: Nomos, 1993); "The United States and European Integration," in Clemens Wurm, ed., *Western Europe and Germany: The Beginnings of European Integration, 1945–1969,* (Oxford: Berg, 1995); and "Atlantic Partnership and European Integration: American-European Policies and the German Problem, 1947–1969," in Geir Lundestad, ed., *No End to Alliance: The United States and Western Europe: Past, Present and Future* (New York: St. Martin's, 1998).

common and that those interests were distinct from those of the United States. The events of late 1950 helped push the Europeans—especially the French and the Germans—to that conclusion: it helped get them to see why they had to put their differences aside and come together as a kind of strategic unit. This episode thus plays an important role in the history of European integration, and indeed in the history of the western alliance as a whole.

CHAPTER FIVE

The Making of the Western Defense System:
France, the United States, and MC 48

In December 1954 the NATO Council formally adopted a document called MC 48, a report by the Alliance's Military Committee on "The Most Effective Pattern of NATO Military Strength for the Next Few Years." In approving this document, the Council authorized the military authorities of the Alliance to "plan and make preparations on the assumption that atomic and thermonuclear weapons will be used in defense from the outset."[1]

This article was originally written in French for delivery at a conference on France and NATO held in Paris in February 1996. That version was published in Maurice Vaïsse, Pierre Mélandri, and Frédéric Bozo, eds., *La France et l'OTAN, 1949–1996* (Paris: Éditions Complexe, 1996), and appears here in English for the first time.

[1] See Note de la Direction Politique, "Guerre atomique," December 13, 1954, *Documents diplomatiques français: 1954* (Paris, 1987), pp. 906–7; henceforth cited in this form: DDF 1954, pp. 906–7. On MC 48, see also U. S. Department of State, *Foreign Relations of the United States: 1952–1954*, vol. 5 (Washington, D.C., 1983), pp. 482–562 (henceforth cited in this form: FRUS 1952–54, 5:482–56); Robert J. Watson, *History of the Joint Chiefs of Staff*, vol. 5: *The Joint Chiefs of Staff and National Policy 1953–1954* (Washington, D.C.: Office of Joint History,1986), pp. 304–17; and three British documents: "Report by the Military Committee on the Most Effective Pattern of NATO Military Strength for the Next Few Years," Annex A to J.P.(54) 77 (Final), August 19, 1954, "Standing Group Report to the Military Committee on SACEUR's Capability Study, 1967," Annex to J.P.(54) 76 (Final), September 2, 1954, and "The Most Effective Pattern of NATO Military Strength for the Next Few Years: Report by the Joint Planning Staff," J.P.(54) 86 (Final), October 21, 1954, all in DEFE 6/26, British National Archives, Kew. As for the French sources, the most important ones—those found in the Blanc Papers in the Service Historique de l'Armée de Terre in Vincennes—will be cited below. But there is also one rather unusual source that should be cited: the "Mons notes," found at the end of Philippe Bernert, *Roger Wybot et la Bataille pour la D.S.T.* (Paris: Presses de la Cité, 1975). Robert Wampler is one of the few historians to have recognized the importance of MC 48 and his analysis is fundamental: Robert Wampler, "Ambiguous Legacy: The United States, Great Britain, and the Foundations of NATO Strategy, 1948–1957" (Ph.D. diss., Harvard University, 1991), chap. 9. For a summary, see Robert Wampler, "NATO Strategic Planning and Nuclear Weapons, 1950–1957," Nuclear History Program Occasional Paper 6 (College Park, Md.: Center for International Security Studies, 1990), pp. 11–19. [I should also note that after this article was originally written, the full text of MC 48 has been declassified and is available on the NATO Archives website (http://www.nato.int/docu/stratdoc/eng/a541122a.pdf). The September 2 British document cited above is now also available online (http://www.php .isn.ethz.ch/collections/colltopic.cfm?lng=en&id=18485&navinfo=14968). It was posted in 2002 as part of a collection of documents relating to NATO planning put together by William Burr and Robert Wampler under the auspices of the Parallel History Project called "Lift-

This was an event of absolutely fundamental importance in the history of the Atlantic Alliance. NATO was adopting a strategy which, as the French Chiefs of Staff noted, "for the first time would make it possible to actually defend Europe effectively."[2] The NATO Commander, General Alfred Gruenther, shared that view. Gruenther, who along with his very good friend Dwight Eisenhower was the principal architect of the new strategy, laid out his thinking in his "Capabilities Study," one of the key documents on which MC 48 was based. The adoption of this plan, Gruenther believed, would make it possible for the western forces, in the event of a Soviet attack, to hold the line in Europe even if they were outnumbered by the enemy. But he emphasized the point (as the French military authorities paraphrased his line of argument) that "this hope, which NATO can aspire to for the first time since it had come into being, was absolutely dependent" on three key conditions: (a) "the massive and immediate use of atomic and thermonuclear weapons, at the very start of hostilities," (b) "the effective participation of German forces in the defense effort," and (c) the reworking of the western defense structure, and the development of appropriate tactical doctrine, so that western forces could operate in an atomic environment.[3]

The basic idea here was simple. In a European war—and that meant *any* war between NATO and the USSR that broke out in Europe, including a war, for example, that resulted from a Soviet attack on Yugoslavia—there was only one option: "the only means of providing for the defense of Europe in the event of a Soviet attack is to unleash an immediate atomic and thermonuclear counter-attack."[4] The attack had to be massive, concentrated, and above all extremely rapid: "The Supreme Commander of Allied Forces in Europe (SACEUR) has built his thinking on the basic postulate that *the new weapons will be used at the first sign of hostility (dès la première manifestation d'hostilité)*." It was vital, in his

---

ing the Veil on Cosmic: Declassified US and British Documents on NATO Military Planning and Threat Assessments of the Warsaw Pact" (http://www.php.isn.ethz.ch/collections/colltopic.cfm?lng=en&id=14968).]

[2] "Avis du Comité des Chefs d'État-Major au sujet des problèmes soulevés par le Plan des Possibilités du Commandant Suprême Allié en Europe," September 6, 1954, Blanc Papers (fonds 1K145), box 2, Service Historique de l'Armée de Terre [SHAT], Vincennes. Emphasis in the original text.

[3] "Examen du 'Plan des Possibilités' établi par le commandement suprême des forces alliées en Europe," Blanc Papers (fonds 1K145), box 2, SHAT.

[4] "Examen du 'Plan des Possibilités'" (see n. 3), p. 10. For the reference to the different ways a war could begin (including the case of a Soviet attack on Yugoslavia), see p. 8: "all these different cases, which in political terms involve particularly delicate problems, in military terms have to be dealt with the same way—a way based on SACEUR's strategic concept."

view, that "NATO's air-atomic counter-attack" be launched "without loosing a minute."[5] The attack would be mounted with both tactical and strategic weapons—that is, against the sources of the enemy's military power in Russia itself, and, at the same time, against the enemy's forces and their supporting infrastructure in the European theater of operations. A covering force in Europe, using the "new weapons" and prepared to fight on a nuclear battlefield, could hold the line and defend western Europe during the relatively brief period at the beginning of the war when the Soviet threat was very great; after the air offensive had destroyed the sources of Soviet power in Russia itself, the threat to Europe would diminish quite rapidly. But to protect western Europe in such a war, it was absolutely essential to strike quickly. NATO's first order of business would be to attack the enemy's "atomic potential and his key positions: in this area, where the time factor is crucial, measures need to be taken to reduce to a minimum the time for decision," and for the implementation of the decision once it was made.[6]

The MC 48 strategy was thus a real strategy for the *defense* of Europe. It was not simply a strategy of deterrence. In the event of war, there was a good chance that western Europe could actually be protected; the Soviet Union, on the other hand, would be totally destroyed. But to shield Europe from Soviet retaliation—and the strategy was viable only if European society could be protected—it was essential to neutralize the nuclear potential of the adversary at the very start of the war. It was for this reason that it was crucial, according to SACEUR, to be able to "stop or to intercept the attack as soon as and wherever it was mounted"[7]— and that meant in practice that one had to destroy Soviet aircraft before they got off the ground, since active air defenses could not provide anything close to the necessary degree of assurance. The implication was that the Soviet air-atomic force had to be destroyed before it could actually launch an attack. It was for that reason that an extremely rapid and massive military operation was viewed as indispensable: the survival of western Europe in the event of war would depend on it.

This was why the adoption of this strategy was so extraordinarily important. In effect, NATO was contemplating preemptive war. To be sure, the language in the formal strategy documents was more ambiguous. But the real thinking is quite clear from the U.S. documents that are now available: nuclear weapons would be used; it was essential that the Soviet Union not be the first power to launch an atomic attack; it was therefore necessary that NATO strike first. It is, however, important to note that this was not an aggressive strategy: it first had

---

[5] "Avis du Comité des Chefs d'État-Major" (see n. 2); emphasis in the original text.
[6] "Examen du 'Plan des Possibilités'" (see n. 3).
[7] Ibid.

to be clear that war was unavoidable and that the Soviets were to blame for it. But as soon as it became clear that war was imminent, the attack had to be mounted without losing a minute. According to MC 48, the "immediate use" of nuclear weapons was essential; "any delay in their use—even measured in hours—could be fatal."[8] As President Eisenhower himself said, "[W]e must not allow the enemy to strike the first blow."[9]

So it was essential to act quickly. A long process of consultation within NATO was intolerable. But who would have the authority to launch the attack? This was "the most delicate question."[10] Key officials in Britain, France, and the United States understood the logic that lay at the heart of the strategy: rapid action was absolutely essential if Europe was to survive; but if decisions were to be made very quickly, the deci-sion-making process would have to be highly centralized. Indeed, one of the basic ideas that lay at the heart of the new strategy was that SA-CEUR himself would be making the crucial decisions. As Gruenther put it in his "Capabilities Study," the "authority to implement the planned use of atomic weapons must be such as to ensure that no delay

[8] Sullivan memorandum for General Norstad on the history of NATO doctrine, June 1, 1962, Norstad Papers, box 90, file "NATO General (2)," Dwight D. Eisenhower Library, Abilene, Kansas. President Eisenhower took the same line. "Victory or defeat," he said, "could hang upon minutes and seconds used decisively at top speed or tragically wasted in indecision." Eisenhower to Churchill, January 22, 1955, cited in Wampler, "Ambiguous Leg-acy," p. 648.

[9] Cited in David Rosenberg's very important article, "The Origins of Overkill: Nuclear Weapons and American Strategy, 1945-1960," *International Security* 7, no. 4 (Spring 1983): 47.

[10] "Examen du 'Plan des Possibilités'" (see n. 3), p. 12. It was important, according to this document, to work a procedure that would allow SACEUR to respond to a Soviet attack by launching an "instantaneous air counter-attack" ("une contre-attaque aérienne instan-tanée"). The procedure that had to be worked out well before the onset of hostilities, had to take into account both "serious concerns about military effectiveness, and especially about the importance of rapid response, which SACEUR has emphasized," and had "to avoid tak-ing the initiative too impulsively in an area as serious as this one." The British were also worried about how to strike the right balance. Here, for example, is a passage from a British document on Gruenther's "Capability Study": "Politically the implications of initiating atomic warfare are so grave that there would be the greatest objection to delegating the deci-sion to use atomic weapons to SACEUR. Militarily there is no question now as to the impor-tance of instant atomic retaliation to any major attack whether with or without the use of atomic weapons; this will be of even greater importance by 1957 since SACEUR's forces will be committed to the atomic warfare strategy. . . . The proposal in the Standing Group Draft goes some way towards meeting SACEUR's requirement but still leaves open the question of what will happen in the event of there not being time for SACEUR to obtain the Council's consent to a General Alert. Militarily it is desirable to give SACEUR discretion in this event, politically this is probably impossible." Standing Group Report to the Military Committee on SACEUR's Capability Study, 1957, September 2, 1954, Annex to J.P. (54) 76 (Final), DEFE 6/26, PRO.

whatsoever will occur in countering a surprise attack." And, as it turned out, a large measure of predelegation was, in fact, part and parcel of the MC 48 system. SACEUR, at least until the Kennedy era, had a significant amount of predelegated authority in this very fundamental area.[11]

But could the Europeans really go along with the idea that a foreigner, and in fact a military officer, would be making this life-or-death decision essentially by himself? The extraordinary thing is that whatever qualms they might have felt, they *did* accept it, quite willingly. The MC 48 strategy was not forced on them by the Americans. The Europeans did not simply go along with it reluctantly or grudgingly. Key British officials fully agreed with the U.S. point of view, and the French—at least in military circles—were also quite pleased with the new strategy.

To be sure, the Americans dominated the process that led to MC 48. General Dwight Eisenhower, the first SACEUR, and president since January 1953, knew what he wanted. He did not like the strategy adopted by his successor as NATO commander, General Matthew Ridgway. Ridgway, in his view, was too conservative, too unwilling to take the "new weapons" into account. One major objection was that Ridgway's plans did not take the effects of the U.S. strategic offensive into account. It was as though NATO and the U.S. Strategic Air Command (SAC) were going to fight two entirely separate wars—and this was obviously absurd, for all kinds of reasons. So Eisenhower took a series of decisive actions. He got rid of the Joint Chiefs of Staff (JCS) that he had inherited—a very unusual act in the American political system. He then brought Ridgway back to Washington as the new Army Chief of Staff; the other Chiefs whom he appointed, especially Admiral Radford, the new JCS chairman, and General Twining, the new Air Force Chief of Staff, placed a much heavier emphasis on the air-atomic offensive. Eisenhower thus guaranteed that the JCS would be divided on the most fundamental issues of military strategy, and that he himself would be the arbiter. And by moving Ridgway to Washington, he had created an opening at NATO headquarters, which he soon filled by making Gruenther the new SACEUR. And Gruenther, with the full support of the president, was able to stage-manage the process that led to the adoption of the new strategy.

But if the Americans dominated the process, that does not mean that the Europeans accepted it reluctantly. One can almost say the opposite. The French military authorities had for quite some time shared Gruenther's point of view. The Ridgway strategy was bankrupt: the West

---

[11] Gruenther is quoted in the British document on the Capabilities Study cited in n. 1. On the predelegation arrangements, see especially Wampler, "Ambiguous Legacy," and Rosenberg, "The Origins of Overkill."

simply did not have the resources to build an effective defense on the basis of his ideas. The French authorities, in fact, had called for a new strategy in 1953. They felt that it was necessary to take account of the effects of the SAC air offensive—above all, its ability to neutralize the Soviet nuclear capability. And they also agreed that NATO, in its operations in the European theater, had to adjust to the nuclear revolution—that is, it had to be prepared to fight on a nuclear battlefield.[12] The JCS and the British Chiefs of Staff were more reticent, but Lord Ismay, the NATO Secretary-General, agreed fully with the French point of view. And at the three-power Bermuda summit conference of December 1953, the two most important European allies supported Ismay's proposal to take a "new look at NATO defense"; "NATO strategy," the French foreign minister said, "must take into account [the] use [of] new weapons."[13]

So it is not at all surprising that the French Chiefs of Staff endorsed the MC 48 strategy. For the French military authorities, "the fact that Europe cannot be defended against an attack from the east without the use of atomic weapons leads to the acceptance of the principle that this weapon will be used, first of all to discourage the aggressor, and if necessary to defeat him." From their point of view, the key question was simple: could Europe be defended if SACEUR's basic thesis was rejected? "The answer is no;" "on this point, the opinion of the highest Military Authorities is formal and unanimous."[14] The French military leaders fully accepted the principle that the new weapons would be used "at the first sign of hostility." They also officially approved of the idea that nuclear weapons would be fully integrated into the western defense structure, and that forces in the theater would be tied closely to the American strategic force, arrangements, they said, which "up to the present the French authorities have never stopped calling for."[15] This

[12] See Pierre Billotte, *Le passé au futur* (Paris: Stock, 1979), pp. 41–42, 58–59; Alphonse Juin, *Mémoires*, vol. 2 (Paris: Fayard, 1960), pp. 255–58; Bernard Pujo, *Juin, Maréchal de France* (Paris: A. Michel, 1988), pp. 294–96, and, above all, a memorandum from the French État-Major des Forces Armées (English translation), November 11, 1953, Ismay Papers III/12/13a, Liddell Hart Centre for Military Archives, King's College, London. See also various documents in the Blanc Papers, box 2, SHAT, Vincennes.

[13] See, for example, summaries of foreign ministers' meetings, December 6, 1953, FRUS 1952–54, 5:1789–93.

[14] "Examen du 'Plan des Possibilités'" (see n. 3).

[15] "Avis du Comité des Chefs d'État-Major (see n. 2). In other documents, the French military authorities claimed credit for having pressed for a strategy of this sort. General Blanc, for example, the Army Chief of Staff, in some remarks he made to the Conseil Supérieur des Forces Armées shortly before MC 48 was officially adopted by the NATO Council, made a point of noting the major role the French military authorities had played in the process that had led to the new strategy. He referrred specifically to "the reform of the military system and to the way the forces are structured, an idea put forward by General Ely in the NATO

was the only way that the "forward strategy"—a strategy of defending Europe as far to the east as possible—could be made viable. And from the French point of view, it was essential that the forward strategy be adopted: it was the only alternative to the so-called "peripheral strategy"—that is, to the abandonment, in the event of war, of all of continental western Europe. And the forward strategy was necessary for another fundamental reason, for France and for the West as a whole: it was essential if West Germany was to be brought into the western system; the Germans had to feel that they were being defended, that NATO was protecting them.

And in fact it was within the framework of the new strategy that the French military authorities reaffirmed their acceptance of German rearmament: the forward strategy, which now had a real chance of being effective thanks to MC 48, meant that the Federal Republic had to be rearmed. This was, as the French Chiefs of Staff put it, a "necessity resulting from geography." NATO would be preparing to fight a war on German soil; it could make the necessary preparations only if the Germans themselves actively approved of, and in fact participated in, the common defense effort.[16] That was SACEUR's opinion, and the French military leaders fully agreed with the conclusions he had reached.

And the government headed by Pierre Mendès France accepted this whole analysis. On September 10, 1954, the Comité de Défense Nationale officially approved the new strategy. Mendès, to be sure, thought that the core issue was "too serious to leave entirely in the hands of the military authorities," and that in an emergency the fundamental decisions would have to be made by the political leadership. "The need to act with extreme rapidity" meant that it would not be possible to consult "with all the members of NATO." The French instead proposed that the key decision would be made by the political equivalent of the three-power NATO Standing Group: the ultimate decision, that is, would be made by the United States, Great Britain, and France.[17]

The U.S. government was against this idea, but it did not oppose the

---

Standing Group as early as 1950, and supported by General Valluy with a tenacity that is today bearing its fruit." Général Blanc's remarks in the Conseil Supérieur des Forces Armées, November 5, 1954, Blanc Papers (fonds 1K145), box 4, SHAT.

[16] "Avis du Comité des Chefs d'État-Major" (see n. 2). This side of the story has been emphasized by Pierre Guillen in his important article, "Les Chefs militaires français, le réarmement de l'Allemagne et la CED (1950–1954)," *Revue d'histoire de la deuxième guerre mondiale et des conflits contemporains*, no. 129 (janvier 1983): 6–7.

[17] Mons to Chevallier, October 9, 1954, Blanc Papers (fonds 1K145), box 2, SHAT; Dulles-Mendès meeting, November 11, 1954, "Secretary of State's Memoranda of Conversation, November 1952 to December 1954," *Foreign Relations of the United States*, microfiche supplement, no. 800; Mons notes (see n. 1); Mendès to Bonnet, November 30, 1954, and Note de la direction politique: Guerre atomique, December 13, 1954, DDF 1954, nos. 399, 444.

French head on. It agreed in principle that the civilian authorities would make the final decision, but it stressed the point that it was important to avoid setting up formal machinery that might make it hard to take extremely rapid action—something that might have to be done if Europe was to be defended effectively. It therefore accepted the principle that there should be informal consultations at the political level—but only when there was time for that. The key thing here, however, is that the Americans did not want to give up their freedom of action.

The Mendès France government had little trouble going along with this arrangement, even though it knew full well what was at stake. It understood that the "political authorities' freedom of decision will, in practice . . . be considerably limited, when the western forces as a whole are prepared only to fight an atomic war."[18] But it was essential that the public not understand the real significance of what was in the process of being decided. The "political sensitivity" of the decision on MC 48, Mendès insisted, had to be "emphasized to the allies." Secrecy had to be maintained; if the decision became known, the effect could be disastrous; the French government felt, in fact, that such a turn of events had to be "absolutely avoided."[19]

But as far as the substance of the new strategy was concerned, there is no doubt what the French attitude was. The Mendès France government fully agreed with France's allies. It fully supported MC 48. To be sure, its "freedom of decision would be limited." But the freedom of action of the American political authorities would also be limited—and this was an element of balance, quite important for the Europeans. In accepting MC 48, Britain, France, and the other countries of western Europe were giving up a lot, but the concessions they were making were not totally one-sided. The new strategy might have limited their sovereignty—that is, their ability to decide between war and peace—in a rather extraordinary way, but a loss for them was not a pure gain for the United States. Under MC 48, military imperatives dominated the situation; the hands of the political authorities in Washington were also, to a certain extent, tied; the authority that had been delegated to SACEUR, in his capacity as the U.S. commander in Europe (CINCEUR), meant that the freedom of action of the U.S. political leadership in Washington was also limited. And it is important to realize that in cre-

---

[18] Dulles-Mendès meeting, November 11, 1954; Dulles-Makins meeting, December 4 and 8, 1954; Dulles-Eisenhower meeting, December 14, 1954; tripartite meeting, December 16, 1954; all in "Secretary of State's Memoranda of Conversation, November 1952 to December 1954" (see n. 17), nos. 800, 827. 838, 849, 853; Note de la Direction Politique: Guerre atomique, December 13, 1954, DDF 1954, no. 444.

[19] Mendès remarks in Mons notes (see n. 1); Mons to Chevallier, October 9, 1954, Blanc Papers (fonds 1K145), box 2, SHAT, Vincennes.

ating that system, the U.S. government knew what it was doing. Eisenhower remained at heart a military man, and it was as a military professional that he approached the problem of the defense of western Europe.

One very important consequence of the new strategy from the European point of view had to do with what was called "nuclear sharing"—that is, with the provision of American nuclear weapons to the NATO allies. The basic idea that military imperatives were of absolutely fundamental importance and that all other considerations had to take a back seat to them implied that all the NATO armies should be organized and armed according to the same principles—that is, that one could not discriminate between the various national armies. As U.S. Secretary of State John Foster Dulles put it, "As far as we are concerned, we did not think it possible to contemplate a situation in which there were first and second class powers in NATO."[20] The basic principle that NATO strategy was built on—the idea that the forces should be used without regard to national differences, and that they should be armed and deployed on the basis of functional military criteria—implied that the European forces should be armed the same way the American army was, and that they should all be organized in accordance with a single overarching strategic concept. MC 48 thus implied the nuclear armament of western Europe. After all, the fundamental assumption here was that a war in Europe would be nuclear from the very outset. Nuclear weapons would thus be normal. They would be the only weapons that mattered. And it was quite clear to top U.S. officials that it was impossible to say that these weapons were normal and at the same time that the European countries could not have them. Such a situation was not healthy, Dulles and Eisenhower thought, and the Atlantic alliance would "fall apart" if the U.S. government tried to keep those weapons out of the hands of its allies.[21] So the Americans agreed that the new strategic concept meant that "everyone will have an atomic capability"—this, in fact, was the "implication of MC 48."[22]

The nuclear sharing policy was thus a fundamental element of the Eisenhower strategy. The truth here is very simple, even if, for a vari-

[20] Dulles-Brentano meeting, November 21, 1957, 740.5/11-2157, Department of State Central Files, RG 59, U.S. National Archives, College Park, Md.

[21] According to Dulles, the United States could not tell its allies "in effect that these new weapons are becoming conventional weapons, and at the same time tell them that they cannot have such weapons. He [Dulles] felt that now is the time for a decision in this matter—the alternative is that the alliances will fall apart." Eisenhower-Dulles meeting, October 22, 1957, Ann Whitman File, Dwight Eisenhower Diaries, box 27, October '57 Staff Notes (1), Eisenhower Library, Abilene, Kans.

[22] Anglo-American meeting, December 11, 1956, FRUS 1955–57, 4:125. See also the Goodpaster memoranda of November 4 and 16, 1954, FRUS 1952–54, 5:533–35.

ety of reasons, the main western governments had an interest, especially from 1961 on, in keeping people from seeing it: the Eisenhower administration *wanted* to share America's nuclear weapons with the main European allies. At the beginning of 1956, for example, Dulles "spontaneously" outlined basic U.S. policy in this area in a meeting with Maurice Couve de Murville, at that time the French ambassador in Washington. The Secretary of State, to be sure, was not in favor of the manufacture of nuclear weapons in Europe: a wasteful duplication of effort within the western alliance was to be avoided. But (as Couve reported his remarks) "since the United States had such a lead in this area and was able to produce atomic weapons relatively inexpensively," Dulles "had never understood why the allies should spend money and make a major effort to build them." But the arming of the Europeans with weapons built in America was another matter entirely. "The only problem," according to Dulles, was the legal problem having to do with the "American law forbidding the transfer of such weapons to foreign countries." U.S. leaders were going to try to change the legislation in this area, but there would be "strong resistance" in Congress to any change in the law. Dulles, however, was "convinced that the necessary authorizations would be forthcoming." It was essential, he said, "that the American government be able to supply the armies of its European allies with atomic weapons, and it didn't matter much whether those weapons were transferred to them right away or whether they were simply stockpiled in Europe for the Europeans to use when the time came."[23]

Dulles's concerns about Congress proved to be warranted, and the administration did not succeed in its attempt to bring about a radical change in the McMahon Act (as the Atomic Energy Act was often called). A frustrated Eisenhower, convinced that the act was unconstitutional (it both violated the basic constitutional principle of the separation of powers and infringed on the president's constitutional prerogatives as commander-in-chief) felt entitled to do an end-run around the law. The delivery systems would be given to the allies; the warheads would remain officially in U.S. custody, which meant that technically the government would not be violating the law; but custody arrangements were designed to be so weak that the European allies would have effective control of the weapons.

This was the policy that Dulles explained to the French leaders in November 1957. The United States, he said, "hoped to be in a position to station intermediate range missiles in NATO countries towards the end of 1958. He hoped that it would be possible that such missiles could be

---

[23] Couve de Murville to Massigli (Secretary General at the Quai d'Orsay), February 2, 1956, Massigli Papers, vol. 96, French Foreign Ministry Archives, Paris.

available for use by any NATO country concerned in the event of hostilities in accordance with NATO strategy. The nuclear warheads would have to remain *technically* under U.S. custody"—"*nominalement* sous garde américaine," in the French record of the meeting. But the warheads, Dulles assured the French, "would be located where best use could be made of them; the troops of the country concerned would be stationed in the vicinity; the country *would be assured that in the event of war the warheads located there would be made immediately available to it.*"[24]

Dulles took the same line in a meeting with General Charles de Gaulle in 1958. The United States, he said, "was seeking to develop within the limits of our legislation a concept and practice for modern weapons, particularly tactical nuclear weapons, to be available in the NATO area under such conditions that the countries concerned would have complete confidence that such weapons would in effect be used in accordance with plans worked out in advance, rather than to have to depend on a political decision from far away." He wanted to work out arrangements with the French that would "ensure that in the event of a major attack on French or U.S. forces in Europe, nuclear weapons available to NATO would be used immediately without having to depend on a U.S. political decision, concerning which the French might have some doubts."[25]

And in fact, by the end of the Eisenhower period, U.S. nuclear weapons were effectively in the hands of the NATO allies. The U.S. custody arrangements were essentially nominal. This was the result of a deliberate policy. As Eisenhower himself said, the United States was "willing to give, to all intents and purposes, control of the weapons. We retain titular possession only."[26]

This policy of nuclear sharing was in fact one of the key elements in the history of this period. A nuclearization of the alliance meant in particular a nuclearization of West Germany, and that question lay at the heart of the great Berlin crisis of 1958–62, the central episode of the Cold War. And the dropping of the nuclear sharing policy by the Kennedy administration in 1961 was one of the most important events in the history of the Atlantic alliance, and the fundamental cause of the NATO crisis of the early 1960s.

The history of NATO during the 1950s and in the Kennedy period is not well understood even today. Most of the historians who have dealt

[24] Dulles-Pineau meeting, November 19, 1957, 740.5/11-1957, Department of State Central Files, USNA. For the French record, see DDF 1957, 2:712. Emphasis added (for both documents).

[25] Franco-American talks, July 5, 1958, FRUS 1958–60, 7:II:55–56. For the French record, see DDF 1958, 2:24.

[26] Eisenhower-Norstad meeting, June 9, 1959, FRUS 1958–60, 7:I:462.

with this period write as though the nuclear sharing policy never existed. As for MC 48, its importance is rarely appreciated. But it is not by chance that historical interpretation has these blind spots. The political interests of governments on both sides of the Atlantic have certainly come into play. In the United States, the idea that American policy has been consistent—that every U.S. administration from 1945 on, including the Eisenhower administration, was against the spread of nuclear weapons—provided an easy defense of the policy most U.S. governments have pursued since 1961. And it is obviously for that reason that for years the documents that showed the contrary were redacted (or "sanitized," to use the standard but very revealing term) before they were released.[27] In France, the same myth about America's unwillingness to see nuclear weapons in the hands of her allies provided a certain rationale for the policies pursued by General de Gaulle and his successors. It was clear, according to the Gaullists, that no American government could pursue a generous policy in this area; France therefore had little choice but to pursue the policy whose basic lines had been laid out by General de Gaulle.

But that's the past. Today we have a good deal of evidence—above all American, but also British, French, and German—bearing on this question. For the first time, it is possible to write the history of this extraordinary period the way its history in general needs to be written: by putting political preconceptions aside and trying to tell the story as it's revealed in the documents. Now that the Cold War is over, and evidence has become much more freely available, we're finally in a position to rethink this whole period. The end of the Cold War marks the beginning of a golden age for historians of the nuclear era.

[27] For two examples, see the second and third documents linked to a short piece I wrote on "declassification analysis" (http://www.sscnet.ucla.edu/polisci/faculty/trachtenberg/documents/doclist.html).

CHAPTER SIX

The Structure of Great Power Politics, 1963–75

JOHN F. KENNEDY's most fundamental goal as president of the United States was to reach a political understanding with the Soviet Union. That understanding would be based on a simple principle: America and Russia were both very great powers and therefore needed to respect each other's most fundamental interests. The United States was thus prepared, for its part, to recognize the USSR's special position in eastern Europe. America would also see to it that West Germany would not become a nuclear power.[1] In exchange, the Soviets would also have to accept the status quo in central Europe, especially in Berlin. If a settlement of that sort could be worked out, the situation in central Europe would be stabilized. The great problem that lay at the heart of the Cold War would be resolved.

But to reach a settlement based on those principles, Kennedy, in effect, had to fight a war on two fronts. He had to get both the USSR and his own allies in Europe to accept this sort of arrangement. The Soviets, however, were not particularly receptive when it became clear to them, beginning in mid-1961, what the president had in mind. The Americans, in their view, were making concessions because they were afraid the Berlin Crisis would lead to war. Why not see what more they might get by keeping the crisis going?

As for the Europeans, they by no means welcomed the new Kennedy policy with open arms. The West German government was especially distraught. Germany was divided and there was obviously not much

This is an expanded version of a paper that was published in the second volume of Melvyn P. Leffler and Odd Arne Westad, eds., *The Cambridge History of the Cold War* (Cambridge, England: Cambridge University Press, 2010). Reprinted with permission.

[1] Note especially Kennedy's comments to Soviet leader Nikita Khrushchev at the Vienna summit conference in June 1961. Kennedy assured his Soviet counterpart that the United States did not "wish to act in a way that would deprive the Soviet Union of its ties in Eastern Europe" and that it was also "opposed to a buildup in West Germany that would constitute a threat to the Soviet Union." Khrushchev would have had no problem understanding what Kennedy was driving at. Kennedy-Khrushchev meetings, June 4, 1961, *Foreign Relations of the United States* [FRUS], *1961–1963*, vol. 14, pp. 87–98 (the quotations are on pp. 91 and 95); henceforth cited in the form: FRUS 1961–63, 14:87–98. That Kennedy was telling Khrushchev that the United States recognized eastern Europe as a Soviet sphere of influence is also suggested by the fact that the U.S. government found that statement of his embarrassing as late as 1990: the sentence about eastern Europe, published in 1993 on p. 95 of the FRUS volume, had been "sanitized" out of the version of the document released three years earlier.

anyone could do about it. But for years the German government—the conservative government that Konrad Adenauer had led since the founding of the Federal Republic in 1949—had insisted that those "realities" could not be officially recognized. To do so would put a kind of seal of approval on the division of their country. Nor was the Adenauer government pleased by what the Americans had in mind with regard to Germany's nuclear status. A Germany with no nuclear forces under her own control would be utterly dependent on the United States for her security. Could any great nation rely so totally on a foreign power for its protection and accept the sort of extreme political dependence that such a situation implied? The Germans, of course, knew they had to pay a price for what their country had done during the Hitler period, and this meant that for the time being certain constraints in this area had to be accepted. But the German government also felt it needed to do what it could to keep the Federal Republic's nuclear options open, and so it did not take kindly to the idea of formalizing Germany's non-nuclear status, above all as part of a general settlement with the USSR.

The French, for other reasons, did not like the way Kennedy was playing the western hand. It was not that they objected in principle to the sort of understanding with the Soviets he had in mind, but they felt he was giving away too much too quickly at a time when a lot more in the way of backbone was in order. Even the British were somewhat taken aback, in late 1961, by the Kennedy policy. But the president was prepared to move ahead regardless: the Europeans would have to "come along or stay behind."[2]

He was particularly rough with the Germans. The conflict came to a head in early 1963, albeit in a much harsher way than Kennedy had wanted. A line was drawn in the sand. If the Germans wanted to pursue an independent policy—a policy based on a strong alignment with the France of Charles de Gaulle, a policy, that is, with a distinct anti-American edge—they could just forget about American military protection. If they wanted America to provide for their security, they would have to follow America's political lead. They would have to cooperate, in other words, with the policy Kennedy was now pursuing vis-à-vis Russia. And the Germans made their choice. Adenauer was forced out as chancellor and the Federal Republic more or less formally declared loyalty to the NATO alliance and to the United States.

By that point, the conflict with Russia had come to a head. The Cuban Missile Crisis of October 1962 was the climax of the great Berlin Crisis of 1958–62. The Soviets had not been willing to make peace on Kennedy's terms and had instead threatened the United States with war. The situation in Europe had actually worsened in mid-1962. But now, after

[2] Kennedy to Rusk, August 21, 1961, FRUS 1961–63, 14:359.

the missile crisis, that Soviet policy was clearly bankrupt. The Soviets were still unwilling to make a formal deal, but the major powers reached certain more or less tacit understandings: the status quo in Berlin would be respected, and West Germany would be kept non-nuclear. Indeed, one of the main goals of the Limited Nuclear Test Ban Treaty, negotiated in Moscow in July 1963—a treaty which the Germans were essentially made to sign—was to help guarantee that West Germany would not be able to build nuclear weapons. But this was not a simple gift to the Russians. It was linked to other understandings, most notably relating to Berlin, that mainly benefited the western powers.

Taken as a bloc, those understandings provided the basis for a relatively stable international order. But many Germans—the German "Gaullists," as now ex-Chancellor Adenauer and those who basically shared his views were called—were bitter about the course that events had taken. German interests, as they saw it, had been sacrificed so that the United States could pursue its own goals. The Germans, as one of them put it, were the "victims of America's détente policy."[3] But in West Germany in 1963 that was a minority view, even in Adenauer's own party. Most Germans were coming to see things in a rather different light.

It was important, Kennedy argued, in a speech he gave during his famous visit to Berlin in June 1963, "to face the facts as they are, not to involve ourselves in self-deception." It was "not enough," he said, "to mark time, to adhere to a status quo, while awaiting a change for the better."[4] His meaning was clear: the rigid German policy of the past had to be abandoned. But the German people, by and large, were not appalled by those remarks. The Adenauer approach had not brought reunification any closer, so maybe it was time for something new. There was also a certain sense that the Federal Republic could not be too out-of-step with her western partners, none of whom (as de Gaulle often put it) were in any rush to see Germany reunified.[5] The Federal Republic could not afford to pursue a totally independent policy. The country had to frame its policy with an eye to what its allies, and especially the United States, were willing to support.

Egon Bahr, who served as chief advisor to Willy Brandt (the mayor of

[3] Krone diary, August 5, 1963, *Adenauer-Studien* 3 (1974): 178.

[4] Address at the Free University of Berlin, June 26, 1963, in *Public Papers of the Presidents: John F. Kennedy: 1963* (Washington, D.C.: GPO, 1964), p. 527.

[5] See Helga Haftendorn, *NATO and the Nuclear Revolution: A Crisis of Credibility* (Oxford: Clarendon, 1996), pp. 10, 22 n.27; and Thomas Schwartz, *Lyndon Johnson and Europe: In the Shadow of Vietnam* (Cambridge, Mass.: Harvard University Press, 2003), pp. 22–23, 134–35. Note also Klein to Bundy, August 5, 1964, Declassified Documents Reference System (online version), document number CK3100499982; henceforth cited in this form: DDRS/CK3100499982.

West Berlin and the leading figure in the German Social Democratic Party), made the key point in a famous speech he gave in July 1963, just three weeks after Kennedy's visit to Berlin. The Americans were pursuing a peace policy, he said, a policy based on the idea that "the interests of the other side had to be recognized and taken into account"—on the idea, that is, that the status quo, for the time being at least, had to be accepted. In such circumstances, the old German hard-line policy was "hopelessly antiquated and unreal." It was simply "senseless." The Germans, on the other hand, could play a positive role in the détente process. Indeed, if they did not want to exclude themselves and just sit on the sidelines as America pursued that policy, they would have to pursue an active détente policy of their own.[6] A détente policy, a policy that sought to relax tensions in central Europe, might eventually lead to major changes in the Cold War status quo. At the very least, in the view of people like Bahr, better relations with the Soviet Union might reduce the Federal Republic's extraordinary dependence on the United States, and thus might create more room for maneuver: Germany would be better able to pursue a policy based on her own national interests.

By the end of the decade Brandt had become chancellor and Bahr was his right-hand man. Their way of thinking had strong support, not only in their own party, but also in the Free Democratic Party (FDP), the junior partner in the governing coalition. It was also supported to one degree or another by important elements in the conservative parties. Brandt and Bahr were thus able to pursue their policy of improving relations with the east—their Ostpolitik. The Soviets were receptive, their western partners were supportive (for the time being at least), and by 1973 a whole package of agreements had been signed and ratified: treaties providing for the "inviolability" of existing borders in central Europe, a treaty establishing a framework for relations between the two German states; a four-power treaty securing the status quo in Berlin; and the Nuclear Non-Proliferation Treaty (NPT), whose importance for

---

[6] Bahr Tutzing speech, July 15, 1963, *Dokumente zur Deutschlandpolitik*, 4th series, vol. 9, part 2, pp. 572–75. The idea that the Ostpolitik was rooted in the sense that the Federal Republic had to adjust to the changing international environment is a major theme in the German historical literature in this area. See, for example, a number of works by Werner Link: "Die Aussenpolitik und internationale Einordnung der Bundesrepublik Deutschland," in Werner Weidenfeld and Hartmut Zimmermann, eds., *Deutschland-Handbuch: Ein doppelte Bilanz 1949–1989* (Munich: Carl Hanser Verlag, 1989), p. 579; "Détente auf deutsch und Anpassung an Amerika: Die Bonner Ostpolitik," in Detlef Junker, ed., *Die USA und Deutschland im Zeitalter des Kalten Krieges 1945–1990* (Stuttgart: Deutsche Verlags-Anstalt, 2001), 2:55–65; and above all his contribution to Karl Dietrich Bracher, Wolfgang Jäger, and Werner Link, *Republik im Wandel 1969–1974: Die Ära Brandt*, vol. 5, part I, of the *Geschichte der Bundesrepublik Deutschland* (Stuttgart: Deutsche Verlags-Anstalt, 1986), esp. pp. 276–78.

the Soviets lay mainly in the fact that it would help keep Germany non-nuclear.

This was, of course, very similar to what Kennedy had wanted, and it is tempting to see this set of arrangements as essentially a formalization of the sort of system that had more or less come into being in a much less official way in 1963. It is tempting, in other words, to view the Ostpolitik treaties as just the icing on the cake—to assume that the system of great power relations in Europe, the heart of the international political system, was already quite stable, and that the only difference now was that this fact was getting a kind of formal recognition. But in reality the system had a basic structural flaw: the military foundation on which it rested was not rock-solid. How stable the system would end up being would depend, in large measure, on how that military problem was dealt with.

THE NATO NUCLEAR PROBLEM

During the Cold War, western Europe lived in the shadow of Soviet military power, and the NATO countries obviously had to be concerned with the military balance on the continent. If there were no effective counterweight to Soviet power in Europe, the Europeans would be at the mercy of the USSR. Even if the Red Army never actually invaded western Europe, an imbalance of military power, it was assumed, would almost certainly have far-reaching political consequences.

What sort of counterweight could be put in place? During the heyday of American nuclear superiority, the period from late 1952 through mid-1963, this question had a very simple answer: the Soviets could be deterred from invading western Europe by the threat of U.S. nuclear retaliation. And this was a threat the U.S. government might actually execute in extreme circumstances: if the U.S. attack was massive enough and was launched quickly enough, America would not suffer really heavy damage from whatever counterattack the Soviets were able to mount. But by September 1963 the U.S. government had reached the conclusion that even if the United States were to "attack the USSR first, the loss to the U.S. would be unacceptable to political leaders." It was understood at once that the United States could no longer, even in theory, respond to an act of aggression in Europe with a full-scale attack on the USSR.[7]

How then could NATO Europe be protected? In principle, there was

---

[7] NSC meeting, September 12, 1963 (Report of Net Evaluation Subcommittee), FRUS 1961–63, 8:499–500.

a simple solution to the problem. If the Europeans allies—and especially West Germany, the most exposed country—would some day no longer be able to count on the American nuclear deterrent, maybe they would have to build deterrent forces they themselves could control. This logic was clear enough even in the mid-1950s, and the Germans in particular were quite interested in acquiring a nuclear force of their own, perhaps as part of some kind of European nuclear force. The idea that the Germans were never interested in anything of the sort is simply a myth. Adenauer, for example, certainly wanted Germany to have nuclear weapons—"we must produce them," he said in 1957—and Ludwig Erhard, who succeeded him as chancellor, told President Johnson in 1965 that "it was impossible to assume that Germany will go forever without a nuclear deterrent."[8] The Germans very much wanted

[8] Adenauer quoted in Hans-Peter Schwarz, *Adenauer*, vol. 2 (Stuttgart: Deutsche Verlags-Anstalt, 1991), p. 396; Johnson-Erhard meeting, December 20, 1965, FRUS 1964–68, 13:291. In November 1964, Adenauer explained why, as Chancellor, he had immediately accepted the American proposal for a multilateral force. He was convinced, he said, that in all probability things would develop in such a way that "in the near future somehow or other we would manage to get nuclear weapons" ("dass hochstwährscheinlich die Entwicklung in der Welt so verlaufen werde, dass wir irgendwie auch in die Nähe der nuklearen Waffen kommen müssen"). Notes of CDU/CSU parliamentary group, November 3, 1964, in Corinna Franz, ed., *Die CDU/CSU-Fraktion im Deutschen Bundestag: Sitzungsprotokolle 1961–1966*, 2:1248. This, according to one leading scholar, was the standard view in the German political leadership at the time. Klaus Hildebrand, *Von Erhard zur Grossen Koalition 1963–1969*, vol. 4 of the *Geschichte der Bundesrepublik Deutschland* (Stuttgart: Deutsche Verlags-Anstalt, 1984), p. 102—Hildebrand quotes that Adenauer comment in this passage. Note also Adenauer's comments in the parliamentary group's executive committee, October 11, 1965, in *Die CDU/CSU-Fraktion im Deutschen Bundestag*, 3:1569. Erhard was more cautious, but it is clear he thought that Germany needed to participate in some sort of nuclear defense system—that Germany could not remain a nonnuclear power forever—and he was particularly interested in seeing if some kind of nuclear relationship could be worked out with France. See his comments in *Die CDU/CSU-Fraktion im Deutschen Bundestag*, 2:1344 (Jan. 26, 1965—especially the phrase "not at this moment"); 3:1573 (October 11, 1965); 3:1980 (September 20, 1966); 3:1996 (October 4, 1966); and, with regard to the overtures to France, 3:1593 (October 20, 1965) and 3:1750 (March 15, 1966). The Germans had long hoped to work out some kind of collaborative arrangement with France, and during the Adenauer period de Gaulle had sometimes made encouraging noises along these lines. The issue played a certain role in the mid-1960s. See especially Matthias Schulz, "Integration durch eine europäische Atomstreitmacht? Nuklearambitionen und die deutsche Europa-Initiative vom Herbst 1964," *Vierteljahrshefte für Zeitgeschichte* (2005, no. 2), and especially Benedikt Schoenborn, *La mésentente apprivoisée: De Gaulle et les Allemands, 1963–1969* (Paris: PUF, 2007), pp. 79, 158, 163–65, 288, 291–92, 295, 298. Even Brandt thought NATO might be replaced by some sort of European nuclear force built in cooperation with France. Germany, he told the French in 1973, did not seek nuclear weapons for herself, but in a European defense organization it was out of the question, he said, that that country would "play the role of the infantry." Quoted in Georges-Henri Soutou, *L'Alliance incertaine: Les rapports politico-stratégiques franco-allemands, 1954–1996* (Paris: Fayard, 1996), p. 339.

to keep their nuclear options open—and as it became increasingly clear that they would not be allowed to build a purely national force, their hopes came to focus on some international alternative, a NATO force or a European nuclear force over which the Federal Republic would have some control. For Germany to be shut out entirely, for Germany to be permanently dependent on her allies for protection, would mean that Germany would be politically impotent. If it were at all possible, that situation had to be avoided.

It was thus important to keep the door at least somewhat open, and it was for this reason that many German leaders in the late 1960s did not want their country to sign the Non-proliferation Treaty. Adenauer, for example, declared that the NPT was even worse than the Morgenthau Plan from World War II. Franz-Josef Strauss, the long-time head of the Christian Social Union, the Bavarian affiliate of Adenauer's Christian Democratic Union, and for years one of the most prominent figures in German political life, called it a "Versailles of cosmic dimensions."[9] Even Chancellor Kiesinger referred in this context to U.S.-Soviet "atomic complicity."[10] Henry Kissinger, visiting Germany in early 1966, was "amazed by the depth of German feelings on this subject"; in November 1967, the head of the State Department's Office of German Affairs thought that "among the 50 or 60 top politicians and officials" in West Germany, there was "*not one* who supports the NPT."[11]

But the Soviets were dead set against the very idea of a German nuclear force and opposed anything that pointed in that direction. This was one issue, it seemed, that the USSR might actually go to war over. This concern, in fact, largely explained its willingness to negotiate the

[9] See Schwarz, *Adenauer*, 2:974, and Susanna Schrafstetter and Stephen Twigge, *Avoiding Armageddon: Europe, the United States, and the Struggle for Nuclear Nonproliferation, 1945-1970* (Westport: Praeger, 2004), pp. 182-183, 197 n.89. See also Strauss to Kiesinger, February 15, 1967, quoted in Dirk Kroegel, *Einen Anfang finden! Kurt Georg Kiesinger in der Aussen- and Deutschlandpolitik der Grossen Koalition* (Munich: Oldenbourg, 1997), p. 92.

[10] See Kroegel, *Einen Anfang finden!*, p. 109ff; and Schwartz, *Lyndon Johnson and Europe*, p. 152.

[11] Henry Kissinger, "Summary of Conversations in Germany, January 24-30, 1966," p. 6, Digital National Security Archive (http://nsarchive.chadwyck.com/home.do), item number NP01164; henceforth cited in this form: DNSA/NP01164; Fried to Rostow, November 3, 1967, FRUS 1964–68, 15:593. Emphasis in original. For Kissinger's assessment in 1968, see Imhof to Puhan, January 10, 1968, ibid., p. 618. Note also the editor's comment about the almost universal dislike for the NPT in the CDU in Günter Buchstab, ed., *Kiesinger: "Wir leben in einer veränderten Welt": Die Protokolle des CDU-Bundesvorstands 1965-1969* (Duesseldorf: Droste, 2005), p. xxvi, and also the comment of François Seydoux, the French ambassador in Federal Republic at the time, that "l'Allemagne aspirait à s'approcher de l'arme nucléaire," in François Seydoux, *Dans l'intimité franco-allemande: Une mission diplomatique* (Paris: Albatros, 1977), p. 62. On the NPT issue in German politics at this time in general, see Kroegel, *Einen Anfang finden!*, pp. 90–114, 235–63.

NPT: "Soviet interest in non-proliferation," according to Secretary of State Dean Rusk, was "95 percent centered" on West Germany.[12] As for the Federal Republic's allies, the British were totally opposed to the notion of a German nuclear capability from the very outset. The French attitude, somewhat ambivalent in the late 1950s and early 1960s, hardened dramatically after Franco-German relations went downhill in 1963. By the mid-1960s, de Gaulle was also very much against the idea of the Germans getting their hands on nuclear weapons.

And the Americans, by that time, were absolutely determined to keep the Federal Republic from acquiring a nuclear force. President Johnson had no doubt that the Germans would want to build such a force as soon as they could— if he were in their shoes, he said, he would certainly want to go in that direction—but he also thought it would be disastrous if Germany went nuclear.[13] The U.S. government tried to deal with this problem by pushing its plan for a "multilateral force" (MLF); the huge effort it put into that very dubious project, especially in 1964, is a good measure of the seriousness with which it took this problem. It eventually gave up on that idea and thus needed to deal with the problem in a more direct way. The Americans, in fact, ended up laying down the law to the Germans, who were warned that their country "might well be destroyed" if they tried to develop an independent nuclear capability.[14] The Germans could scarcely resist this sort of pressure, and by the end of the decade it was clear that the Federal Republic was not going to become a nuclear power.

But if a German nuclear deterrent was out of the question, and if the American nuclear deterrent could no longer, in itself, keep the Red Army at bay, how then could Europe be protected? U.S. leaders thought that in principle at least the answer was obvious. NATO, in their view, needed to move away from nuclear deterrence and instead rely essentially on conventional forces. But there were two problems with the conventional strategy. First of all, the forces needed to sustain such a strategy were simply not available. Throughout the 1960s, the United States, and Britain as well, were under pressure to cut back on their military presence in central Europe for balance of payments and other

[12] Rusk meeting with Gilpatric Committee, January 7, 1965, FRUS 1964–68, 11:155.

[13] Johnson-Wilson meeting, December 5, 1964, p. 3, DDRS/CK3100076994. Bundy memo of phone conversation with Johnson, December 7, 1964, DDRS/CK3100317751. Note also Bundy to Johnson, December 6, 1964, FRUS 1964–68, 13:136. See also Schwartz, *Lyndon Johnson and Europe*, pp. 62–63; and Frank Costigliola, "Lyndon B. Johnson, Germany, and the 'End of the Cold War,'" in Warren Cohen and Nancy Bernkopf Tucker, eds., *Lyndon Johnson Confronts the World: American Foreign Policy, 1963–1968* (Cambridge, England: Cambridge University Press, 1994), esp. pp. 175, 177, 189, 201.

[14] Rostow-Barzel meeting, February 23, 1968, FRUS 1964–68, 15:637. See also McGhee to Rusk, August 25, 1966, ibid., p. 395.

reasons, some connected with the Vietnam War.[15] Indeed, and despite the emphasis U.S. leaders placed on conventional forces at that time, U.S. force levels in Europe declined substantially during that period, and the NATO defense ministers were told in 1968 to get ready for yet further cuts.[16] France's withdrawal in 1966 from the NATO military system, of course, further aggravated the problem.

The second problem was more basic: no matter what sort of conventional defense was put in place, NATO would still have to worry about the possibility of a Soviet nuclear attack. People wanted to build up NATO's conventional defenses because they assumed the United States would not be willing to use nuclear weapons against the USSR no matter what was happening in a conventional war for fear of provoking a Soviet nuclear attack on the United States. But would the threat of escalation be any less great if nuclear weapons were used in response to a Soviet *nuclear* attack on Europe? Why would the United States, in such circumstances, be any more likely to take action that could lead to a Soviet attack on America? Wouldn't the United States in that case be likely to accept defeat, or at most use nuclear weapons only against battlefield targets and targets in eastern Europe, avoiding Soviet territory entirely? But if Soviet territory was treated as a "sanctuary," then what exactly was the USSR being threatened with? What deterrent value would the western forces then have?

U.S. officials generally dismissed this problem out of hand.[17] But the Europeans were not convinced that a nuclear war in which the two superpowers' homelands were spared was simply out of the question and their concerns had some basis in fact. The Soviets, it seems, had by no means ruled out the possibility of a war in which "the use of nuclear weapons would remain restricted to the theater level, leaving both homelands inviolate."[18]

---

[15] On these issues, see Francis Gavin, *Gold, Dollars, and Power: The Politics of International Monetary Relations, 1958–1971* (Chapel Hill: University of North Carolina Press, 2004), esp. chap. 6; Hubert Zimmermann, *Money and Security: Troops, Monetary Policy and West Germany's Relations with the United States and Britain, 1950–1971* (Cambridge, England: Cambridge University Press, 2002); and Andreas Wenger, "Crisis and Opportunity: NATO and the Multilateralization of Détente, 1966–1968," *Journal of Cold War Studies* 6, no. 1 (Winter 2004): esp. pp. 48–51.

[16] Department of Defense talking paper, c. July 1968, FRUS 1964–68, 13:727 n.1 and 729–30. See also NSC minutes, May 22, 1968, FRUS 1964–68, 15:675, and Wenger, "Crisis and Opportunity," p. 58.

[17] See "Secretary McNamara's Remarks to NATO Ministerial Meeting, December 15–17, 1964," p. 5, attached to Rusk to U.S. embassies in Europe, December 23, 1964, DNSA/NH00999.

[18] For the French view, see, for example, de Gaulle-Bohlen meeting, November 23, 1964, summarized in FRUS 1964–1968, 13:126n. For the German view, see Bowie to Rusk, July 20, 1967, FRUS 1964–68, 13:596; and Haftendorn, *NATO and the Nuclear Revolution*, p.

And that meant that the nuclear issue could not be dismissed as un-real. One could not just assume that nuclear weapons were "unusable" for both sides, that the two nuclear arsenals simply "cancelled each other out," and that the conventional balance was the only thing that really mattered. One had to think about how nuclear weapons would be used, if a conventional defense proved ineffective or the enemy used nuclear weapons first in a European war. It obviously made little sense to launch an all-out attack in such circumstances; if nuclear weapons were used at all, they would certainly have to be used in a more limited and more controlled way. And NATO in fact adopted a strategy of con-trolled escalation.[19] But how would that strategy work? What "philoso-phy" would govern the use of NATO's nuclear forces?

The key issue here had to do with tactical nuclear weapons—that is, with the question of how the thousands of such weapons NATO had in Europe would be used in the event of war. But the NATO countries had a hard time coming up with an answer to this question. The basic prob-lem was clear enough. On the one hand, if the goal was to deter a Soviet

---

69. For the quotation about the Soviets, see William Odom, *The Collapse of the Soviet Mili-tary* (New Haven: Yale University Press, 1998), p. 69; note also p. 71. See in addition Vo-jtech Mastny, "Imagining War in Europe: Soviet Strategic Planning," in Vojtech Mastny, Sven Holtsmark, and Andreas Wenger, eds., *War Plans and Alliances in the Cold War*, ed. (London: Routledge, 2006), pp. 24–25. Note, finally, Secretary of Defense James Schlesing-er's judgment in 1975: Warsaw Pact "forces, current doctrine and training indicate a readiness, however, for conducting a war in Europe with theater-wide, large scale nuclear strikes." James Schlesinger, "The Theater Nuclear Force Posture in Europe: A Report to the United States Congress in compliance with Public Law 93-365," p.2, available on the Defense Department's Freedom of Information website (http://www.dod.mil/pubs/foi/reading_room/237.pdf).

[19] MC 14/3, "Overall Strategic Concept for the Defense of the North Atlantic Treaty Organization Area," January 16, 1968 (http://www.nato.int/docu/stratdoc/eng/a6801 16a.pdf), esp. paragraphs 33(b) and 34(b). The United States had been trying to get NATO to adopt a strategy of this sort for some time. See the "statement of a suitable military strategy for NATO" that the Pentagon had worked out in 1963, attached to McNamara to Rusk, December 3, 1963 (DNSA/NH00988), especially the reference to the "controlled use of tactical nuclear weapons" in paragraph 3. For more on the working out of the of-ficial NATO strategy embodied in MC14/3, see Haftendorn, *NATO and the Nuclear Revo-lution*, chap. 2; Jane Stromseth, *The Origins of Flexible Response: NATO's Debate over Strategy in the 1960s* (New York: St. Martin's, 1988); and John Duffield, *Power Rules: The Evolution of NATO's Conventional Force Posture* (Stanford: Stanford University Press, 1995), chap. 5. A number of documents relating to NATO strategy in this period can be found in William Burr and Robert Wampler, eds., "Lifting the Veil on Cosmic: Declassified US and British Documents on NATO Military Planning and Threat Assessments of the Warsaw Pact" (http://www.php.isn.ethz.ch/collections/colltopic.cfm?lng=en&id=14968). For Euro-pean views on these issues, see Beatrice Heuser, *NATO, Britain, France, and the FRG : Nu-clear Strategies and Forces for Europe, 1949–2000* (New York: St. Martin's, 1997), and Chris-toph Bluth, *Britain, Germany, and Western Nuclear Strategy* (Oxford: Clarendon, 1995), esp. chap. 4.

attack on Europe, the USSR itself could not be treated as a "sanctuary." Use of the weapons would therefore have to be part of a process, perhaps a process no one could fully control, that might conceivably lead to nuclear attacks on the USSR itself. Those attacks, to be sure, might in turn lead to a Soviet nuclear strike on the United States. But as long as there was only a *chance* of this happening—as long as the U.S. government did not have to take action that it knew with absolute certainty would lead to a general nuclear war—NATO, the argument ran, should be willing to run the risk.[20]

On the other hand, there was a real aversion, not just on the part of the Americans but in practice on the part of the Europeans as well, to deliberately running any real risk of general nuclear war. Given what was at stake, a strategy of that sort seemed utterly irresponsible. The risk of escalation was not a phenomenon to be exploited; it was a danger to be minimized. The Americans made it clear at the time that they had no stomach for engaging in what Thomas Schelling called a "competition in risk taking"—for deliberately playing on the possibility that events might spin out of control, and thus for arranging things so that no one could be sure that the conflict would not escalate. Nor were the Europeans really committed to such a strategy: U.S. leaders thought (quite correctly in my view) that whatever the Europeans said in peacetime, if the moment of truth ever came they would draw back from any use of nuclear weapons.[21]

In any event, U.S. leaders wanted to keep the lid on the escalatory

[20] For the general argument that one could credibly threaten to set off a process that just might lead to a nuclear holocaust, see Thomas Schelling, *Arms and Influence* (New Haven: Yale University Press, 1966), chap. 3 and esp. pp. 97–98. See also the excerpts from some unpublished Schelling writings quoted in Marc Trachtenberg, *History and Strategy* (Princeton: Princeton University Press, 1991), p. 16. The United States, Schelling thought, needed to adopt a strategy of this sort. "Until we can manipulate the risk of general war and engage in competitive risk-taking with the Soviets," he wrote, "I don't think we are going to learn to take care of Berlin, much less to take care of Indonesia and Finland when the time comes." David Abshire and Richard Allen, eds., *National Security: Political, Military and Economic Strategies in the Decade Ahead* (New York: Praeger, 1963), p. 646. In theory, the major European governments were inclined to place all their chips on deterrence and thus, in the event of an attack, to take actions that would force the Soviets to face the risk of general thermonuclear war. For a discussion of the NATO allies' "concepts for the defense of Europe," see "Project 1d First Interim Report," May 18, 1964, Part I, pp. 3–4, and Part III, pp. 1–6, DNSA/NH00991. See also (in addition to the works cited in the previous footnote) Frédéric Bozo, *Deux stratégies pour l'Europe: De Gaulle, les États-Unis et l'Alliance atlantique* (Paris: Plon, 1996).

[21] See especially Secretary of Defense Robert McNamara's Draft President Memorandum on tactical nuclear forces in NATO strategy, January 15, 1965, p. 30, DNSA/NH01000. Secretary Rusk shared that view; see Rusk to McNamara, November 28, 1964, FRUS 1964 -68, 10:183. See also Weiss to U. A. Johnson, May 27, 1964, DNSA/NH00993, pp. 1-2, and Stromseth, *Origins of Flexible Response*, p. 127.

process—or, as they put it even in official pronouncements, to keep the fighting at the "lowest level of violence consistent with NATO's objectives."[22] But this seemed to imply that if the Soviet attack was limited to Europe, the American response would also be limited to Europe. The USSR and the United States would be treated as "sanctuaries," but both eastern and western Europe would be incinerated. But the problem here, of course, is that with this sort of strategy—with the Soviet homeland insured against attack—NATO's nuclear forces would have little deterrent value. This strategy, moreover, would give the Soviets the upper hand in a crisis: if the two sides were faced with the prospect of a Europe-only war, it was obvious which side would be more likely to draw back. And there was yet another problem with such a strategy, one that contemplated a war in which Europe would be destroyed but America would get off virtually scot-free: it was bound to poison relations between the United States and the European allies, especially if east-west relations were bad and the threat of war had to be taken seriously.

Thus the problem of controlled escalation had no easy solution, and in fact the U.S. government in this middle period of the Cold War had no clear sense for how the escalatory process was to be managed. It had

---

[22] Secretary of Defense James Schlesinger, "The Theater Nuclear Force Posture in Europe," p. 1. For later official references to the "lowest possible level of violence," see Secretary of Defense Caspar Weinberger's statement to the Senate Foreign Relations Committee, December 14, 1982 (http://www.nuclearfiles.org/menu/key-issues/nuclear-weapons/history/cold-war/strategy/testimony-senate-weinberger1982-12-14.htm), and Secretary of Defense Frank Carlucci's statement, January 17, 1989 (http://www.nuclearfiles.org/menu/key-issues/nuclear-weapons/history/cold-war/strategy/report-carlucci-deterrence_1989-01-17.htm). An important internal document, the top secret summary report for NSSM 169 (DNSA/PR01168, p.4) also contained language of this sort. This had, in effect, been U.S. policy since 1961, and by the late 1960s NATO's official strategy also called for meeting aggression "at the place, time, and intensity it is launched." See MC 48/3(Final), "Measures to Implement the Strategic Concept for the Defence of the NATO Area," December 8, 1969, para. 13 (http://www.nato.int/docu/stratdoc/eng/a691208a.pdf). Note also the view of an exceptionally well-informed British observer that the Americans, in the NATO strategy discussions in the late 1960s, supported the tactical nuclear option "because it offered the best hope of preventing a major land battle in Europe from escalating to an all-out strategic exchange." The Europeans, on the other hand, he said, supported it precisely because any use of nuclear weapons would make escalation more likely, and thus the threat of theater use would have a broader deterrent effect. J. Michael Legge, *Theater Nuclear Weapons and the NATO Strategy of Flexible Response* (Santa Monica, Calif.: Rand, 1983), p. 10. This is in fact a common theme in the documents: "The Europeans," one U.S. official, for example, wrote in late 1967, "continue to emphasize deterrence and stress the need to pose the risk of escalation in order to deter attack or stop it if it occurs. Increasingly, we have stressed the need to avoid escalation in order to limit damage should a war occur." Farley to Kohler, December 1, 1967, DNSA/NH01026.

no clear sense, in particular, for the role that tactical nuclear weapons were to play. Over and over again in the documents you find people complaining about a "void" in this area. In 1965, for example, the U.S. Secretary of Defense, Robert McNamara, told his German counterpart "that in his judgment there exists no rational plan for the use of nuclear weapons now located in Europe." In 1971 Henry Kissinger, now President Richard Nixon's national security advisor, complained that "we still don't have a clear doctrine for their use."[23] In Kissinger's view, if such issues were not taken seriously—if the United States gave the impression that it was "not interested in fighting"—then the other side would conclude that America was just bluffing. Deterrence, he thought, had "to be based on a war-fighting capability."[24]

So the whole military situation was far from satisfactory. It was clear that the security of the NATO allies, and especially West Germany, did not rest on a solid military foundation. As President Johnson was told by his top advisors in 1966, there were "gaping holes in all strategic options": massive retaliation would be "virtually suicidal"; an effective conventional defense "seems less attainable than heretofore"; and "tactical nuclear war" was "full of uncertainties."[25] President Nixon in 1970 felt the same way.[26] And indeed observers outside the government often made the same point. Lawrence Freedman's view was typical. "An inadequate conventional defense backed by an incredible nuclear guarantee"—this, he said, was what the NATO strategy of "flexible response" really boiled down to.[27]

The assumption, in other words, was that nuclear deterrence was something of a sham. The United States would never launch a fall-scale nuclear attack on the Soviet Union in the event of a European war. Kissinger himself, in a famous speech, later admitted that America's "strategic assurances" had been empty.[28] Even the tactical nuclear option

[23] Cleveland to State Department, November 29, 1965, FRUS 1964–68, 13:280; NSC meeting, August 13, 1971, p. 3, DNSA/KT00332. This was a very common theme throughout this period. See, for example, Thompson to Howard, November 20, 1964, FRUS 1964–68, 10:174–75; Cleveland to McNamara, December 10, 1966, FRUS 1964–68, 13:510 (for the term *void*); and Kissinger meeting with British officials, April 19, 1973 (document dated April 24, 1973), pp. 8–9, DNSA/KT00707 (second document at this location). See also Henry Kissinger, *White House Years* (Boston: Little Brown, 1979), pp. 218–20, and also Kissinger's famous and extraordinarily frank Brussels speech of September 1979, in Henry Kissinger, *For the Record: Selected Statements, 1977–1980* (Boston: Little Brown, 1981), pp. 236, 242.

[24] Minutes of DPRC meeting, February 22, 1971, p. 5, DNSA/KT00236.

[25] McNamara and Rusk to Johnson, May 28, 1966, FRUS 1964–68, 13:402–403.

[26] NSC meeting, November 19, 1970, p. 9, DNSA/KT00211.

[27] Lawrence Freedman, "NATO Myths," *Foreign Policy*, no. 45 (Winter 1981–82): 55.

[28] Kissinger, *For the Record*, p. 240.

was unreal. "We will never use the tactical nuclears," Nixon said. The "nuclear umbrella in NATO," in his view, was "a lot of crap."[29]

What all this meant was that in strategic terms, even if the Soviets could never be certain that a European war would not escalate, the western position was not very strong. In the event of a crisis, the West would be at a disadvantage; the Soviets would have the upper hand. The NATO powers thus had an enormous incentive to make sure that they did not come anywhere near the point where an armed conflict was a real possibility. They had an enormous incentive, that is, to reach a political accommodation with the USSR.

The point applied with particular force to the case of West Germany. Willy Brandt thought in 1968 that "West Germany cannot really depend on the Americans"; he thought that "as things now stand the United States would not be in a position to meet by military means a serious Soviet military offensive in Europe."[30] The implication was that Germany could not afford to risk a confrontation with the USSR—that it instead needed to try to mend fences with her great neighbor to the east. His chief advisor, Egon Bahr, was even more explicit. With nuclear parity, Bahr told Kissinger, the Americans would certainly not launch a nuclear attack on the Soviet Union "if the Russians took Hamburg." Détente, he said, was therefore "our only option."[31] His country thus had a strong "structural incentive," as one astute German observer put it, to pursue a "policy of partial appeasement."[32]

[29] NSC meeting, November 19, 1970, p. 9, DNSA/KT00211; NSC meeting, February 19, 1969, quoted in William Burr, "The Nixon Administration, the 'Horror Strategy,' and the Search for Limited Nuclear Options, 1969–1972," *Journal of Cold War Studies* 7, no. 3 (Summer 2005): 48 n.31.

[30] "Foreign Minister Brandt's Musings on West German Foreign Policy Before Visiting Paris," September 13, 1968, available in the CIA's Electronic Reading Room (http://www.foia.cia.gov/), document number EO-2002-00148. Other western leaders were quite familiar with the Brandt government's views on the subject. As Nixon pointed out to French President Georges Pompidou in December 1971, "[I]t was no secret that the Germans felt the U.S. could not be depended on," and that in particular "the U.S. could not be counted upon to risk its survival to defend Europe in a nuclear war." Nixon-Pompidou meeting, December 13, 1971, William Burr, ed., *The Kissinger Transcripts: The Top Secret Talks with Beijing and Moscow* (New York: Free Press, 1998), p. 35.

[31] Dana Allin, *Cold War Illusions: America, Europe and Soviet Power, 1969–1989* (New York: St. Martin's, 1994), p. 40.

[32] Josef Joffe, *The Limited Partnership: Europe, the United States, and the Burdens of Alliance* (Cambridge, Mass.: Ballinger, 1987), p. 23. The point that the antagonism with the East that the Federal Republic's existing policy had led to was "extraordinarily dangerous, given the tremendous military potential of the Soviet Union—a force which was overwhelmingly concentrated against Germany" was quite clear at the time, even to those of a relatively conservative bent. The quotation comes from an October 17, 1966, memorandum by Karl Carstens, at the time State Secretary in the German Foreign Office, in *Akten zur auswärtigen Politik der Bundesrepublik Deutschland* 1966, vol. 2, p. 1380; henceforth cited

But a source of weakness for the West was a source of strength for the Soviets. The structural incentives cut both ways. The western countries, and especially the Germans, might feel that they needed to ease tensions with the USSR. But the Soviets might feel freer to take a tougher line in their dealings with the western powers, especially on European questions.

RUSSIA'S CHOICE

Given the basic structural weaknesses in the western system, which way would Russia go? Would the Soviets try to exploit NATO's vulnerabilities by pursuing a forward policy in central Europe or would they seek instead to stabilize the existing system? As the Soviets grappled with this question, they were pulled in more than one direction. The USSR, to be sure, clearly had a certain interest in expanding its influence in western Europe. The Soviets would obviously not be upset if the countries there had to live more in the shadow of Soviet power—if the Europeans, that is, had to be more sensitive to Soviet wishes, more accommodating politically, militarily, and economically. The USSR might therefore want to "Finlandize" western Europe—that is, draw that part of the world, to one degree or another, into the Soviet orbit. That sort of thinking was bound to have a certain appeal, and Soviet leaders clearly took seriously the idea that the USSR should pursue a policy of that kind.[33]

---

in this form: AAPD 1966, 2:1380. Henry Kissinger also interpreted the shift in German policy in these terms. "If Europe could no longer rely on American strategic preeminence and if Europe would not—or in terms of its domestic politics could not—make the effort to defend itself, Europe and, above, all the Federal Republic had to seek safety in relaxation of tensions with the East." Henry Kissinger, *Years of Upheaval* (Boston: Little, Brown, 1982), p. 147.

[33] See Arkady Shevchenko, *Breaking with Moscow* (New York: Knopf, 1985), p. 171. In a statement that somehow slipped by the censor (as Hannes Adomeit notes), one Soviet commentator actually complained that the "'balance of forces' that would suit the Western countries in that area [central Europe] is one which would rule out the possibility of the socialist countries influencing international events *beyond their frontiers.*" V. M. Kulish, "Detente, International Relations and Military Might," *Coexistence* (Glasgow) 14, no. 2 (1977): 190, quoted in Hannes Adomeit, "The Political Rationale of Soviet Military Capabilities and Doctrine," in European Security Study, *Strengthening Conventional Deterrence in Europe: Proposals for the 1980s* (London: Macmillan, 1983), p. 89; emphasis added by Adomeit. Kulish was the editor of what Robert Legvold characterized as "the most thorough Soviet analysis of the political role of military power." Robert Legvold, "Military Power in International Politics: Soviet Doctrine on its Centrality and Instrumentality," in Uwe Nerlich, ed., *The Soviet Asset: Military Power in the Competition over Europe*, (Cambridge, Mass.,: Ballinger, 1983), p. 131.

And in fact this kind of thinking did play a certain role in shaping Soviet policy, especially on the German question, and above all on the German nuclear question. The Federal Republic, clearly, was to have a special status in this area. Not only, in the Soviet view, would West Germany not be allowed to develop a nuclear force of her own. Not only would it not be allowed to participate in any sort of NATO nuclear force, even a force that was something of a charade—a force, like the MLF, explicitly designed to prevent that country from getting her finger on the nuclear trigger. But the Germans, ideally, would not even be allowed to take part in NATO nuclear planning.[34] And later on, in the post-1979 period, the USSR of course strongly objected to the stationing of medium-range American missiles in western Europe, including West Germany, even though Soviet missiles had been targeting that area for years. In their view, they had a certain *droit de regard* over that whole region, especially where defense issues were concerned. As Josef Joffe says, what was at issue in that dispute "was the Soviet claim to a veto right over NATO's nuclear choices, that is, over the terms of protection offered by the United States to its European allies. If successful, the Soviet Union would have won a historic victory; Moscow would have gained the power to act as arbiter of Europe's security."[35]

And the Soviets could achieve that general goal, in principle, by building up their military power. During the Brezhnev period (1964–82), the Soviets made an enormous effort in this area, steadily building up their forces at every level—strategic nuclear, theater nuclear, and conventional—and straining every muscle to do it. The defense burden was very high: defense spending accounted for a much higher share of the national income than it did in the West.[36]

---

[34] Soviet foreign minister Gromyko's remarks, reported in Kohler to State Department, December 23, 1965, and Soviet Prime Minister Alexei Kosygin to President Johnson, delivered January 11, 1966, in FRUS 1964–68, 11:274–76, 280–81. These Soviets demands were eventually softened; see various documents in ibid., pp. 333, 378, 381. Note incidentally that the French at this time shared the Soviet view. Bozo, *Deux stratégies pour l'Europe*, p. 146.

[35] Joffe, *The Limited Partnership*, p. 174.

[36] The Soviets were apparently spending at least 15 percent of their national income on defense in the 1970s. As one well-respected economist put it, the defense burden in the USSR in the 1970s was "at least three times" what it was in the western countries. Gur Ofer, "Soviet Economic Growth: 1928–1985," *Journal of Economic Literature* 25, no. 4 (December 1987): 1787; Ofer is commenting here on the data shown on line 11 of the table presented on p. 1788. See also Noel Firth and James Noren, *Soviet Defense Spending: A History of CIA Estimates, 1950–1990* (College Station: Texas A&M Press, 1998), esp. pp. 116, 128–35. According to Firth and Noren (pp. 116, 149), the Soviets were outspending the United States by a very considerable margin in the 1970s. The CIA estimates, the basis for most scholarly discussions, were attacked from both the left and the right—that is, for either overestimating or underestimating the Soviet defense burden. Some scholars, for

Observers in the West were bound to ask why the USSR was making that kind of effort. If détente was "truly the Soviet purpose in Europe," one analyst wondered, "then why the steady and unprecedented military build-up at the same time?"[37] The USSR was Clausewitzian to the core: the Soviets thought of military power in political terms; military forces were of value, in large measure, because of the political shadow they cast. If the Soviets were making a major military effort, then presumably this was because they had some major political purpose in mind—that they were interested, in other words, in pursuing a policy that was not purely defensive in nature. And if that was the case, then what could the goal be if not to deepen Soviet influence in western Europe?

But while the temptation to push ahead in Europe clearly played a certain role, it was not the only factor that entered into the equation. There was, in fact, a whole series of reasons why the Soviet Union might be expected to pursue a less ambitious policy.

First of all, if one were trying to predict the course of Soviet foreign policy, the basic character of the regime would certainly have to be taken into account. Over the years the USSR had lost most of its revolutionary élan, and by the 1970s the regime had become heavily bureaucratic and conservative. During the Brezhnev period, the aging leadership created "a kind of bureaucrats' paradise," but the price of the "quiet life" was "social and economic stagnation."[38] "The decrepit members of Brezhnev's Politburo," Dmitri Volkogonov writes, "valued stability above all, an unchanging course and bland decisions."[39] And this general attitude was bound to affect the way they, and Brezhnev in particular, dealt with other countries. That was certainly Kissinger's impression. At least "part of Brezhnev," he thought, "sincerely sought,

---

example, think that the Soviets were spending perhaps 22 percent of their national income on defense around 1980. See Paul Gregory, "Soviet Defense Puzzles: Archives, Strategy and Underfulfilment," *Europe-Asia Studies* 55, no. 6 (2003): 935, citing an unpublished 2003 paper by Mark Harrison. For an analysis, see James Noren, "The Controversy Over Western Measures of Soviet Defense Expenditures," *Post-Soviet Affairs* 11, no. 3 (1995): esp. pp. 254–57; see also Firth and Noren, *Soviet Defense Spending*, chap. 6, and Ofer, "Soviet Economic Growth," pp. 1788–89, n. 26.

[37] Eliot Goodman, "Disparities in East-West Relations," *Survey* 19, no. 3 (Summer 1973): 89.

[38] Adam Ulam, *The Communists: The Story of Power and Lost Illusions, 1948–1991* (New York: Scribner's, 1992), p. 246; Peter Rutland, *The Politics of Economic Stagnation in the Soviet Union* (Cambridge, Mass.: Cambridge University Press, 1993), p. xi, quoted in Alex Dowlah and John Elliott, *The Life and Times of Soviet Socialism* (Westport, Conn.: Praeger, 1997), p. 165.

[39] Dmitri Volkogonov, *Autopsy for an Empire: The Seven Leaders Who Built the Soviet Regime* (New York: Free Press, 1998), p. 275.

if not peace in the Western sense, then surcease from the dangers and risks and struggles of a lifetime."[40]

And the Soviets clearly had a lot to worry about at home. "The Soviet economy," as one scholar put it, "seemed to be gradually running out of steam, being dragged to stagnation and decline by some inexorable underlying process."[41] The problem was in fact clear at the time, but the regime seemed unable to deal with it.[42] And the deepening economic problem was bound to affect Soviet foreign policy in all sorts of ways. The self-confidence of the regime would be shaken, and the Soviets would have to worry about the USSR's ability to sustain a costly military rivalry with a coalition of much richer and more technologically

[40] Henry Kissinger, *White House Years* (Boston: Little Brown, 1979), p. 1143.

[41] Gertrude Schroeder, "Reflections on Economic Sovietology," *Post-Soviet Affairs* 11, no. 3 (1995): 209, 225.

[42] It was claimed, especially in the early 1990s, that both the CIA and analysts outside the government had failed to see the problems with the Soviet economy and in particular had overestimated Soviet economic performance. Those charges turn out to have little basis in fact. Economists specializing in this area were talking about the problem—the term *crisis* was sometimes used—even in the 1960s. See Schroeder, "Reflections on Economic Sovietology," pp. 223–24 and the sources cited there, and especially the 1966 *Slavic Review* round-table discussion (where the term "crisis" was used on pp. 233 and 234). Note also the economist Joseph Berliner's impressions following a visit to the USSR in 1967, quoted in Alexander Dallin, "Causes of the Collapse of the USSR," *Post-Soviet Affairs* 8, no. 4 (1992): 283. On the CIA estimates, see David Kotz with Fred Weir, *Revolution from Above: The Demise of the Soviet System* (London: Routledge, 1997), pp. 38–40; Abram Bergson, "The USSR Before the Fall: How Poor and Why," *Journal of Economic Perspectives* 5, no. 4 (Autumn 1991): 40–41; Angus Maddison, "Measuring the Performance of a Communist Command Economy: An Assessment of the CIA Estimates for the USSR," *Review of Income and Wealth* 44, no. 3 (September 1998); Vladimir Kontorovich, "Economists, Soviet Growth Slowdown and the Collapse," *Europe-Asia Studies* 53, no. 5 (July 2001): 689–91; Abraham Becker, "Intelligence Fiasco or Reasoned Accounting? CIA Estimates of Soviet GNP," *Post-Soviet Affairs* 10, no. 4 (1994); and Jeffrey Richelson, "The CIA Vindicated: The Soviet Collapse Was Predicted," *The National Interest* (September 22, 1995). Note also the more analytical CIA reports cited in James Noren, "CIA's Analysis of the Soviet Economy," in Gerald Haines and Robert Leggett, eds., *Watching the Bear: Essays on CIA's Analysis of the Soviet Union*, (Washington, D.C.: GPO, 2001), pp. 20–21. The idea that the Soviets had to deal with very serious economic problems, and that this situation was having a major impact on their political behavior, was also a common theme in the European diplomatic documents. For typical examples, see Wilson-Erhard meeting, January 15, 1964, AAPD 1964, 1:50 (esp. n. 6); and de Gaulle-Heath meeting, November 22, 1965, *Documents diplomatiques français: 1965*, vol. 2, p. 24. See also Cyrus Sulzberger, *An Age of Mediocrity: Memoirs and Diaries 1963–1972* (New York: Macmillan, 1973), pp. 155 (for Adenauer) and 181 (Llewellyn Thompson). There is also the question of whether the Soviet leadership was itself aware of the problem. It turns out that "the top echelons of the Soviet leadership had been getting confidential reports critical of the economy's performance since the 1960s," but during the Brezhnev period key reports "met hostility" or "were ignored." See Michael Ellman and Vladimir Kontorovich, "The Collapse of the Soviet Union and the Memoir Literature," *Europe-Asia Studies* 49, no. 2 (March 1997): 260.

advanced powers. The Soviets might feel they could not risk provoking a great increase in U.S. defense spending. They might prefer instead to ease tensions with the West, especially since that might help them get access to western technology and credits, which were particularly important given the nature of the economic problem they were faced with at home.

And of course geopolitical factors, especially the conflict with China, were bound to loom large in Soviet thinking. If the Chinese were hostile, the Soviets would obviously want to improve their relations with the West.[43] The Soviet leadership had a certain interest in getting the United States to side with the USSR in its conflict with China, or at the very least in preventing the Americans from forming a *de facto* alliance with the Chinese. But to have any chance at all of achieving those goals, they would have to pursue a relatively moderate course of action in other areas, above all in Europe.[44]

The Soviets, in other words, might be tempted in such circumstances to think in terms of a U.S.-Soviet "condominium," and that kind of thinking might have had a certain bearing on how specific political issues, and especially European issues, were approached. They might, for example, be attracted to the idea of a divided Europe, with the USSR controlling the east and the Americans controlling the west. An American withdrawal from Europe might lead to some kind of European nuclear force, and thus possibly to the Federal Republic getting her finger on the nuclear trigger.[45] It might be better, therefore, to keep the Americans in, so that West Germany could be contained in a structure dominated by American power.[46] Even a Germany unified under Com-

---

[43] See the document quoted in Anatoly Dobrynin, *In Confidence* (New York: Times Books, 1995), p. 158.

[44] The Soviets actually tried to form a *de facto* alliance of their own with the United States, to be directed against China. See William Hyland, *Mortal Rivals: Superpower Relations from Nixon to Reagan* (New York: Random House, 1987), pp. 61, 63; Henry Kissinger, *Years of Upheaval* (Boston: Little Brown, 1982), pp. 233, 294–95, 1173–74; Henry Kissinger, *Diplomacy* (New York: Simon & Schuster, 1994), p. 730; Burr, *Kissinger Transcripts*, pp. 131, 143, 171, 300. Nothing came of the proposal, but the mere fact that they thought something of this sort was possible shows that the hope that America might side with them against China had entered into their calculations.

[45] See Michael Sodaro, *Moscow, Germany, and the West from Khrushchev to Gorbachev* (Ithaca: Cornell University Press, 1990), p. 30 and the sources cited there (n. 16); note also an article by Gromyko's son, discussed by Sodaro on p. 223. Note also John Erickson, "Soviet Military Posture and Policy in Europe," in *Soviet Strategy in Europe*, ed. Richard Pipes (New York: Crane, Russak, 1976), p. 200. Note finally the Soviet comment cited in Soutou, *L'Alliance incertaine*, p. 264.

[46] American observers were struck by the fact that Brezhnev agreed to take part in the European force reduction talks just days before the Mansfield amendment, which called for unilateral U.S. troop withdrawals from Europe, was due to come to a vote. This was

munist rule might not make much sense from the Soviet point of view, given what had happened with China. "We don't need a united Germany at all," Soviet Foreign Minister Gromyko told one of his advisors in 1977, "not even a socialist one. The united socialist China is enough for us."[47]

So the Soviets were pulled in both directions: toward exploiting the position they had acquired and toward reaching an accommodation with the West. Which way would they go? The answer might depend to a certain degree on decisions the western governments made—above all, on the policies pursued by West Germany and the United States. How did those governments try to deal with the USSR during this period, and what effect, if any, did their policies have on Soviet behavior?

What effect, in particular, did the German Ostpolitik, certainly one of the most important developments of the period, have on the way the Soviets struck the balance? During its first years in office, the Brandt government pursued a policy of "accepting realities"—of accepting the division of Europe, the East German state, and indeed the whole Cold War political system. But that was not an end in itself, and Brandt and his associates had more ambitious goals in mind. The long-term goal was to end the bloc system—to dissolve both NATO and the Warsaw Pact, and to get both American and Soviet forces out of central Europe.[48]

"widely interpreted as a sign of Moscow's preference for an American military presence on the continent, at least for the foreseeable future." Sodaro, *Moscow, Germany, and the West*, p. 225. See also Raymond Garthoff, *Détente and Confrontation: American-Soviet Relations from Nixon to Reagan*, revised ed. (Washington, D.C.: Brookings, 1994), p. 133.

[47] Valentin Falin, *Politische Erinnerungen* (Munich: Droemer Knaur, 1993), pp. 238–39, quoted in Hannes Adomeit, *Imperial Overstretch: Germany in Soviet Policy from Stalin to Gorbachev* (Baden-Baden: Nomos, 1998), p. 125.

[48] Bahr had actually outlined a plan of this sort in an interview with an American scholar in January 1969. That scholar published extensive notes of the interview a few years later. See Walter Hahn, "West Germany's Ostpolitik: The Grand Design of Egon Bahr," *Orbis* 16, no. 4 (Winter 1973): 867–71, esp. p. 871. Note also a 1968 Bahr memorandum, which was leaked and published in the September 27, 1973, issue of *Quick*. That document was eventually also published in the *Akten zur Auswärtigen Politik der Bundesrepublik Deutschland 1968*, vol. 1 (Munich: Oldenbourg, 1999), doc. 207. On the general issue of Brandt government's ultimate goals, see Werner Link's discussion in *Republik im Wandel: Die Ära Brandt*, pp. 169–79; Andreas Vogtmeier, *Egon Bahr und die deutsche Frage: Zur Entwicklung der sozialdemokratischen Ost- and Deutschlandpolitik vom Kriegsende bis zur Vereinigung* (Bonn: Dietz, 1996), esp. pp. 84–85, 170n.; Georges-Henri Soutou, *La Guerre de Cinquante Ans: Le conflit Est-Ouest 1943–1990* (Paris: Fayard, 2001), pp. 491, 501; and Alexander Gallus, *Die Neutralisten: Verfechter eines vereinten Deutschland zwischen Ost und West 1945–1990* (Düsseldorf: Droste, 2001), pp. 296–306. For more evidence on the Brandt-Bahr policy from French sources, and for French concerns, even in the 1960s, about the sort of policy they stood for, see Schoenborn, *Mésentente apprivoisée*, pp. 63, 183, 280–84, 343–45, 359.

The hope was that in that post-Cold War system the two parts of Germany could come together in a single state.

But what effect did all this have on the USSR? A Soviet hardliner could interpret the Brandt phenomenon—not just the move toward détente, but even more Brandt's apparent willingness to move toward a "European peace order" in which NATO would no longer exist—as a direct result of the buildup of Soviet military power, as indeed it was to a certain degree.[49] It could be interpreted, in other words, as a good example of "Finlandization" in action. On the other hand, a Soviet leader interested in reaching an accommodation with the West could view the Brandt phenomenon in a very different light—as proving that Germany posed no threat, that a moderate policy was workable, and that there were governments in the West that would cooperate with such a policy. "Without Ostpolitik no Gorbachev!"—that was how a key mid-level Soviet policymaker later put the point.[50] But since both arguments could be made and neither was intrinsically more compelling than the other, it is hard to see how the Brandt episode could have played a major role in determining how the Soviets struck the balance.

The same general point can be made about U.S. policy during the Johnson period (1964–68). Johnson, as George Ball put it, "desperately wanted to be a peace president."[51] His goal was to "end the Cold War."[52] That policy was not able to make much headway because of the Vietnam conflict. But Johnson was determined, especially toward the end of his term of office, to move ahead, above all on arms control. Nonproliferation was taken quite seriously as a goal, and Johnson also very much wanted to reach a strategic arms limitation agreement with the Soviets.[53] In 1968, his last year in office, he tried hard to get the arms

[49] One Soviet text from the period, in fact, explicitly linked the Ostpolitik to the growth of Soviet military power: the "ruling circles in Bonn" had opted for a more reasonable policy because they had come to understand that the Federal Republic was now "perilously vulnerable militarily and strategically." V.I. Popov et al., *A Study of Soviet Foreign Policy* (Moscow: Progress, 1975), p. 257, quoted in David Finley, "Some Aspects of Conventional Military Capability in Soviet Foreign Relations," UCLA Center for International and Strategic Affairs, ACIS Working Paper No. 20 (February 1980), pp. 39–40. See also Adomeit, *Imperial Overstretch*, pp. 113, 137.

[50] Valentin Falin, quoted in Timothy Garton Ash, *In Europe's Name: Germany and the Divided Continent* (New York, Random House, 1993), p. 119. But note that Garton Ash goes on to point out that "this same Falin could say, in an interview with *Die Zeit* in 1992, that the Americans had arms-raced the Soviets to death."

[51] Quoted in Hal Brands, "Progress Unseen: U.S. Arms Control Policy and the Origins of Détente, 1963–1968," *Diplomatic History* 30, no. 2 (April 2006): 255.

[52] Costigliola, "Lyndon B. Johnson, Germany, and the 'End of the Cold War,'" esp. p. 197.

[53] See Francis Gavin, "Blasts from the Past: Proliferation Lessons from the 1960s," *International Security* 29, no. 3 (Winter 2004–2005); Hal Brands, "Rethinking Nonprolifera-

negotiations started; even the Soviet invasion of Czechoslovakia in August did little to slow him down.[54] The plan for a Johnson visit to Russia to begin talks on this subject was dropped only after it was made clear to the Soviets in December that the incoming Nixon administration very much disapproved of the idea.[55]

What impact did that policy have on Soviet behavior? Once again, one can argue both sides of the issue. On the one hand, Johnson in late 1968 seemed "fixated" on strategic weapons—that is, on an area where the stability of the balance was never really in danger.[56] The really important military questions—above all, those relating to the defense of Europe, an area where there really was a stability problem—did not receive much attention. The administration, in fact, seemed willing to give away the store in what came to be called the "Eurostrategic" area: it was prepared to enter into an agreement that would allow the Soviets to keep the large number of missiles they had targeted on western Europe, but which would prevent the United States from deploying any missiles of its own on European soil.[57] This sort of policy would scarcely deter the Soviets from trying to "Finlandize" western Europe. If anything, it would have the opposite effect.

On the other hand, Soviet leaders interested in reaching an accommodation with the United States might have reacted positively to the

---

tion: LBJ, the Gilpatric Committee, and U.S. National Security Policy," *Journal of Cold War Studies* 8, no. 2 (Spring 2006); and Brands, "Progress Unseen."

[54] See the editorial note, FRUS 1964–68, 11:716–17; note also Rostow to Johnson, December 11, 1968, and Johnson's marginal notes on that memo, ibid., p. 757, and especially notes 2 and 3. See also the message from the Soviet government to President-elect Nixon, December 18, 1968, FRUS 1964–68, 14:788–89. For criticism of that move, see Bohlen to Rusk , October 15, 1968, and McCloy to Johnson, December 12, 1968, ibid., pp. 738–39 and 782–86.

[55] Kissinger to Nixon, December 18, 1968, ibid., pp. 790–91.

[56] Schwartz, *Lyndon Johnson and Europe*, p. 218.

[57] "Strategic Missile Talks: Basic Position Paper," August 24, 1968, part II, para. 3, FRUS 1964–68, 11:706. This was not a new idea. Even in 1964, the U.S. government had proposed a freeze on delivery systems which would allow the USSR to keep the missiles it had targeted at western Europe, but which would also prevent NATO from deploying missiles in Europe that would be targeted at the Soviet Union. The French and the Germans very much disliked the plan at the time and disliked the way the U.S. government claimed it had the sovereign right to negotiate with the Soviets on this basis no matter what the Europeans thought. For the U.S. proposal, see Adrian Fisher statement, April 16, 1964, *Department of State Bulletin* 40, no. 1298 (May 11, 1964): 756–59; for various internal documents related to the proposal, see FRUS 1964–68, 11:docs. 2, 8, 14, 19, and 21. For German objections to the plan (and to the high-handed way the United States had moved ahead with it), see AAPD 1964, doc. 38 (esp. n. 13) and doc. 120 (esp. n. 2); for French objections to the way the U.S. government had turned down the NATO commander's request for Medium Range Ballistic Missiles to be deployed on European soil, see ibid. p. 1262.

Johnson policy. It was not just that the idea of a strategic arms control agreement had a certain visceral appeal. They also might have been encouraged by Johnson's policy on Germany, the policy of keeping German power limited. The basic idea that the two superpowers had overlapping interests in this area was by no means new. John Foster Dulles himself, despite his reputation as a hard-liner, thought that America and Russia had a common interest in making sure that Germany, whether united or divided, was kept under "some measure of external control."[58] But under Johnson that attitude was blunter, cruder, and less nuanced than it had been under Eisenhower or even under Kennedy. And the Soviets could reasonably see that policy as providing the basis for a political understanding between the two superpowers. So again the policy could cut both ways, and what effect it had in practice would depend on how the Soviets were disposed to approach the general problem of their relations with the West.

Can the same be said of U.S. policy during the Nixon period (1969–74)? In principle, Nixon and Kissinger wanted to build a "global structure of peace." In theory, they wanted a world where the major powers, pursuing their interests "rationally and predictably," balanced each others' power and kept each other in check. The United States, they said, needed to create such a system. America could most effectively promote her own interests by balancing between the other great states, and above all between the USSR and China. She could best promote her interests, that is, by keeping her options open—by retaining as much room for maneuver as possible, by making sure that each of the Communist giants understood it had something to gain from better relations with America and something to lose if relations were to deteriorate.[59]

Thus the U.S. opening to China, Kissinger later insisted, was not directed against Russia. The aim was "not to collude against the Soviet Union but to give us a balancing position to use for constructive ends— to give each Communist power a stake in better relations with us. Such an equilibrium could assure stability among the major powers, and even eventual cooperation, in the Seventies and Eighties."[60] That meant that the United States had to pursue a relatively complex and nuanced policy, not too militant, but not too committed to "peace" either. "If the

[58] Notes of NSC meeting, February 6, 1958, pp. 7–8, Ann Whitman File, NSC Series, box 9, Eisenhower Library, Abilene, Kans.

[59] See especially Kissinger, *Diplomacy*, p. 705, and Kissinger, *White House Years*, pp. 165, 190. For the term *global structure of peace*, see the president's 1971 "state of the world" report: Richard Nixon, "U.S. Foreign Policy for the 1970's: Building for Peace," February 25, 1971, *Department of State Bulletin* 64, no. 1656 (March 22, 1971): 344.

[60] Kissinger, *White House Years*, p. 192. See also ibid., p. 764.

quest for peace," Kissinger wrote, "turns into the *sole* objective of policy, the fear of war becomes a weapon in the hands of the most ruthless."[61] The United States should therefore be willing to use its power, but in a relatively measured and restrained way, in order to bring about the sort of "global equilibrium" that could serve as the basis of a stable international order.[62]

This, of course, was quite different from the policy Johnson had pursued, and Nixon and Kissinger obviously disliked the image of the United States as a "reluctant giant," "seeking peace and reconciliation almost feverishly." The Soviets were taking their measure of America, and the ability of the U.S. government to influence the sorts of choices the Soviets would be making would depend on the conclusions they reached about the United States—on how serious they thought the United States was as an actor in global politics.[63] The goal, therefore, was to structure the incentives within which the Soviets would operate—to dangle carrots and brandish sticks, so that when the Soviets made a calculation about the sort of policy that would be in their interest, they would reach what the Americans viewed as the right conclusion.[64]

So that was the theory, and if the policy had actually worked that way, it might have had a major impact on Soviet behavior. The problem was that U.S. policy, as it emerged in practice, was not really cut from that cloth. The United States, during the Nixon-Kissinger period, was not really interested in balancing *between* the Soviet Union and China. It was interested instead in balancing *against* the USSR, by helping China build up her power and by entering into a "tacit alliance" with the PRC.[65] But that policy, U.S. leaders understood, could not be pursued in a straightforward way. The United States needed to make sure the Soviets did not attack China before the Chinese became strong enough to deter the USSR on their own. To do that, the United States not only needed to develop a certain relationship with China; it also needed to try to hold back the Soviets by pursuing a détente policy with the USSR at the same time. The American strategy, as Kissinger told French President Georges Pompidou in May 1973, was "perhaps complex, but it was not stupid." The goal was to "gain time, to paralyze the USSR."[66]

---

[61] Ibid., p. 70; emphasis his. See also Henry Kissinger, *For the Record*, p. 192.

[62] Kissinger, *White House Years*, pp. 55, 192.

[63] "The Modern World, a Single 'Strategic Theater,'" September 29, 1969 (no author given), with Nixon's comments, FRUS 1969–72, 1:120; note esp. Nixon's comments in notes 11 and 12.

[64] Kissinger talk to U.S. chiefs of mission in east Asia, November 14–16, 1973, quoted in Burr, *Kissinger Transcripts*, p. 10.

[65] See Evelyn Goh, "Nixon, Kissinger, and the 'Soviet Card' in the U.S. Opening to China, 1971–1974," *Diplomatic History* 29:3 (June 2005), p. 485.

[66] See Georges-Henri Soutou, "Georges Pompidou and U.S.-European Relations," in

This, Kissinger admitted (especially in talks with the Chinese), was not a particularly heroic policy, but the U.S. government needed to use such "complicated methods." It needed to "maneuver," not just because of the Soviet threat to China, but also because of its domestic situation, and because of the political situation in Europe as well.[67]

The situation within the United States was of particular importance. Thanks to the Vietnam War, the country was now in a semi-isolationist mood, inclined to cut back not just on foreign entanglements but on military spending as well.[68] The administration thus had to fight a kind of guerrilla war on the home front. The actions it took, and the way it packaged its policies, were designed also with an eye to European opinion. Its goal was to take the wind out of its critics' sails by "pursuing policies which adopt their rhetoric." "We have to do certain things," Kissinger said, "and say certain things designed to paralyze not only our Left but the European Left as well."[69] Negotiations to reduce force levels in Europe, for example, were primarily "a device to keep the Senate from cutting our forces unilaterally."[70]

The United States, Kissinger said, had to engage in a lot of "shadow-boxing," but it was important, he insisted, to "distinguish between appearances and reality."[71] The U.S. government had "no illusions about the world today."[72] The West, in his view, had to be on its "guard against detente." Indeed, it had to be prepared to use détente "quite cold-bloodedly to justify as hard a policy line" as it could.[73]

It is scarcely surprising, therefore, as Kissinger himself admitted in 1974, that the Soviets were "getting nothing from détente." The United States was "pushing them everywhere." The Soviets, on the other hand, had "tried to be fairly reasonable all across the board." You could not

---

Between Empire and Alliance: America and Europe during the Cold War, ed. Marc Trachtenberg (Lanham, Md.: Rowman and Littlefield, 2003), p. 181. For the U.S. record of the meeting, see DNSA/KT00728 . See also Kissinger's comments to Chinese UN Ambassador Huang Hua, August 4, 1972, and July 6, 1973, in Burr, *Kissinger Transcripts*, pp. 73, 145.

[67] See various documents in Burr, *Kissinger Transcripts*, pp. 94, 177–78, 303, 386.

[68] U.S. defense spending, in fact, declined substantially during the Nixon-Ford period, even after discounting for decreases associated with the winding down and eventual termination of the Vietnam War. See Finley, "Some Aspects of Conventional Military Capability in Soviet Foreign Relations," p. 20, citing figures from Barry Blechman et al., *The Soviet Military Buildup and U.S. Defense Spending* (Washington, D.C.: Brookings, 1977), chap. 1.

[69] Kissinger-Deng meeting, November 27, 1974, in Burr, *Kissinger Transcripts*, pp. 304, 311.

[70] Kissinger-Huang meeting, September 8, 1972, p. 4, DNSA/KT00552

[71] Kissinger-Deng meeting, November 26, 1974, Burr, *Kissinger Transcripts*, p. 290.

[72] Kissinger-Debré meeting, July 11, 1972, p. 2, DNSA/KT00525.

[73] Kissinger meeting with high British officials, April 19, 1973, p. 4, DNSA/KT00707 (second document at that location).

find a single place, he said, "where they have really tried to make serious trouble for us. Even in the Middle East where our political strategy put them in an awful bind, they haven't really tried to screw us. Their tactics haven't been exactly brilliant but they haven't been particularly destructive either."[74]

The Nixon-Kissinger policy in theory was supposed to draw the Soviet Union into a closer, more cooperative relationship with the West. But there was a huge gap between rhetoric and reality, and the Soviets could scarcely be expected to respond positively to the policy the U.S. government actually pursued during that period. The rhetoric of détente might serve America's political purposes in the short run, but in the long run the chickens would probably come home to roost. There was a good chance the Soviets would feel that they had been played for fools and would react accordingly.

A STABLE SYSTEM?

The détente policy was thus something of a charade. Kissinger and Nixon had not set out to build a "global structure of peace" based on cooperation with the USSR. Their goal instead was to keep the Soviets in line by making sure they had to worry about a strong China on their Asian border. The U.S. government, that is, as Kissinger told Pompidou in May 1973, was interested in "playing China against the Soviet Union." It therefore wanted to prevent the Soviets from "destroying China." To do that, the Americans needed to develop a certain political relationship with the PRC, so that the Soviets could not be sure the United States would remain passive if China were attacked. But that would take time, and while that relationship was developing the USSR would somehow have to be kept from attacking that country. That was why U.S. policy could not "*seem* to be directed against the Soviet

---

[74] Kissinger meeting with State Department and White House officials, March 18, 1974, Burr, *Kissinger Transcripts,* pp. 224-225. This was in fact one of Kissinger's basic themes at the time. "If I were in the Politburo," he said on March 11, "I could make a case against Brezhnev for détente—more so than against us." "What have the Soviets gotten from détente?" he wondered on March 19. "The psychic satisfaction of reducing the chance of war and gaining equality with the U.S. Nothing else. We have defused the peace movement here. The Middle East must be painful to the Soviets." And on April 23 he made the same sort of assessment. Maybe the Soviets had an interest in good relations with the United States, he said, "but I think Brezhnev is a political idiot and has given us all sorts of gains." Kissinger-Schlesinger meetings, March 11, March 19, and April 23, 1974, National Security Adviser: Memoranda of Conversations, 1973-1977, box 3, Gerald Ford Library; also available online in the Digital Ford Presidential Library (http://www.ford librarymuseum.gov/library/docs.asp).

Union"; that was why détente had to be "carried on in parallel with the Soviet Union"; that was why (as he told the Chinese) the U.S. government needed to "do enough with the Soviet Union to maintain a *formal* symmetry." As China was making her way through the danger zone, the United States could not seem to be ganging up with that country against the USSR.[75] The United States had to make it seem that it was also developing a relationship with the Soviet Union. The Soviets had to be made to feel they had something to lose if they moved against China.

The focus was thus on appearances, not substance. Kissinger and Nixon were not really interested in working with the Soviets on fundamental political problems. The Arab-Israeli question, for example, was obviously of central importance for all sorts of reasons, and it seemed that the USSR, especially after the 1973 Yom Kippur War, was willing to cooperate with the United States in working out a solution. But the U.S. government was not interested in working together with the Soviets in this area no matter what position they took. Indeed, as Kissinger himself said, the United States was not particularly interested in the "merits of the dispute." "Our whole policy," he said, was to avoid "settling it cooperatively with the Soviet Union."[76]

The most important U.S.-Soviet negotiations thus dealt not with political but with military questions. A number of agreements were in fact reached in that latter area, and the SALT agreements, limiting the size of each side's strategic nuclear arsenals, were considered quite important at the time. Looking back, though, it seems that their importance had to do mainly with what those agreements seemed to symbolize. They made it seem that the two sides were determined to move away from the Cold War and put their relations on a more solid basis.

But putting symbolism aside, it is hard to see how the SALT agreements had a major stabilizing effect. With or without an agreement, neither side could hope to disarm the other. With or without an agreement, neither side therefore had any incentive to preempt. In such circumstances, what exactly could an agreement in this area hope to accomplish? How exactly could a strategic arms agreement make for a more stable international order? But those fundamental questions were

---

[75] Kissinger-Pompidou meeting, May 18, 1973, p. 4, DNSA/KT00728; Kissinger-Huang meeting, August 4, 1972, in Burr, *Kissinger Transcripts*, p. 73. Emphasis added.

[76] Kissinger-Mao meeting, November 12, 1973, and Kissinger-Deng meeting, October 20, 1975, in Burr, *Kissinger Transcripts*, pp. 188, 382. For a summary assessment of the USSR's policy on the Arab-Israeli dispute by a well-known specialist in this area, see Galia Golan, "The Soviet Union and the Outbreak of the June 1967 Six-Day War," *Journal of Cold War Studies* 8, no. 1 (Winter 2006): 17.

not addressed. The negotiations on offensive weapons, Schelling later wrote, were evidently not governed by any "guiding philosophy." Arms control, he said, was pursued "for its own sake, not for the sake of peace and confidence."[77] It is difficult to quarrel with those judgments. In fact, it is hard to see how even the agreement limiting the deployment of defensive anti-ballistic missile systems—the famous ABM treaty of 1972—played a major role in stabilizing the U.S.-Soviet strategic relationship. Given that ABM systems could easily and cheaply be overwhelmed by additional offensive weapons, even a massive defensive effort was bound to be futile and would thus have had little impact on that relationship.

But the arms control negotiations and the SALT agreements received a huge amount of attention at the time. Strategic arms control was viewed as the heart of the détente process. It seemed that the two great powers were dealing seriously with the military side of the Cold War, and that made it easier to ignore the fact that the really important military problems, the problems relating to the defense of Europe, were not being dealt with effectively.

Kissinger, of course, understood those problems—not just the military problems in the narrow sense, but the whole complex of problems, political as well as military, rooted in the waning of the American nuclear guarantee. This set of issues had been his main concern as a scholar since the mid-1950s, and those problems were certainly on his mind when he was in power in Washington. Even in December 1976, on the eve of his departure from office, Kissinger had no doubt that that the European defense problem—and problems relating to the defense of other regions as well—were still of "overwhelming" importance.[78]

But did the European defense problem really have to be taken so seriously? No one, after all, thought the Soviets were about to invade western Europe. The real problem was less overt. The West, even in the official view, had to worry instead about "a more subtle mix of military, psychological and political pressures."[79] But if that was all there was to the threat, how much danger were the western countries really in? Kissinger himself might have thought that Europe was on the verge of an "abyss," that Brandt, if he continued on his present course, would end up giving the Soviets a "veto over German policy," and that in about

[77] Thomas Schelling, "What Went Wrong with Arms Control?" *Foreign Affairs* 64, no. 2 (Winter 1985–86), pp. 225, 228.

[78] NSC meeting, December 15, 1976, p. 8 (http://www.fordlibrarymuseum.gov/library/document/nscmin/761215.pdf). See also Kissinger, *White House Years*, pp. 84, 196, 198.

[79] Nixon, "U.S. Foreign Policy for the 1970s," p. 342.

five years the point would "be reached where no German Chancellor [could] afford the hostility of the Soviet Union."[80] But while those fears were not absurd, they seem exaggerated, and not just in retrospect. The real risk was probably never that great.

But that is not the same as saying that there was nothing to be worried about. Maybe the Soviets would never use nuclear weapons in Europe. Maybe they would calculate that the risk was just too great—that no one, not even the Americans themselves, could tell for sure what the U.S. government would do if those weapons were actually used, and maybe that core uncertainty would have a very powerful deterrent effect. But it was also possible that the Soviets would come to the conclusion that the United States would never attack Soviet territory, no matter what the Red Army was doing in Europe; maybe they would somehow try to take advantage of that situation. Who could tell what they would do five or ten years down the road? Who could tell how the western countries would assess the threat or how they would deal with it? Events could take their course in all kinds of ways and no one could predict with any confidence how things would develop.

Extreme pessimism may not have been warranted, but there was no deep stability in this system. There were just too many unresolved questions—questions about the future of Russia and the future course of Soviet policy, about the future of Europe and the future of America's commitment to Europe, even about the future of the Sino-Soviet relationship. And one has the sense, studying this period, that those issues would not be left hanging forever— that sooner or later those questions would be answered, and that change, perhaps even fundamental change, was inevitable. But what sort of world would emerge as that process ran its course? Change there would be, but to what?

[80] Kissinger meeting with "Wise Men," November 28, 1973, p. 31, DNSA/KT00928; Kissinger-Zhou meeting, November 11, 1973, in Burr, *Kissinger Transcripts*, p. 175; Kissinger-Jobert meeting, May 22, 1973, p. 13, DNSA/KT00736.

CHAPTER SEVEN

The French Factor in U.S. Foreign Policy during the Nixon-Pompidou Period

WHEN RICHARD NIXON took office as president of the United States in early 1969, he and his national security advisor Henry Kissinger wanted to put America's relationship with France on an entirely new footing. Relations between the two countries in the 1960s, and especially from early 1963 on, had been far from ideal, and U.S. governments at the time blamed French President Charles de Gaulle for the fact that the United States was on such poor terms with its old ally. But Nixon and Kissinger took a rather different view. They admired de Gaulle and indeed thought of themselves as Gaullists.[1] Like de Gaulle, they thought that America in the past had been too domineering. "The excessive concentration of decision-making in the hands of the senior partner," as Kissinger put it in a book published in 1965, was not in America's own interest; it drained the alliance of "long-term political vitality."[2] The United States needed real allies—"self-confident partners with a strongly developed sense of identity"—and not satellites.[3] Nixon took

---

This paper, which was originally written for a conference on Georges Pompidou and the United States held in Paris in 2009, was published in the winter 2010–11 issue of the *Journal of Cold War Studies*. Copyright © Journal of Cold War Studies, MIT Press, Cambridge, Massachusetts. Reprinted by permission. A much shorter version of the paper is due to come out in a volume of conference papers being put out by the Association Georges Pompidou. A version of this article with links to copies of most of the documents cited is available at http://www.sscnet.ucla.edu/polisci/faculty/trachtenberg/ffus/FrenchFactor.pdf.

[1] See, for example, Nixon-Pompidou meeting, May 31, 1973, 10 a.m., p. 3, Digital National Security Archive (http://nsarchive.chadwyck.com/home.do), Kissinger Transcripts collection, document KT00742; henceforth documents from this source will be cited in this form: DNSA/KT00742. Note also Kissinger meeting with Rusk, Bundy, McCloy, et al., November 28, 1973, p. 8, DNSA/KT00928; and Henry Kissinger, *Years of Upheaval* (Boston: Little, Brown, 1982), p. 919.

[2] Henry Kissinger, *The Troubled Partnership: A Re-appraisal of the Atlantic Alliance* (New York: McGraw Hill, 1965), p. 233.

[3] Ibid., p. 235. See also Henry Kissinger, *White House Years* (Boston: Little, Brown, 1979), pp. 86, 106. This had been Kissinger's view for some time. See, especially, his important article "NATO's Nuclear Dilemma," *The Reporter* (March 28, 1963)—an article which President John F. Kennedy at the time referred to as a "disaster." Richard Neustadt notes of a conversation with Carl Kaysen, June 1, 1963, Richard Neustadt Papers, box 22, folder "Memcons—US," John F. Kennedy Library [JFKL], Boston.

the same line in meetings both with de Gaulle in March 1969 and with his successor as president, Georges Pompidou, in February 1970. It was "not healthy," he told Pompidou, "to have just two superpowers"; "what we need," he said, "is a better balance in the West."[4]

When Kissinger and Nixon argued along these lines, they were thinking above all of France. And indeed, if they were serious about recasting American policy along these lines, ending what Kissinger later called the "brutish quarrel" with that country was bound to be of fundamental importance.[5] The relationship needed to be rebuilt, and they thought this goal was within reach. French foreign policy under Pompidou, in Kissinger's view, was "serious and consistent."[6] The British, in comparison, were no longer interested in playing a major role: "with every passing year they acted less as if their decisions mattered. They offered advice, usually sage; they rarely sought to embody it in a policy of their own. British statesmen were content to act as honored consultants in our deliberations."[7] As for the Germans, both Nixon and Kissinger were worried about the Federal Republic, and especially about where the policy of the new Willy Brandt government—its Ostpolitik, its policy of improving relations with the East—was leading. They knew they had to go along with that policy, at least for the time being.[8] But they were worried about German nationalism and German neutralism, about the Germans' interest in eventually doing away with NATO, about the possibility that the present leaders like Brandt, although per-

---

[4] Nixon-de Gaulle meeting, March 1, 1969, p. 3, Nixon Presidential Library website, Virtual Library; and Nixon-Pompidou meeting, February 24, 1970, p. 6, DNSA/KT00103. See also Kissinger, *White House Years*, pp. 81–82, 86, 106, 390, 418, and Kissinger, *Troubled Partnership*, pp. 233–36.

[5] Kissinger, *Years of Upheaval*, p. 5.

[6] Kissinger, *White House Years*, p. 420; see also p. 963.

[7] Kissinger, *White House Years*, p. 421.

[8] As Kissinger put it in a National Security Council meeting in 1970, "We can't afford to oppose Brandt but we can't support his policy too strongly either." NSC meeting, October 14, 1970, DNSA/KT00198. He took a dim view of the agreements that were eventually reached: the German settlement, he told the British in April 1973, was "pernicious"; the U.S. government, he told them that November, had "hair-raising intelligence on what the Germans were saying to the Russians." Kissinger meeting with British officials, April 19, 1973, p. 4, DNSA/KT00707; Cromer to Douglas-Home, November 24, 1973, in *Documents on British Policy Overseas*, series III, vol. 4, ed. Keith Hamilton and Patrick Salmon, CD-ROM (New York: Routledge, 2006), doc. 412; henceforth cited in this form: DBPO III:4:412. On this general issue, see Stephan Fuchs, *"Dreiecksverhältnisse sind immer kompliziert": Kissinger, Bahr und die Ostpolitik* (Hamburg: Rotbuch Verlag, 1999); Holger Klitzing, *The Nemesis of Stability: Henry A. Kissinger's Ambivalent Relationship with Germany* (Trier: Wissenschaftlicher Verlag Trier, 2007); and also Klitzing's article "To Grin and Bear It: The Nixon Administration and *Ostpolitik*," in Carole Fink and Bernd Schaefer, eds., *Ostpolitik, 1969–1974: European and Global Perspectives* (Cambridge, England: Cambridge University Press, 2009).

sonally committed to the West, might be setting off a process they would not be able to control.[9] This meant that the United States could not have the same sort of relationship with Germany that Nixon and Kissinger hoped to have with France: too much independence for Germany would be too dangerous; Germany was viewed more as a problem than as a partner. Kissinger explained U.S. thinking in this area to Pompidou in May 1973. A strong Europe, in the American view, was as essential as a strong China, and in that strong Europe, "France would play a pivotal role. We do not believe that Germany is sufficiently strong psychologically, and we believe it is too open to Soviet pressures to be able to contribute to develop a Europe in this sense." It was "of great importance," he told Pompidou, "that you understand our real policy"; "we have never discussed this so openly with another leader."[10]

So France was of central importance, and Nixon and Kissinger tried to develop a close relationship with the Pompidou government. They admired Pompidou as a person.[11] They liked the way the French tended to think in cool, realistic, power political terms.[12] They tended to view France as the most "European" of the European allies, saying things that the other European governments did not dare to say out loud— and this meant that in dealing with France as something of a privileged partner, they were really in a sense dealing with western Europe as a whole.[13] And they were willing, they said, to live with the fact that French and American interests and policies diverged in a number of key areas. In a December 1970 meeting with Hervé Alphand, the top permanent official in the French foreign ministry, Kissinger "remarked

---

[9] See Kissinger, *White House Years*, pp. 408–9, and Kissinger, *Years of Upheaval*, p. 146. Note also Nixon's comments in a meeting with Pompidou, December 13, 1971, in William Burr, ed., *The Kissinger Transcripts: The Top Secret Talks with Beijing and Moscow* (New York: New Press, 1998), pp. 36–37, and Kissinger's comments in a meeting with Zhou Enlai, November 10, 1973, ibid., p. 175. See also Kissinger-Jobert meeting, May 22, 1973, p. 13, DNSA/KT00736. Kissinger had been aware of those trends for some time. See, especially, his notes of an April 10, 1965, meeting with Egon Bahr, Brandt's most important advisor. Bahr told him that in the "scheme he and Brandt were considering," "a unified Germany would leave NATO" and "foreign troops would be withdrawn from its territory." Declassified Documents Reference System [DDRS], document CK2349120291.

[10] Kissinger-Pompidou meeting, May 18, 1973, p. 7, DNSA/KT00728.

[11] See Kissinger, *White House Years*, pp. 389, 419, and Kissinger, *Years of Upheaval*, p. 129.

[12] See Kissinger, *White House Years*, pp. 105, 421; and Kissinger, *Troubled Partnership*, p. 58. This basic attitude was reflected in a comment Nixon made in his February 1970 meeting with Pompidou. "What we really need," he had told his colleagues, "was a healthy dose of French skepticism or cynicism in dealing with the Soviet Union." Nixon-Pompidou meeting, February 24, 1970, pp. 4–5, DNSA/KT00103.

[13] See, for example, Kissinger, *Troubled Partnership*, p. 72, and Kissinger, *White House Years*, p. 109. The references there are to de Gaulle, but that way of looking at things applied also to the France of Georges Pompidou.

that we did not have nervous breakdowns every time a Franco-American disagreement appeared; that was the custom when Alphand was the Ambassador here in another period but it was not so now."[14]

Those attitudes would have had a major impact on relations between the two countries even if de Gaulle had remained in power. As it was, the French for their part had also shifted course in 1969. Pompidou, who also came to power that year, was a Gaullist but he was not de Gaulle. His was a "rationalized Gaullism," as Georges-Henri Soutou calls it, a Gaullism shorn of the General's eccentricities. The new president did not want to see the United States play only a peripheral role in European affairs. There needed to be a counterweight to Soviet power in Europe, and in his view only the United States could provide it. On that issue he and the new American leadership saw eye-to-eye. And on the other great issue in European politics, the German question, they also took basically the same line. Neither of them was entirely thrilled by what Brandt was doing, but for now at least neither would stand in his way.[15]

Given all this, it would have been amazing if relations between the two countries did not improve dramatically, and in fact in the early Nixon-Pompidou period the two governments were on very good terms. Kissinger, in his memoirs, referred to a "degree of sharing of views unprecedented among allies," and some of his meetings with Pompidou were indeed quite extraordinary.[16] But what was going on in

[14] Kissinger-Alphand meeting, December 14, 1970, p. 5, National Security Council Files [NSCF], box 677, folder "France vol. VII," now at the Nixon Presidential Library [NPL], Yorba Linda, Calif.; henceforth cited in this form: NSCF/677/France vol. VII/NPL. Alphand was ambassador in Washington from 1956 to 1965.

[15] On the Pompidou policy, a series of works by Georges-Henri Soutou are of fundamental importance: "L'attitude de Georges Pompidou face à l'Allemagne," in Association Georges Pompidou, *Georges Pompidou et l'Europe: Colloque, 25 et 26 novembre 1993* (Brussels: Éditions Complexe, 1995); "Le Président Pompidou et les relations entre les États-Unis et l'Europe," *Journal of European Integration History* [JEIH] 6, no. 2 (2000)—an English translation was published in Marc Trachtenberg, ed., *Between Empire and Alliance: America and Europe during the Cold War* (Lanham, Md.: Rowman and Littlefield, 2003); and "La problématique de la Détente et le testament stratégique de Georges Pompidou," *Cahiers du Centre d'Études d'Histoire de la Défense*, cahier no. 22 (2004). See also Andreas Wilkens, *Der unstete Nachbar: Frankreich, die deutsche Ostpolitik und die Berliner Vier-Mächte-Verhandlungen 1969–1974* (Munich: Oldenbourg, 1990); and Gottfried Niedhart, "Frankreich und die USA im Dialog über Détente und Ostpolitik, 1969–1970," *Francia: Forschungen zur westeuropäischen Geschichte* 31, no. 3 (2004): 65–85; see esp. the final two pages in this article.

[16] Kissinger, *White House Years*, p. 964. See especially the record of their May 18, 1973, meeting (DNSA/KT00728). Note also Soutou's discussion of this meeting in his article "Le Président Pompidou et les relations entre les États-Unis et l'Europe,"pp. 133–34 (corresponding to pp. 180–81 in the translated version published in Trachtenberg, ed., *Between Empire and Alliance*). China was the only other government with which Kissinger

the nuclear area was of even greater importance.[17] From the very start, both governments were interested in developing a certain relationship in this area.[18] Nixon and Kissinger wanted to support the French nuclear program. As Kissinger told the French ambassador in April 1973, de Gaulle "was basically right," it was "too dangerous to have one country as the repository of nuclear weapons. We would like France to be a possessor."[19] American policy in this area, as Nixon told Pompidou in 1973, had shifted 180 degrees from what it had been in the 1960s.[20] And as for Pompidou, he very much wanted to get American help for the French nuclear program. He was not held back by any doctrinaire Gaullist notions that the French could not even talk to the Americans about such matters—that for the sake of French independence, they would have to do everything entirely on their own. When Kissinger asked Pompidou in February 1970 whether he could talk about defense matters on his forthcoming visit to Washington, he said, "I can and I want to."[21] On the other hand, the U.S. leadership, knowing how sensitive the French could be on the subject of independence, decided that no political preconditions would be laid down, and that in particular the U.S. negotiators would *"not* suggest that U.S. assistance" be "tied to greater French cooperation in NATO."[22]

---

was so open; on May 30 he in fact gave the Chinese a copy of the record of his meeting with Pompidou. See Kissinger-Huang meeting, May 29, 1973, p. 4, DNSA/KT00740.

[17] On this issue, see especially Pierre Mélandri, "Aux origines de la coopération nucléaire franco-américaine," in Maurice Vaïsse, ed., *La France et l'atome: études d'histoire nucléaire* (Brussels: Bruyant, 1994); Pierre Mélandri, "Une relation très spéciale: la France, les États-Unis et l'Année de l'Europe," in *Georges Pompidou et l'Europe*, esp. pp. 106–110; Soutou, "La problématique de la Détente," esp. pp. 91–92, 97–98, and above all Maurice Vaïsse, "Les 'relations spéciales' franco-américaines au temps de Richard Nixon et Georges Pompidou," *Relations internationales*, no. 119 (Fall 2004).

[18] See Vaïsse, "Les 'relations spéciales' franco-américaines," p. 360, and also the discussion on p. 3 of the more extensive manuscript version of this article (provided to me by Professor Vaïsse).

[19] Kissinger meeting with Ambassador Jacques Kosciusko-Morizet, April 13, 1973, p. 9, DNSA/KT00702. Note also his comments to a high-level British official, Sir Burke Trend, on April 19, 1973, in Trend's memo to the Prime Minister (dated April 24, 1973), pp. 2–3, DNSA/KT00707.

[20] Quoted in Mélandri, "Aux origines de la coopération nucléaire franco-américaine," p. 247.

[21] Kissinger-Pompidou meeting, February 23, 1970, DNSA/KT00100.

[22] Sonnenfeldt to Kissinger, June 25, 1970, NSCF/677/France vol. VI/NPL. Emphasis in original text. It should be noted that Secretary of Defense Melvin Laird had assumed that the U.S. government should ask for something in return for the nuclear assistance it would be offering—for example, "French participation in NATO defense studies." Laird draft memo for the president, enclosed in Laird to Kissinger, April 2, 1970, p. 3, in the same file. That Laird suggestion was now being overruled. It should be noted, incidentally, that in Kissinger's view the whole question of French relations with NATO was not very important in any case. "It is clear," he wrote earlier that year, "that much of the dis-

So it is not too surprising, given those attitudes, that a certain relationship did develop. The Americans began to provide some very important information relating especially to France's existing systems, especially information that would help French missiles penetrate Soviet defenses. The French, for their part, were quite pleased with the information the Americans were giving them.[23] So American policy toward France had shifted in a fairly fundamental way, and what this suggests is that the language the new U.S. leadership was now using has to be taken seriously.

But if all this is true, how then are we to understand what happened in the final year of the Nixon-Pompidou period? For in 1973, as many observers have noted, relations between the two countries took a sharp turn for the worse. What had gone wrong? Why did the attempt to develop a close relationship fail? My goal here is to look at this issue in the light of a remarkable body of source material—not just French and American, but German and British as well—that has become available in the past few years. What light does that new evidence throw on this question?

THE END OF BRETTON WOODS

It is easy enough for two countries to cooperate when they see eye-to-eye on key issues. But what happens when they disagree on some issue of major importance? The first great test of the new relationship between

---

cussion of integration versus national freedom of action is artificial and theological. In the end, all NATO members retain the capacity for unilateral military action; at the same time, in practice, they are unlikely to use them unilaterally except under most unusual and extreme circumstances." Kissinger memo for Nixon on Military Relations with France, February 23, 1970, NSCF/916/France—Pompidou Visit Feb. '70 (1 of 3)/NPL. And it is important to note also that the French government, even under de Gaulle, and despite all of the General's complaints about NATO, did not take the NATO structures too seriously: the only really important question was whether the U.S. president would decide to go nuclear if the alliance ever faced its moment of truth; the plans that had been worked out in the NATO framework and the strategy documents that had been adopted would not have much bearing on the sort of decision that was made. See, for example, Couve de Murville's comments in a meeting with U.S. ambassador Charles Bohlen, December 2, 1963, *Documents diplomatiques français* 1963, 2:576. For confirmation of the point that the Americans did not ask for anything in exchange for the nuclear help they were offering, see Defense Minister Debré to Pompidou, March 11, 1972, quoted in Mélandri, "Une relation très spéciale," p. 107.

[23] See especially the Debré to Pompidou letter cited in n. 22. For a discussion of how the nuclear relationship had developed, of how matters stood in the spring of 1973, and how things might progress, see the Defense Department response to NSSM 175, May 11, 1973, NSCF/679/France—vol. XI/NPL.

France and the United States that had developed early in the Nixon-Pompidou period came in 1971 with the collapse of the Bretton Woods system of fixed exchange rates. The two countries had very different policies in that area. How well were they able to manage their differences? Some new international monetary system had to be worked out, and in fact a new system of market-based (or "floating") exchange rates did eventually come into being. What does a study of the story here tell us about the basic nature of Franco-American relations in this period?

The collapse of the Bretton Woods system in August 1971, with the American decision to close the "gold window"—that is, to no longer allow foreign governments to convert the dollars they had accumulated into gold at the official price of $35 an ounce—came as no surprise. By the time the end came, it was quite clear that the system was in crisis and that the basic problem had to do not with the policy of any particular government but rather with the system itself. The Bretton Woods regime was in practice, if not quite in theory, a system of more or less fixed exchange rates. The dollar was convertible into gold at a fixed rate, and other currencies were convertible into dollars (considered, at the start, to be as "good as gold"), again at fixed rates. [24] The problem with such a system is that, given that different governments pursue different policies, especially monetary policies, payments imbalances are almost inevitable. If the U.S. rate of inflation is higher than that of America's main trading partners, American goods (in a fixed rate regime) would become increasingly overpriced abroad, and foreign goods would become a better deal in the United States. The balance of trade would thus shift, and other key elements in the balance of payments—above all, capital movements—would be affected in much the same way. And as it happened by 1971 the United States was running a large balance of payments deficit, spending more for foreign goods, for foreign assets, and for foreign exchange that it wanted for other purposes (most notably to meet the needs of the American armed forces stationed abroad) than it was taking in from the sale of U.S. goods abroad, from U.S. investment earnings abroad, and in other more or less normal ways. That deficit was possible only because foreign governments and their central banks were in effect willing to finance it by holding those excess dollars or their equivalents. In theory, they were entitled to cash in the dollars they were accumulating for gold, but in practice it was clear that the Americans would view that as an unfriendly act; in any case, an unending U.S. gold hemorrhage would lead to an official closing of the gold window, and few foreign govern-

[24] See, for example, John Williamson, *The Failure of World Monetary Reform, 1971-1974* (New York: New York University Press, 1977), p. 4.

ments wanted to bring down the par value system by forcing the Americans to do that.

So the key question then had to do with how those persistent payments imbalances could be dealt with. In principle, under the Bretton Woods system, the parities could be adjusted in such cases. But in practice the surplus countries were reluctant to revalue their currencies upward, mainly because they did not want to hurt their export industries, and the deficit countries were reluctant to devalue, largely because devaluation was viewed as something of a humiliation.[25] A devaluation of the dollar, moreover, was especially problematic, given that other countries were holding substantial parts of their reserves in dollars. One of the reasons those countries were holding dollars was that they had been told that those dollar reserves were as "good as gold"; a devaluation of the dollar might be seen almost as a breach of faith, an admission that the surplus countries had been misled and that their dollar reserves were not as "good as gold" after all.[26] If the dollar were devalued, their reserves, moreover, would be worth less in terms of gold; those countries might then lose faith in the dollar and cash in their dollar reserves for gold even at the new price. A devaluation, in other words, might actually lead to a run on the dollar, and thus to a collapse of the system. And beyond that there was a certain sense that a devaluation might not have much of an effect on actual exchange rates and thus on the payments imbalance: a top European Economic Community official predicted that if the United States devalued, "all European currencies would be devalued by the same percentage on the same day."[27]

This situation was not to anyone's liking. The United States was in effect living beyond its means, and the Europeans, together with the Japanese, were picking up the tab. This naturally led to a certain amount of resentment on the part of the surplus countries. De Gaulle, of course, was especially outspoken on this issue. But the Americans did not feel they were benefiting from the system.[28] They were not happy to be run-

[25] See, for example, French Finance Minister Valéry Giscard d'Estaing's characterization of de Gaulle's attitude, quoted in Benedict Schoenborn, *La mésentente apprivoisée: De Gaulle et les Allemands, 1963–1969* (Paris: Presses Universitaires de France, 2007), p. 116.

[26] "An increase in the official gold price would break faith with all those who have helped us for a decade by holding large amounts of dollars." Kissinger to Nixon, June 25, 1969, U.S. Department of State, *Foreign Relations of the United States, 1969–1976*, vol. 3, p. 349; henceforth cited in this form: FRUS 1969–76, 3:349.

[27] Hendrik Houthakker, "The Breakdown of Bretton Woods," in Werner Sichel, *Economic Advice and Executive Policy: Recommendations from Past Members of the Council of Economic Advisors* (New York: Praeger, 1978), p. 54. See also George Shultz and Kenneth Dam, *Economic Policy Beyond the Headlines* (New York: Norton, 1977), p. 114.

[28] On this point, see the important study by Francis Gavin, *Gold, Dollars, and Power: The*

ning a payments deficit—quite the contrary. The payments deficit was for them a burden. It constrained their freedom of action both at home and abroad. They would have preferred, for example, to set policy on troop levels in Europe without having to take balance of payments considerations into account. And they would have preferred to manage the U.S. economy without, say, having to worry about how the low interest rates needed to deal with unemployment might affect the payments deficit. As Nixon put it, "[W]e just can't have the American domestic economy constantly hostage" to the "international monetary situation."[29] The payments deficit was in fact disliked for all sorts of reasons—not least because of the controls and protectionist pressures it had led to[30]—and by 1971 the U.S. government was more open to fundamental systemic change than one might think.

By that point many economists had begun to concern themselves with these problems. Some of them wanted to move to a system of floating exchange rates, where rates would be set by the market.[31] The major advantage of that system, as the economist Milton Friedman pointed out, is that it "completely eliminates the balance-of-payments problem," or as the British-born economist Harry Johnson, another champion of the market-based system, put it, it would automatically ensure balance of payments equilibrium.[32] The exchange rate would

---

Politics of International Monetary Relations, 1958-1971 (Chapel Hill: University of North Carolina Press, 2004).

[29] Nixon meeting with economic advisors, March 3, 1973, tape transcript, FRUS 1969–76, 31:59.

[30] Note for example Paul Krugman's comment on a paper by Richard Marston about capital controls under Bretton Woods: "The most striking result of the paper is its demonstration that the Bretton Woods system bore very little resemblance to the golden age of financial markets that many people now think that they remember. Capital controls were pervasive, and they led to large, systematic interest differentials." In Michael Bordo and Barry Eichengreen, eds., A Retrospective on the Bretton Woods System: Lessons for International Monetary Reform (Chicago: University of Chicago Press, 1993), p. 539.

[31] Robert Roosa, a leading proponent of the fixed-parity system, thought in 1967 that at least 90 percent of academic economists seemed to accept the "theoretical case for fluctuating rates." Milton Friedman and Robert Roosa, The Balance of Payments: Free Versus Fixed Exchange Rates (Washington, D.C.: American Enterprise Institute, 1967), p. 177. The real figure was in all likelihood not nearly that high, although most economists probably did favor the introduction of more flexibility into the system—for example, a "crawling peg," or wider bands within which rates would be allowed to fluctuate. See Friedman's own comments on this issue in ibid., pp. 133–34.

[32] Ibid., p. 15; Harry Johnson, "The Case for Flexible Exchange Rates, 1969," republished in Harry Johnson, Further Essays in Monetary Economics (London: George Allen and Unwin, 1972), p. 199. It should be noted, however, that it was not just the pro-market monetarist right of the economics profession that disliked the par value system. The Keynesian left was also uncomfortable with a regime that made it more difficult for gov-

simply be set at the point where demand for a particular currency was equal to the supply—the point, that is, at which payments were in balance with each other.

And it was not just academic economists who tended increasingly to favor a more flexible system. After a decade of chronic balance of payments problems, support for the Bretton Woods regime was no longer rock solid, and some people in business, government and even banking circles were open to the idea of fairly fundamental change. In the United States, the most influential "floater" was George Shultz, an economist by training, a friend, disciple, and former colleague of Friedman, and in 1971 head of the Office of Management and Budget at the White House. Some key European officials, especially in Germany and Italy, also favored a more flexible regime. But most officials, and probably most economists as well, were not quite ready to go all the way and replace Bretton Woods with a market-based system. There was still a strong feeling that without fixed parities the world might well revert to the chaos of the 1930s, with its competitive devaluations and pernicious "beggar-thy-neighbor" monetary policies. This view was not based on a serious historical analysis of that period. It ignored the fact, for example, that the world did not have a simple floating exchange rate system in the 1930s; indeed, the very term *competitive devaluations* implied that currencies were still being pegged to a fixed standard.[33] But the myth about the 1930s was very strong, and it was in large part because of a visceral fear that radical change might lead to a 1930s-style disaster that the Bretton Woods system had the support it did.

So the Nixon administration, even in 1971, did not set out to bring

---

ernments to pursue the monetary and fiscal policies that the domestic economic situation seemed to call for. Keynes himself in the interwar period had pointed out the problems with the gold exchange standard; the term *golden fetters* that Barry Eichengreen used as the title of one of his books—*Golden Fetters: The Gold Standard and the Great Depression* (New York: Oxford University Press, 1992)—was taken from a passage in an essay that Keynes published in 1932.

[33] As Ragnar Nurkse pointed in out in 1944, the "monetary authorities in most countries" in the 1930s "had little or no desire for freely fluctuating exchanges." Ragnar Nurkse, *International Currency Experience: Lessons of the Inter-War Period* (Geneva: League of Nations, 1944), p. 122. Scholars incidentally tend to argue nowadays that the historical beliefs that sustained the Bretton Woods system were essentially incorrect. See, for example, Michael Bordo, "The Bretton Woods International Monetary System: A Historical Overview," in Bordo and Eichengreen, *Retrospective on the Bretton Woods System*, p. 31; Barry Eichengreen and Jeffrey Sachs, "Exchange Rates and Economic Recovery in the 1930s," *Journal of Economic History* 65 (1985): 925–46; and Eichengreen, *Golden Fetters*, esp. pp. 4, 21–22. Thus Eichengreen writes, "According to the conventional wisdom, the currency depreciation made possible by abandoning the gold standard failed to ameliorate conditions in countries that left gold and exacerbated the Depression in those that remained. Nothing could be more contrary to the evidence" (p. 21).

down the system. Its primary goal was to deal with the payments deficit, and that meant that it had to get its trading partners to accept a more reasonable structure of exchange rates. It would achieve that goal by not actively defending the dollar if it came under pressure; the United States would also make it clear, either formally or informally, that it would not allow other countries to cash in the dollars they had accumulated for gold at the official price; the surplus countries would then have to choose whether to revalue their currencies upward or go on accumulating dollars. The assumption was that they would probably opt to revalue and the world would get a better system of fixed parities. But if they went the other route, that would not be a major problem for the Americans. The surplus countries would be soaking up dollars because they had chosen to do so, not because the U.S. government had come to them, hat in hand, and had asked them to do so.[34]

But although an exchange rate realignment was an important immediate goal, a number of key U.S. officials were interested in getting something more than just a one-shot set of revaluations. Some of them were also, from the start, interested in bringing about a fundamental reform of the system—in cooperation with the surplus countries if possible, but unilaterally if those cooperative efforts failed. And those who favored this course were under no illusions that the sorts of reforms they had in mind would be easy to achieve.

The crisis, though long expected, came to a head in mid-1971. The new secretary of the treasury, John Connally, laid out the policy in May. The crisis would be allowed to develop "without action or strong intervention by the U.S." At an appropriate time, the gold window would be closed and trade restrictions would be imposed. This would lead, at least for the time being, to a system of floating rates. The main goal was to get the surplus countries to revalue their currencies, but it would be made clear—both for bargaining purposes and as a fallback position if revaluation negotiations failed—that the United States could live with the floating rate system indefinitely. [35] Nixon approved this course of

[34] Houthakker, "The Breakdown of Bretton Woods," pp. 50–53; Hendrik Houthakker, "Cooling Off the Money Crisis," *Wall Street Journal*, March 16, 1973, p. 10. Houthakker was a Harvard economics professor who served on Nixon's Council of Economic Advisors from 1969 to 1971. Note also Kissinger to Nixon, June 25, 1969, FRUS 1969–76, 3:345–51; see especially the recommendation on p. 351 that the U.S. should "pursue a passive balance of payments policy while pursuing the negotiations for monetary reform." (Kissinger obviously did not draft this document; as he often admitted, this was not his area of expertise.) The aim of the June 25 memorandum was to prepare the president for an important meeting on international monetary policy. No record of that meeting has been found (ibid., p. 345 n. 3), but it is discussed in Houthakker, "Breakdown of Bretton Woods," p. 53.

[35] Treasury paper, May 8, 1971, FRUS 1969–76, 3:423–427, esp. p. 425.

action and in fact wanted to "move on the problem," and not "just wait for it to hit us again."[36] The new measures were announced on August 15: the gold window was closed, a border tax was imposed. Nixon had gone on the offensive. The whole tone of U.S. policy in this area was quite nationalistic. The emphasis was still on getting the Europeans and the Japanese to accept a substantial realignment of exchange rates, but the goal of systemic change had by no means disappeared entirely. According to Shultz, who was certainly in a position to know, the August 15 package "was designed to be a signal that the United States was seeking a fundamental change not only in existing exchange rates but also in the monetary system itself."[37]

And Shultz's influence was on the rise. By late 1971, Nixon had evidently come to share the Shultz view that a major structural reform was in order, and that it would be a mistake to go back to the "old system of parities, but with different exchange rates."[38] It was probably for this reason that the question of a devaluation of the dollar in terms of its gold price was now so important: if the price of the dollar could be set in terms of gold, then why shouldn't all the exchange rates be set by international agreement? That was the old system, and the basic goal now for Shultz and, increasingly, for Nixon as well, was to move on to something better. But Connally, who was being criticized for his rough tactics, was under pressure to settle, and he in effect offered to devalue the dollar as part of a rate realignment package.[39] Nixon was angry. He had made it clear that he did not favor devaluation.[40] But it was too late to go back on the Connally offer. A series of negotiations—between the

[36] Huntsman to Connally, June 8, 1971, ibid., p. 443. The Nixon tapes provide some extraordinary insights into U.S. policy-making at this point. Some key passages were transcribed and presented in chapter 3 of Luke Nichter, "Richard Nixon and Europe: Confrontation and Cooperation, 1969–1974," unpublished diss., Bowling Green State University, Ohio, 2008.

[37] Shultz and Dam, *Economic Policy*, p. 115.

[38] Editorial note, FRUS 1969–76, 3:521–22. Note also a September 8, 1971, letter to the Under Secretary of the Treasury for Monetary Affairs Paul Volcker from Shultz's Assistant Director Kenneth Dam (he and Shultz later wrote a book together), cited in FRUS 1969–76, 3:179 n. 1, warning (in the editor's paraphrase) that "focusing on quantitative goals before agreeing on the type of international monetary system the administration wanted might constrain long-term options." See also Nixon-Kissinger telephone conversation, October 28, 1971, Digital National Security Archive (http://nsarchive.chadwyck.com/home.do), Kissinger Telephone Conversations Collection, item number KA06727; henceforth cited in this form: DNSA/KA06727.

[39] See, for example, Paul Volcker and Toyoo Gyohten, *Changing Fortunes: The World's Money and the Threat to American Leadership* (New York: Times Books, 1992), pp. 85–87.

[40] Nixon memo, November 2, 1971, and editorial note, FRUS 1969–76, 3:528, 582. See also Nixon-Kissinger phone conversation, October 28, 1971, DNSA/KA06727; Allen Matusow, *Nixon's Economy: Booms, Busts, Dollars, and Votes* (Lawrence: University Press of Kansas, 1998), pp. 173, 176; and Robert Leeson, *Ideology and the International Economy: The*

Germans and the French, then between Nixon, Kissinger, and Pompidou in the Azores, and finally in late December 1971 among all the major trading nations at the Smithsonian Institution in Washington—followed in rapid order, leading to an agreement that set new parities, but which did not restore convertibility.

The Americans, however, did little to "defend" the new rates.[41] Shultz had taken over from Connally as secretary of the treasury in early 1972 and that policy choice was in line with Shultz's basic approach to the problem. His goals were more ambitious than Connally's had been: he wanted a fundamentally new system, a system where the market would play the central role in setting exchange rates. But he was no Texas cowboy: his methods were subtle and indirect. He thought of himself as a strategist who sought to "understand the constellation of forces present in a situation" and tried to arrange them so that they pointed "toward a desirable result." The aim was not to dictate the terms of a settlement, but rather "to get the right process going" and allow things to take their course.[42]

It was thus not Shultz's style to try to force his views directly on other people. He was a "conciliator and consensus builder" and could "work with almost inhuman patience to bring a group into agreement upon a decision that all could support, at times submerging his own preferences."[43] The most striking example of this was his willingness in mid-1972 to accept a "par value system supported by official convertibility of dollar balances," provided the burden of adjustment was shared equally by both surplus and deficit countries.[44] A plan of that sort (which, however, would also allow countries to "float their currencies") was announced in September 1972.[45] It was well received, since it showed that the U.S. government was serious about reform. For Shultz, however, a negotiation based on this kind of plan was not the only way to bring a new system into being. For him, the road to reform had two lanes, "one of negotiations and the other of reality. A conclusion would

---

Decline and Fall of Bretton Woods (Houndmills, England: Palgrave Macmillan, 2003), pp. 140–41.

[41] See Volcker and Gyohten, *Changing Fortunes*, pp. 103–4.

[42] George Shultz, *Turmoil and Triumph: My Years as Secretary of State* (New York: Scribner's, 1993), pp. 30, 31.

[43] Volcker and Gyohten, *Changing Fortunes*, p. 118.

[44] Ibid., p. 119.

[45] See "Major Elements of Plan X," July 31, 1972, and editorial note, FRUS 1969–76, 3:646, 655. The text of Shultz's September 26, 1972, speech laying out this proposal was published in the *New York Times* on September 27. It is interesting to compare the accounts of this plan that Shultz and Volcker give in their memoirs; one would hardly think they were describing the same proposal. See Volcker and Gyohten, *Changing Fortunes*, pp. 119–20; Shultz and Dam, *Economic Policy*, pp. 126–27.

be reached only when these two lanes merged and the formal system and the system in actual practice came together."[46] A system of floating exchange rates came into being *de facto* with the collapse of the Smithsonian agreement in early 1973; the two lanes converged when the reality of the floating rate system was recognized by the Jamaica agreement of January 1976.

What does this story tell us about U.S. policy toward Europe in this period? Does it give us any insight into the question of why Franco-American relations took the course they did in the Nixon-Pompidou period? The first point to note is that the floating exchange rate system did not come about by accident. It was not as though everyone wanted fixed rates, but just could not agree on what sort of fixed rate system to set up. By early 1972 the Americans had a strategy; key officials like Shultz, backed to a certain extent by Nixon, knew what they were doing. They were not trying to maintain a system in which the United States had special rights. The French had complained, under both de Gaulle and Pompidou, that in the Bretton Woods system the Americans had enjoyed a kind of right of seignorage. They could run deficits and the rest of the world would have to finance those deficits by holding dollars that in effect could not be cashed in for gold. They could pay for what they wanted, they could buy up European firms, with dollars they could create at will.[47] But in a floating exchange rate system, no foreign government would have to hold dollars if it did not want to. The "privileges" that America "enjoyed" under Bretton Woods would disappear. The dollar would become a more normal currency. And that was the way U.S. leaders wanted it. For them Bretton Woods was a straitjacket. They complained constantly about the "asymmetries" of the system. They wanted, as Shultz put it, "to gain for the United States some of the freedom of action for its own exchange rate that was available to all other countries."[48]

The French were much more committed to the basic idea of a fixed rate system, but they were by no means horrified by the new American policy. They were not too upset even by the nationalistic rhetoric Nixon and Connally adopted when the gold window was closed in August 1971. As a politician, Pompidou appreciated the way Nixon had turned

[46] Shultz and Dam, *Economic Policy*, p. 127. Shultz had in fact used the two-track metaphor at the time. See Nixon-Kissinger-Shultz meeting, March 3, 1973, tape transcript, and Nixon meeting with Shultz, Ash and Stein, January 21, 1974, FRUS 1969–76, 31:83, 216.

[47] See, for example, de Gaulle press conference, February 4, 1965, in Charles de Gaulle, *Discours and messages*, vol. 4 (Paris: Plon, 1970), p. 332; Alain Peyrefitte, *C'était de Gaulle*, vol. 2 (Paris: Fayard, 1997), p. 77; and Pompidou press conference, September 23, 1971, in Georges Pompidou, *Entretiens et discours*, vol. 2 (Paris: Plon, 1975), p. 40.

[48] Shultz and Dam, *Economic Policy*, p. 119.

a potential liability—something that could easily be portrayed as practically a confession of national bankruptcy—into a political asset.[49] As a Gaullist, he could hardly blame the United States for pursuing a policy based on its own national interest. And after complaining for years about Bretton Woods, and especially about the American deficits and the special role the dollar played in the system, the French could scarcely complain now that the Americans were determined to put an end to the deficits and make the dollar a more normal currency. Their president, in fact, recognized that "the reserve role of the dollar is actually a burden"; he agreed that "no currency should have this theoretical privilege."[50]

Pompidou certainly believed that a fixed rate system of some sort was essential. This was in part because he accepted the conventional view about the 1930s—a view which one of the main French officials involved with these matters at the time, Claude Pierre-Brossolette, later characterized as a "myth."[51] It was also in part because he wanted to maintain a slightly undervalued franc for domestic economic purposes, something possible only with a regime of fixed, or at least managed, exchange rates.[52] (The irony here, of course, is that policies that sought to keep exchange rates artificially low in order to stimulate the domestic economy had a certain 1930s-style "beggar thy neighbor" feel.[53]) But Pompidou and other key French officials were clearly intelligent enough to see that there was something to the U.S. case. The Americans

[49] Pompidou, *Entretiens et discours*, 2:42.

[50] Pompidou-Kissinger meeting, December 14, 1971, p. 3, DNSA/KT00410.

[51] Pompidou, *Entretiens et discours*, 2:37; Comité pour l'histoire économique et financière de la France, *La France et les institutions de Bretton Woods, 1944–1994: Colloque tenu à Bercy les 30 juin et ler juillet 1994* (Paris: Ministère de l'Économie, des Finances et de l'Industrie, 1998), pp. 111–12. Note also a comment made at that conference by Pompidou's economics advisor Jean-René Bernard. Pompidou, he said, "éprouvait une très grande difficulté à concevoir un système radicalement différent du système des parités fixes: je pense qu'il s'agit là d'une opinion quasi métaphysique, quasi religieuse…" Ibid., p. 125. Bernard's own views, as this passage suggests, were probably more moderate at the time. See Soutou, "L'attitude de Georges Pompidou face à l'Allemagne," p. 311 n. 88.

[52] See Bernard's remarks to that effect at another conference: Éric Bussière, ed., *Georges Pompidou face à la mutation économique de l'Occident, 1969–1974: Actes du Colloque des 15 et 16 novembre 2001 au Conseil économique et social* (Paris: Presses Universitaires de France, 2003), p. 109; note also Éric Bussière, "Georges Pompidou et la crise du système monétaire international," ibid., p. 85.

[53] Note in this context Connally's reaction when the EEC representative rejected the American proposal to totally end the payments deficit (with the argument that the proposed change was "too ambitious" because the world had gotten used to the situation that had developed). The U.S. government, Connally replied, could not accept the idea that "the export market should be used or can be used for the purpose of providing prosperity at home to the detriment of other nations around the world." Quoted in Luciano Segreto, "États-Unis, Europe et crise du système monétaire international (1968–1973)," p. 37.

were not just being selfish; the argument that the fixed rate system was fundamentally defective and that radical change might be necessary was perhaps not to be dismissed out of hand. The sense seemed to be growing that maybe France was behind the curve intellectually, that maybe the whole idea of a market-based system deserved to be taken more seriously, that maybe French thinking was a bit too rigid, too locked into the clichés of the past.[54] So while the French were not thrilled by what the United States was doing in this area, they were by no means prepared (as Pompidou told the German foreign minister in November 1971) to "go to war" with the United States over this issue. The Europeans were neither strong enough nor united enough to pursue a really tough anti-American policy, and even if they had been, it would not have been to their interest to act in that way.[55]

To be sure, French policy hardened after it became clear that the Smithsonian agreement was empty—that the Americans did not intend to defend the December 1971 parities and were thus reneging on the assurances they had given at the Azores meeting.[56] That new situation

[54] Thus, for example, almost certainly referring to the Americans, Pierre-Brossolette said at the time, "[L]a flexibilité n'était pas seulement dans les taux de change; elle était également dans les esprits." J.-R. Bernard meeting with Pierre-Brossolette, March 30, 1973, quoted in Bussière, "Georges Pompidou et la crise du système monétaire international," ibid., p. 102. The implication was that the French were still too rigid in comparison. Note also a commentary published at the time by Raymond Aron, who among other things was France's most distinguished political analyst: "Fin des parités fixes?" September 7, 1971, in Georges-Henri Soutou, ed., *Raymond Aron: Les articles de politique internationale dans* Le Figaro *de 1947 à 1977*, vol. 3 (Paris: Éditions de Fallois, 1997), p. 982. Aron viewed the whole question of fixed vs. floating exchange rates as very much an open issue, even intellectually. Looking back on the period, Bernard felt that the French had not been prepared intellectually to deal with these issues, and that it was only later that their way of thinking became more like that prevailing in the international financial community as a whole. See his comments in Bussière, *Georges Pompidou face à la mutation économique de l'Occident*, p. 111. It strikes me as quite likely that a vague feeling that this was the case had already begun to take shape at the time. Pompidou was more attached to the par value system, but as he himself admitted, despite his background in banking he had no particular expertise in this area. See Pompidou-Schmidt meeting, February 10, 1973, *Akten zur auswärtigen Politik der Bundesrepublik Deutschland 1973*, pp. 223–24; henceforth cited in this form: AAPD 1973, pp. 223–24. This suggests that he was perhaps more open to the views of other people in this area than one might have thought.

[55] For Pompidou's comment to German foreign minister Scheel, see Segreto, "États-Unis, Europe et crise du système monétaire international," p. 40. For the German text, see Pompidou-Scheel meeting, November 19, 1971, AAPD 1971, p. 1767. For the softening of the French view in late 1971, see also McCracken to Nixon, November 24, 1971, 1969–76, 3:567–68.

[56] "On a été déloyal avec nous," Pompidou said in this context in early 1973. See Jobert notes of February 14 and March 7, 1973, cabinet meetings, Association Georges Pompidou, Paris, cited in Laurent Césari, "Les relations personnelles entre Nixon, Pompidou et leurs entourages," unpublished paper, p. 8. For the U.S. assurances, see Pompidou-

led to certain major changes in French policy. The European countries, generally speaking, were not going to defend the Smithsonian parities entirely on their own by absorbing however many dollars they had to in order to keep their own exchange rates from rising, and the French in particular would obviously not go along with a pure dollar standard of that sort. If a par value system was desirable, then it made sense, if the Americans refused to be part of it, to try to establish at least a European monetary system of some kind.[57] And in fact, when the Smithsonian system collapsed in early 1973 and the world moved *de facto* to a floating exchange rate regime, Pompidou accepted the notion, which the Germans had been suggesting for some time, of a joint European float against the dollar.[58] But he had been slow to accept this idea. He might have agreed in theory that there should be some sort of European counterweight to American power in this area, but in practice he had from the start been reluctant to move ahead too quickly toward the establishment of a European monetary system, and had rejected the idea of a joint float when the Germans had proposed it in 1971 and 1972.[59] And in deciding to participate in the joint float in March 1973, the French were by no means making an irrevocable decision. They in fact left the European "snake," as it was called, and floated their own currency in January 1974, just ten months later.

Did the plan fail, at least for the time being, because the Americans disliked the idea of a free-standing Europe, and thus of a monetarily and economically united Europe, and had set out to torpedo it?[60] This issue is more complex than one might think. On the one hand, the U.S. officials most deeply involved with these monetary problems, and

---

Kissinger meeting, December 13, 1971, p. 3, DNSA/KT00407. Nixon-Kissinger-Pompidou meeting, December 13, 1971, 4 p.m., pp. 6, 11, DNSA/KT00408; Pompidou-Kissinger meeting, December 14, 1971, p. 1, DNSA/KT00410.

[57] See Soutou, "L'attitude de Georges Pompidou face à l'Allemagne," pp. 292–293.

[58] Ibid., p. 292.

[59] See Robert Frank, "Pompidou, le franc et l'Europe," in *Georges Pompidou et l'Europe*, pp. 348–63, esp. pp. 356, 361, 362; and Pompidou's comments quoted in Gérard Bossuat, "Le président Georges Pompidou et les tentatives d'Union économique et monétaire," *Georges Pompidou et l'Europe*, p. 422. The issue, incidentally, had already come up in the 1960s. De Gaulle had proposed a single European currency to the Germans in 1964—without, according to Giscard, fully understanding its political implications—but the Germans rejected the idea. The French brought up the issue again in 1968–69. See Schoenborn, *Mésentente apprivoisée*, pp. 116–19, 139.

[60] Note, for example, Segreto, "États-Unis, Europe et crise du système monétaire international," p. 32, where the author refers to the alleged U.S. goal (in 1971) of ending what remained of a "common European position with regard to the problems with the U.S. currency." On this issue, see also Dimitri Grygowski, "Les États-Unis et l'unification monétaire de l'Europe: bilan d'ensemble et perspectives de recherche, 1968–1998," *JEIH* 13, no. 1 (2007): 119–22.

above all Treasury Secretary Shultz, had no objection in principle to "Europe floating against the United States"—certainly not on economic grounds.[61] Shultz, in fact, welcomed the idea, since it would in effect bring a floating exchange rate system into being; his top assistant in this area told the French finance minister in February 1973 that "a joint European float would be fine with the U.S., and it would be consistent with the evolution of international monetary arrangements." The treasury secretary understood that the joint float would be accompanied by "anti-American rhetoric," but he was prepared to accept that kind of thing philosophically. He certainly did not think the U.S. government should oppose it for that reason.[62]

On the other hand, neither Nixon nor Kissinger approached the issue in quite the same way. The president, to be sure, by this point agreed with Shultz about what made sense in purely economic terms.[63] But his feeling was that the issue could not be decided solely on that basis, and that the political side of the problem was of fundamental importance. To take the Shultz view—that the United States should not intervene in the foreign exchange markets in any massive way but should basically just let the dollar float—would give the wrong message. That would, Nixon said, be "just too much of a 'To hell with the rest of the world'" sort of policy.[64] If the Americans went that route, he thought, the Europeans would "pull together [and say] 'The United States doesn't care,' and that hurts our bigger game with regard to Europe."[65] A more active

---

[61] Volcker quoted in Leeson, *Ideology and the International Economy*, p. 137. Note also Volcker's account in *Changing Fortunes*, pp. 112–13, of Shultz's views on the subject, and also the report of a top British official on his meetings with Shultz, Volcker, and Federal Reserve Chairman Arthur Burns in February 1973: "[T]hey were not opposed to a common European monetary policy including a common float." Cromer to Foreign Office, February 16, 1973, DBPO III:4:26. One of the arguments for a U.S. policy of suspending convertibility, in fact, was that it might "provide a major impetus toward closer European integration." Kissinger (but obviously not drafted by him) to Nixon, June 25, 1969, FRUS 1969–76, 3:348. For the views of a number of leading U.S. economists on the question, none of whom were very alarmed by the prospect of joint European action in this area, see the record of a conference held at the time and cosponsored by the State Department and the Brookings Institution: Lawrence Krause and Walter Salant, eds., *European Monetary Unification and Its Meaning for the United States* (Washington, D.C.: Brookings, 1973), esp. pp. 183 (Max Corden), 297 (Henry Wallich), and 309 (Harry Johnson).

[62] Volcker report of meeting with Giscard, February 11, 1973; Nixon meeting with economic advisors, March 3, 1973, tape transcript; Nixon-Kissinger-Shultz meeting, March 3, 1973, tape transcript; in FRUS 1969–76, 31:44, 56, 75–76, 81.

[63] See, for example, Nixon meeting with economic advisors, March 3, 1973, tape transcript, and Nixon-Kissinger-Shultz meeting, March 7, 1973, tape transcript, ibid., pp. 69, 106.

[64] Nixon-Shultz-Burns meeting, February 6, 1973, tape transcript, ibid., p. 12.

[65] Nixon-Kissinger-Shultz meeting, March 3, 1973, tape transcript, ibid., p. 74. See also Nixon meeting with economic advisors, March 3, 1973, tape transcript, ibid., p. 69.

policy would mean that the U.S. government would have "a leadership role with the Europeans that we don't have otherwise"—although he went on to add (quite revealingly, I think), "Now, I don't [know] what the hell we do with it."[66]

But Nixon's basic feeling was that "political considerations must completely override economic considerations" in this area. This, he noted, was "going to be a bitter pill for Shultz to swallow but he must swallow it."[67] So the treasury secretary was instructed to "be forthcoming" with the Europeans, more forthcoming than he himself was inclined to be.[68] This applied especially to the Germans. Kissinger told Shultz, "We don't want [German Finance Minister Helmut Schmidt] to be in a domestic position at home where he turned to the Americans" and "got totally kicked in the teeth," because if the Nixon administration was blamed for the measures the German government would have to take, that would "shift the whole pattern within Germany."[69]

This did not mean, however, that Nixon and Kissinger basically wanted to cooperate with the Europeans in this area. It did not mean, in particular, that on the issue of the joint float they wanted America to play a helpful role. There was a "growing tendency," Nixon thought, for the Europeans to "turn inward" and to distance themselves from the United States.[70] The policy of "building Europe," it seemed, was coming to have an increasingly sharp anti-American edge; French policy especially was interpreted in those terms. Paul Volcker, Under Secretary of the Treasury for Monetary Affairs, was afraid that the French were using the "so-called European solution" for political purposes. The "European solution," he said, was simply "a euphemism for saying 'Let's leave the United States out of the world—and go our independent course.'" That, he said, was the French view. Their goal was "to posture Europe vis-à-vis the United States politically." But it wasn't just the French. There was a risk that western Europe as a whole would move in that direction.[71]

And Nixon seemed to agree. Both he and Kissinger now wondered whether European integration was in America's interest.[72] The presi-

---

[66] Nixon-Kissinger-Shultz meeting, March 3, 1973, tape transcript, ibid., p. 84.

[67] Nixon to Kissinger, March 10, 1973 (draft), ibid., p. 119.

[68] Nixon-Kissinger-Shultz meeting, March 7, 1973, tape transcript, ibid., pp. 106, 111.

[69] Ibid., p. 110; see also p. 112. What Kissinger probably had in mind here was that if the Americans were not "forthcoming," the Germans might feel they had to float their currency on a national basis, a move that might lead to a dramatic appreciation of the mark, with devastating consequences for the Federal Republic's export-oriented economy.

[70] Nixon meeting with economic advisors, March 3, 1973, tape transcript, ibid., p. 69.

[71] Ibid., pp. 62–63, 70.

[72] Nixon-Kissinger-Shultz meeting, March 3, 1973, tape transcript, ibid., pp. 74, 79.

dent, in fact, thought that there was a risk that Europe would turn into a "Frankenstein monster"; the reason he was interested in an interventionist monetary policy was that "it might serve our interests in keeping the Europeans apart."[73] Kissinger also thought it might be a good idea "if we can force [the Europeans] to deal separately with us."[74] And the U.S. government now made it clear to Willy Brandt (who had informed Nixon that the Europeans were considering possible "joint action" that they could take in the monetary area) that European integration was no longer viewed as an end in itself, but only as a "step towards increased Atlantic cooperation."[75]

So the whole point of an interventionist policy in this area was not to help the Europeans with their monetary problems. The main goal was to keep the Europeans from coming together as a bloc, and the idea was that the United States might be able to achieve that goal by intervening selectively, on a country-by-country basis. But it was taken for granted that the U.S. government could not oppose the Europeans head on: "We couldn't bust the common float without getting into a hell of a political fight," Kissinger said; the Americans had to do what they could "to prevent a united European position without showing our hand." And he emphasized the point that this policy was not based on an assessment of America's economic interests: his objection to what the Europeans wanted to do "was entirely political." He had in fact learned from intelligence reports that all of America's enemies in the German cabinet "were for the European solution"; it was this information that had pretty much decided the issue for him.[76] A year later, at a time when America's problem with Europe was coming to a head, he laid out his thinking on the issue in somewhat greater detail. "We are not," he said, "opposed to a French attempt to strengthen the unity of Europe if the context of that unity is not organically directed against us. So I am not offended by the float idea as such, or by common institutions. If, however, it is linked to the sort of thing that is inherent in the Arab initiative [i.e., the Europeans' plan at that point for a "dialogue" with the Arabs, which, as will be seen, Kissinger viewed as a hostile

[73] Nixon to Kissinger, March 10, 1973 (draft), ibid., p. 119; and Nixon-Kissinger-Shultz meeting, March 3, 1973, tape transcript, ibid., p. 83.

[74] Nixon-Kissinger-Shultz meeting, March 3, 1973, tape transcript, ibid., p. 79.

[75] Brandt to Nixon, March 2, 1973, and Nixon to Brandt, March 3, 1973, ibid., pp. 49, 92.

[76] Kissinger-Simon telephone conversations, March 14 and 15, 1973, DNSA/KA09752 and KA09779. Some extracts were also published in FRUS 1969–76, 31:123, 126. The following month another intelligence report about Brandt was circulated to top U.S. officials. "Apparently," Federal Reserve chief Arthur Burns wrote in his diary, "we know everything that goes on at German cabinet meetings." Arthur Burns Journal II, p. 60, entry for April 3, 1973, available online in the Digital Ford Presidential Library [DFPL].

move], as it seems to be, then we have a massive problem. Then we have the problem that we have got to break it up now."[77]

It is not clear, however, that the U.S. government actually did much to prevent the joint float from working. The Treasury Department controlled policy at the operational level, and people like Shultz had no wish to torpedo the project. It was not as though the point of a European monetary system was to conduct an economic war against the United States (although it was sometimes interpreted in those terms, both by some U.S. officials at the time and by some scholars more recently).[78] The Europeans were clearly in no position to pursue that kind of policy, and the Americans did not really object to the European plan on economic grounds. Shultz, of course, could not ignore what Nixon and Kissinger were telling him, but they were saying all sorts of different things; the guidance was far from clear. Shultz was told to "be more forthcoming," but Kissinger especially had also made it clear that he did not want to joint float to succeed. That latter goal, as the Treasury Department saw it, meant "less intervention," which was in line with the Shultz position.[79] So the treasury secretary had plenty of wiggle room; he could select which goals to emphasize, and the choices he made were in line with his own policy preferences. In any event, it was hard to see how a policy of selective intervention could actually achieve the goals Nixon and Kissinger had set for themselves. As Volcker pointed out, "[A]lmost inevitably, intervention on our part with appreciating European currencies will contribute to the viability of the snake."[80] If the United States, for example, intervened to limit the rise in the German exchange rate, this would automatically reduce pressure on the other currencies tied to the mark in the system—it would make it easier on the French, for instance, to stay in the snake, since the franc would also not have to rise so sharply.

[77] Secretary's Staff meeting, March 22, 1974 (document dated March 26), p. 50, DNSA/ KT01079. Note also a comment Kissinger made in a March 6, 1974 meeting with Secretary of Defense James Schlesinger: "I am convinced we must break up the EC. The French are determined to unify them all against the United States." National Security Advisor: Memoranda of Conversations, 1973–1977, box 3, Gerald Ford Presidential Library, DFPL, Digitized Memoranda of Presidential Conversations: Nixon Administration; henceforth cited as DMPC:Nixon.

[78] See Watson to Secretary of State, September 20, 1972, Department of State Central Files [DOSCF], Subject/Numeric Files [Subj-Num] 1970–73, box 2278 [POL FR-US 1-10-72], RG 59, U.S. National Archives, College Park, Md. [USNA]; and Bossuat, "Le président Georges Pompidou et les tentatives d'Union économique et monétaire," pp. 425, 427.

[79] Kissinger-Simon telephone conversation, March 14, 1973, DNSA/KA09752; see also FRUS 1969–76, 31:123.

[80] Volcker to Shultz, enclosed in Sonnenfeldt to Kissinger, March 13, 1973, FRUS 1969–76, 31:122.

So if the joint float failed, it was probably not because the Americans had been able to sabotage it. As long as the U.S. government was able to regain its own freedom of action, key officials like Shultz did not really care much what sort of monetary system the Europeans worked out among themselves. The effort failed, it seems, for the same reason the Bretton Woods system had failed. Just as Bretton Woods had resulted in an overvalued dollar, so the European snake, by tying the franc so tightly to the strong German mark, had resulted in an overvalued franc.[81] A belief in the importance of a united Europe was not enough to override basic economic realities. This was particularly true, since for Pompidou as for Nixon, political and economic autonomy was from the start what mattered most; the French national interest was more important than "building Europe."[82] And from the French point of view there was also a special problem having to do with the central role the German mark played in the European monetary system. The fear was that in a European monetary system too much power might be concentrated in German hands. The French president, as he himself said, did not want to exchange the dollar standard for a mark standard.[83]

Pompidou certainly did not like the basic thrust of American policy in this area, but it really is an exaggeration to say that the "limited improvement in U.S.-French political relations" that had taken place in the early part of the Nixon-Pompidou period "was overwhelmed by the increasingly poisonous atmosphere created by U.S.-European economic tensions."[84] Economic issues played a key role in the story, but in themselves they by no means drove the two countries apart. The United States, for example, did not oppose the joint float for economic reasons; in a different political context, America would have had no objection to the plan. And the French position on monetary issues more generally did not pose any real problem for the U.S. government: the tough line the French took in the negotiations meant that a formal agreement would be harder to achieve, but the Americans were content to live with the existing "floating" arrangements indefinitely. Nor was the French government overly concerned with this set of issues. Indeed, when Pompidou met with U.S. leaders in Iceland in mid-1973, he played down the political importance of these issues. He saw "no great difficulty concerning economic relations between the U.S. and the Eu-

[81] See Frank, "Pompidou, le franc et l'Europe," p. 365.

[82] Ibid., pp. 349–55.

[83] Frank, "Pompidou, le franc et l'Europe," p. 359, and Soutou, "L'attitude de Georges Pompidou face à l'Allemagne," pp. 290–91.

[84] Frank Costigliola, *France and the United States: The Cold Alliance since World War II* (New York: Twayne, 1992), p. 173.

ropean Community"; those sorts of problems, he thought, were "easy to solve."[85] The real problem lay elsewhere.

THE YEAR OF EUROPE

On April 23, 1973, Henry Kissinger gave a major speech called "The Year of Europe." The Atlantic alliance, he argued, was in trouble. America and Europe were drifting apart. "In economic relations the European Community" had "increasingly stressed its regional personality," whereas the United States tended to think in terms of a "wider international trade and monetary system." In the political sphere, one had the same sort of structural problem. The United States was a global power, whereas the Europeans had essentially "regional interests." The time had come to deal with the tensions this situation had given rise to, and indeed one had to deal with them comprehensively. "The political, military, and economic issues in Atlantic relations," he said, "are linked by reality, not by our choice nor for the tactical purpose of trading one off against the other. The solutions will not be worthy of the opportunity if left to technicians." They had to be "addressed at the highest level." In 1972 Nixon had transformed America's relationship with her two Cold War adversaries, the Soviet Union and China. In 1973, the main goal would be to reinvigorate the western alliance by working out a "new Atlantic charter," a "blueprint" for a "revitalized Atlantic partnership."[86]

Kissinger was worried about the future of the alliance—worries which, as we have seen, were coming into focus in part as a result of

[85] Pompidou-Nixon meeting, May 31, 1973, 10 a.m., p. 8, DNSA/KT00742. He used the same language in the French record of the meeting, quoted in Éric Roussel, *Georges Pompidou, 1911–1974*, new ed. (Paris: J.C. Lattès, 1994), pp. 555–56; and took a very relaxed line, in particular, on the question of the reform of the international monetary system (ibid., p. 564). The original document is in the Pompidou Presidential Papers, collection 5AG2, box 1023, Archives Nationales, Paris, henceforth cited in this form: 5AG2/10235/AN. On this general issue, see also Pompidou-Heath meeting, May 22, 1973, DBPO III:4:98, pp. 4, 6.

[86] "The Year of Europe," address by Henry Kissinger in New York, April 23, 1973, *Department of State Bulletin*, May 14, 1973, pp. 593–98. A number of works dealing with the Year of Europe and related issues have appeared in recent years. See Daniel Möckli, *European Foreign Policy during the Cold War: Heath, Brandt, Pompidou and the Dream of Political Unity* (London: Tauris, 2008), esp. chap. 4; Jussi M. Hanhimäki, "Kissinger et l'Europe: entre intégration et autonomie," *Relations internationales*, no. 119 (2004): 319–32; Silvia Pietrantonio, "L'anno che non fu? L'anno dell'Europa e la crisi nelle relazioni transatlantiche, 1973–1974," Ph.D. diss., University of Bologna, 2008; and Aurélie Gfeller, "Reenvisioning Europe: France, America and the Arab World, 1973–74," Ph.D. diss., Princeton University, 2008, chap. 1.

what was happening on the economic front. Could the U.S. government just sit on its hands and allow the confrontation with Europe to develop? Maybe it was possible to head it off; maybe some sort of dramatic move was called for. In September 1972 he gave a preview of the policy to Franz-Josef Strauss, the leader of one of the main opposition parties in Germany, the Christian Social Union. It was "absolutely essential," he told Strauss, that after the U.S. presidential elections in November "we have a fundamental review" of U.S.-European relations. If the basic problems were not worked out, Europe and America would find themselves "fighting about individual issues year after year. And after a while the economic problems will make it impossible to maintain the security relationship."[87]

He made the same sort of argument to the French ambassador, Jacques Kosciusko-Morizet, the following March, about a month before the Year of Europe speech:

> Our basic thinking is this: We believe that if we go into trade negotiations without a framework, confrontation will almost certainly result. If our President has to make each decision one at a time, on its own merits, he will be motivated by domestic political pressures. We also have defense issues to discuss. It is helpful to get an overall framework to discuss economics, defense and political issues. We cannot have a monetary crisis every six months, and we both have an energy crisis.[88]

He elaborated on the point in another meeting with Kosciusko-Morizet a couple of weeks later, this time laying greater emphasis on the political issues. He knew, for example, that the French were worried "that maybe some sort of condominium between the US and the USSR could emerge." To make sure that no one would think that something like that was possible, he argued, you had to change the whole tenor of the U.S.-European relationship. Above all, you had to put an end to all the squabbling—you had to avoid getting into a "guerrilla type of situation between Europe and the United States in which the public considers we have endless disagreements and no common action."[89] The two sides, in Kissinger's view, needed to look at the larger picture and deal comprehensively with all the major issues they faced.

The Europeans, and especially the French, did not respond the way Kissinger had hoped. The Americans, it seemed to them, were trying to group the allies around the United States. Their goal was to set policy for the alliance as a whole. The sort of system they were trying to create,

---

[87] Kissinger-Strauss meeting, September 10, 1972, p. 5, DNSA/KT00553.
[88] Kissinger-Kosciusko-Morizet meeting, March 29, 1973, p. 2, DNSA/KT00690.
[89] Kissinger-Kosciusko-Morizet meeting, April 13, 1973, pp. 6–7, DNSA/KT00702.

Pompidou himself later said, implied a "certain subordination" of the allies to the United States.[90] Michel Jobert, the foreign minister, used stronger language. Kissinger's geopolitical vision, he wrote, was quite clear: the whole world would revolve around American power; Europe would be "confined to a purely regional role"; the process the Americans hoped to begin would "consecrate American hegemony over the western world." [91]

Although U.S. leaders had gotten some sense that there might be problems, it was not clear at first that the official French reaction would be so negative.[92] After Kissinger's March 19 meeting with Kosciusko-Morizet in which he explained the initiative, the ambassador flew to Paris to brief the head of state in person. "Yes, I agree," Pompidou said, giving what Kosciusko called the "green light" for the Year of Europe speech.[93] And when Kissinger met with Pompidou on May 18, the

[90] Pompidou meeting with Japanese prime minister Tanaka, September 18, 1973, quoted in Mélandri, "Une relation très spéciale," p. 97.

[91] Michel Jobert, *Mémoires d'avenir* (Paris: Grasset, 1974), pp. 231–32. Jobert made much the same point in another volume of memoirs published two years later: "Je tournais les pages du discours d'Henry Kissinger: quelle tranquille assurance, dans l'affirmation de la primauté américaine sur le monde occidentale, quelle détermination dans la volonté d'organiser son camp, en répartissant les tâches et en assignant les places, quelle brutalité aussi pour exiger de l'Europe, dans son organisation économique et sa défense, la subordination et une contribution en échange de l'exercice du droit de suzeraineté." Michel Jobert, *L'Autre regard* (Paris: Grasset, 1976), p. 288. Note also the following comment made in 1994 by Jean de Lipkowski, in 1973 Secretary of State in the Foreign Ministry: "Lorsque Kissinger—qui ne manquait pas d'humour—décréta l'année de l'Europe c'est-à-dire un système qui cherchait à la réduire au silence, il ne trouva sur sa route que la France." Jean de Lipkowski, "Succéder au Général," Bernard Pons et al., *Georges Pompidou: vingt ans après* (Paris: Table Ronde, 1994), p. 108. This sort of interpretation, incidentally, can still be found even in the American historical literature. Frank Costigliola, author of the most important U.S. study of Franco-American relations in the post–World War II period, views the speech as a "blunt reassertion of American hegemony." Kissinger, he says, was asking for a "near veto over the EEC's economic decisions"; this, in his view, is what the passage in the speech about how economic, military and politics issues were linked really meant. Costigliola, *France and the United States*, pp. 174–75.

[92] According to Jobert's later account (*Mémoires d'avenir*, p. 237), he had warned Kissinger when he was in Paris before the Iceland summit conference that France was deeply opposed to the project. The U.S. record of Jobert's May 22, 1973, meeting with Kissinger, however, has Jobert predicting that Pompidou would take a rather conciliatory line on the issue when he met Nixon in Reykjavik: "President Nixon will have to outline the concrete lines, the framework, of his conception. I don't think Mr. Pompidou will be opposed to the idea." Kissinger-Jobert meeting, May 22, 1973, p. 5, DNSA/KT00736.

[93] Kosciusko-Morizet comment in *Georges Pompidou et l'Europe*, p. 209. Kissinger told the British much the same thing at the time. Kissinger meeting with British officials, May 10, 1973, p. 15, Henry A. Kissinger Office Files [HAK OF]/62/HAK London Trip/NPL. Jobert gave a rather different account in *L'Autre regard*, p. 288. The Europeans, he says, had not been consulted and the speech came as a surprise. But factual accuracy was not his strong suit. On the immediately preceding page (p. 287), for example, he made the

208 • Chapter 7

French president did not seem at all hostile. He was "not particularly shocked" by the much-criticized passage in the speech that referred to the Europeans' "regional" interests. And he agreed that while it was necessary to consider each specific problem "in its own context" it was also important to keep the broader picture in mind "on all occasions." "If some were shocked by your ideas," he told Kissinger, "I personally did not find your ideas so far from reality."[94]

The French president, as Kissinger saw it, was the key to the whole Year of Europe plan and in his view the main goal of the Nixon-Pompidou meeting that was scheduled to begin in Reykjavik at the end of May was to set in motion the whole process of drafting a new Atlantic charter.[95] It therefore came as something of a shock to him, after a long late-night talk with Jobert shortly after his arrival in Iceland, that "the

---

rather astonishing claim that Eisenhower owed his reelection in 1956 to his establishment of the Berlin airlift. Eisenhower, of course, had little to do with the airlift. He had resigned from the Army in February 1948 and was serving as president of Columbia University at the time the blockade was imposed a few months later. And the Berlin airlift of 1948–49 was not even an issue in the 1956 presidential campaign. But it was not just Jobert who falsely claimed that the Europeans had not been consulted. The British prime minister, Edward Heath, often made the same sort of claim, despite the fact that the Americans prior to the speech had made it quite clear what they had in mind and had asked explicitly for British views. For Heath's claims, see Armstrong to Acland, June 19, 1973 (an account of Heath's meeting the previous day with W.W. Rostow), DBPO III:4:133; Cabinet minutes, June 20, 1973, DBPO III:4:137; Catherine Hynes, *The Year That Never Was: Heath, the Nixon Administration and the Year of Europe* (Dublin: University College Dublin Press, 2009), pp. 103, 208; and Heath's remarks in a 1990 interview, quoted in Peter Hennessy and Caroline Anstey, *Moneybags and Brains: The Anglo-American 'Special Relationship' Since 1945* (Glascow: University of Strathclyde, 1990), p. 17. For evidence that the British knew what the Americans had in mind and were in fact consulted in advance about the U.S. initiative, see, for example, Acland to Armstrong, December 19, 1972, DBPO III:4:8, p. 2, and especially Kissinger meeting with Brimelow, Cromer and Sykes, March 5, 1973, DBPO III:4:44, pp. 24–29; see also Hynes, *Year That Never Was*, esp. pp. 65, 88, 124. For the British side of the Year of Europe story, see also Alastair Noble, "Kissinger's 'Year of Europe,' Britain's Year of Choice," in Matthias Schultz, Thomas A. Schwartz, and Bernd Schäfer, eds., *The Strained Alliance: Conflicts and Cooperation in Transatlantic Relations from Nixon to Carter* (Cambridge, England: Cambridge University Press, 2009); Niklas Rossbach, *Heath, Nixon and the Rebirth of the Special Relationship: Britain, the US and the EC, 1969–74* (Basingstoke, England: Palgrave Macmillan, 2009); and Keith Hamilton, "Britain, France, and America's Year of Europe, 1973," *Diplomacy and Statecraft* 17 (2006)—Hamilton was co-editor of the DBPO volume on the Year of Europe.

[94] Kissinger-Pompidou meeting, May 18, 1973, pp. 1–2, DNSA/KT00728. See also the French account of this meeting in 5AG2/117, where the point is made even more strongly. Pompidou, incidentally, made the same point in a meeting with Heath on May 21, 1973, quoted in Roussel, *Pompidou*, p. 548 (5AG2/1015/AN); Heath's reaction to that part of the Kissinger speech was a good deal more hostile.

[95] "Proposed Outcome of Meeting Between Presidents Nixon and Pompidou in Iceland," and Kissinger to Nixon, "Meeting with President Pompidou—Iceland," both undated, both in NSCF/949/Pompidou-Nixon Meeting, May–June 1973, 1 of 3/NPL.

French clearly harbor the most deep-seated suspicions of our motives in launching our Atlantic initiative." It was evident, he wrote Nixon, that "Pompidou is laboring under certain serious misapprehensions regarding our purposes."[96] It was therefore important to clear up those misconceptions, and that effort had begun even before the Reykjavik meeting, triggered in all probability by what had appeared in the newspapers.

Above all, it had to be made clear to the Europeans, and especially to the French, what America's real goals were. "They think we are aiming at a perpetuation of U.S. hegemony," Kissinger told the president and other top officials on May 25. "This is not our objective at all."[97] He had taken the same line in a meeting with Kosciusko on May 14. It did not make sense, he said, for someone like himself who admired de Gaulle to want to "return to the Kennedy period, and the same for the President. . . . We don't disagree with your views." "We have no view or no intention," he said, "to create one undifferentiated Atlantic Community in which the Europeans have to follow Washington directly." The passage in his speech about the regional role of Europe had been taken entirely out of context. If Europe wanted to play a global role, America would welcome it. And as for the argument that by linking economic, political, and military issues the Americans were trying to "blackmail" Europe—that is, that they were implicitly threatening the Europeans that the security relationship would be put at risk if they did not give way on economic matters—Kissinger said that this too was based on a misunderstanding. If the United States wanted to play hardball, the political leadership would simply leave the economic negotiations to the economic agencies. Putting them in a political framework would lead to a more conciliatory U.S. stance. But the basic point was that America was not pursuing a hostile or confrontational policy. He wanted to pursue the initiative together with the French. "We believe in a strong France," he said; in particular, the U.S. leaders "would be prepared to listen to your ideas in the nuclear field."[98]

Kissinger hammered away on these points in subsequent meetings with Jobert and Pompidou.[99] And Nixon, on his advice, made much the same argument in his May 31 meeting with Pompidou in Reykjavik.[100]

[96] Kissinger to Nixon, May 30, 1973, NSCF/949/Pompidou-Nixon Meeting, May–June 1973, 1 of 3/NPL.

[97] Kissinger meeting with Nixon et al., May 25, 1973, DNSA/KT00738.

[98] Kissinger-Kosciusko-Morizet meeting, May 14, 1973, pp. 2–3, DNSA/KT00723.

[99] Kissinger-Jobert meeting, May 17, 1973, and Kissinger-Pompidou meeting, May 18, 1973, DNSA/KT00727 and KT00728.

[100] Kissinger to Nixon, May 30, 1973, NSCF/949/Pompidou-Nixon Meeting, May–June 1973, 1 of 3/NPL; and Nixon-Pompidou meeting, May 31, 1973, 10 a.m., DNSA/KT00742.

The whole notion that in pushing the Year of Europe project the Americans were "seeking hegemony" was just not true, Kissinger told Jobert on May 17. He and Nixon were "not against French autonomy," he said. Why, given everything they had said and done, would they pursue such a policy? "It would be insane to first humiliate our friends and then face the Soviet Union alone," he said. "That can't be an American objective."[101] And Kissinger's meeting with Pompidou the next day was particularly important, because once again he linked the basic concept to the U.S. policy of helping the French nuclear program:

> We do not seek to dominate Europe, on the contrary. We want a strong Europe. We have always supported the European nuclear effort. As I recently told your Ambassador, we are not pushing but we are ready to discuss with you, either directly or if you prefer through the British, what we could do to strengthen your military capacity.

And in a Europe of that sort, the French, he said, would play the key role. The fact that the United States was willing to move forward with its policy of helping the French nuclear program proved that these assurances about U.S. policy were not to be dismissed as mere words— this, it seems, was what Kissinger was now suggesting.[102]

The Americans, in fact, were now ready to deepen the nuclear relationship with France. Nixon and Pompidou agreed at Reykjavik to move the discussion into a new area, the "holy of holies," as Soutou puts it, the design of the nuclear cores themselves.[103] Kissinger had made it clear in April, even before he gave the Year of Europe speech, that he was prepared to do more for the French nuclear weapons program. Most of the State Department, he said, "would like to throttle" the whole French nuclear program "because they are in the year 1965," but he was willing to move ahead. The U.S. government was prepared to discuss the issue with the new French armed forces minister, Robert Galley, and "we are waiting for you to approach us."[104] And after Reykjavik, Kissinger still seemed determined to proceed with that policy. "Some of our experts," he told Jobert on June 8, "think you don't appreciate the characteristics of Soviet defenses. If you wanted, you could send quietly some of your technical experts to Washington, so our experts could explain this and how you could deal with it. Warhead design, and some suggestions. Without changing your program."[105]

[101] Kissinger-Jobert meeting, May 17, 1973, pp. 2–3, DNSA/KT00727.

[102] Kissinger-Pompidou meeting, May 18, 1973, p. 7, DNSA/KT00728. On the linkage with the nuclear question, see also Kissinger-Jobert meeting, May 17, 1973, p. 4, DNSA/KT00727.

[103] Soutou, "La problématique de la Détente," p. 97.

[104] Kissinger-Kosciusko-Morizet meeting, April 13, 1973, pp. 8–9, DNSA/KT00702.

[105] Kissinger-Jobert meeting, June 8, 1973, p. 17, DNSA/KT00748. For a discussion of

But the French were not convinced by Kissinger's arguments about the meaning of the Year of Europe initiative, and even the prospect of a much closer nuclear relationship did not induce them to go along with the Kissinger policy. At Reykjavik, it seemed that Pompidou might be willing to cooperate. He and Nixon agreed on a procedure, more or less. Kissinger would meet with his French, British, and German counterparts, but not as a group; eventually the deputy foreign ministers of all the allied countries would meet to see if some statement of principles could be worked out.[106] But then in July the procedure was changed. The Europeans announced (in Kissinger's words at the time) that "they planned to get together as the Nine to prepare their response and that in the meantime they would not communicate with the U.S."[107] (This, it should be noted, was in spite of the fact that at Reykjavik Pompidou had said that it was hard to imagine the European Community serving as America's negotiating partner on this issue because the European Community had no political substance, but was simply an economic entity.[108]) When the E.C. had drafted the plan, it would be presented to the United States by the Danish foreign minister, but he was "only a messenger." He could not negotiate on behalf of Europe as a whole.

The whole situation, as Kissinger saw it, was absurd: "the countries who can negotiate with us won't talk and those who can talk with us can't negotiate."[109] The Americans felt they were being given the run-

---

some of the problems the French bomber force had in penetrating Soviet air defenses, see Central Intelligence Agency, "French Development of Nuclear Weapons Delivery Systems," n.d. (but probably written in the late 1960s), available in the CIA's Electronic Reading Room [CIA/ERR] (http://www.foia.cia.gov/search_options.asp).

[106] Nixon-Pompidou meeting, May 31, 1973, 10 a.m., pp. 7, 10, 12-13, DNSA/KT00742, and Nixon-Pompdou meeting, May 31, 1973, 3 p.m., pp. 3–4, DNSA/KT00743. See also Kissinger, *Years of Upheaval*, pp. 178–179.

[107] Kissinger meeting with Rusk, Bundy, McCloy, et al., November 28, 1973, p. 5, DNSA/KT00928. See also Kissinger, *Years of Upheaval*, pp. 188–189, 701, and Hynes, *Year That Never Was*, pp. 156–159. A top British official, Sir Thomas Brimelow, had noted in March that this sort of procedure "would, of course, rule out any question of a meaningful dialogue." Meeting between Kissinger and British officials, March 5, 1973, DBPO III:4:44, p. 28.

[108] Nixon-Pompidou meeting, May 31, 1973, 10 a.m., p. 8, DNSA/KT00742. Kissinger was "totally amazed [he told Jobert's successor Jean Sauvagnargues in July 1974] when your Government decided to oppose" the Year of Europe initiative. "Jobert," he said, "told me that the one thing France did not want was for the U.S. to talk to the E.C. He said that he preferred for us to deal with the French and not build up the E.C. and make it move faster." Kissinger-Sauvagnargues meeting, July 4, 1974, DNSA/KT01240. And indeed in the immediate post-Reykjavik period the French were "unwilling to participate in or agree to any common European approach to the trans-Atlantic relationship." Douglas-Home to Cromer, June 8, 1973, DBPO III:4:116. Note also, in this context, Jobert's remarks in his meeting with Heath and Douglas-Home, July 2, 1973, DBPO III:4:146, pp. 4 and 10, and Hynes, *Year That Never Was*, pp. 126, 146.

[109] Kissinger meeting with Rusk, Bundy, McCloy, et al., November 28, 1973, p. 5,

around. Kissinger was bitter. It was clear that the Europeans, and especially the French, had no interest in cooperating with the United States in this area. To one extent or another, they were hostile to the whole Year of Europe idea. It was particularly galling to him that they were not even willing to use the word *partnership* in the declaration.[110] The initiative was supposed to improve America's relationship with Europe, but it had been "turned almost into a European-American confrontation."[111] As a result, no matter what draft was eventually worked out—and Kissinger assumed (correctly as it turned out) that it would be "finished in a tolerable way"—the "emotional content" had been "drained from the declaration exercise."[112] But then again this showed how foolish it had been, as he himself later admitted, to try to "base foreign policy on an abstract quest for psychological fulfillment."[113]

So what is to be made of the whole Year of Europe affair? Looking back, the whole episode comes across as a little bizarre. "In Europe," as Helmut Schmidt later wrote, Kissinger's proclamation of a Year of Europe "aroused only disbelieving astonishment, mixed with mockery," and it is not hard to understand why people reacted that way.[114] There were certainly serious problems in the U.S.-European relationship, but could you really deal with them by drafting a declaration of principles? It is hard to see, in fact, how a declaration of this sort, which was bound to be full of platitudes and generalities, would change anything of substance. The inclusion of the word *partnership* in the text, for example,

---

DNSA/KT00928. Kissinger used this sort of phrase repeatedly to characterize the situation. See, for example, Kissinger-Jobert meeting, September 26, 1973, p. 7, DNSA/KT00815, and also Kissinger, *Years of Upheaval*, p. 189. For Kissinger's reaction at the time, see Kissinger meeting with British officials, July 30, 1973, DBPO III:4:179.

[110] Kissinger meeting with Rusk, Bundy, McCloy, et al., November 28, 1973, p. 7, DNSA/KT00928. Again, he made this point on many occasions. See, for example, Kissinger-Scheel meeting, March 3, 1974, pp. 13, 20, DNSA/KT01052; Kissinger meeting with German Ambassador von Staden, October 26, 1973, p.7 (doc. dated Oct. 27), in National Security Archive Electronic Briefing Book No. 98, "The October War and U.S. Policy," doc. no. 81; henceforth cited in this form: NSAEBB98/81/7; Kissinger meeting with British Ambassador Lord Cromer, October 31, 1973, NSAEBB98/90/2. The European Community had come up with a draft declaration of September 20, 1973. The sentences containing the word *partnership* were in a revised draft the Americans proposed on September 29. The first document was published in the *New York Times* on September 24, 1973, and the second on November 9, 1973. On French objections to the word *partnership*, see Gfeller, "Re-envisioning Europe," pp. 69–70. 79–81.

[111] Nixon to Brandt (drafted by Kissinger), July 30, 1973, Kissinger, *Years of Upheaval*, p. 191.

[112] Kissinger meeting with Rusk, Bundy, McCloy, et al., November 28, 1973, pp. 5, 7, DNSA/KT00928.

[113] Kissinger, *White House Years*, p. 381.

[114] Helmut Schmidt, *Men and Powers: A Political Retrospective* (New York: Random House, 1989), p. 150.

would scarcely have made the United States into more of a hegemon than it would otherwise have been.

On the other hand, for the same reason, the plan for a "new Atlantic charter" was essentially harmless, and the only thing that made the episode important politically was the fact that the Europeans, led by the French, opposed it. A mere declaration would change nothing of substance. If America wanted to pursue a "linkage" policy—if the U.S. government, for example, wanted to force the Europeans to make concessions in the economic area by making it clear that the security relationship was at risk—it would scarcely need a formal "charter" to do so.[115] A "new Atlantic charter" would not enable the United States to rule over a bloc of countries it would otherwise not dominate in that way. As Kissinger pointed out to Soviet leader Leonid Brezhnev in March 1974, "[T]he ultimate independence and freedom of action of a country depend on its specific weight, not its declarations."[116]

Given that fairly obvious point, it is hard to understand why the French reacted as negatively as they did to the Year of Europe initiative. Looking back, Kissinger was puzzled by the fact that "we found ourselves embroiled with France in the same sort of nasty confrontation for which we had criticized our predecessors." "The reasons for it," he wrote, "are not fully clear to me even today."[117] He blamed Jobert for the conflict. He thought the French foreign minister was pursuing "the old Gaullist dream of building Europe on an anti-American basis."[118] But Pompidou, and not Jobert, was calling the shots on the French side, and Pompidou was not, as he himself put it, an *Européen acharné*—that is, he was not fiercely committed to the idea of "building Europe."[119] He certainly wanted the Europeans to develop an identity of their own, and for that to happen he knew that the Americans would have to be kept at arm's length. But his general view had been that one had to

---

[115] Nixon and Kissinger certainly did think that all these issues had to be linked, but for the sorts of linkages they had in mind, see, for example, their comments in a meeting with Shultz, March 3, 1973, tape transcript, and Kissinger-Shultz telephone conversation, August 15, 1973, FRUS 1969–76, 31:84–85, 88, 191–93. Note also the record of Nixon's farewell meeting with German Ambassador Pauls, March 7, 1973, AAPD 1973, pp. 352–54, and Nixon's discussion of that meeting in a telephone conversation with Kissinger that same day, in which he talked about how important it was to "let these people know that they can't have it both ways"—meaning that the Europeans could not oppose America on economic issues and still expect the United States to defend them; DNSA/KA09695. See also Hynes, *Year That Never Was*, p. 86.

[116] Kissinger-Brezhnev meeting, March 26, 1974, p. 24, DNSA/KT01086. Kissinger and Brezhnev were talking at that point of their conversation about France and the French insistence on retaining a free hand.

[117] Kissinger, *Years of Upheaval*, p. 163.

[118] Ibid., p. 165.

[119] See Roussel, *Pompidou*, p. 338.

proceed cautiously. It was not wise, as he saw it, to force the pace of that process, or to alienate America unnecessarily as the European countries came together, first economically and then politically.[120] He understood that for the time being Europe, as a unified political entity, did not really count for much: the European Community, as he told Nixon in May 1973, had "no political reality," it was "only an economic reality." He was prepared, however, to live with that situation: "But Europe is what it is; there is nothing we can do about it."[121]

And yet even as Pompidou uttered those words his attitude was shifting. He had already begun to take a more "European" line, a line that suggested that the Europeans should come together by separating themselves more from the United States. In the final analysis, he said, the whole problem of a common European policy came down to "a common attitude toward America": "an independent Europe will define itself essentially by its relationship with the United States."[122] Europe would have to pursue its own policy, a policy that differed from America's, almost as an end itself. As Jobert put the point in a meeting with the German foreign minister in March 1974, "There is no doubt that if we are too obliging with [the Americans], we will count for nothing."[123]

Why the shift in policy? It was not that Pompidou's basic feelings about "building Europe" had suddenly changed. The real taproot lay elsewhere. The United States was now dealing directly and seriously

[120] See, for example, Pompidou's remarks in a meeting with Brandt, January 22, 1973, AAPD 1973, p. 84. Note also his comments in another meeting with Brandt, held on December 4, 1971, quoted in Roussel, *Pompidou*, p. 650: "Toute la difficulté des années à venir consistera à pousser vers un progrès politique de l'Europe—et économique bien sûr—sans inquiéter les États-Unis, sans se couper d'eux, sans les rendre hostiles, ce qui empêcherait nos progrès" (5AG2/1011/AN). Note also Pompidou's comment on a November 1972 telegram from Kosciusko, quoted in Mélandri, "Une relation très spéciale," p. 119. For Pompidou's thinking on the general issue of the "construction of Europe," see Roussel, *Pompidou*, pp. 17–21, 494–96.

[121] Pompidou-Nixon meeting, May 31, 1973, 10 a.m., pp. 5–6, 8, DNSA/KT00742. See also the French record of the meeting, which has Pompidou saying much the same thing: Roussel, *Pompidou*, pp. 555–56 (5AG3/1023/AN). Pompidou's rather cautious attitude on the issue of "building Europe" comes out over and over again in the documents: on the monetary issue, as Robert Frank has stressed (see n. 59 of this chapter); on the military question (see n. 204 of this chapter); and on the issue of political cooperation (see, for example, the evidence cited in Gfeller, "Re-envisioning Europe," pp. 94, 116–17).

[122] Pompidou interview with the Italian magazine *Epoca*, reported in *Le Monde*, February 10, 1972, p. 2, and quoted in AAPD 1973, pp. 1241–42, n. 10. Note also the comments of the German ambassador in Paris on this issue, von Braun to Foreign Office, October 11, 1973, AAPD 1973, p. 1542.

[123] The German document quotes the Jobert comment verbatim: "À coup sûr, si nous sommes complaisants avec eux, nous serons complètement effacés." Jobert-Scheel meeting, March 1, 1974, AAPD 1974, p. 268.

with the Soviet Union, and it was very natural to worry about where that process might lead. Were the two superpowers going to settle major issues, including European issues, by themselves, over the heads of the Europeans? It was obvious, he thought, that the U.S.-Soviet rapprochement might be at Europe's expense.[124] Given the kinds of negotiations that were either going on or were planned—the Strategic Arms Limitation talks (SALT), the Mutual and Balanced Force Reduction talks (MBFR), the talks leading to the U.S.-Soviet agreement on preventing nuclear war (PNW)—this was a major source of concern, not just in France but in Germany as well. Pompidou and his top advisors were increasingly worried about the prospect of a U.S.-Soviet "condominium"—of America and Russia becoming too intimate with each other, and of the Europeans being eclipsed.[125] The Year of Europe project was seen in that context. The condominium idea implied that each superpower would dominate its own bloc; the proposal for a more solid western alliance, it seemed, might well be rooted in this kind of thinking.

Over and over again, Kissinger and Nixon denied, as explicitly as they could, that their goal was to bring about a world of this sort.[126] From their point of view, the whole argument that the Year of Europe initiative was to be understood in such terms made little sense. If the United States wanted to deal with the Soviet Union *à deux*, it would just do so.[127] If their policy was to ignore the Europeans, why were they try-

[124] "Un tel rapprochement," he told Helmut Kohl in late 1973, "risque obligatoirement de se faire aux dépens de l'Europe." Pompidou-Kohl meeting, October 15, 1973, in Roussel, *Pompidou*, p. 657 (5AG2/1012/AN). See also Soutou, "La problématique de la Détente," p. 92.

[125] For French fears along these lines, see Jean-Bernard Raimond's comments of May 1973 quoted in Soutou, "La problématique de la Détente," p. 96. See also Marie-Pierre Rey, "Georges Pompidou, l'Union soviétique et l'Europe," *Georges Pompidou et l'Europe*, p. 163; Jean-Bernard Raimond, "Georges Pompidou et l'Union soviétique," ibid., pp. 181–83; and Roussel, *Pompidou*, p. 17 and chap. 27. Some American scholars, on the other hand, find it hard to believe that this was seen as a real problem. See, for example, Raymond Garthoff, *Détente and Confrontation: American-Soviet Relations from Nixon to Reagan*, rev. ed. (Washington, D.C.: Brookings, 1994), p. 383. The text of the PNW agreement, signed on June 22, 1973, was published in the *Department of State Bulletin*, no. 1778 (July 23, 1973). For the Germans, the NPT was of particular concern in this context: Franz-Josef Strauss, for example, thought that with the NPT a "super-cartel of the world powers" would come into being. Strauss to Kiesinger, February 15, 1967, quoted in Dirk Kroegel, *Einen Anfang finden! Kurt Georg Kiesinger in der Aussen- and Deutschlandpolitik der Grossen Koalition* (Munich: Oldenbourg, 1997), p. 92.

[126] See, for example, Nixon-Pompidou meeting, May 31, 1973, 10 a.m., pp. 4, 5, DNSA/KT00742.

[127] See, for example, Kissinger-Scheel meeting, March 3, 1974, pp. 3–4, 14, DNSA/KT01052.

ing so hard to develop a stronger relationship with the European allies, and especially with France?

Kissinger, in fact, went to great lengths to explain what the United States was up to in some of the areas that most concerned the French, especially the PNW agreement and MBFR. Contrary to what Jobert suggested, both at the time and in his memoirs, the PNW agreement came as no surprise. The French government had not only been told about the negotiations, but it also had been given a clear sense for what the Americans had objected to in the original Soviet draft, why they were insisting on changes, and why they felt it was desirable to reach some agreement with the Soviets in this area.[128] In his extraordinary May 18, 1973, meeting with Pompidou, Kissinger explained in some detail how the PNW agreement fit into America's larger foreign policy.

[128] For the claim that the French were kept in the dark, see Jobert, *L'Autre regard*, p. 289. Kosciusko-Morizet later said that Pompidou, at his May 18 meeting with Kissinger, did not conceal the fact that he did not agree with the policy the Americans were pursuing in this area, "parce ce qu'on revenait à l'ancienne politique américaine de domination, tout au moins à l'habitude calculée de mettre ses alliés et amis devant le fait accompli, sans aucune consultation." Kosciusko-Morizet comment in *Georges Pompidou et l'Europe*, p. 210. Note also Kissinger's comment at the time about how "the folklore in Europe" was that the PNW agreement "was sprung without any warning." Jobert, he added, "says this constantly and no one contradicts him." Kissinger meeting with Rusk, Bundy, McCloy, et al., November 28, 1973, p. 12, DNSA/KT00928. And in fact Jobert did claim in a meeting with British leaders "that the Americans had not consulted the Europeans before reaching their agreements with the Soviet Union." Jobert-Heath-Douglas-Home meeting, July 2, 1973, DBPO III:4:146, p. 5. Some scholars also claim that the Europeans were not informed. See, for example, Costigliola, *France and the United States*, p. 176. It has, however, been known for some time that this view is incorrect. See especially Mélandri, "Une relation très spéciale," pp. 106, 113. For the U.S. briefings of the French on this issue, see Kissinger-Kosciusko-Morizet meeting, September 6, 1972, NSCF/HAK OF/24/HAK's Germany, Moscow, London, Paris Trip 9/72—Misc. Cables and Documents/NPL; Kissinger-Pompidou meeting, September 15, 1972, quoted at length in Roussel, *Pompidou*, 524–27; Kissinger-Kosciusko-Morizet meeting, April 13, 1973, p. 6, DNSA/KT00702; and Kissinger-Kosciusko-Morizet meeting, May 14, 1973, pp. 4–5, DNSA/KT00723. The British were also kept informed, and indeed a British official (Thomas Brimelow) played a key role in drafting the agreement—something that made British opposition to the agreement particularly galling. As Kissinger put it at the time, "[W]e are fed up because Brimelow drafted the nuclear agreement and then didn't back it." See Kissinger, *Years of Upheaval*, p. 286; Hynes, *Year That Never Was*, pp. 120–121; and especially Stephen Twigge, "Operation Hullabaloo: Henry Kissinger, British Diplomacy, and the Agreement on the Prevention of Nuclear War," *Diplomatic History* 33, no. 4 (September 2009). For Kissinger's irritation with British behavior on this issue, see, for example, Kissinger-Schlesinger meeting, December 5, 1973, p. 3, DMPC:Nixon/DFPL; see also Kissinger-Schlesinger meeting, August 9, 1973, in that same collection. For Kissinger's initial briefing of the British on this affair, see Record of Discussion with Dr. Kissinger at Washington on 28th July, 1972, annex, attached to Trend to Prime Minister, July 31, 1972, PREM 15/1362, British National Archives, Kew; also in DNSA/KT00533. Other British documents relating to the PNW affair are in DBPO III:4, numbers 15, 17, 22, 32, 44, 59, 61, and 95.

The détente policy, he said, should not be misunderstood. The United States was not opting for the Soviet Union over China:

There is no sense in choosing the strongest against the weakest. If the Soviet Union managed to render China impotent, Europe would become a Finland and the United States would be completely isolated. It is therefore consistent with our own interests not to want and to try not to permit that the Soviet Union should destroy China. In fact, it is more a question of playing China against the Soviet Union. We have never used such frankness in discussing this with another Head of State. It is extremely important that you understand our real strategy. How can one support China? Today, such an idea would not be conceivable for American opinion. We need several years to establish with China the links which make plausible the notion that an attack directed against China could be an attack on the fundamental interests of the United States. This is our deliberate policy. We have the intention to turn rapidly toward China in the space of two or three years.

It is nevertheless important that this movement not serve as a pretext for a Soviet attack against China. It is consequently necessary that our policy be such that it does not seem to be directed against the Soviet Union and that détente is carried on in parallel with the Soviet Union; that the Soviet Union uses its power in conditions of peace and not of tension; finally that there would be a certain juridical obligation which would be violated if the Soviet Union undertook a military attack against China.

U.S. policy in the PNW affair, Kissinger pointed out, was to be understood in this context. "We aimed to gain time, to paralyze the Soviet Union"; the question was not whether the Soviets should be resisted, but rather how it should be done. The Americans knew what they were doing: their strategy might "be complex, but it is not stupid." They were not capitulating to the Soviets; they were trying "to enmesh them," and it was "absolutely essential" that Pompidou understand what the Americans were up to.[129]

[129] Kissinger-Pompidou meeting, May 18, 1973, pp. 4–6, DNSA/KT00728, and also (for the French record) 5AG2/117/AN, pp. 4–8. Although he was not quite so explicit, Nixon had taken a somewhat similar line in a meeting with the British prime minister in February; see Nixon-Heath meeting, February 2, 1973, DBPO III:4:22, p. 2. Note also Kissinger's comments about the point of the PNW talks in Twigge, "Operation Hullabaloo," pp. 692 and 697: "the nuclear Treaty," in Kissinger's view, "would be a kind of carrot, dangling perpetually just ahead of the Soviet donkey's nose until the poor animal was finally lured into some suitable stable where it could not do much harm." It is important to realize, more generally, that for Nixon and Kissinger the policy of détente was a tactic; the real aim was to deal with what they saw as a growing Soviet threat. See, for example,

This was a very important statement of American policy and Pompidou understood it as such. He did not object to the policy that Kissinger outlined; from his point of view, there was little to object to.[130] And indeed, even on the face of it, it is hard to understand why the French (and other Europeans) found the PNW agreement so distasteful. The key provision that people objected to, Article IV in the final June 22 agreement, simply called on the two superpowers to consult with each other if a situation developed that could lead to a nuclear war in which either or both of them might be involved. Was there any reason why they should not talk to each other in such a case? And what exactly would the signing of such an agreement actually change? If it was to the interest of the two governments to talk about any issue, then they would talk. The PNW agreement would not change the fundamental situation one way or the other. So why then was there a problem?

The U.S. government also tried to explain to the French why they should not be troubled by what the Americans were doing on the force reduction issue. The French did not like the idea of an MBFR agreement. It implied that central Europe would have a special military status, and this was viewed as a step toward the neutralization of that area. Pompidou, moreover, did not want a reduction of the U.S. troop presence in Europe.[131] But again Kissinger and Nixon, in confidential talks (not just with the French, but also with the British and the Chinese) explained what American policy in this area really was. The U.S. government was "using these negotiations on mutual force reductions primarily as a device to keep the Senate from cutting our forces

---

Kissinger-Pompidou meeting, December 20, 1973, DNSA/KT00968, p. 2, and (for the French record) Roussel, *Pompidou*, p. 603. (In the French record, Kissinger referred explicitly to the "*tactique de la détente*.") For Kissinger's account of the PNW affair, see *Years of Upheaval*, pp. 274–86, and also his comment on p. 926.

[130] Kissinger-Pompidou meeting, May 18, 1973, pp. 7–8, DNSA/KT00728. See also Soutou's account, based on the French record of this meeting in the Pompidou Papers, in "Le Président Pompidou et les relations entre les États-Unis et l'Europe," pp. 134–35 (pp. 181–82 in the translated version in *Between Empire and Alliance*). These remarks were so sensitive that Kissinger was not able to give an accurate account of what he had told Pompidou when he published his memoirs nine years later. Among other things, in introducing the seven-sentence extract from the record of the May 18 meeting that appeared in *Years of Upheaval*, p. 169, he claims he had told Pompidou that the United States would "prefer not to have to choose" between Russia and China, although the document itself does not show him saying anything of the sort, and he deleted the sentence in that passage about "playing China against the Soviet Union." He obviously did not want to reveal just how anti-Soviet American policy had been in 1973.

[131] See especially Soutou, "La problématique de la Détente," pp. 92–93, 99–100. The Americans were well aware of French feelings in this regard. See Shriver to Secretary of State, December 12, 1969, DOSCF/Subj-Num 1967–69/2103 [POL FR-US 1-1-69]/RG 59/ USNA.

unilaterally."[132] MBFR was regarded in Washington "essentially as a means of anticipating the domestic pressure for some reduction of United States troops in Europe and of dealing with that pressure on a basis which would do the minimum of damage to the conventional defence of Europe."[133] At Reykjavik, Nixon told Pompidou that neither of them really wanted an MBFR agreement, but that the talks had an important domestic political function: "I keep dangling this in front of Congress to keep them from cutting funds" for the U.S. troops in Europe.[134]

But none of those explanations and assurances had the desired effect.[135] In France, the fear of an emerging U.S.-Soviet "condominium" remained very much alive. But even if those concerns were warranted, there was more than one way to deal with them. One might, for example, have expected the French to press for greater political intimacy with the United States—for deeper forms of cooperation—so that France and the other European countries would not be marginalized. And some key French officials agreed with the Americans that the U.S.-European relationship needed to be reexamined and that the two sides needed to engage in a serious dialogue.[136] But Pompidou chose to move in the opposite direction, toward a more Gaullist policy, a policy with a sharper anti-American edge. That choice was probably rooted in a visceral sense that increased self-assertiveness—a greater emphasis on "building Europe" and a greater effort to keep the Americans at arm's length—was the only real answer to the "condominium" problem.[137]

So by mid-1973 the shift in French policy was quite clear and the

[132] Kissinger-Huang Hua meeting, September 8, 1972, p. 4, DNSA/KT00552.

[133] Personal Record of a Discussion [with Kissinger] in the British Embassy, Washington DC, on 19th April, 1973, pp. 7–8, attached to Sir Burke Trend to Prime Minister, April 24, 1973, PREM 15/1362, British National Archives, Kew; also in DNSA/KT00707.

[134] Nixon-Pompidou meeting, May 31, 1973, p. 10, DNSA/KT00742. Note also Kissinger's comments in a meeting with French foreign minister Maurice Schumann on September 22, 1972, pp. 7, 9, NSCF/679/France vol. X/NPL; also in DNSA/KT00570.

[135] Note, for example, Jobert's sharp attack on the PNW agreement in the NATO Council on December 10, 1973, in U.S. Embassy London to Department of State, December 12, 1973, Department of State Central Foreign Policy Files, Electronic Telegrams (1973), RG 59, USNA, retrieved from the National Archives' Access to Archival Databases (AAD) website for that file, document number 1973LONDON14640; henceforth cited in this form: DOSCFPF/Telegrams(1973)/1973LONDON14640.

[136] See, for example, Jean-Bernard Raimond note for Pompidou, May 10, 1973, cited in Soutou, "La problématique de la Détente," p. 96.

[137] Note in this context some remarks he made in a cabinet meeting in 1970: "URSS/USA parlent entre eux plus qu'ils nous disent. . . . Ce n'est pas plaisant pour nous. . . . Il faut durcir notre position et se démarquer de tous. . ." Jobert notes of April 29, 1970, cabinet meeting, Association Georges Pompidou, Paris, quoted in Laurent Césari, "Les relations personnelles entre Nixon, Pompidou et leurs entourages," unpublished paper, p. 7.

Americans were not slow to react. The U.S. government had earlier taken a relatively conciliatory line on monetary issues, but in mid-August Kissinger told Shultz to "hang tough" in this area. The Europeans, he said, had been "bastards"—he was thinking especially of the "Year of Europe" affair—and whatever concessions the U.S. government was prepared to make in the monetary field could be made only "as part of a more global negotiation." Kissinger did not like the fact that the French and German finance ministers were quite happy about the way the negotiations in this area were progressing. The Europeans were getting a degree of cooperation in this area free of charge; they should be made to give something in exchange in the political sphere. When he had spoken to Valéry Giscard d'Estaing, the French finance minister, he had told him, "[Y]ou know what you people don't understand is if you made a political concession we could be more generous in the economic field." And Giscard had answered: "Like what? What could you do that Shultz isn't already doing?" The Europeans, Kissinger said, were "trying to build their identity in confrontation with us and they are doing it by picking the areas where it is safe. And sucking us dry in the areas where it isn't and we've just got to put a stop to that."[138]

But the most striking change was in the nuclear area. It seemed in the summer that American assistance to France would be stepped up; the French armed forces minister, Robert Galley, came over for talks in late July and again in late August.[139] But by then the American attitude had cooled. "What we want," Kissinger told Secretary of Defense James Schlesinger on August 9, "is something which makes Galley drool but doesn't give him anything but something to study for a while." The goal was to "lead [the French] on without giving up anything," "to get a handle on them without [their] knowing it."[140] Kissinger's goals in

---

[138] Kissinger-Shultz telephone conversation , August 15, 1973, DNSA/KA10631; also in FRUS 1969–76, 31:191–93.

[139] Soutou, "La problématique de la Détente," p. 97. It is clear from the notes of Galley's meetings with top U.S. officials during this period (July 27 and August 31, 1973) that the French government was quite interested in deepening the nuclear relationship. As the French representatives said at the July 27 meeting, "Il s'agit donc bien d'échanges d'informations sur la base d'une liste de sujets très classés dans le domaine des missiles et des armes nucléaires" (Balladur Papers, *fonds* 543 AP at the Archives Nationales, Paris, box 32, folder "États-Unis"; extract provided by François Dubasque). At about this time, the French were in particular requesting specific information about Soviet surface-to-air and medium- and intermediate-range ballistic missile sites. See CIA Director Colby to Kissinger and Schlesinger, August 6, 1974, "French Request for Data on Locations of Soviet Missile Sites," CIA/ERR.

[140] Kissinger-Schlesinger meeting, August 9, 1973, DMPC:Nixon/DFPL. For the program that was to be presented to Galley on September 25, see Sonnenfeldt to Kissinger, 24 September 1973, and the attached Defense Department "memorandum for the record," NSCF/679/France—vol. XI/NPL. Limited assistance in the area of warhead design was

this area are not totally clear. At times it seemed that he wanted to keep a certain nuclear relationship alive—not to "let loose yet" with full co-operation, but to do "something moderate" in the nuclear area in order to drive a wedge between France and the other European countries. The policy of "building Europe" was now directed against the United States; the Americans were therefore "going to try to bust the Europeans"—to "break their unity." Developing a certain bilateral nuclear relationship with the French was "essential" if the U.S. government was to achieve that goal. The Americans could work with Galley and then at some point, he calculated, the other Europeans would say to the French, "you bastards, you talk about unity and then you go this bilateral route" with the United States.[141]

But although Kissinger in late 1973 and early 1974 occasionally argued along these lines, it seems that the basic thrust of his policy in this area at that time was not that subtle, and that his main goal was to get the French to change their basic policy. On September 5, for example, he told Schlesinger not to "conclude anything with Galley" when he came to America that month. He now thought he could get something in exchange for the nuclear assistance he was prepared to give France: "The real quid pro quo is the basic orientation of French policy. Galley said he understood but it would take them time."[142] Pompidou, however,

---

included here, as well as help with strategic warning. On the warning issue (which was linked to the question of a French option for launch on warning), see especially the Defense Department paper summarizing Foster's talks with the French, drafted 24 May 1973, attached to Kennedy to Hyland, 27 June 1973, NSCF/679/France—vol. IX/NPL. The obvious solution here involved tying the French into the U.S. satellite warning system, an arrangement, however, that might have made France more dependent on the United States than she otherwise would have been. But as the Kissinger comment about "getting a handle" on the French suggests, the Americans were not above thinking in such terms, even if getting influence over France was never the main point of the nuclear assistance program. But it was a factor. See, for example, the reference to "opportunities to exert influence" in the May 24 document just cited, or the comment about how allowing the French to test at the U.S. underground testing facility in Nevada "could establish a degree of U.S. control or influence over the pace of French nuclear weapons development," in Defense Department response to NSSM 175, 11 May 1973, p. 20, NSCF/679/France—vol. XI/NPL.

[141] Kissinger-Schlesinger-Foster meeting, August 17, 1973, pp. 1–3, DMPC:Nixon/DFPL; Kissinger-Schlesinger meeting, December 5, 1973, DMPC:Nixon/DFPL; and Kissinger-Schlesinger meeting, January 8, 1974, p. 3, DMPC:Nixon/DFPL. Note also Kissinger's comment in a September 5, 1973 meeting with Schlesinger (p. 4): "We want to keep Europe from developing their unity against us. If we keep the French hoping they can get ahead of the British, this would accomplish our objective." DMPC:Nixon/DFPL. The notes of Kissinger's August 31 meeting with Galley in that collection were exempted from declassification in 2008.

[142] Kissinger-Schlesinger meeting, September 5, 1973, p. 1, DNSA/KT00800. A less sanitized version is available online in the DFPL DMPC collection.

was obviously not going to give way on something that basic, and the U.S. government, for its part, was no longer willing to deepen the nuclear relationship with France. "The Americans don't want to give us anything any more," Pompidou told Michel Debré in February 1974.[143] But the nuclear relationship had effectively been put on hold months earlier, in September 1973.[144]

The collapse of that relationship thus has to be understood in political terms. It did not end because the Americans wanted to learn too much about what the French were doing in the nuclear area—it did not end, that is, because the Americans in the final analysis were insisting on terms that would compromise French nuclear independence.[145] It is quite clear, in fact, that the Pompidou government did not feel it had to keep the Americans in the dark in this area as a matter of principle. In June 1971, for example, a U.S. delegation was sent to Paris to work out arrangements for the missile cooperation program; a key U.S. goal was "to obtain a more detailed understanding of French missile programs so that [an] effort to implement the program of assistance could be initiated." The French had no problem giving the Americans the information they had asked for. In fact, they were "very forthcoming in the technical discussions. They described their land and sea-based systems

---

[143] Michel Debré, *Entretiens avec Georges Pompidou 1971-1974* (Paris: Albin Michel, 1996), p. 210. See also Soutou, "La problématique de la Détente," pp. 97–98, and Mélandri, "Aux origines de la coopération nucléaire franco-américaine," p. 252. The American evidence also indicates fairly clearly that the relationship was suspended in late 1973. See Kissinger-Schlesinger meeting, December 5, 1973, p. 4, DMPC:Nixon/DFPL. One should note, however, that according to Pompidou's successor, Giscard d'Estaing, a nuclear relationship still existed when he took over as president, a point Mélandri mentions in his article. Giscard alluded specifically to a breakfast meeting he had with Kissinger on July 5, 1974, in which the Secretary of State asked him if he wanted that relationship to continue. See Valéry Giscard d'Estaing, *Le pouvoir et la vie*, vol. 2, *L'affrontement* (Paris: Cie. 12, 1991), pp. 186–91. There is, however, no record of that meeting in the DNSA's Kissinger Transcripts collection. Perhaps the relationship had not been completely suspended, or perhaps Giscard had misunderstood or misremembered what Kissinger said. But the important point is that even if certain contacts continued, the relationship had cooled quite significantly.

[144] This sort of thing, incidentally, had happened twice before, first at the end of the Eisenhower period in August 1960 and then under Kennedy in December 1962–January 1963. For an account of those episodes, see Marc Trachtenberg, *A Constructed Peace: The Making of the European Settlement, 1945–1963* (Princeton: Princeton University Press, 1999), pp. 228–29, 365–69. It is interesting to note in this connection that Richard Ullman, in a well-known 1981 article based on interviews, said that the cooperation program *began* shortly after Galley's September 1973 trip to Washington. See Richard Ullman, "The Covert French Connection," *Foreign Policy*, no. 75 (Summer 1989): 11.

[145] For a somewhat different view, see Mélandri, "Aux origines de la coopération nucléaire franco-américaine," pp. 250–251, and Soutou, "La problématique de la Détente," pp. 90–91, 97–98.

generally, so as to place matters in context, and went into greater detail on specific problem areas. They took the U.S. delegation to Bordeaux to tour propulsion fabrication and missile assembly facilities. Actual missiles were examined at close hand."[146] Another document referred to the "frank manner in which [French defense minister] Debré has provided [General Vernon] Walters [the U.S. representative in the talks with the French on Soviet ABMs] with information concerning French military developments."[147]

Even in the area of what Soutou calls the "software"[148]—that is, the basic thinking and planning about how nuclear weapons would actually be used—the French government was more willing to work with the Americans than one might have thought. The main reason was that Pompidou (unlike de Gaulle in the mid-1960s) took the Soviet threat quite seriously. Other key French officials were also worried about what the Soviets were up to. The USSR was clearly increasing its military power; General Maurin, the armed forces chief of staff, thought the whole point of that buildup was to support a "policy of expansion aimed at dominating western Europe."[149] The defense of Europe, as the French now saw it, depended on a strong American military presence. But there was a danger that U.S. troop levels might be reduced and an even greater danger that American strategic forces might be "decoupled" from the defense of Europe.[150] The great fear was that America and Russia were moving toward a certain understanding, based on the idea that no matter what happened in Europe, neither America's nor Russia's homeland would be subject to nuclear attack. But whether that would be possible turned, in large measure, on the question of how a European war would be fought, and in particular on the question of how and when, if it all, nuclear weapons would be used in such a war. Perhaps, French officials were now coming to think, the old strategy of simply threatening massive retaliation was no longer viable; perhaps nuclear weapons, if they were used at all, needed to be used in a more discriminate way, first in the theater and then beyond; perhaps a more subtle strategy of controlled escalation was now in

---

[146] Laird to Kissinger, July 29, 1971, DNSA/PR00608.

[147] Sonnenfeldt to Kissinger, September 7, 1972, NSCF/HAK OF/24/HAK's Germany, Moscow, London, Paris trip 9/72, Misc. Cables and Documents/NPL.

[148] Soutou, "La problématique de la Détente," p. 90.

[149] General Maurin (Chief of Staff of French armed forces) meeting with Ambassador Irwin, November 15, 1973 (document dated Nov. 16), DOSCFPF/Telegrams(1973)/1973PARIS29551.

[150] Irwin to Kissinger and Schlesinger, October 6, 1973, reporting views of Galley's diplomatic advisor Seillière, DOSCFPF/Telegrams(1973)/1973PARIS26207. Those French fears were by no means baseless. See the discussion in chapter 6, pp. 162–65.

order.[151] But since the Americans were bound to play a fundamental role in this area, it made sense to try to work closely with them on these matters—to try to think through with them all of the problems relating to the use of nuclear weapons, and especially tactical nuclear weapons, in a European war.

And Galley made it quite clear that the French government was prepared to discuss these issues. He met with the U.S. ambassador on September 21; he was about to fly to Washington and wanted to let the Americans know what he wanted to talk about, and coordinating policy on tactical nuclear weapons was one of the top items on his agenda. "Nothing can be done seriously," he said, "in France or Europe in the area of security without extensive discussions with the U.S. Secretary of Defense Schlesinger. As an example of his last point, Minister Galley noted that the French air force had received tactical nuclear bombs some time ago and that the French army was scheduled to receive the Pluton tactical nuclear missile system in May 1974. These developments require that the U.S. and France discuss the new situation because France now finds itself, like the NATO forces, with a broad tactical nuclear capability."[152] He made the same point a few days later in a meeting in Washington with Deputy Secretary of State Kenneth Rush and Leon Sloss, an important State Department official who specialized in politico-military affairs. Further talks between French and American military officers, Galley thought, would be "extremely useful. The French were beginning to develop a serious tactical nuclear force. There would soon be a certain number of tactical nuclear weapons for French fighter aircraft and for the French ground forces. This introduction posed problems of cooperation that have to be discussed frankly."[153] A couple of weeks later, Galley's diplomatic advisor Ernest-Antoine Seillière brought up the issue again in a meeting with an American official: "Seillière volunteered that the French High Council of National De-

---

[151] Irwin to Kissinger, November 16, 1973, reporting a conversation between Seymour Weiss, an important State Department official involved in nuclear issues, and Jacques Martin, Deputy Secretary General of the French Secretariat Général de la Défense Nationale, DOSCFPF/Telegrams(1973)/1973PARIS29553. The French official outlined his government's thinking in this area in some detail; Ambassador Irwin commented that his exposition was "one of the most detailed and authoritative we have received." On French nuclear strategy in the 1960s, see especially de Gaulle's note on the "Défense atomique de l'Europe," May 1, 1963, Couve de Murville Papers, box CM8, Centre d'Histoire, Fondation Nationale des Sciences Politiques, Paris, discussed in Jeffrey Vanke, "De Gaulle's Atomic Defence Policy in 1963," *Cold War History* 1, no. 2 (January 2001).

[152] Irwin to Kissinger, Rush, and Schlesinger, September 21, 1973, DOSCFPF/Telegrams(1973)/1973PARIS24957.

[153] Rush-Galley conversation, September 25, 1973 (document dated Sept. 26), DOSCFPF/Telegrams(1973)/1973STATE191313.

fense (nearest French equivalent to the NSC, and normally chaired by the president) is addressing the question of France's future doctrine regarding tactical nuclear weapons. A decision should be reached 'in several weeks.' Once France has established its tactical nuclear policy, Seillière thought they would be in a position to examine the question of discussing with the U.S. the problems of cooperation posed by these weapons."[154] All of this has to be understood in the light of the fact that Galley, as Kosciusko had told Kissinger, was Pompidou's man; what that implies is that the president himself was behind this general policy.[155]

The French government, in other words, was quite prepared at this point to work closely with the Americans in the nuclear area. French officials were willing to discuss fundamental strategic issues—"software" issues—with their American counterparts; it seemed that they might even be willing to work out a common strategy for the nuclear defense of Europe. But the nuclear relationship, as important as it was, could not exist in a vacuum, and as political relations deteriorated, a strong defense relationship could scarcely be sustained. The problem, as a U.S. diplomat in Paris put it at the time, was that the French government "regards us as a partner in defense only, while in all other matters the E.C. and the U.S. are to interact as separate, independent entities."[156] But an arrangement of that sort the U.S. government was simply unwilling to accept.

So by September 1973 the nuclear relationship had been put on hold. And the date here is quite significant. It means that political relations

---

[154] Irwin to Kissinger, October 8, 1973, DOSCFPF/Telegrams(1973)/1973PARIS26222. The NATO commander, General Andrew Goodpaster, also wanted to move ahead in this area. The whole question of tactical nuclear weapons, he told Nixon, had "been stagnant for 10 years. He feels we are now at the point where we have done enough preparatory work that we can begin to take a new position of this troublesome issue. Goodpaster also noted that he was trying to extend the areas of cooperation with the French and he felt the French military were very much in favor of closer cooperation." Nixon-Goodpaster meeting, February 15, 1973, DMPC:Nixon/DFPL. And the Defense Department more generally was very much in favor of closer cooperation in this area and had been disappointed by French Defense Minister Debré's reluctance to pursue this issue when he met with his American counterpart in July 1972. See Laird to Nixon, 5 July 1972; talking points memo, p. 4, attached to Sonnenfeldt to Kissinger, 5 July 1972; and especially Defense Department response to NSSM 175, 11 May 1973, pp. 7, 30; all in NSC Files, boxes 678 and 679, France—vols. IX and XI, NPL.

[155] Kissinger-Kosciusko-Morizet meeting, April 13, 1973, p. 8, DNSA/KT00702. Pompidou himself told German chancellor Brandt in June 1973 that the French and the Americans needed to discuss the tactical nuclear weapons issue. Brandt-Pompidou meeting, June 21, 1973, AAPD 1973, p. 1026.

[156] Stone to Stoessel, November 29, 1973, DOSCFPF/Telegrams(1973)/1973PARIS30642.

had taken a sharp turn for the worse even before war broke out in the Middle East the following month.

THE MIDEAST WAR AND ITS AFTERMATH

In October 1973, war broke out between Israel and her Arab neighbors. The Americans supported Israel (within limits), and the Soviets supported the Arabs, at one point threatening to intervene unilaterally—a threat that led directly to the famous American nuclear alert of October 24. If a nuclear war broke out, NATO Europe could obviously not stand on the sidelines, but the U.S. government had not consulted with its allies before ordering the alert.[157] And the Europeans basically did not agree with the United States on the Arab-Israeli issue. They generally took a more pro-Arab line, in large part, as they themselves freely admitted, because of their much greater dependence on Arab oil.[158] The Arabs, in fact, were now openly using oil as a political weapon.

So as the war ran its course, the Europeans by and large sought to distance themselves from the United States. They objected to American efforts to resupply Israel from U.S. stocks in Europe. They refused to permit U.S. transport planes to overfly their territory—even though the Soviets were allowed (as Kissinger notes) to use NATO airspace "without challenge."[159] And it was not just the French who dissociated themselves from the United States in that way. The German government, for

---

[157] I should note, however, that on the issue of the alert the French were perhaps a bit more understanding than one might have expected. Kosciusko-Morizet, for example, in a frank exchange with a key State Department official on the general issue of consultations on November 27, said that "France understood [the] need for quick action in calling [the] alert under the circumstances and he felt [the] French had no complaints on that score." And Galley told the U.S. ambassador on October 30 that he personally felt the "US government was right to go on alert in order to keep Soviet paratroopers from inserting themselves along the Suez Canal," and that that unilateral U.S. action was in line with de Gaulle's view that the use of U.S. forces would be determined by the Americans themselves, adding, "We French do not object. You are playing your role exactly as we expected. You are Americans first and that is right." And indeed on Pompidou's instructions the French put their own forces in Germany on alert and allowed allied warplanes to pass through French airspace. Kissinger to U.S. Embassy Paris, November 30, 1973, and Irwin to Kissinger, November 31, 1973, both in *Richard M. Nixon National Security Files, 1969–1974* (microfilm), Western Europe series (Bethesda, Md.: Lexis/Nexis, 2005), reel 10 [the original documents are NSCF/679/France vol. XI (2 of 2)/NPL]; and General Alain de Boissieu account in *Georges Pompidou hier et aujourd'hui: témoignages* (Neuilly: Éditions Breet, 1990), p. 221.

[158] See, for example, Pompidou's comments to Kissinger in a December 20, 1973 meeting, p. 7, DNSA/KT00968. For a recent overview of French policy in the crisis, see Pauline Peretz, "La France et la Guerre du Kippour," *Revue d'histoire diplomatique*, no. 2 (2006).

[159] Kissinger, *Years of Upheaval*, p. 709.

example, publicly announced that weapons deliveries from U.S. depots in the FRG "cannot be allowed."[160]

The Europeans, of course, had their own grievances. They complained above all about inadequate consultation, but "the real trouble," as Kissinger later pointed out, "was a clash in political perspectives that no amount of consultation" would have been able to remove.[161] He also felt that there was something disingenuous about that complaint. The United States, as he told the German ambassador on October 26, had in the past tried repeatedly to consult with the allies and "work out common positions," but the Europeans had not been interested. On the Arab-Israeli question in particular, they had instead chosen to dissociate themselves from America and pursue policies of their own. In such circumstances, he said, "when their fundamental attitude was either slightly or openly hostile," they were hardly in a position to "insist on a right to private briefings."[162]

It is important to note, however, that Kissinger did not dismiss the European case in this general area as frivolous. A serious argument could certainly be made that America had been too passive before the war, that the U.S. government needed to force the Israelis to withdraw from the areas they had occupied in 1967, and that a comprehensive peace had to be the goal. The U.S. view was different: even a full Israeli withdrawal would not necessarily lead to peace; to tilt toward the Arab side, to give way to Arab oil power, would strengthen the radicals within the Arab camp; the situation was such that a comprehensive peace was unachievable in the near future, and a more modest step-by-step approach was in order.[163]

The Americans had a strategy. The key thing was to capitalize on Israeli dependence on the United States. That meant that the Arabs would have to deal with the United States since only the Americans could influence Israeli policy. The U.S. government could take advantage of that position to build a relationship with the Arab moderates and to marginalize the radicals within the Arab world (and their Soviet supporters). To do that, it would have to show that moderation paid off and that bit by bit a reasonable accommodation could be worked out. And as the Arabs moved toward a reasonable policy, the Israelis would

---

[160] Ibid., p. 714. On British policy during the crisis, see Matthew Ferraro, *"Tough Going": Anglo-American Relations and the Yom Kippur War of 1973* (New York: iUniverse, 2007).

[161] Kissinger, *Years of Upheaval*, p. 720.

[162] Kissinger-von Staden meeting, October 26, 1973 (doc. dated Oct. 27), NSAEBB98/81/4 and 6. The German account of this meeting, which generally has Kissinger taking a somewhat softer line, is in AAPD 1973, no. 341; the account of this particular exchange appears on p. 1665.

[163] Kissinger, *Years of Upheaval*, pp. 707–8.

also become more accommodating—or could more easily be pushed in that direction. In pursuing this sort of strategy, there was some hope that a settlement of this almost intractable conflict could eventually be worked out.

The Europeans, of course, saw things differently, but for Kissinger at this point the issue was no longer who could make the better case. Even if the Europeans had been right about American policy before the war, it made little sense for them to try to sabotage American policy now. They had no viable alternative strategy that they were capable of pursuing themselves. To undercut what the U.S. government was doing— to encourage the Arab radicals, to give them the sense that they, and not the Americans, were in the driver's seat—could not, in his view, be in the interest of the West as a whole.[164]

And indeed one would not have expected the Europeans, and especially the French, to have opposed the Americans in this area as strongly as they did. On the core issue the two sides were not that far apart. All the major European countries were committed to the survival of Israel, while the Americans, for their part, did not intend to give the Israelis a blank check. As Kissinger told Pompidou in December 1973, the Israelis had "a diplomacy which leads to suicide."[165] The implication was that basic Israeli policy had to change. On that point both he and Pompidou agreed. The argument was thus over strategy, not fundamentals. In such circumstances one might have thought that given the basic realities of the situation, the Europeans would not try to sabotage American policy.

And yet that, as Kissinger saw it, was precisely what they did. "Europe, it emerged increasingly," he said, "wanted the option to conduct a policy separate from the United States and in the case of the Middle East objectively in conflict with us."[166] This was something the U.S. government could not accept. Did the Europeans really think they could pursue a totally independent and indeed anti-American policy and still expect the United States to defend them? Did anyone really think that "America should be accorded the great privilege of defending Europe, but have no other role" in European affairs?[167] To his mind, and to Nix-

[164] Ibid., pp. 707–8, 711, 716.

[165] Kissinger-Pompidou meeting, December 20, 1973, p. 4, DNSA/KT00968. Kissinger was convinced, he told the British that same month, "that Israel would have to withdraw from the occupied territories." Record of December 13, 1973, Cabinet meting, CM(73)61st, in CAB 128/53, British National Archives, Kew.

[166] Kissinger, *Years of Upheaval*, p. 716. For Kissinger's views at the time, see Secretary's Staff Meeting, November 20, 1973 (notes dated Nov. 21), esp. pp. 13–21, DNSA/KT00914.

[167] Kissinger-Kosciusko-Morizet meeting, December 3, 1973, p. 2, DNSA/KT00932. Note also Kissinger's remarks to the NATO Council, March 4, 1974, AAPD 1974, pp. 309, 314.

on's as well, the European view (as the German ambassador expressed it in a meeting with Kissinger) that it was wrong to link "the Near East issue to broader alliance questions," and that "these matters should be kept separate," was absurd.[168] In particular, he felt that it had to be made clear to the main European governments that the line they were taking on the Arab-Israeli question was putting their alliance with America at risk. It had to be made clear to them that there were "limits to our store of good will." They had to be made to "recognize the abyss before which they stand."[169] The Europeans, he told the French ambassador on October 26, had behaved in the crisis "not as friends but as hostile powers." The U.S. government was going to reassess its relationship with the NATO allies in light of their behavior in the area.[170] And Kissinger took certain actions designed to give the allies the impression that America's commitment to Europe was weakening. He instructed U.S. officials, for example, to stop "the compulsory reassuring of the Europeans on a nuclear guarantee."[171] And he also made it clear that he was no longer interested in the Year of Europe declarations. "They have been drained of any significance," he told the French ambassador on December 3. He was in fact washing his hands of the entire affair.[172]

The whole problem, Kissinger was coming to think, could no longer be swept under the rug. America needed to have it out with the European allies. It was "morally disgraceful" for the Europeans to be "beholden to the Arabs."[173] The Europeans were "craven," they were appeasers; when one saw the intelligence reports "of what the U.K. and

[168] Kissinger-von Staden meeting, October 26, 1973, NSAEBB98/81/4 (doc. dated Oct. 27); Kissinger in Secretary's Staff meeting, October 23, 1973, NSAEBB98/63/7-8. For Nixon's view, see his well-known public comment on March 15, 1974, quoted in Kissinger, *Years of Upheaval*, p. 932.

[169] Kissinger meeting with Rusk, Bundy, McCloy, et al., November 28, 1973, pp. 29, 31, DNSA/KT00928.

[170] Kissinger-Kosciusko-Morizet meeting, October 25, 1973, NSAEBB98/75/2-3 (doc. dated Oct. 26); and also Kissinger's remarks in Secretary's Staff meeting, October 23, 1973, NSAEBB98/63/7-8. See also Ferraro, *"Tough Going,"* pp. 82–83, 103; Kissinger-von Staden meeting, October 26, 1973, NSAEBB98/81/1 (doc. dated Oct. 27); and especially Secretary's Staff Meeting, October 25, 1973 (notes dated Oct. 29), pp. 21–24, DNSA/KT00869.

[171] Kissinger, in Secretary of State's staff meeting, November 27, 1973, pp. 1, 16, DNSA/KT00927.

[172] Kissinger-Kosciusko-Morizet meeting, December 3, 1973, pp. 7–8, DNSA/KT00932. See also Secretary's Staff Meeting, October 25, 1973 (notes dated Oct. 29), DNSA/KT00869, pp. 21–22, and Kissinger meeting with key advisors, March 11, 1974, p. 5, Helmut Sonnenfeldt Papers [USNA entry no. 5339]/4/HS Chron – Official – Jan–Apr 1974/RG 59/USNA.

[173] Kissinger-Jobert meeting, December 19, 1973, p. 5, DOSCF/Subj-Num 1970-73/2278 [POL FR-US 1-10-73]/RG 59/USNA.

the French are saying to the Arabs, it is worse than it was in the thirties."[174] "We are aware of French approaches in Arab capitals," he told the French ambassador on December 3, "and our reports suggest that your position has been critical of the United States. I see no reason under these conditions for a cooperative relationship."[175] He made much the same point two months later in a telephone conversation with John McCloy: "I cannot tell you on the phone" (again presumably because this information came from intelligence sources) but the French were "pursuing a more active anti-US policy in the Middle East than the Russians."[176] And again, a month after that in a talk with the German foreign minister: "And let's not forget what the French are saying in the Middle East as they talk against our policies. If [Soviet Foreign Minister] Gromyko had said such things we would say it was the end of détente."[177]

The issue, in Kissinger's view, could not be allowed to fester. He was increasingly inclined to "bring matters to a head" with the Europeans, and especially with the French.[178] In January 1974 the main oil-importing countries were invited to a conference in Washington. The goal was to organize the oil purchasers, but the Europeans did not like the idea of a consumers' cartel. They were afraid that the oil producers, who of course had an active cartel-like organization of their own, would find the notion provocative. The French were particularly hostile to the plan. But the U.S. government wanted a showdown. If the plan for energy cooperation did not work, Kissinger told McCloy, the Americans would "have to take on the French in an all-out confrontation"; "I have reached the point, Jack, where I believe we have to take the French on."[179]

---

[174] Kissinger meeting with Rusk, Bundy, McCloy, et al., November 28, 1973, p. 23, DNSA/KT00928; Kissinger quoted in C.L. Sulzberger, "United States and France: I," *New York Times*, March 16, 1974, p. 31.

[175] Kissinger-Kosciusko-Morizet meeting, December 3, 1973, p. 3, DNSA/KT00932.

[176] Kissinger telephone conversation with John McCloy, February 8, 1974, 11:10 a.m., U.S. Department of State Electronic Reading Room, Kissinger Transcripts series; henceforth cited as DOS ERR/KT.

[177] Kissinger-Scheel meeting, March 3, 1974, p. 8, DNSA/KT01052. Note also the discussion in Kissinger, *Years of Upheaval*, p. 904, and Kissinger-Rush telephone conversation, March 30, 1974, DNSA/KA12252.

[178] Kissinger, *Years of Upheaval*, p. 901.

[179] Kissinger phone conversations with John McCloy, February 8, 1974, 11:10 a.m. and 9:40 p.m., DOS ERR/KT. It is interesting to note, however, that Pompidou, in his important May 18, 1973, meeting with Kissinger, actually proposed establishing a western-dominated cartel to control supplies of wheat, another very important commodity: "I think it is possible," he said, "to reach an understanding among France, the United States, Canada and perhaps Argentina, to constitute a sort of OPEC to direct the [wheat] market." Kissinger-Pompidou meeting, May 18, 1973, pp. 2–3, DNSA/KT00728. Pompidou, in fact, in a June 1973 meeting with Brandt, said he favored organizing the oil-consuming

As it turned out, the French were isolated in Washington. The other main consumer countries succumbed to U.S. pressure and supported the American proposal to set up an international energy agency.[180] But that U.S. victory, such as it was, did not settle the issue. A month later there was a new confrontation. The Americans had long wanted to make sure that the European Community did not take action on the Arab-Israeli question that would tend to undermine U.S. policy. To that end, Kissinger thought the European Community should consult with the U.S. government before it made any major move in that area.[181] In early March, the E.C. met in Brussels and adopted a plan for a European-Arab dialogue, to culminate in a foreign ministers' meeting—a move taken without consultation with the United States, and indeed after assurances had been given (by German Foreign Minister Scheel) that the "dialogue" would be a more low-key affair.[182] As Kissinger later noted, Scheel (then speaking for the European Community) could not have been under the illusion that the U.S. government would be pleased by the E.C.'s decision.[183]

Kissinger, in fact, was livid. "We were determined to draw the line," he later wrote. What had happened was unacceptable. "We now had divergent policies in areas we considered vital."[184] He had warned Scheel on March 3 about what was at stake. "The Saturday before the Energy Conference," he told him, "I had a long discussion with the President and for the first time we discussed seriously the possibility of unilateral US troop withdrawal. If Europe pursues this policy toward opposition—if Europe is going to move toward neutralism anyway—we may as well make our decisions unilaterally as well."[185] He wanted U.S. representatives in the field to be told that the administration intended to take a hard line with the allies: "I want to get it into the system so that our God damned embassies understand that we are deadly serious about this and they are not running a psychiatric social service

---

countries to "resist certain operations by the producing countries." See Willy Brandt, *People and Politics: The Years 1960–1974* (Boston: Little Brown, 1976, pp. 272, 466; and Brandt-Pompidou meeting, June 21, 1973, AAPD 1973, p. 1030.

[180] As Kissinger later noted, he had told the German foreign minister that rather than be "party to a confusing outcome in which rhetoric obscured failure," the U.S. government "would rather announce disagreement and draw the political consequences—a thinly veiled threat that this time intransigence would not be free." Kissinger, *Years of Upheaval*, p. 907. For an interesting discussion of U.S. tactics for the conference, see Kissinger-Sonnenfeldt telephone conversation, February 8, 1974, DNSA/KA11995.

[181] Ibid., pp. 899–900.

[182] See Kissinger-Scheel meeting, March 3, 1974, p. 7, DNSA/KT01052.

[183] Kissinger, *Years of Upheaval*, p. 930.

[184] Ibid., pp. 930–31.

[185] See Kissinger-Scheel meeting, March 3, 1974, p. 17, DNSA/KT01052.

for distraught Europeans."[186] The United States, he wrote Scheel shortly after the Brussels decision was announced, would now also feel free to take steps that it considered to be in its own national interest and "to report on them to the Community thereafter"—and the Americans in his view were much better able to pursue that sort of policy than the Europeans were.[187] As he had warned Scheel on March 3, "If we had wanted to be predominant, we wouldn't consult on such areas as the Middle East but instead we would allow our foreign policy to float. We could achieve domination because of our greater weight."[188]

The issue of the "dialogue" was not in itself of enormous importance, but Kissinger was trying to make a point. He was using this occasion to make it clear to the Europeans that the procedure they had used, of taking action in an area where U.S. interests were affected in a major way without consulting with the Americans, "will never be accepted again."[189] By the end of the month, he thought that goal had been achieved. "I think now," he told McGeorge Bundy on March 23, "no European government is going to vote on something that affects our interest without getting it to us one way or another."[190] And France was

[186] Kissinger meeting with key advisors, March 18, 1974, pp. 3, 5–6, Sonnenfeldt Papers/4/HS Chron – Official – Jan–Apr 1974/RG 59/USNA; also at DNSA/KT01073.

[187] See Kissinger, *Years of Upheaval*, pp. 901–2, 930.

[188] Kissinger-Scheel meeting, March 3, 1974, pp. 3–4, DNSA/KT01052; see also p. 14.

[189] Kissinger-Sonnenfeldt telephone conversation, March 5, 1974, DOS ERR/KT. Note also the line he took in a March 11, 1974, meeting with Sonnenfeldt and other key State Department officials: "The question is what would be the greatest shock to the Europeans?" (p. 5); "They keep saying that if they are forced to choose between France and the US, they will choose the US. Well, maybe we should give them the choice now" (p. 6); "We have never gone for the jugular. Maybe it is time to do it" (p. 7); "I am tired of a crisis with them every six months. Maybe we should push them to the wall" (p. 8); "if we don't [reaffirm the alliance], we scare the hell out of them and they show extreme caution before another initiative without consultation" (p. 10); and so on. Kissinger meeting with key advisors, March 11, 1974, Sonnenfeldt Papers/4/HS Chron – Official – Jan–Apr 1974/RG 59/USNA.

[190] Kissinger-Bundy telephone conversation, March 23, 1974, DOS ERR/KT. A week earlier he had told his staff, "I want our embassies to understand that this is a damned serious process, that we are winning—that in fact we have won because the Europeans have no guts for a real fight. In fact, when I consider how much they screamed when we asked for cooperation and how quiet they are when we are kicking them around, it really makes me wonder." Kissinger meeting with key advisors, March 18, 1974, p. 3, DNSA/KT01073. And it does seem that the Europeans did in fact essentially give way. See Werner Link, "Aussen- under Deutschlandpolitik in der Ära Brandt 1969–1974," in Karl Dietrich Bracher, Wolfgang Jäger, and Werner Link, *Republik im Wandel 1969–1974: Die Ära Brandt* (Stuttgart: Deutsche Verlags-Anstalt, 1986), pp. 260–66, esp. p. 265. The more recent scholarship takes much the same line. Note, especially, the interpretation of the Gymnich agreement of April 21, 1974 (ultimately reflected in a "gentleman's agreement" of June 10, 1974), which Link views as fundamental in this context. "The Gymnich agreement," Gfeller, for example, writes, "and its enshrinement in a non-paper practically en-

the main target. "French policy," he told his advisors, "is not only obstructionist, but antagonistic: in Syria, and other places as well. They are organically hostile to the US and now clearly constitute the greatest global opposition to US foreign policy."[191] And the French were trying to get Europe as a whole to back that policy: in formulating its own Mideast policy, Europe, he thought, would in Jobert's view be issuing "a sort of declaration of independence from the United States."[192] But for Kissinger, as he told Scheel on March 3, it was "intolerable to us that the only way Europe seems to be able to establish its identity is in opposition to the US."[193] And he did not conceal these views from the French. In a meeting with Kosciusko-Morizet in late March, just a few days before Pompidou's death, he laid out his grievances in considerable detail. The bottom line was quite simple: "The Alliance is basic to our policy but the American defense of Europe cannot continue so that Europe is free to pursue anti-American policies."[194]

By that point, French policy had also hardened. The dying president laid out his views in an important document, his "strategic testament" of February 1, 1974. "When our core interests are at stake," Pompidou wrote, "we must never give way or pull back. Being isolated does not matter, threats and pressures do not matter, France must never give in to anyone, even the most powerful. When the national interest is at stake, it is necessary to display an iron will."[195] The time had come, in other words, to stand up to America—to return, that is, to a purer more

---

sured that EC states would no longer bear a joint influence on world events in any way that could antagonize the US." Gfeller, "Re-envisioning Europe," p. 280. See also Möckli, *European Foreign Policy during the Cold War*, pp. 3, 316–22.

[191] Kissinger meeting with key advisors, March 11, 1974, p. 4, Sonnenfeldt Papers/4/ HS Chron – Official – Jan–Apr 1974/RG 59/USNA.

[192] Kissinger, *Years of Upheaval*, p. 926.

[193] Kissinger-Scheel meeting, March 3, 1974, p. 4, DNSA/KT01052.

[194] Kissinger-Kosciusko-Morizet meeting, March 22, 1974, p. 10, DNSA/KT01080. On these matters, see also Kosciusko-Morizet to Jobert, March 7, 1974 (titled "La grande colère de M. Kissinger"), Balladur Papers (543 AP), box 32, folder "Correspondance J. Kosciusko-Morizet, ambassadeur de France aux État-Unis, à M. Jobert, ministre des Affaires étrangères (classée secret)," Archives Nationales, Paris (provided by François Dubasque). This was a long report based on notes of Kissinger's (taped) remarks to American journalists during his recent trips to Europe and the Middle East. Note also Kissinger's comments during the March 1974 meeting of the North Atlantic Council, and especially his threat to "break" France if that country continued its obstructionist policy, quoted in Maurice Vaïsse, *La Puissance ou l'influence? La France dans le monde depuis 1958* (Paris: Fayard, 2009), p. 194; the quotation is drawn from the unpublished memoirs of Paul Carraud, the diplomat representing France at that meeting.

[195] For a discussion of Pompidou's "testament," see Soutou, "La problématique de la Détente," esp. pp. 105–107, and also Georges-Henri Soutou, "Georges Pompidou et Valéry Giscard d'Estaing: deux réconciliations et deux ruptures avec les États-Unis," *Relations Internationales*, no. 119 (Fall 2004), pp. 311–12. The quotation is from the extract from

orthodox Gaullist political line. On February 1, the very day it was signed, Pompidou showed a copy of the document to the arch-Gaullist Michel Debré: "Vous voyez, Michel, je ne trahis pas la France!"[196]

MAKING SENSE OF THE STORY

So by the end of the Nixon-Pompidou period the relationship that had begun so promisingly in 1969 lay in pieces on the floor. Kissinger was totally baffled by what had happened after mid-1973.[197] "What," he wondered, "have we done to these people?"[198] From his point of view, he and Nixon had from the start practically bent over backward to build a strong relationship with France. They had "always believed," he told the French ambassador on March 22, 1974, "that Europe must be organized around France." "The confrontation which has come about," he said, was "certainly not by our choice." "The French," he said, were "the aggressors in this situation."[199]

So what had gone wrong? The two countries had an obvious interest in cooperating with each other. Why then was it so hard for them to do so? In Pierre Mélandri's view, the answer is simple. The basic policies of the two countries, he says, were essentially "incompatible": the French sought to develop a distinct European identity, while the Americans were out to reaffirm "Atlantic solidarity" and their own "leadership" within the Atlantic alliance.[200] Soutou's interpretation is somewhat different. The U.S. government, as he sees it, did not really want Europe (and Japan) to play a more independent role in world affairs. In the world of Nixon and Kissinger, he says, only three powers—the United States, China, and the Soviet Union—really mattered. All the rest—all the talk about the allies playing an important role—was essentially just window-dressing.[201] But the French in the final analysis could scarcely

the document quoted in Jean de Lipkowski, "Succéder au Général," in Bernard Pons et al., *Georges Pompidou,* pp. 114–15.

[196] Debré, *Entretiens avec Georges Pompidou,* p. 209.

[197] Kissinger-Sauvagnargues meeting, July 4, 1974, DNSA/KT01240. His perplexity comes out in many documents from the period. Note, for example, a comment he made in a meeting with the French ambassador at the end of 1973: "We are rapidly approaching in our bilateral relations the conditions of 1962 and this in an administration more francophile than any could conceivably imagine." Kissinger-Kosciusko-Morizet meeting, December 3, 1973, DNSA/KT00932.

[198] Nixon-Kissinger telephone conversation, February 11, 1974 (6:30 p.m.), DOS ERR/KT.

[199] Kissinger-Kosciusko-Morizet meeting, March 22, 1974, pp. 8, 14, DNSA/KT01080.

[200] Mélandri, "Une relation très spéciale," p. 124.

[201] Georges-Henri Soutou, *La Guerre de Cinquante Ans: Le conflit Est-Ouest 1943–1990* (Paris: Fayard, 2001), pp. 524–25.

accept being marginalized in that way. Those French fears about where the détente policy was leading—the fear of an emerging U.S.-Soviet "condominium"—meant, he argues, that the relationship with America could only go so far.[202] When tested, Pompidou's basic Gaullist instincts were practically bound to reassert themselves.

What is to be made of these arguments? I think, first of all, that the idea that Pompidou's fundamental goal was to build a Europe with a political personality of its own is a bit overdrawn. He certainly wanted Europe to develop a greater degree of political cohesion and independence, but his basic inclination was to proceed slowly and carefully and without putting what he saw as Europe's vital security relationship with America at risk.[203] And too "European" a policy was distasteful for another reason: a policy of "building Europe" might give Germany too much power, and it was in large part for that reason that Pompidou had not been eager to move ahead toward an autonomous European defense structure or even toward a European monetary union.[204]

In fact, it is important to note that for all the talk about "building Europe," the French were much more interested even at this point in working with the Americans on defense issues than with the Germans. According to a high French official, the Germans had made it clear that they were prepared to work out a "joint defense arrangement" with France "which would include reliance on the French strategic nuclear

[202] Soutou, "La problématique de la Détente," esp. p. 92.

[203] See Roussel, *Pompidou*, pp. 486, 496, 650. On the importance of the security relationship with the United States, note especially a comment he made in his May 21, 1973, meeting with Heath, quoted ibid., p. 549: "Nos relations avec les États-Unis sont, en réalité, dominées par un fait: la défense européenne dépend avant tout de la puissance américaine" (5AG2/1015/AN).

[204] Note especially Pompidou's comments on the issue of a European defense system in a March 19, 1973, meeting with Heath, quoted in Roussel, *Pompidou*, p. 506 (5AG2/1015/AN), and the discussion in Gfeller, "Re-envisioning Europe," pp. 92–93. "Nous ne sommes nullement pressés de parler défense ," he noted in August 1972. "Il faut d'abord une base politique à l'Europe et elle est loin d'être en place." Pompidou note on "Grande-Bretagne," August 18, 1972, 5AG2/1014, quoted in ibid., p. 93 n. 91. The French were not particularly interested even in nuclear cooperation with the British, even though it was quite clear that this sort of arrangement would not prejudice their nuclear relationship with the Americans. The U.S. government, in fact, seemed to favor Anglo-French nuclear cooperation, and apparently preferred an arrangement à trois with France and Britain to separate bilateral relationships—but that idea the French dismissed out of hand. See Möckli, *European Foreign Policy during the Cold War*, pp. 86–90, 216–17, 344 (Nixon's comments about Anglo-French cooperation are quoted on p. 89); and Vaïsse, "Les 'relations spéciales' franco-américaines" (manuscript version—the key passages do not appear in the published version), pp. 23–24, 28. On these and related issues, see also Möckli, *European Foreign Policy during the Cold War*, pp. 85–91, 213–19, and 342–46. On French policy on the question of a European monetary union, see Robert Frank, "Pompidou, le franc et l'Europe," pp. 349–55, 359.

force. Coupled with this proposal was an offer to make a substantial financial contribution to the further development of the French strategic nuclear forces." But the French were not interested in anything of the sort: they were determined not to allow the Germans to share in any way in the control of their strategic nuclear forces.[205] And that was just one of a number of nuclear overtures the German authorities were making to the French during this period; the French response was invariably quite tepid.[206] French officials, incidentally, were well aware of the fact that their reluctance to allow Germany to play a major role in this area meant that there was a limit beyond which the policy of "building Europe" could not go.[207] But defense cooperation with America was another matter entirely.[208] As already noted, the French government very much wanted to develop a nuclear relationship with the Americans—a policy that remained intact even as political relations deteriorated sharply in mid-1973.

This whole question of how to organize the defense of western Europe, and in particular the question of how much emphasis to give to "European" as opposed to "Atlantic" structures, was of course of fundamental importance, and indeed throughout the Cold War period the

[205] Report of comments made by Achille-Fould, the secretary of state in the Armed Forces Ministry, in Irwin to Kissinger, September 14, 1973, *Richard M. Nixon National Security Files, 1969–1974* (microfilm), Western Europe series (Bethesda, Md.: Lexis/Nexis, 2005), reel 10. The original document is in NSCF/679/France vol. XI (2 of 2)/NPL.

[206] See Georges-Henri Soutou, "Willy Brandt, Georges Pompidou et l'Ostpolitik"; Hans-Peter Schwarz, "Willy Brandt, Georges Pompidou und die Ostpolitik"; and Wilfried Loth, "Willy Brandt, Georges Pompidou und die Entspannungspolitik," all in Horst Müller and Maurice Vaïsse, eds., *Willy Brandt und Frankreich* (Munich: Oldenbourg, 2005), pp. 147–48, 156, 163, 175–79. Soutou had previously discussed this issue in his article "L'attitude de Georges Pompidou face à l'Allemagne," pp. 298-304, and again in his book *L'alliance incertaine: les rapports politico-stratégiques franco-allemands, 1954-1966* (Paris: Fayard, 1996), pp. 339-341. The German record of the key meeting between Brandt and Pompidou was published in AAPD 1973, esp. pp. 1024-1025. The record of another important meeting (between Scheel and Jobert on November 9, 1973) at which this issue was discussed is also in AAPD 1973, no. 367, esp. p. 1794; see also ibid., docs. 274, 390, and 393.

[207] See, for example, André Bettencourt (*ministre délégué auprès du ministre des Affaires étrangères*) meeting with U.S. Assistant Secretary of State Irwin, October 23, 1972, 5AG2/117/AN: "L'une des raisons fondamentales de la faiblesse de l'Europe," Bettencourt said, "c'est que les Neuf ne peuvent pas élaborer une politique de défense à cause de l'Allemagne."

[208] Indeed, even under de Gaulle the French had been interested in seeing if something could be worked out: on June 15, 1962, the NATO commander's French liaison officer told him that the French foreign minister would raise the issue of "coordination of US-French nuclear forces" with Secretary of State Rusk. "US-French Nuclear Cooperation," n.s., June 18, 1962, Richard Neustadt Papers, box 19, folder "Government Consulting— Skybolt/NATO/Atlantic Affairs, 2 of 3," JFKL. Another document refers to French interest in the issue in late 1965: Kissinger-Grandville meeting, January 23, 1966, pp. 8–9, DDRS/CK3100490686.

French had to figure out how to strike the right balance between Germany and America. Obviously there had to be a counterweight to Soviet power in Europe; almost as obviously, that counterweight had to be based on American power. But there also had to be a European counterweight to American power within the western alliance, and, given the main thrust of British policy for most of this period, that counterweight had to be based on some sort of Franco-German entente. But the French could not tilt too far in that direction: a free-standing Europe meant a strong—perhaps a too strong—German state. A decent relationship with the United States would thus provide a degree of reinsurance, a hedge against the risks of pursuing too "European" a policy. It was not that every French leader in the Cold War period thought in those terms, but Pompidou basically did, at least until the final year of his presidency when he seemed to take a more "European" line. But he did not take that line because he had suddenly become an *"Européen acharné"* (to use his own term); the shift in policy was a result of changes in the global political conjuncture, above all the dramatic improvement in U.S.-Soviet relations and the "condominium" fears that it had given rise to.

But did this mean that a confrontation with the United States was unavoidable? Pompidou certainly wanted to do what he could to make sure that the European countries, and especially France, were not just American satellites. He did not really share de Gaulle's view that the Americans were in Europe simply because they had a basic interest in preventing that key part of the world from being absorbed into the Soviet sphere—and that France could therefore pursue a totally independent policy since whether the United States stayed in Europe or withdrew would be determined by America's own interests and not by anything the French did or did not do.[209] Pompidou's views were by no means that extreme: for him, Europe's dependence on America was a

---

[209] Perhaps the most striking example of this attitude was de Gaulle's justification for his refusal in 1964 to take part in the ceremonies marking the twentieth anniversary of the Normandy landings. The Anglo-Saxons in 1944 were pursuing their own interests; the French thus owed them no debt of gratitude for what they had done: "Les Américains ne se souciaient pas plus de délivrer la France que les Russes de libérer la Pologne." See Peyrefitte, *C'était de Gaulle*, 2:84–87. Jobert saw things much the same way. See, for example, Jobert-Bahr meeting, November 19, 1973, AAPD 1973, p. 1862. This basic point about U.S. policy was expressed more elegantly by Maurice Couve de Murville, formerly de Gaulle's foreign minister, in a number of speeches he gave after leaving office. America, he said, was "too great a nation" not to base its policy on a judgment about where its true interests lay; security for Europe was therefore not a function of the "degree of docility" the Europeans showed toward the United States. See, for example, his speech to the Semaine Européenne de l'École Centrale, January 23, 1974, pp. 4–5, and his Hanover speech of March 11, 1974, p. 18, both in Maurice Couve de Murville Papers, box CM5, Fondation Nationale des Sciences Politiques, Paris.

simple fact of life that had to be taken into account when the Europeans were working out their own policies. But that did not mean that the Americans had to be followed blindly; within very broad limits, France had to be able to make choices of her own.

But was that incompatible with American policy? Kissinger said that the U.S. government wanted a strong Europe—that a "strong Europe [was] as essential as a strong China"—and that the only thing it objected to was the "attempt to organize Europe, to unify Europe, on an anti-American basis, or at least on a basis in which criticism of the United States becomes the organizing principle."[210] In reality, things were not quite that simple. A strong Europe would be a Europe that could pursue policies that differed from those of the United States in perhaps fundamental ways. But as U.S. leaders saw it, there were limits beyond which the Europeans could simply not go. Even on economic issues, they expected the Europeans to take American interests "fully into account."[211] Indeed, the basic U.S. view from 1961 on was that the western European countries were in the final analysis dependent on America for their security and in such circumstances could not pursue totally independent foreign policies. If the Europeans wanted to be completely independent politically, they would have to be independent militarily as well: they would have to be prepared to defend themselves. But if they wanted American protection, they could not oppose U.S. policy in any major way.[212]

Does this mean, however, that the French were right in thinking that the U.S. goal in pressing for a "revitalized" alliance was to create a system in which the policies of the European governments would be subject to American control? Again, things are not quite that simple. Kissinger and Nixon certainly wanted the main western allies to work out what amounted to a common policy, but that does not in itself mean that they thought the U.S. government would essentially determine

[210] Kissinger-Pompidou meeting, May 18, 1973, p. 7, DNSA/KT00728; Kissinger in Secretary's Staff Meeting, December 26, 1973, DNSA/KT00973, p. 2.

[211] See National Security Decision Memorandum 68, "U.S. Policy Toward the European Community," July 3, 1970, National Security Council Institutional Files, box H-208, NPL.

[212] For U.S. views on this subject during the Kennedy period, see Trachtenberg, *Constructed Peace*, pp. 303, 338–39, 376. Note also the U.S. reaction to Mitterrand's 1991 plan for a "European Confederation." The U.S. government made it clear that it would not accept "being used by the Europeans for security and held apart from other domains." German paraphrase of U.S. views conveyed to the French government on March 5, 1991, quoted in Frédéric Bozo, *Mitterrand, the End of the Cold War, and German Unification* (New York: Berghahn, 2009), p. 356. The Baker and Bush comments quoted in Mary Sarotte, *1989: The Struggle to Create Post–Cold War Europe* (Princeton: Princeton University Press, 2009), pp. 146, 175, point in the same general direction.

what that policy would be.[213] Kissinger especially did not want to transform the European countries into American satellites; even in December 1973, he still admired France for being the only ally to "have the guts to stand up against us," and that was linked in his mind to the fact that the French were the only ones making a "serious defense effort." It was for that reason that he wanted to "back them down without breaking them."[214]

But even putting considerations of that sort aside, it was simply a fact of life that the United States did not have anything like total control over what the European countries did; from the U.S. point of view, the future of Germany, in particular, was very much up in the air. That meant that what the Europeans did really mattered; the French especially would play a key role, in large part because France could help determine how firmly Germany was anchored in the West. And that in turn meant that the European countries, and especially France, would have a certain amount of bargaining power vis-à-vis the United States—that countries like France could not be treated as satellites, and that their views would carry weight in the western system.

And in institutional terms, the sort of system the Americans wanted to create would scarcely have tended to marginalize the Europeans. The U.S. aim—and this had been a goal of Kissinger's for quite some time—was to create a kind of "directorate," a system in which the four main western countries would essentially work out policy for the alliance as a whole. The plan was to create a "very high-level working group," composed of Kissinger and his French, German, and British counterparts (Jobert, Egon Bahr, and probably Sir Burke Trend), which would discuss all the key issues. That group, meeting secretly, would play a key role in the process by which a common policy would be worked out.[215] In that group the Europeans would thus outnumber the

---

[213] See [Henry Kissinger], "Proposed Outcome of the Meeting between Presidents Nixon and Pompidou in Iceland," undated but evidently written in late May 1973, NSCF/949/Pompidou-Nixon Meeting May–June 1973/NPL. Kissinger's name does not appear there, but he is identified as its author in Jean-Bernard Raimond, note for Pompidou, May 29, 1973, 5AG2/1021/AN, which comments on (and follows in the file) a French translation of that document. Note also Nixon's comment in a meeting with Jobert a month later: "quels que soient les problèmes . . . nous devons parler d'une voix aussi forte que possible à partir d'une position concertée." Nixon-Jobert meeting, June 29, 1973, 5AG2/117/AN. According to Raimond, Nixon's remarks to Jobert "se situent au coeur de la proposition Kissinger (concertation avec rôle dirigeant pour les États-Unis, directoire, etc.)." Raimond note for Pompidou, July 4, 1973, 5AG2/1023/AN, file "Jobert-Kissinger."

[214] Kissinger-Schlesinger meeting, December 5, 1973, DMPC:Nixon/DFPL.

[215] Kissinger laid out his ideas in a meeting with top British officials on April 19, 1973. Trend to Heath, April 24, 1973, p. 2, and Trend's notes of Kissinger's meeting with British

American three-to-one; that fact alone meant that their views would carry a certain weight.[216]

The basic idea behind the plan for a "directorate," the idea that the allies should try to work out a common policy, was by no means absurd. It is natural that allies should try to work together if they can; indeed, no ally can act as though the alliance did not exist and still expect the alliance to be meaningful politically. An alliance, if it has any substance at all, is bound, to some degree, to constrain the policies of its members. The real issue here was whether, in the U.S. view, the Europeans were expected to essentially rubber-stamp policies that had been decided upon in Washington, or whether, as Kissinger and Nixon insisted, the common policy would be hammered out in serious discussions among the four main allies.

Was it reasonable to think that discussions of that sort could lead to a policy that all the allies could support? The fundamentals were such that an accommodation was not out of the question. Even on the Middle East, the gap between Europe and America was by no means unbridgeable. At the end of 1973 Kissinger was in fact willing to admit

---

officials, April 19, 1973, p. 4, both in DNSA/KT00707; note also the official record of this meeting in DBPO III:4:69, p.3, and also Trend's discussion of the plan in Trend to Heath, May 2, 1973, DBPO III:4:81, p. 3. On May 22, Kissinger brought up the idea with Jobert, who seemed to like it. DNSA/KT00736, p. 6. The plan was presented to the French in a more formal way in the "Proposed Outcome" document, cited in n. 213. The "directorate" concept was then discussed at some length at Reykjavik, and Nixon brought it up again in his meeting with Jobert in late June. Pompidou-Nixon meeting, May 31, 1973, 10 a.m., pp. 7, 10, 12–13, DNSA/KT00742; Nixon-Pompdou meeting, May 31, 1973, 3 p.m., pp. 1-2, DNSA/KT00743; Roussel, *Pompidou*, 555, 558, 559, 562, 563; Nixon-Jobert meeting, June 29, 1973, p. 3, 5AG2/117/AN. Note also Jobert's comments about the plan in a meeting with German foreign minister Scheel, March 1, 1974, AAPD 1974, pp. 257–58. On Kissinger's early support for an arrangement of this sort, see Jeremi Suri, *Henry Kissinger and the American Century* (Cambridge, Mass.: Belknap Press of Harvard University Press, 2007), p. 171, and Kissinger, *Troubled Partnership*, p. 246. The whole idea of a "directorate" was, of course, by no means new. The proposal de Gaulle had put forth in his well-known September 1958 memorandum is the most famous example, but ideas of this sort had surfaced at various points in the 1950s and 1960s. See Schoenborn, *Mésentente apprivoisée*, pp. 32, 34, 244, 245, 357; and Trachtenberg, *Constructed Peace*, pp. 167, 242–44.

[216] To understand the importance of the proposal, one need only compare it with the main alternatives. On the one hand, the Americans could have proposed that issues of interest be discussed in a body in which all the allies were represented. But in such a large group, no meaningful give-and-take would have been possible. As a top British official pointed out at the time, "[I]t would be difficult to get down to real business or drafting in such a forum." Sir Burke Trend in Kissinger-Douglas-Home meeting, May 10, 1973, p. 4, DBPO III:4:89. On the other hand, the U.S. government could have proposed that the issues be discussed with the allies on a purely bilateral basis, but in that case it could certainly have been accused of pursuing a "divide and rule" policy (to use a phrase that crops up in the British documents at the time).

that the policy the U.S. government had pursued in this area had been a mistake, and he seemed to think that a new policy, much more in line with European thinking, was now in order.[217]

To be sure, the Americans had their grievances. The French, and indeed the Europeans in general, Kissinger often said, wanted to have it both ways.[218] They wanted America to pursue a détente policy, but were quick to complain about an emerging "condominium" when U.S.-Soviet relations improved. They complained about the agreements that were signed with the USSR, even though they themselves had already signed their own "political cooperation" agreements with that country.[219] Each major ally wanted the right to pursue an independent foreign policy, but when the United States exercised that same sort of right, the Europeans were quick to complain about American "unilateralism." France and Germany, Kissinger wrote, while eager to "circumscribe *our* freedom of action were not prepared to pay in the coin of a coordinated Western policy."[220] The assumption was that in trying to have it both ways, the Europeans were not acting responsibly, and that was why it fell to the U.S. government to make "the ultimate decisions on the most critical issues."[221]

But the Europeans, for their part, had more fundamental concerns. The basic problem from their point of view was that the Americans were retreating from the nuclear defense of Europe. If war broke out, U.S. leaders might be willing to use nuclear weapons in Europe proper, but they would not attack targets on Soviet territory, for fear of triggering an attack on the United States. Western Europe, and especially West Germany, would in such circumstances become increasingly vulnerable to Soviet power, and increasingly inclined to reach an accommodation with the USSR, on Soviet terms.

These were all serious issues, but they were the sorts of issues that allies should be able to discuss. And the Americans very much wanted

[217] See van Well to Frank, December 10, 1973, AAPD 1973, p. 2012, and "Dr. Kissinger's Visit to Europe – A Balance Sheet," enclosed in Brimelow to Sykes, January 18, 1974, DBPO III:4:513. Note also Kissinger's comments about the importance of working out a common policy in this area: Secretary's Staff Meeting, November 20, 1973 (notes dated Nov. 21), pp. 18–21, DNSA/KT00914.

[218] See Kissinger, *White House Years*, pp. 94, 387, 963–64; Kissinger, *Years of Upheaval*, pp. 135–36, 731; Kissinger, "The Year of Europe," pp. 593–94.

[219] See Kissinger, *White House Years*, p. 1273, and Kissinger meeting with Rusk, Bundy, McCloy, et al., November 28, 1973, p. 10, DNSA/KT00928. On the Franco-Soviet political cooperation agreement of October 13, 1970, see Marie-Pierre Rey, "Georges Pompidou, l'Union soviétique et l'Europe," p. 155.

[220] Kissinger, *Years of Upheaval*, p. 731 (emphasis in original text); see also Kissinger, *White House Years*, p. 387.

[221] Kissinger, *White House Years*, p. 964.

to talk with their allies—or at least with the three major European powers—about this whole complex of issues, and above all about the very
fundamental problem of the nuclear defense of Europe.[222] Stripped to
its essentials, the whole point of the Year of Europe initiative was to get
a discussion of this sort started. Did the torpedoing of that initiative
serve anyone's interests? One well-placed observer, Jacques Kosciusko-
Morizet, the French ambassador in Washington at the time and a man
no one would ever accuse of being excessively pro-American, thought,
looking back twenty years later, that an important opportunity might
well have been lost, and this is a view I tend to share.[223]

An alliance, Kissinger wrote, is not just a legal contract. A real alliance, he thought, has to be based on something more fundamental. The
western alliance, in particular, had to be "sustained by the hearts as
well as the minds of its members."[224] But emotions are what they are; a
government's ability to shape the feelings of its own people is quite
limited. So in analyzing these issues, it makes more sense to focus on
the intellective side of the relationship. The members of an alliance are
of course sovereign states, each with interests of its own. But they also
have an interest in working together, and perhaps even in developing
common policies on key political issues. And working things out in that

[222] U.S. leaders brought up the European defense issue repeatedly in meetings with the
allies. "We sometimes say," Kissinger, for example, told the NATO ambassadors in June
1973, "that conventional defense is within reach, and the Europeans say we must use
nuclear weapons immediately. And we ask how to use them, but we have only agreed on
using three. Does anyone believe that three will stop the Soviets? We have thousands of
tactical nuclear weapons, but no rational plan for using them; perhaps the only thing sav-
ing us is Soviet uncertainty. We need a realistic discussion; if the decision is for much
earlier use, then we need to decide how to do it." Kissinger meeting with NATO ambassadors, June 30, 1973, DNSA/KT00767, p. 14. In referring to the plan for the use of three
weapons, he was alluding to the "Provisional Political Guidelines for the Initial Defensive Tactical Use of Nuclear Weapons by NATO" (commonly called the "PPGs"), which
had been developed by NATO's Nuclear Planning Group in the late 1960s. On the PPGs,
see especially J. Michael Legge, *Theater Nuclear Weapons and the NATO Strategy of Flexible
Response* (Santa Monica, Calif.: Rand, 1983), pp. 17–25. The basic point here—the idea that
NATO needed a "rational" defense concept and that a fundamental reappraisal of NATO
strategy was in order—was one of the Nixon administration's standard arguments. See,
for example, Nixon-Heath meeting, February 2, 1973, 4 p.m., pp. 2, 4, DBPO III:4:20, and
Kissinger meeting with British officials, April 19, 1973, pp. 8–9, DNSA/KT00707. And
indeed Kissinger continued to complain throughout the 1970s that NATO did not have a
rational plan for the use of tactical nuclear weapons. See chapter 6, p. 166, n. 23.

[223] Kosciusko-Morizet comment in *Georges Pompidou et l'Europe*, p. 211. Even at the
time, Kosciusko thought that a positive response to the Kissinger speech was in order: he
saw in this speech an "ouverture faite à l'Europe, et un esprit de concertation." Quoted in
Raimond note for Pompidou, May 3, 1973, 5AG2/1021/AN. Kosciusko's April 23 dispatch is also quoted in Gfeller, "Re-envisioning Europe," p. 35.

[224] Kissinger, *Years of Upheaval*, p. 730.

way is in large part an intellective process. When countries have common interests, they can think those issues through together; in principle, they can try to work out a common course of action. It is perhaps a cause for regret that in 1973–74 no real effort of this sort was made. But that does not mean that it could not have been done at the time, and it does not mean that countries like France and the United States are simply incapable of working together.

PART III

Policy

CHAPTER EIGHT

Preventive War and U.S. Foreign Policy

On September 11, 2001, the United States suddenly found itself in what seemed to be a new world, a perplexing world, a world where the old guideposts no longer seemed adequate. How was the nation to deal with the enormous problems it now faced? Above all, what could it do to make sure that "weapons of mass destruction," and above all nuclear and biological weapons weapons, would not be used against it?

President George W. Bush and his top advisors soon came up with some basic answers to those very fundamental questions. A new national security policy was worked out, and the main lines of that policy were by no means kept secret. U.S. policy, the Bush administration declared quite openly, could no longer be based on the principle of deterrence. The nation could not "remain idle while dangers gather." It had to identify the threat and destroy it "before it reaches our borders" and "take whatever action [was] necessary" to protect itself. It had to be prepared to move "preemptively"—and, indeed, alone if necessary—against "rogue states and their terrorist clients before they are able to threaten or use weapons of mass destruction against the United States and our allies and friends." America, in other words, had to seize the initiative, "take the battle to the enemy, disrupt his plans, and confront the worst threats before they emerge." "In the new world we have entered," the president declared, "the only path to peace and security is the path of action."[1]

That new strategy of "preemption," as it was called, did not go unnoticed, either in the United States or in the world as a whole.[2] Presi-

---

This article was published in *Security Studies* 16, no. 1 (January–March 2007). A slightly different version was published at more or less the same time in Henry Shue and David Rodin, eds., *Preemption: Military Action and Moral Justification* (Oxford: Oxford University Press, 2007).

[1] Bush West Point speech, June 1, 2002; Cheney speech, August 26, 2002; and "The National Security Strategy of the United States of America" (with Bush introduction), September 2002; all available on the White House website (http://www.whitehouse .gov).

[2] As it was called, that is, mainly by the administration and its supporters; many observers, especially in the academic world, strongly object to the use of the term *preemption* in this context. That term, they believe, should be reserved for cases where a country strikes in the belief it is about to be attacked; if no attack is viewed as imminent, they think the term "preventive war" should be used. But not all scholars take that view. Paul

dent Bush, as one European commentator put it, had in fact "stunned the international community" by declaring "that taking preemptive military action was an acceptable option for coping with the new threat environment characterized by transnational terrorism and the proliferation of weapons of mass destruction."[3] The new policy, it was said, marked a total break with American tradition. In the past, the argument ran, the United States had had a more cautious, more purely defensive policy—a policy whose watchwords during the Cold War were containment and deterrence, a policy marked by respect for legal norms and for the sovereign rights of other countries. America had traditionally refrained from the use of force until it, or one of its allies, had been attacked. But now the government had broken with that tradition and had opted for a far more active—or, as the critics would put it, a far more aggressive—policy.[4] Now the idea was that the country could not "let our enemies strike first"—that America, if the danger was great enough, might have to move "preemptively."

The administration, of course, defended its new policy, but it did not really take issue with the basic historical claim here: that the Bush policy was radically different from the sort of policy the country had pursued in the past. To be sure, from time to time certain historical precedents were cited, and Secretary of Defense Donald Rumsfeld occasionally pointed out that throughout history countries had moved "preemptively" when they saw a threat developing—that is, that there was nothing new to the idea of anticipatory self-defense.[5] But basically

---

Schroeder, for example, a strong critic of the Bush strategy, has no problem referring to it as a strategy of preemption. See his "Iraq: The Case against Preemptive War," *American Conservative*, October 21, 2002. In this article, however, when I use terms like *preemptive war* (in quotation marks), I will be referring to what most academic writers prefer to refer to as "preventive war." For an historian's analysis of the shifting and at times rather problematic relationship between these two very distinct concepts, see Hew Strachan, "Preemption and Prevention in Historical Perspective," in Henry Shue and David Rodin, eds., *Preemption: Military Action and Moral Justification* (Oxford: Oxford University Press, 2007).

[3] Karl-Heinz Kamp, "Preemption: Far from Forsaken," *Bulletin of the Atomic Scientists*, March–April 2005, p. 26. The author was security policy coordinator at the Konrad Adenauer Foundation in Berlin.

[4] Note the title, for example, of one of Arthur Schlesinger's writings on the subject: "Seeking Out Monsters: By Committing Himself to Preventive War, George Bush Has Overturned Two Centuries of U.S. Thinking on Global Diplomacy," *The Guardian* (London), October 19, 2004. See also his article "The Immorality of Preemptive War," *New Perspectives Quarterly* 19, no. 4 (Fall 2002), and his book *War and the American Presidency* (New York: Norton, 2004), pp. 21–23. But this sort of argument is by no means limited to politically active writers like Schlesinger. It is quite common in the more academic literature as well. See, for example, Robert Pape, "Soft Balancing against the United States," *International Security* 30, no. 1 (Summer 2005): esp. 7, 25–26, 28.

[5] Charles Lambroschini and Alexandrine Bouilhet, "Donald Rumsfeld: 'La Guerre Préventif est aussi vieille que l'Histoire," *Le Figaro*, February 10, 2003; and Rumsfeld in-

the administration did not dispute the idea that policy had shifted dramatically. It instead took the line that new circumstances, the combined threat of terrorism and "weapons of mass destruction," meant that the country had to break with tradition—that it could not just sit on its hands and wait for its enemies to attack, but instead had to go on the offensive and do whatever was necessary to neutralize the threat.

Historical arguments have thus played a certain role in these very fundamental political debates, and this suggests that historical analysis can have a certain bearing on the way we think about these basic issues of policy. For if it turns out that U.S. policy has historically been considerably more active—more willing to use force "preemptively"—than people have tended to assume, then this might lead us to look at the Bush policy in a rather different light. A degree of historical continuity always suggests that what is going on has to be understood, at least to some extent, in structural terms, and not just in terms of the particular personalities of those who happen to be in power at the time. And indeed international relations theorists have argued that the basic structure of the international political system leads states to act "preemptively"—that is, that it leads them to adopt aggressive policies for essentially defensive purposes. This claim, if valid, should certainly affect the way we think about these questions of policy, and a historical analysis might throw some light on this very basic theoretical issue.

So I would like to bring an historian's perspective to bear on this problem. Has the Bush administration really broken with American tradition in this area by adopting what it calls a "preemptive" strategy (but which most academic writers prefer to call a "preventive war" strategy)? The goal here is to get at the issue by looking at how other American administrations dealt with this kind of problem.

THE EARLY COLD WAR

Let me begin with Truman and Eisenhower. What role did preventive war thinking—that is, the idea that the United States might have to move against its principal adversary before the threat posed by the enemy became too great—play in American policy in the late 1940s and 1950s?

I once spent some time looking into this issue and was amazed by what I found. I got involved with this question because I saw political scientists arguing that the prospect of a shift in the strategic balance could have an enormous impact on state behavior—and arguing in par-

terview with Bob Woodward, October 23, 2003 (http://www.defenselink.mil/tran
scripts/2004/tr20040419-secdef1362.html).

ticular that when a country sees itself losing its strategic edge, it might well decide to bring matters to a head with its enemies and take action before it too late. I understood the logic of the argument, but I just did not think that in practice this sort of thing was very important. I assumed that during the Cold War, for example, only the lunatic fringe took those preventive war arguments seriously. Responsible leaders, it seemed to me at that time, would never have come close to thinking in those terms. And I thought that by studying the issue of the shifting strategic balance during the early nuclear age—and the balance was changing quite dramatically from year to year at that time—I could get a handle on those theoretical issues. I thought I would be able to show that the political scientists were wrong and that their whole way of looking at things was misguided.

But after studying the evidence I was forced to admit that I was the one who had been wrong. It turned out that when you look at the evidence from this period, you find preventive war arguments all over the place. A whole series of major figures were very worried about what would happen if matters were allowed to drift and nothing were done to prevent the USSR from building a nuclear force. They wanted the United States to do what it had to in order to prevent the Soviets from building such a force. It was just astonishing how many people were thinking along those lines—scientists, mathematicians, and philosophers (like Leo Szilard, John von Neumann, and Bertrand Russell), leading journalists and major political figures (including a number of senators), and, above all, a whole series of high-ranking military (and especially Air Force) officers. Even distinguished diplomats like George Kennan and Charles Bohlen seemed to think that it would not have been too bad if war with the USSR had broken out before that country had developed a large nuclear force. And not just Americans: a number of leading European political figures were also thinking along these lines. Winston Churchill, for example, argued repeatedly in the late 1940s that matters needed to be brought to a head with the Soviets before it was too late, while the United States still enjoyed a nuclear monopoly. And Charles de Gaulle told an American journalist in 1954 that the "United States made a great mistake by not pursuing a policy of war" when it still had a "definite atomic lead." Europe, he thought, would have supported America in such a policy: "When you took your stand in Korea the free world was with you and was ready to be led into war. But you cannot expect other nations to adopt a real self-sacrificing military attitude if you do not pursue a policy of war." But it was too late, he said regretfully, for anything like that now.[6]

[6] See Marc Trachtenberg, "A 'Wasting Asset': American Strategy and the Shifting Nu-

So preventive war thinking was surprisingly widespread in the early nuclear age, the period from mid-1945 through late 1954. What, however, is to be made of all this? Was it all just talk, or did this kind of thinking have any real effect on U.S. policy? Were ideas of this sort taken seriously in high policy-making circles? Or was it the case that only isolated individuals were attracted to this kind of policy? What role, if any, did this way of looking at things play during the Truman period?

It turns out that the preventive war philosophy, in terms of its effect on policy, was not very important in the late 1940s. To be sure, President Truman himself fantasized about starting a war in 1946: "Get plenty of Atomic Bombs on hand—drop one on Stalin, put the United Nations to work and eventually set up a free world."[7] But daydreams of that sort (if you can call them that) did not count for much, and it was only after 1949—that is, after the Soviets had broken the American nuclear monopoly and had begun to build an atomic arsenal of their own, and after Dean Acheson had taken office as Secretary of State—that preventive war thinking came into play in a major way.

People tend to assume that U.S. policy during the Cold War was from the very start based on the idea of containment. But it is important to understand that Acheson's goal was rollback—that he did not just want to stabilize the situation as it was. The aim was to bring about a "retraction" of Soviet power by creating "situations of strength." The goal, according to one very well-known document from that period, NSC 68, was to "check and to roll back the Kremlin's drive for world domination." The "policy of gradual and calculated coercion" that NSC 68 explicitly called for would, it was understood, be possible only if U.S. power were first built up to quite extraordinary levels, and in fact, beginning in late 1950, the U.S. began to rearm on an absolutely massive scale. The idea, according to Paul Nitze, then head of the State Depart-

---

clear Balance, 1949–1954," in Marc Trachtenberg, *History and Strategy* (Princeton: Princeton University Press, 1991), esp. pp. 103–7 and p. 118 n. 62. For de Gaulle, see C. L. Sulzberger, *The Last of the Giants* (New York: Macmillan, 1970), p. 52. See also Russell D. Buhite and William C. Hamel, "War for Peace: The Question of an American Preventive War against the Soviet Union, 1945–1955," *Diplomatic History* 14, no. 3 (Summer 1990), and Steven Casey, "Selling NSC-68: The Truman Administration, Public Opinion, and the Politics of Mobilization, 1950–51," *Diplomatic History* 29, no. 4 (September 2005): 663–64, 675–76, 687–89.

[7] Truman desk note of June 1946, in *Strictly Personal and Confidential: The Letters Harry Truman Never Mailed*, ed. Monte Poen (Boston: Little Brown, 1982), p. 31. This was not the only time Truman fantasized about starting, or threatening to start, a nuclear war as a way of settling things with the Communists. See also his journal entries from 1952 published in Barton Bernstein, "Truman's Secret Thoughts on Ending the Korean War," *Foreign Service Journal* (November 1980): 33, 44.

ment's Policy Planning Staff and the main author of that document, was to "lay the basis" for a policy of "taking increased risks of general war" with the USSR "while her stockpile of atomic weapons was still small."[8] And Nitze, it should be noted, was very close to Acheson at that time.

By late 1952 the rearmament program had achieved its goal. By that point, the United States had very much the upper hand in strategic terms. But the U.S. government as a whole, it seemed, was not willing to take advantage of that situation and go on the offensive. Nitze complained, in fact, at the very end of the Truman period, that the United States was becoming "a sort of hedge-hog, unattractive to attack, but basically not very worrisome," and that the goals laid out in documents like NSC 68 were not being taken "sufficiently seriously as to warrant doing what is necessary to give us some chance of seeing these objectives attained."[9] And the coming to power of the Republicans did not make much of a difference, from the point of view of people like Nitze and Acheson. By mid-1953, just a few months after Dwight D. Eisenhower took office, Acheson was already complaining also about the new administration's "weakness"—about its failure to take advantage of the fact that, thanks to its predecessor's policies, it was now in a position to press the Soviets hard.[10] But Acheson, now an outsider, scarcely knew what the new administration was thinking.

In their first two years in office, Eisenhower and his associates were in fact strongly tempted to pursue a policy that no one would ever call "weak." They were very much concerned with the problem of the growing Soviet nuclear capability. Eisenhower himself wondered whether "our duty to future generations did not require us to *initiate* war at the most propitious moment that we could designate."[11] Secretary of State John Foster Dulles, however, thought that America's allies, by and large, would not support a "tough policy" and in particular a policy of pressing "the Russians hard during the few years in which" the country "would retain atomic superiority." Eisenhower's reply was quite revealing. "[I]f this were indeed the situation," he said, "we should perhaps come back to the very grave question: Should the United States now get

[8] See Trachtenberg, *History and Strategy*, pp. 109–11, 112 n. 41.

[9] Nitze to Acheson, January 12, 1953, in U.S. Department of State, *Foreign Relations of the United States, 1952–1954*, vol. 2, p. 205; henceforth cited in this form: FRUS 1952–54, 2:205.

[10] Acheson to Truman, May 28, 1953, box 30, folder 391, and Acheson memorandum of conversation, June 23, 1953, box 68, folder 172, both in Dean Acheson Papers, Sterling Library, Yale University, New Haven, Conn.

[11] Eisenhower to Dulles, September 8, 1953, FRUS 1952–54, 2:461. Emphasis in original text.

ready to fight the Soviet Union?" He had "brought up this question more than once" at earlier National Security Council meetings, and he had "never done so facetiously."[12]

The United States, of course, never actually implemented a "preventive war" strategy of this sort, but that does not mean that this kind of thinking had no effect on policy. It was, in fact, one of the elements in the policy mix—one of the ingredients in the matrix out of which policy emerged, one of the main factors that led U.S. leaders to take a relatively tough line on a whole range of specific issues. The idea was that if war was inevitable, maybe it would not be the worst thing in the world to have it come sooner rather than later—to have it come while the United States was still in a relatively strong position. By taking a tough line, the United States could take its measure of Soviet policy— that is, it could see in this way just how "inevitable" a showdown with the Soviet Union was. If the Soviets were unwilling to pull in their horns even when they were weak, then perhaps war with them really was inevitable, in which case it might have been important to have it out with them before matters became totally unmanageable. Their reaction would serve as a kind of touchstone: U.S. policy could go either way, depending on the kind of country the Americans found themselves dealing with.

This, incidentally, bears a certain resemblance to the sort of policy Germany pursued toward Russia in 1914. The Germans at that point, like the Americans forty years later, were deeply concerned about the growth of Russian power. Taking a tough line in the showdown over Serbia was a way of seeing what Russian policy was. As one German put it at the time, it "would be the touchstone [for determining] whether Russia meant war or not."[13] If the Russians did not give way when they were weak, there would be no living with them when they became strong; war would then have to be seen as inevitable, and if that was the case, an early war was much better than a later one. In 1914, the "preventive war" philosophy was a key element in the policy mix. The policy of "bringing matters to a head" with Russia and thus of taking a tough line in political disputes was rooted in part in preventive war thinking, but this sort of thinking was also an element in American policy in the 1952–54 period.[14]

[12] "Discussion at the 204th Meeting of the National Security Council, Thursday, June 24, 1954," Dwight D. Eisenhower Papers as President of the United States (Ann Whitman File), pp. 11–12, box 5, Eisenhower Library, Abilene, Kans., and also available on the Declassified Documents Reference System website.

[13] Hoyos-Naumann meeting, July 1, 1914, in *July 1914: The Outbreak of the First World War, Selected Documents*, ed. Imanuel Geiss (New York: Scribner's, 1967), p. 66.

[14] See Trachtenberg, *History and Strategy*, esp. pp. 132, 136–37, 148–49.

The United States at that time—the period when U.S. strategic superiority was at its height—took a tough line on all sorts of issues, just as Germany had in 1914, in part for the same general reason. In structural terms, the two situations were quite similar. If war came in 1914 but not in 1954, this was not because Eisenhower pursued a more complaisant policy or was less concerned with the problems created by the changing strategic balance. That the two situations had such different outcomes had to do mainly with Russia—with the fact that Russia in 1914 chose war despite her strategic weakness, while Russia in the early 1950s accommodated to American power. From 1912 on, Tsarist Russia had been playing with fire in the Balkans.[15] But from 1952 on—that is, even before the death of Stalin—Communist Russia pursued a very mild policy in her dealings with the West. The Soviets, so bellicose around 1950, by 1952 were purring like pussycats, and the change had to do mostly with the fact that the Soviets understood how the strategic balance had shifted and why their policy had to be adjusted accordingly. The Communist regime was far more cold-blooded, far more calculating in its attitude toward power, than its predecessor had been—so much so that if you're looking for a historical justification for the Bolshevik Revolution, it's in this area, I think, that you will find it.

THE KENNEDY PERIOD

The Truman and Eisenhower periods are of real historical interest, but Americans do not relate to them the same way they relate to the Kennedy period. This latter period evokes stronger emotions: people in the United States even today feel a more direct bond with Kennedy than with Eisenhower or Truman. It is for this reason that arguments about Kennedy's policy have a special salience in contemporary American

[15] Paul Schroeder, for example, refers to the "very bold offensive policy" that Russia had been pursuing before 1914, a characterization that strikes me as right on target. Paul Schroeder, "Embedded Counterfactuals and World War I as an Unavoidable War," in Paul Schroeder, *Systems, Stability, and Statecraft: Essays on the International History of Modern Europe* (New York: Palgrave Macmillan, 2004), p. 186. One key episode was Russia's sponsorship of the Balkan League in 1912. When the Russians showed the treaty establishing the League to French Prime Minister Raymond Poincaré, the French leader—by no means a Germanophile—remarked that it "contained the seeds not only of a war against Turkey, but of a war against Austria as well." Poincaré notes of meeting with Russian foreign minister Sazonov, August 1912, *Documents diplomatiques français: 1871–1914*, 3rd series, 3:34. For the key evidence on Russia's Balkan policy at the time, see Barbara Jelavich, *Russia's Balkan Entanglements, 1806–1914* (Cambridge, England: Cambridge University Press, 1991), pp. 246–47; Bernadotte Schmitt, *The Coming of the War, 1914*, 2 vols. (New York: Scribner's, 1930), 1:135; and Luigi Albertini, *The Origins of the War of 1914*, 3 vols. (London: Oxford University Press, 1952–57), 1:375, 486.

culture, and this holds true in particular for arguments about Kennedy and the "preemptive" use of force.

When the Bush strategy of "preemption" was first revealed to the press, key officials made a point of arguing that Kennedy, during the Cuban Missile Crisis in 1962, had opted for a "preemptive" strategy.[16] Critics of the Bush policy, including some veterans of the Kennedy administration, reacted by basically denying that Kennedy had pursued a policy of this sort. According to Ted Sorensen, President Kennedy and most of his key advisers at the time of missile crisis "forcefully rejected" the idea of a preemptive strike on the missiles in Cuba "as would any thoughtful American president or citizen."[17] According to Arthur Schlesinger, a preventive war strategy is simply immoral, and during the Kennedy period moral considerations ruled out anything of the sort. When Robert Kennedy, the president's brother, said a "preventive attack" on the missiles in Cuba would be a "Pearl Harbor in reverse," Schlesinger says, he "swung the ExCom—President Kennedy's special group of advisors—from an airstrike to a blockade."[18] The Bush administration was also criticized for claiming that it had the right under international law to use force in self-defense, even if no attack was imminent. According to Bruce Ackerman, a law professor at Yale, that argument "went far beyond any claim made by previous American governments." Again, this criticism was supported by a claim about the missile crisis, the claim that in 1962 "President Kennedy did not invoke any notion of 'anticipatory self-defense.'"[19]

What is to be made of these arguments? What light, in fact, does a study of the Kennedy period throw on this whole complex of issues? The key point to note here is that Kennedy—and not just in the context of the Cuban Missile Crisis—was far more willing to take preventive action than most people think. He was quite concerned, for example, about what would happen if China developed a nuclear capability. He in fact thought that a nuclear China "would be intolerable."[20] He thought the Chinese nuclear facilities might therefore have to be attacked and destroyed, and approached the Soviets in the context of the Moscow

---

[16] David Sanger, "Bush to Formalize a Defense Policy of Hitting First," *New York Times*, June 17, 2002.

[17] Sorensen letter to the editor, *New York Times*, July 1, 2002.

[18] Schlesinger, "The Immorality of Preemptive War."

[19] Bruce Ackerman, "But What's the Legal Case for Preemption?" *Washington Post*, August 18, 2002.

[20] Kennedy's views as described by his National Security Advisor McGeorge Bundy in a January 10, 1963, meeting with CIA director McCone, quoted in William Burr and Jeffrey Richelson, "Whether to 'Strangle the Baby in the Cradle': The United States and the Chinese Nuclear Program, 1960–64," *International Security* 25, no. 3 (Winter 2000/2001): 67.

Test Ban Treaty negotiations in July 1963 to see if the USSR would go along with such a policy.[21] All of this is sometimes dismissed as mere talk, but (as William Burr and Jeffrey Richelson point out in their important article on the subject) it is quite clear that "Kennedy and his advisers did much more than talk."[22] The Chinese nuclear facilities were of course never attacked, but this was not because the U.S. government rejected this kind of policy out of hand. Nothing was done, in part because the Soviet Union at that point refused to go along with such a policy, in part because Kennedy was assassinated before any final decision had been made. It is very much an open question what would have happened if Kennedy had not been shot or if the Soviet reaction in 1963 had been different—that is, if the Soviet government had been as open to the idea of a "preemptive" attack on the Chinese nuclear facilities in 1963 as it was during the Nixon period just a few years later.[23]

But as important as this episode is, it is the case of the Cuban Missile Crisis that plays the key role in the public debate, so that's what I want to focus on here. And in fact there's a whole series of points to be made about this episode. First of all, there is the obvious point that the United States was prepared to attack Cuba if the missiles were not withdrawn—even though a launch of the missiles was never considered imminent; even though Cuba, as a sovereign state (more sovereign, in fact, than Iraq was in 2003) had as much right to allow Soviets missiles to be deployed on her territory as (say) Turkey had to host American missiles

---

[21] All this is fairly well known by now. The Burr and Richelson article cited in the previous footnote is by far the best study of the question, but note also the earlier article by Gordon Chang, "JFK, China, and the Bomb," *Journal of American History* 74, no. 4 (March 1988): 1287–310, and see the evidence cited in Marc Trachtenberg, *A Constructed Peace: The Making of the European Settlement, 1945–1963* (Princeton: Princeton University Press, 1999), pp. 385–86. Documents relating to the Burr and Richelson article are available online (http://www.gwu.edu/~nsarchiv/NSAEBB/NSAEBB38/).

[22] Burr and Richelson, "'Strangle the Baby,'" p. 55.

[23] On the question of a possible Soviet attack on the Chinese nuclear facilities during the latter period, see Henry Kissinger, *White House Years* (Boston: Little, Brown, 1979), pp. 183–86; Henry Kissinger, *Years of Upheaval* (Boston: Little Brown, 1982), p. 233; Henry Kissinger, *Diplomacy* (New York: Simon and Shuster, 1994), pp. 722–23; Raymond Garthoff, *Détente and Confrontation: American-Soviet Relations from Nixon to Reagan* (Washington, D.C.: Brookings, 1985), pp. 208–10; Rosemary Foot, *The Practice of Power: U.S. Relations with China since 1949* (Oxford: Clarendon, 1995), p. 190; and especially William Burr, ed., *The Kissinger Transcripts: The Top-Secret Talks with Beijing and Moscow* (New York: New Press, 1998), pp. 126, 142–44, 183. A number of documents dealing with the question are available online in the National Security Archive Electronic Briefing Book on "The Sino-Soviet Border War, 1969" (http://www.gwu.edu/~nsarchiv/NSAEBB/NSAEBB49/). These documents are discussed in William Burr, "Sino-American Relations, 1969: The Sino-Soviet Border War and Steps Toward Rapprochement," *Cold War History* 1, no. 3 (April 2001).

in 1962; and even though the U.N. had by no means authorized the United States to use force against Cuba.[24]

But putting this rather obvious point aside, what is to be made of the other claims people make about the missile crisis in this context? What, in particular, is to be made of the argument that for the U.S. government at the time, moral considerations were of fundamental importance? Is Schlesinger, for example, right in arguing that Robert Kennedy, by raising the moral issue, was able to swing the ExCom "from an airstrike to a blockade"? The truth here, to put it mildly, is not quite that simple. The president's brother was by no means a "dove from the start."[25] He was by no means dead set against the idea of an air strike or of decisive military action in general. To be sure, at the start of the crisis Robert Kennedy argued against a simple air strike, but this was because he wanted even stronger military action. He in fact wanted to invade Cuba. He repeatedly brought up the issue of an invasion at the very first two top-level meetings held after the discovery of the missiles. There was little point, he said, to just attacking the missile sites. The Americans would be killing "an awful lot of people" and would

---

[24] On this last point, it is often argued that the actions the United States took were legal because they had been authorized by the Organization of American States (OAS). But under the U.N. Charter, regional organizations like the OAS do not have the authority "to operate as the Security Council's surrogate" (as David Rivkin and Darin Bartram point out in their article "The Law on the Road to Baghdad," *National Review Online*, August 28, 2002). Article 53 of the charter is quite explicit in this regard: "no enforcement action shall be taken under regional arrangements or by regional agencies without the authorization of the Security Council." (The single exception to this rule had to do with actions taken against the Axis powers in the "transitional" period immediately following the signing of the charter.) And putting textual analysis aside and just applying the test of logic, it is hard to see why the fact that action is taken by a group of states would in itself make that action any more legal than if it had been taken by just a single state. Would Warsaw Pact authorization have made the Soviet invasion of Czechoslovakia in 1968 any more legal than it would otherwise have been? Would an Arab attack on Israel be any more legal if it were authorized by the Arab League than it would be in the absence of such authorization? Finally, since it is American policy that is being assessed here, it is important to remember that the U.S. government would have taken action—that is, it would have done things in much the same way—even if it had not gotten OAS support. The decision to go to the OAS was made only after the assistant secretary of state for Latin American affairs had given his strong assurance that the United States would be able to get what it wanted from that body. See the record of a top-level meeting, October 19, 1962, FRUS 1961–63, 11:117–18. The administration, it is quite clear, was determined to act no matter what the OAS did. When Kennedy, for example, was asked whether "a blockade would be legal if the OAS did not support it," he answered that "it probably would not; however we would proceed anyway." Kennedy meeting with Congressional leadership, October 24, 1962, ibid., p. 160.

[25] As Arthur Schlesinger, Jr., claims in *Robert Kennedy and His Times* (Boston: Houghton Mifflin, 1978), p. 507.

have to take "an awful lot of heat on it," but to no avail, because the Soviets would just send in the missiles again and threaten the United States with retaliation in Turkey or Iran if it attacked the sites a second time. So if the U.S. government was "going to get into it at all," he wondered, shouldn't it just "take [its] losses" and "get it over with"—that is, shouldn't it just solve the problem once and for all by invading the island? And if that meant war with the USSR—if the Soviets were going to "get into a war over this" after they had stuck in "those kinds of missiles after the warning"—then that, in his view, would simply prove they were so aggressive that America would be facing war with them anyway, six months or a year down the road. So even the prospect of general thermonuclear war was not an argument for restraint. He also wondered in this context whether the United States could find a pretext for military action against Cuba—whether it could "sink the *Maine* again or something."[26]

What about the claim that by raising the Pearl Harbor issue, Robert Kennedy "swung the ExCom" from "an airstrike to a blockade"? The point about an attack being a "Pearl Harbor in reverse" did come up during the first day of meetings on the issue, but it was Undersecretary of State George Ball who raised it. It was only a couple of days later, after Ball had brought up the issue again, that Robert Kennedy said that he thought Ball had a "hell of a good point."[27] But that did not keep him from supporting an air strike later in the crisis—indeed, from preferring it to a blockade. Thus, for example, in the October 25 ExCom meeting, he repeated his view that "we may decide that it is better to avoid confronting the Russians by stopping one of their ships and to react by attacking the missiles already in Cuba."[28] And the record of the October 27 ExCom meeting shows that even at that point in the crisis, Robert Kennedy still favored an air strike. "If we attack a Soviet tanker," he said, "the balloon would go up." It was therefore important to "buy time now in order to launch an air attack Monday or Tuesday"—that is, on October 29 or 30.[29] It is thus quite clear that from his point of view, an attack on Cuba was by no means out of the question—even though neither he nor anyone else felt that the missiles were about to be launched.

What about the international law argument—the claim that the U.S. government at that time "did not invoke any notion of 'anticipatory

---

[26] Transcript of October 16, 1962, meetings, in Ernest May and Philip Zelikow, eds., *The Kennedy Tapes: Inside the White House During the Cuban Missile Crisis* (Cambridge, Mass.: Harvard University Press, 1997), pp. 66, 99, 100–101.

[27] Ibid., pp. 115, 121, 143, 149.

[28] Fifth ExCom meeting, October 25, 1962, FRUS 1961–63, 11:208.

[29] Seventh ExCom meeting, October 27, 1962, ibid., p. 256.

self-defense'"? The fact is that the government *did* defend its policy in those terms. The original draft of Kennedy's October 22 speech to the nation in fact explicitly invoked Article 51 of the U.N. Charter, the article referring to a nation's right to defend itself, as justifying the course of action the government was pursuing. That reference, however, was dropped from the final version, because the State Department legal advisor's office thought it amounted "to a full-scale adoption of the doctrine of anticipatory self-defense."[30] But although Article 51 was not mentioned explicitly, the president in that speech did in substance invoke that doctrine. The situation now, as he laid out the argument, was different from what it had been in the past. Given the threat posed by nuclear weapons, a country did not have to wait until it was actually attacked before it could legitimately use force. The United States, in this case, thus had the right to deal with the threat before the missiles were actually launched. "We no longer live in a world," he declared, "where only the actual firing of weapons represents a sufficient challenge to a nation's security to constitute maximum peril. Nuclear weapons are so destructive, and ballistic missiles are so swift, that any substantially increased possibility of their use or any sudden change in their deployment may well be regarded as a definite threat to peace"—that is, as the sort of threat that warranted military action.[31] And Adlai Stevenson, the U.N. ambassador, made the same basic point in a famous speech he gave at the height of the crisis. "Were we to do nothing until the knife was sharpened?" he asked. "Were we to stand idly by until it was at our throats?"[32] If this was not an argument for "anticipatory self-defense," it is hard to imagine what would be.

The right of self-defense was thus interpreted very broadly in 1962. The fact that U.S. security was threatened provided the justification for

[30] Abram Chayes, *The Cuban Missile Crisis* (New York: Oxford University Press, 1974), p. 63.

[31] See Theodore Sorensen, *Kennedy* (New York: Harper and Row, 1965), pp. 699–700. Article 2 of the U.N. Charter prohibited the use of force for purposes inconsistent with the "Purposes of the United Nations," one of which (as defined in Article 1) was the "prevention and removal of threats to the peace." The use of the phrase "threat to peace" in the president's speech thus had a certain resonance in the international law context: it suggested that the United States had the right under the U.N. Charter to use force in this case. On the related issue of what those charter provisions meant at the time they were being drafted—that is, for the point that they were interpreted as allowing the U.S. government to take whatever action it felt was necessary to "prevent aggression"—see chapter 9, pp. 297–300.

[32] Quoted in Arthur Schlesinger, *A Thousand Days* (Boston: Houghton Mifflin, 1965), pp. 823–24. This was clearly an argument for the legitimacy of preventive military action, but—and this shows just how much people's views on this issue have changed over the years—Schlesinger evidently saw nothing wrong with it when he wrote that book forty years ago.

what the Bush administration would now call "preemptive" action. And it is important to remember that few people quarreled with that principle at the time. Even French President Charles de Gaulle, by no means a blind supporter of U.S. policy, had no doubt that the American action was legal, even though the United States was not being attacked. "President Kennedy wishes to react, and to react now," he told Dean Acheson, who had been sent over to brief him on the affair, "and certainly France can have no objection to that since it is legal for a country to defend itself when it finds itself in danger."[33]

There is one final point about the missile crisis—or really about U.S. policy in general at that time—that relates to the preventive war issue in a perhaps more direct way. This has to do with what was going on in U.S.-Soviet relations at the time the missiles were discovered. Kennedy's goal, from the very beginning of his presidency, had been to stabilize east-west relations by reaching an understanding with the USSR on the whole complex of issues that lay at the heart of the Cold War—the issues relating to the division of Europe, to the status of Germany, and to the situation in Berlin. He wanted both sides to accept things as they were in Europe. He himself was willing to accept eastern Europe as a Soviet sphere of influence, and he also made it clear to the Russians that he understood their concerns about Germany, and especially about

[33] Acheson-de Gaulle meeting, October 22, 1962, FRUS 1961-63, 11:166. The German chancellor, Konrad Adenauer (who Acheson saw the day after he met with de Gaulle on that same mission to Europe), was contemptuous of the idea that the United States had no right under international law to impose even a blockade, and in fact actually urged the United States to invade Cuba. See Hans-Peter Schwarz, *Adenauer: Der Staatsmann, 1952–1967* (Stuttgart: Deutsche Verlags-Anstalt, 1991), pp. 771–773, and Dowling to Rusk, October 24, 1962 (on Acheson's meeting with Adenauer on October 23), available online in the Digital National Security Archive's Cuban Missile Crisis collection. One leading Senator—J. William Fulbright, chairman of the Senate Foreign Relations Committee—made a comment about the blockade that is also worth quoting in this context. "It won't be legal," he told Kennedy at the height of the crisis. "I'm not making the arguments for 'legal.' This is self-defense." Kennedy meeting with Congressional leadership, October 22, 1962, in May and Zelikow, *Kennedy Tapes*, p. 272 (punctuation changed slightly). Fulbright, incidentally, later published a book on American foreign policy called *The Arrogance of Power* (New York: Random House, 1966). Acheson's own views on the general issue of the role of legal norms and moral principles in international politics are also worth noting in this context. He was notoriously contemptuous of the United Nations and of international law in general. International politics in his view was a jungle "where the judgment of nature upon error is death"; in such a world, countries like the United States could not afford to play the game according to legal rules. See Acheson to Truman, December 4, 1956, Acheson Papers, Sterling Memorial Library, Yale University, New Haven, Conn., and Robert Beisner, "Wrong from the Beginning," *Weekly Standard* 8, no. 26 (March 17, 2003). Note especially Acheson's comments on the issue of whether U.S. policy during the missile crisis was legal in the *Proceedings of the American Society of International Law*, 1963, pp. 13–15.

West Germany acquiring nuclear weapons, and was willing to meet their needs in that area too. In return, he wanted the Soviets to also accept the status quo in Europe, and in particular the status quo in Berlin. From his point of view, he was willing to give the Soviets everything they could reasonably ask for while asking for very little in exchange. The problem was that the Soviets were not interested in this kind of deal, and their attitude was such that by the eve of the missile crisis, Kennedy had come to feel that a showdown with them at some point in the near future was practically unavoidable. But as he saw it, if that was the case, it was much better to have it out with them sooner rather than later—that is, while the United States still had a nuclear edge. By early October 1962 his policy on the Berlin question had thus hardened considerably. He was no longer interested in playing for time on this issue, and the reason he gave for rejecting that kind of policy is very significant, given the questions we are interested in here. The softer course of action, the policy of trying to put off a showdown, was rejected because "the military balance was more favourable to us now than it would be later on."[34]

Can it be said, given all this, that the discovery of the missiles provided Kennedy with an opportunity to bring matters to a head with the Soviets sooner rather than later? The point about the changing strategic balance was probably at the back of his mind when the decision was made to confront the USSR on the Cuban issue. That the Berlin issue (where such considerations were already viewed as fundamental) played a very important role during the missile crisis in itself suggests that this was the case. And indeed the sense that a crisis over Berlin was looming served as a spur to action in October 1962. "We've got to do something," the president said on October 19, when U.S. policy was still being worked out, "because if we do nothing, we're going to have the problem of Berlin anyway." "We're going to have this knife stuck right in our guts, in about two months," he added, so "we've got to do something."[35] Kennedy thought that once the nuclear force in Cuba had reached a certain level, the country would be immune to American attack. Military action would then be "too much of a gamble," and the Soviets would have a free hand to build up their bases on the island. They could keep putting in "more and more" missiles. And when they had a large force there, they would be in a position, as the president analyzed the situation, to "squeeze us in Berlin."[36] The implication was

[34] Home to Foreign Office, October 2, 1962, FO 371/163581, British National Archives, Kew, quoted in Trachtenberg, *Constructed Peace*, p. 351. The evidence supporting the interpretation outlined in this paragraph is presented in chapter 8 of that book.

[35] May and Zelikow, *Kennedy Tapes*, p. 176 (record of October 19 meeting).

[36] Ibid., p. 90 (record of October 16 meeting).

that America could not allow events to take that course. The U.S. government, in other words, would have to take a relatively hard line on the Cuban issue because of a calculation about something that might happen down the road—because of something the Soviets might well do in the near future in Berlin.

The Kennedy administration was thus perfectly capable of thinking in "preemptive" terms, and indeed neither it nor the country as a whole saw anything wrong in doing so.

The North Korean Nuclear Crisis, 1993–94

All of the episodes discussed so far took place during the most intense phase of the Cold War, the period from 1949 to 1963. The United States during that period felt that its survival as a nation was quite literally on the line. In such circumstances, it is perhaps not surprising that American leaders were willing to consider extreme strategies of the sort I have been describing. But as the global conflict faded after 1963, did traditional norms about the "sovereign equality of all states" and the impermissibility of "anticipatory self-defense" reassert themselves? Did the end of the Cold War in 1989–91 bring about a return to a more normal "Westphalian" system, a system based on the idea that the sovereign rights of every state had to be respected? Well, not quite, and in fact in some ways international norms in this period seemed to be moving in the opposite direction—or at least that is what the story of the North Korean nuclear crisis of 1993–94 seems to suggest.

The basic lines of the story here are clear enough. North Korea had begun a serious nuclear weapons program around 1980, but in 1985, under Soviet pressure, had signed the Nuclear Non-Proliferation Treaty (NPT). In 1992 International Atomic Energy Agency (IAEA) inspectors were sent to North Korea to check up on what its government had said it was doing in the nuclear area. But there were "discrepancies" between what North Korea had declared to the IAEA and what the inspectors actually found. To get to the bottom of the issue and see what North Korea had actually done, the IAEA wanted to conduct more intrusive inspections. The North Koreans refused, and instead, in March 1993, announced that they were going to withdraw from the NPT—permissible under Article Ten of the treaty, but something no country had ever done before.

North Korea might have had the legal right to withdraw from the treaty, but for the U.S. government a North Korea moving full steam ahead in the nuclear area was "intolerable," and the North Koreans were left in little doubt as to how the Americans felt.[37] In late March, for example, Secretary of Defense William Perry told the *Washington Post* (as that newspaper paraphrased his remarks) that the "United States intends to stop North Korea from developing a substantial arsenal of nuclear weapons even at the potential cost of another war on the Korean peninsula." Confronting the North Koreans on this matter, he realized, might lead to an armed conflict, but "Perry made clear that this danger would not deter Washington from taking whatever actions are needed to prevent North Korea from proceeding with its nuclear program. 'We are going to stop them from doing that,' he declared."[38] In June, moreover, the North Koreans were told directly, in private talks, that "no sitting president of the United States would allow North Korea to acquire nuclear weapons."[39] And in November, President Clinton himself publicly warned the Pyongyang regime that it was playing with fire. North Korea, he declared on *Meet the Press*, "cannot be allowed to develop a nuclear bomb."[40]

It was not just the administration that took this kind of line. The country as a whole was clearly taking the issue very seriously. In June 1994, for example, a poll found that most Americans "favored military action to destroy North Korea's nuclear facilities" if that country "continued to refuse international inspection," and nearly half of those polled thought "it was 'worth risking war' to prevent North Korea from manufacturing nuclear weapons."[41] Even in 1991, according to a South Korean observer, many well-informed Americans had been ready to contemplate a "preemptive strike against North Korea."[42] And as the crisis developed, attitudes hardened. By mid-1994 prominent figures in the press and in the policy world were openly calling for a very tough policy. To give but one example, Brent Scowcroft and Arnold Kanter, who had played key policy-making roles in the previous Re-

---

[37] See Ashton B. Carter and William J. Perry, *Preventive Defense: A New Security Strategy for America* (Washington, D.C.: Brookings, 1999), p. 126. Perry was Secretary of Defense at the time of the crisis; Carter was then a top Pentagon official.

[38] R. Jeffrey Smith, "Perry Sharply Warns North Korea," *Washington Post*, March 31, 1994.

[39] Joel Wit, Daniel Poneman, and Robert Gallucci, *Going Critical: The First North Korean Nuclear Crisis* (Washington, D.C.: Brooking Institution Press, 2004), p. 55. Gallucci was the chief American negotiator on this issue.

[40] Don Oberdorfer, *The Two Koreas: A Contemporary History* (Reading, Mass.: Addison-Wesley, 1997), p. 295.

[41] Ibid., p. 323. See also the polling data cited in Leon Sigal, *Disarming Strangers: Nuclear Diplomacy with North Korea* (Princeton: Princeton University Press, 1998), pp. 302–3 n.36.

[42] Wit, Poneman, and Gallucci, *Going Critical*, p. 28.

publican administration, published an article in the *Washington Post* called "Korea: Time for Action." "We should tell North Korea," they wrote, "that it either must permit continuous, unfettered IAEA monitoring to confirm that no further reprocessing is taking place, or we will remove its capacity to reprocess." The use of military force, they conceded, might mean war, but in their view the North Korean regime—and this was a very standard "preventive war" argument—had to "be made to understand that if war is unavoidable, we would rather fight it sooner than later, when North Korea might have a sizable nuclear arsenal."[43]

To be sure, the American and North Korean governments were talking to each other during this period, and the North Koreans agreed relatively early on to suspend their decision to withdraw from the NPT. But those negotiations failed to settle the dispute. North Korea, moreover, was increasingly at loggerheads with the IAEA—and increasingly determined, it seemed, to move ahead with its nuclear program. What this implied for the Americans was that time was running out—that without an agreement, sanctions would have to be imposed. But sanctions, the North Koreans said, would mean war, and U.S. officials were by no means convinced that the North Koreans were bluffing. But the Americans for their part continued to take a hard line. "Despite the risks" (according to the most authoritative account of U.S. policy on this issue) it was felt that "the United States could not allow North Korea to flout its nonproliferation obligations."[44] That meant that the U.S. government would have to prepare for war, but the preparations it took (as it itself realized) might provoke a North Korean attack. As then-Secretary of Defense Perry later put it, he and other key U.S. officials "knew that we were poised on the brink of a war that might involve weapons of mass destruction."[45] The smell of war was in the air. The top U.S. Air Force general in Korea later told Don Oberdorfer "that although neither he nor other commanders said so out loud, not even in private conversations with one another, 'inside we all thought we were going to war.'"[46]

It is hard to believe that this was all simply a gigantic bluff and that the Clinton administration from the very start had no intention of actu-

[43] Brent Scowcroft and Arnold Kanter, "Korea: Time for Action," *Washington Post*, June 15, 1994. Scowcroft had been National Security Advisor under presidents George H. W. Bush and Gerald Ford; Kanter had been deeply involved with the North Korean question as a key State Department official during the Bush administration. See also Sigal, *Disarming Strangers*, pp. 81–82, 153–54, and esp. 162–63.

[44] Wit, Poneman and Gallucci, *Going Critical*, p. 188.

[45] Carter and Perry, *Preventive Defense*, p. 131. It was believed at the time that North Korea might have already built (and hidden) one or two nuclear weapons.

[46] Oberdorfer, *Two Koreas*, p. 306.

ally using force, no matter how intransigent the North Koreans turned out to be. No one, of course, knows for sure what the government would have done if the crisis came to a head; it is quite possible that Clinton himself did not know at the time precisely how far he was prepared to go. But to the extent the claims of former officials are to be believed—to the extent the administration had actually opted for a policy of keeping North Korea non-nuclear and was willing to risk war to achieve that goal—to that extent, the administration had opted for a kind of preventive war policy.

Note that to make this point, one does not have to argue that the administration had actually decided to start a war with North Korea. In fact, the government had not actually decided, if all else failed, to use military force even on a very limited scale. Certainly this possibility—the possibility of what Scott Sagan calls a "preventive attack" as opposed to a full-scale "preventive war"—was being considered. The idea of an air strike that would destroy the North Korean nuclear facilities—the "Osirak option," as it was called—had by no means been ruled out.[47] And indeed, it seems that "in June 1994 U.S. decision-makers were on the verge of seriously considering a preemptive strike against the Yongbyon nuclear facilities."[48] But none of Clinton's advisors thought at that point that the United States should launch such an attack right away. They certainly wanted to take less violent measures first. But they did think that sooner or later, if all else failed, they might have to go that route. So the "Osirak option" remained a possibility, and in fact when the president met with his top advisors on June 16, 1994, to consider America's military options, one of the purposes of that meeting was "to deliberate further on the 'Osirak option.'"[49]

As it turned out, Clinton did not even have to decide at that meeting on the deployment options that had been prepared for him—options which, it was understood, involved a certain risk of war. He was "within minutes of selecting" one of those options when word came from former president Jimmy Carter in Pyongyang that an agreement with North Korea might be possible, and an arrangement called the Agreed Framework was eventually worked out. The issue was settled, at least for the time being.

[47] Carter and Perry, *Preventive Defense*, pp. 128, 131; and Wit, Poneman, and Gallucci, *Going Critical*, pp. 210–211, 220, 244. For Ashton Carter's interest in this sort of option even prior to taking office, see Henry Sokolski, *Best of Intentions: America's Campaign against Strategic Weapons Proliferation* (Westport, Conn.: Praeger, 2001), pp. 90–92, and the sources cited there. See also Sigal, *Disarming Strangers*, pp. 59–60, referring to a paper written for Carter by Philip Zelikow, a holdover from the Bush administration, recommending an attack on the North Korean nuclear facilities.

[48] Wit, Poneman, and Gallucci, *Going Critical*, p. 406.

[49] Ibid., p. 220.

Still, the episode tells us something important about American policy. It shows that the U.S. government felt it had the right to insist that a sovereign state not develop nuclear weapons on its own territory. It felt it had the right to demand that North Korea remain non-nuclear—indeed, the right to use force against that country if it did not accede to that demand. And America was so sure of its right to act in this way that the administration did not even see the need, at least during the initial phase of the crisis, to offer the North Koreans much in exchange for their accepting a non-nuclear status—and the country as a whole saw even less of a need to do so.[50] Eventually, of course, major concessions were made, but the assumption all along was that the United States had the right to prevent a "rogue" third-world state from going nuclear, by whatever means were necessary.

Was this all that different from the basic thinking of the Bush administration after 2001? Former Secretary Perry (together with Ashton Carter, who had worked under him in the Pentagon) published a book in 1999 called *Preventive Defense: A New Strategy for America*. In that book, Perry and Carter called for "counterproliferation programs that include passive defenses such as defensive chemical suits, active defenses such as theater missile defenses, and counterforce programs." The Bush National Security Strategy document called in very similar terms for "proactive counterproliferation efforts," and in particular for the development in this context of "active and passive defenses, and counterforce capabilities," to help America deal with "the threat before it is unleashed."[51] Those references to counterforce suggest that policymakers in both cases were thinking at least to some extent in "preemptive" terms. Indeed, Perry himself testified, just before the September 11 attacks, that because there could never be any guarantee that direct defense would be "fully effective," the U.S. government needed to "establish a policy" that "we, the United States, will attack the launch sites of

---

[50] Gallucci et al. characterize the initial U.S. position as follows: "The Americans' objective was somehow to nudge the North Koreans back toward full NPT compliance, or at least to buy time while a more enduring solution was sought. And it had to be done without making any substantive concessions." Ibid., p. 55; see also pp. 73, 97. According to Oberdorfer, Gallucci privately "characterized his initial negotiating posture as, 'If they do everything we want, we send them a box of oranges.'" Oberdorfer, *Two Koreas*, p. 291. For the view in important nongovernmental circles, see Wit, Poneman, and Gallucci, *Going Critical*, pp. 236–38 (for reaction to the Carter trip), and pp. 335–39 (reaction to the Agreed Framework).

[51] Carter and Perry, *Preventive Defense*, p. 142; "National Security Strategy of the United States of America," p. 14. On the "counterproliferation" strategy, see also James J Wirtz, "Counterproliferation, Conventional Counterforce and Nuclear War," *Journal of Strategic Studies* 23, no. 1 (March 2000). The mere coining of the term *counterproliferation*, it is important to note, reflected the belief that the old "nonproliferation" policy was too passive and that a far more active policy needed to be adopted.

any nation that threatens to attack the United States with nuclear or biological weapons."[52]

People like William Perry and Ashton Carter understood that the policy the Clinton administration pursued toward North Korea in 1994 was cut from the same cloth as the Bush strategy. Eight years before the Bush administration started talking about "preemption," Perry and Carter pointed out, "the Clinton administration contemplated its own act of preemption against the strange, isolated regime then considered the greatest threat to U.S. national security. The two of us, then at the Pentagon, readied plans for striking at North Korea's nuclear facilities and for mobilizing hundreds of thousands of American troops for the war that probably would have followed."[53] And Perry and Carter were not the only Clinton-era officials to take this kind of line—that is, to take the view that "preemptive" action could not simply be ruled out on moral or legal or even on general political grounds. Walter Slocombe, another high Defense Department official during the Clinton period, published an article in *Survival* in 2003 that basically sided with the Bush administration about "preemption." In Slocombe's view, "a strong case exists that the right of 'self-defence' includes a right to move against WMD programmes with high potential danger to the United States (and others) while it is still feasible to do so."[54] The point here, of course, is not that there was no difference between the Bush strategy and the policy pursued under Clinton. It is simply that there is a greater element of continuity here than people realize.

There is a second point worth making about the North Korean nuclear crisis, and this has to do with the way the other major powers reacted to what the United States was doing at the time. They did not really oppose what America was doing in 1993–94; they were not outraged by the fact that the Americans were willing to take military action if all else failed. You might have expected China, for example, and perhaps also Russia as well, to have pursued something of an anti-American policy in the crisis—a policy aimed at restraining the United States and

---

[52] "The Administration's Missile Defense Program and the ABM Treaty," 107th Congress, First Session, hearing before the Senate Foreign Relations Committee, July 24, 2001, p. 88.

[53] Ashton Carter and William Perry, "Back to the Brink," *Washington Post*, October 20, 2002.

[54] Walter Slocombe, "Force, Pre-emption and Legitimacy," *Survival* 45, no. 1 (Spring 2003): 125. In a footnote appended to this passage, Slocombe says that the fact that countries like North Korea and Iraq were in breach of their obligations under the NPT provided a legal basis for action. "It is certainly arguable," he writes, "that other states are entitled to resort to force to compel compliance with such obligations." Slocombe thus simply ignored the fact that North Korea, under the terms of the treaty itself, had the right to withdraw from the NPT regime.

building up counterweights to American power, especially in their neck of the woods. But you just did not see anything of the sort.[55]

This sort of policy can of course be explained in terms of the particular interests of the countries involved. China did not want a nuclear North Korea, in large part because of the spillover effects. If North Korea went nuclear, South Korea and Japan would probably follow, and maybe, with the whole region going nuclear, Taiwan would be tempted to join the club. But none of that would be to China's liking. Taiwan, moreover, might be tempted to go nuclear even if Japan and South Korea did not; given China's basic policy on the Taiwan issue, it might be to that country's interest to establish the principle that force could be used "preemptively" in such a case. China certainly "reserved the right to use force" if Taiwan tried to develop a nuclear capability, and more or less going along with what the United States was doing with North Korea might lend a degree of legitimacy to such a policy.[56] The same kind of point applied to Russia, which also had a certain interest in establishing the legitimacy of the principle of "preemption," which might provide a sort of legal basis for intervention in Russia's "near abroad." Indeed, Russian officials later argued that they had the right to intervene in Georgia, whose territory, they claimed, was serving as a refuge for Chechen rebels; the U.S.-backed principle of "preemption," they said, would justify such a policy.[57]

But it seems that there is more to the story than that—more to the story than can be explained by pointing simply to the particular interests of the countries in question. It seems that there is something more general at work—a certain sense that the major powers have a common interest in limiting the sovereignty of smaller, less responsible, states. The great powers see themselves as members of a very small and exclu-

---

[55] For the policy of the major powers in question—the four other permanent members of the U.N. Security Council—see the references in the entries for China, Russia, France, and Britain in the index to Wit, Poneman, and Gallucci, *Going Critical*. Note especially pp. 154–155, 198–199, 208–209 (for China); pp. 156, 197, 209 (for Russia); and pp. 153, 156, 158, 194 (for Britain and France, characterized here as "nonproliferation hawks"). On Chinese policy at the climax of the crisis, see also Oberdorfer, *Two Koreas*, pp. 320–321. For more information, pointing in the same general direction, on Chinese policy on this issue more recently, see Denny Roy, "China's Reaction to American Predominance," *Survival* 45, no. 3 (Autumn 2003): 63 and 67, and Alastair Iain Johnston, "Is China a Status Quo Power?" *International Security* 27, no. 4 (Spring 2003): 40–41 and esp. n. 84, plus the sources cited in those passages. Note also what Johnston says here about the Chinese more generally "not trying as hard" as they might to balance against the United States (p. 39), a view shared by most commentators, including Roy.

[56] See Thomas Christensen's contribution to Richard Ellings and Aaron Friedberg, eds., *Strategic Asia 2001–02: Power and Purpose* (Seattle: National Bureau of Asian Research, 2001), p. 48.

[57] See "Putin's Folly," *The Economist* (U.S. edition), September 21, 2002.

sive club, a club that essentially runs the international system as a whole, and they feel that they have a certain interest in perpetuating this kind of arrangement. That means that they cannot really take the principle of the "sovereign equality of all states" too seriously—certainly not when their basic interests, or indeed those of other great powers or of the great powers as a bloc, are threatened. The major powers obviously do not always see eye to eye. Their interests often conflict, sometimes very sharply. But whatever their disagreements, they nonetheless have a certain common interest in supporting a regime that gives the great powers special rights, in fact if not in theory.[58] And their

[58] I touch on some of these issues in an essay called "Intervention in Historical Perspective," published in Carl Kaysen and Laura Reed, eds., *Emerging Norms of Justified Intervention* (Cambridge, Mass.: American Academyi of Arts and Sciences, 1993). The tradition I am alluding to here has been an important (although by no means the dominant) element in great power political thinking for centuries. One associates it in particular with Castlereagh and Metternich—with the Congress of Vienna and the Concert of Europe. But it was also a major element in Roosevelt's thinking during the Second World War. Roosevelt, in fact, originally wanted a postwar international order in which the "Four Policemen"—America, Russia, Britain, and China—would keep everyone else (including countries like France) disarmed, a proposal the Soviets were quick to accept. This proposal for the "enforced disarmament of our enemies and, indeed, some of our friends after the war," as Roosevelt put it, scarcely corresponded to the idea of an international order based on the "sovereign equality of all states." See Roosevelt-Molotov meetings, May 29 and June 1, 1942, *Foreign Relations of the United States* 1942, vol. 3, pp. 568–69, 573, 580. In our own day, this idea of an at least semi-cooperative great power-dominated political system is associated above all with political figures like Henry Kissinger, who of course began his scholarly career with a dissertation on the Vienna settlement. On the idea of China as part of a kind of concert system, a system in which the nonproliferation regime would play a central role, see Carter and Perry, *Preventive Defense*, pp. 119–22. See also Susan L. Shirk, "Asia-Pacific Regional Security: Balance of Power or Concert of Powers?" in David Lake and Patrick Morgan, eds., *Regional Orders: Building Security in a New World* (State College: Pennsylvania State University Press, 1997). Note especially Shirk's argument that the "North Korean nuclear threat" might be "a catalytic event for an emerging cooperation among the Asia-Pacific powers that could evolve into a concert of powers" (p. 246; see also pp. 262–65). Note also the two articles on contemporary Chinese foreign policy cited in n. 55 of this chapter—and especially Roy's prediction (in "China's Reaction to American Predominance") that "as China becomes a great power with an interest in responsible management of international politics, its desire to prevent the spread of WMD will likely grow" (p. 65). One comes across this sort of theme quite a bit in recent years in articles written by specialists in Chinese foreign policy. To take just one example: "Chinese strategists," according to Evan Medeiros and M. Taylor Fravel in an article called "China's New Diplomacy" published in *Foreign Affairs* in November–December 2003, "increasingly see their interests as more akin to major powers and less associated with those of developing nations." Finally, for a brief survey of the development of Chinese policy on the proliferation issue that supports this general interpretation, see Weixing Hu, "Nuclear Nonproliferation," in Yong Deng and Fei-Ling Wang, *In the Eyes of the Dragon: China Views the World* (New York: Rowman and Littlefield, 1999).

policy during the 1993–94 North Korean nuclear crisis should probably be seen in this context.

THE ROAD TO WAR IN 1941

So during the Cold War and even in the post–Cold War period "preemptive" action was by no means out of the question. But there was something very distinctive about all the cases I have mentioned. They all had to do with nuclear weapons—that is, with their acquisition or deployment by a hostile power. But does action of this sort become a live issue only when nuclear weapons enter into the equation, or do the roots run deeper? Is the problem, as many theorists imply, rooted in the basic structure of international politics—in the fact that in a world where states have to provide for their own security, they are under pressure to act aggressively, even for purely defensive purposes?

To get at that issue, it makes sense to examine American policy in the pre-nuclear period. So in this section I would like to look at the pre–Pearl Harbor period, a period when the United States (as many people, even scholars, seem to think) was a country that "asked only to be left alone."[59] If it turns out that this view is incorrect—if it is not quite true that the United States had opted for a purely defensive policy, and if in fact the government was pursuing a far more active and, indeed, in a certain sense, more aggressive policy because of what it viewed as a developing threat to national security—then that historical conclusion would obviously have some bearing on the issue at hand. If the Roosevelt strategy in 1941 is to be viewed in "preemptive" terms, then the Bush strategy might have to be seen as less of an anomaly—as more natural, more rooted in the basic structure of international politics, than people think.

What then is the picture that emerges when you look at U.S. policy in the period before Pearl Harbor, both toward Europe and toward Japan? The first thing you are struck by when you study this period is that the United States was not a country that "asked only to be left alone." America in both areas was very active indeed. By late 1941, the United States was fighting an undeclared naval war against Germany in the

---

[59] The argument I make in this section is developed in much greater detail in the fourth chapter of my book *The Craft of International History: A Guide to Method* (Princeton: Princeton University Press, 2006). For the claim that America at this time "asked only to be left alone," see A.J.P. Taylor, *The Origins of the Second World War* (New York: Atheneum, 1961), p. 278. Note also Randall Schweller's use of that passage from the Taylor book in his article "Bandwagoning for Profit: Bringing the Revisionist State Back In," *International Security* 19, no. 1 (Summer 1994): 94–95.

North Atlantic. America had in fact gone on the offensive. As Admiral Harold Stark, the Chief of Naval Operations, wrote on August 28, "The Good Lord knows if the Germans want an excuse for war, they have plenty."[60] President Roosevelt's policy by that time, as he said, was to "wage war, but not declare it." He would become "more and more provocative," he told Churchill in early August, and "if the Germans did not like it, they could attack American forces."[61]

He also pursued a very active policy in the Pacific at this time. On July 26, following the Japanese move into southern Indochina, the United States (together with the British and the Dutch) ended oil deliveries to Japan, and it is generally recognized that the oil embargo put the United States and Japan on a collision course. To get the oil she needed (if only to avoid a collapse of her military position in China), Japan could in principle seize the oil-producing areas in the Dutch East Indies. But it was clear enough that a move into the Indies would almost certainly mean war with the United States. So to get the oil without provoking a war with America, Japan needed to negotiate an agreement with the United States that would allow oil shipments to resume. The American terms, however, were severe: as part of the agreement, Japan would have to agree to withdraw from China. So Japan had in effect been cornered. She was forced to choose between war and capitulation on the China issue, and the Pearl Harbor attack has to be understood in that context. It is thus quite clear that U.S. policy played a major role in bringing on the war.

But effect is not the same as intent, and most of the scholars who have studied the issue assume that a war with Japan was the last thing the Roosevelt administration wanted at this time. Given that the United States was heading toward war with Germany, why would the Americans also want a second war with Japan, if there was any honorable way to avoid it? But if that view is correct—if Roosevelt really wanted to avoid war with Japan—how then is U.S. policy to be explained? If Roosevelt was in full control of American policy, and if he knew what he was doing—in particular, if he understood what the implications of the embargo were—then the policy would have to be seen as deliberate. So to argue that he did not deliberately put the United States on a collision course with Japan, you have to argue *either* that he did not understand the effect America's hard line would have, *or* that he had lost control of

---

[60] Stark to Admiral Hart, August 28, 1941, U.S. Congress, *Hearings Before the Joint Committee on the Investigation of the Pearl Harbor Attack*, part 16, p. 2451 (Washington, D.C.: GPO, 1946); henceforth cited in this form: PHA, part 16, p. 2451.

[61] Churchill's account to the British cabinet, August 19, 1941, quoted in David Reynolds, *The Creation of the Anglo-American Alliance, 1937–41: A Study in Competitive Cooperation* (Chapel Hill: University of North Carolina Press, 1982), p. 214.

policy. And in fact historical arguments in this area—the arguments that purport to explain how the government adopted a policy that led to a war it very much wanted to avoid—fall into those two categories.

But neither set of arguments really stands up to analysis. There certainly was no miscalculation. Roosevelt and his chief advisers clearly understood what the embargo meant. The president understood that it would "drive the Japanese down to the Dutch East Indies," and would thus, as he said, mean "war in the Pacific."[62] And on the second issue, it is now quite clear that the president had not lost control of American policy. Contrary to what a number of scholars have argued, policy had not been hijacked by people like then-Assistant Secretary of State Dean Acheson. Mid-level officials like Acheson had not defied Roosevelt's wishes and imposed an embargo surreptitiously, without his knowledge or consent. Acheson himself, it turns out, was taking orders from Undersecretary of State Sumner Welles, and given what we know about the Welles-Roosevelt relationship, it is safe to assume the president himself was calling the shots.[63]

But if Roosevelt had decided to impose the embargo on Japan knowing full well what it meant, then he had in effect opted for a course of

[62] Quoted in Patrick Hearden, *Roosevelt Confronts Hitler: America's Entry into World War II* (DeKalb: Northern Illinois University Press, 1987), p. 211. It was in fact because he understood what the embargo meant that he had earlier opposed it so fiercely. See, for example, Robert Dallek, *Franklin D. Roosevelt and American Foreign Policy, 1932–1945* (Oxford: Oxford University Press, 1979; paperback edition, 1981), pp. 273–75. Note also Roosevelt's well-known confrontation with Secretary of the Interior Harold Ickes on the issue in June 1941. The documents were published in *The Secret Diary of Harold L. Ickes,*. 3 vols. (New York: Simon & Schuster, 1954–55), 3:553–60.

[63] The argument about the president losing control of policy was laid out independently by Jonathan Utley and Irvine Anderson. See Jonathan Utley, *Going to War with Japan, 1937–1941* (Knoxville: University of Tennessee Press, 1985); Jonathan Utley, "Upstairs, Downstairs at Foggy Bottom: Oil Exports and Japan, 1940-41," *Prologue* 8 (Spring 1976): 17–28; Irvine Anderson, "The 1941 *De Facto* Embargo on Oil to Japan: A Bureaucratic Reflex," *Pacific Historical Review* 44 (1975): 201–31; and Irvine Anderson, *The Standard Vacuum Oil Company and United States East Asian Policy, 1933–1941* (Princeton: Princeton University Press, 1975). The Utley-Anderson argument has been accepted by a number of major scholars. See, for example, Reynolds, *Anglo-American Alliance,* pp. 235–36; Akira Iriye, *The Origins of the Second World War in Asia and the Pacific* (London: Longman, 1987), p. 150; Dallek, *Roosevelt and American Foreign Policy,* p. 275. For the counterargument, quite compelling in my view, see Waldo Heinrichs, *Threshold of War: Franklin D. Roosevelt and American Entry into World War II* (New York: Oxford University Press, 1988), pp. 141–42, 246–47. The British records of the Argentia meeting in early August also show that Roosevelt and Welles had decided to take a very hard line on the question of oil deliveries to Japan. See especially the extract from a record of a meeting between the prime minister and President Roosevelt on August 11th, 1941, FO 371/27909, and Cadogan minutes of meeting with Welles, August 20, 1941, FO 371/27977, *British Foreign Office Japan Correspondence, 1941–1945* [microfilm publication] (Wilmington, England: Scholarly Resources, 1978), series for 1941, reels 7 and 15 respectively.

action which he knew would in all probability lead directly to war with Japan. U.S. policy toward Japan at this point, in other words, has to be viewed as deliberate. And in fact U.S. leaders in late 1941 saw things quite clearly. They did not think Japan would be deterred by the embargo. They expected war. Japanese leaders, as Welles pointed out in November 1941, had to provide "some justification to their own people after four years of national effort and sacrifice" in China. He therefore found it hard to believe that the Japanese would "agree to evacuate China completely." But "nothing less," he said, would "satisfy [the] United States."[64] Admiral Stark also saw war coming. "Two irreconcilable policies can not go on forever—particularly," he said, alluding to the embargo, "if one party can not live with the set up. It doesn't look good."[65]

But why would Roosevelt pursue that kind of policy? Given especially that he was moving toward war with Germany, why would he have wanted to fight a second war with Japan? You cannot say he pursued the policy he did because he was bound by American principles. Those principles had not prevented him from pursuing a much more forbearing policy prior to July 26. So why did he opt for such a tough policy toward Japan at precisely that time—that is, just a few weeks after the German invasion of the USSR?

You can, of course, dismiss Roosevelt as a bungler. You can assume that on matters of foreign policy Roosevelt was simply incompetent. But before you jump to such conclusions, it might make sense to consider whether there was method to his madness—whether his Japan policy served a rational purpose, a purpose related to his most fundamental foreign policy goals. And since Germany was in his view the real threat, the question has to be whether the Japan policy is to be understood in the context of Roosevelt's European policy, and in particular in the context of his policy of taking the United States into the European war.

How then did Roosevelt and his top advisers approach that more basic issue? His chief military advisers did not mince words on this question. They wanted the United States to enter the European war, and the sooner the better. Admiral Stark, for example, told the president less than two days after the Germans attacked the Soviet Union that he "considered every day of delay in our getting into the war as dangerous." Stark wanted to start escorting convoys immediately, calculating that escorting "would almost certainly involve us in the war."[66]

---

[64] Australian Minister to the United States R. G. Casey to Australian Department of External Affairs, November 14, 1941, Australian Department of Foreign Affairs, *Documents on Australian Foreign Policy, 1937–49,* 5:197.

[65] Stark to Admiral Kimmel, November 7, 1941, PHA, part 16, p. 2220.

[66] Stark to Cooke, July 31, 1941, PHA, part 16, p. 2175. One should note the timing

The military authorities laid out their thinking in much greater detail in an important document, usually referred to as the "Victory Program," which they submitted to President Roosevelt on September 11, 1941, sixty years to the day before the attacks on New York and Washington.[67] They analyzed the issue in what can be considered "preventive war" terms. Germany, they believed, would defeat Russia by the following summer, and would probably need a further full year "to bring order out of chaos in the conquered areas." The Germans would then begin to exploit those areas economically, building up their military power and preparing for a showdown with the United States. A German attack on America was by no means imminent. The Germans might, in fact, "wish to establish peace with the United States for several years" after "conquering all of Europe." But America would be foolish to allow Germany to set the timetable for action. If the United States did not act quickly, the country would be faced in the "not distant future by a Germany strongly entrenched economically, supported by newly acquired sources of vital supplies and industries, with her military forces operating on interior lines, and in a position of hegemony in Europe which will be comparatively easy to defend and maintain." America would then have to fight a "long drawn-out war of attrition." Time was thus "of the essence," according to this document. "The longer we delay effective offensive operations against the Axis," its authors argued, "the more difficult will become the attainment of victory." They therefore called for "active participation in the war by the United

---

here—that is, the fact that Stark put the point to the president so soon after the Soviet Union was invaded—and also that he chose to mention this fact in his letter. This suggests that he was already analyzing the situation along the lines that the military leadership (as will be seen) were to take in the "Victory Program," the key document to be discussed in the next paragraph. But the argument about the implications of the German attack on Russia was not the only factor here, and Stark, it should be noted, had been thinking for some time in terms of getting America into the war as quickly as possible, well before the possibility of a German conquest of the USSR had become an issue. He summed up what his thinking had been in a memorandum he sent to the secretary of state on October 8: "I have assumed for the past two years that our country would not let Great Britain fall; that ultimately in order to prevent this we would have to enter the war and as noted above I have long felt and have stated that the sooner we get in the better." Ibid., p. 2217.

[67] The official title of this document, dated September 11, 1941, was "Joint Board Estimate of United States Over-All Production Requirements." It was signed by Stark and by Army Chief of Staff General George Marshall. A copy was published in Steven Ross, ed., *American War Plans, 1919–1941*, vol. 5 (New York: Garland, 1992). The main study appears on pp. 160–89, but the document also included an "Estimate of Army Ground Forces," published here on pp. 190–201. Extensive quotations from the Victory Program also appear in Robert E. Sherwood, *Roosevelt and Hopkins: An Intimate History* (New York: Harper, 1948), pp. 410–18.

States"—for "a rapidly accelerated all-out effort with a view to conducting decisive, offensive operations against the enemy before he can liquidate or recoup from his struggle with Russia."[68]

It was obvious to America's military leaders that the United States had to be concerned with the European balance of power. It was obvious to them that a German conquest of all of Europe would pose a grave threat to American security. The assumption was that the United States had to be concerned about these things—that it had to deal with these threats while it was still able to, and before they became almost totally unmanageable. The country, that is, could not afford to wait until its own territory was attacked. It instead had to be prepared to move "preemptively."

And it was not just the military leaders who analyzed the situation in these terms. The president himself saw things in much the same way. America, he told the country over and over again, in an extraordinary series of speeches in 1940 and 1941, had to worry about what was going on overseas. America's safety and America's future depended on events unfolding far from her borders. She could not afford to wait until "the enemy has landed on our shores"; it was "stupid to wait until a probable enemy has gained a foothold from which to attack."[69] Indeed, Roosevelt said in September 1941, it would be foolish to hold back simply because Hitler seemed "to be making slower progress than he did the year before." That, in his view, was "the very moment to strike with redoubled force."[70] And in his famous fireside chat of September 11, 1941—again, that date is now hard to forget—the speech in which he announced the policy of shooting first in the Atlantic, he framed the issue in what can be viewed as "preventive war" terms. "One peaceful Nation after another," he said, "has met disaster because each refused to look the Nazi danger squarely in the eye until it actually had them by the throat. The United States will not make that fatal mistake." Now, he said, was "the time for prevention of attack"; "when you see a rattlesnake poised to strike, you do not wait until he has struck before you crush him."[71] He was referring here to the German U-Boat threat, but that remark could be construed in a somewhat broader sense—as referring, that is, to the threat posed by Nazi Germany as a whole.

[68] "Victory Program" in Ross, ed., *American War Plans*, 5:163, 165, 168–169, 193–194.

[69] Radio Address Announcing Proclamation of an Unlimited National Emergency, May 27, 1941, *The Public Papers and Addresses of Franklin D. Roosevelt*, comp. Samuel Rosenman, vol. 10 [for 1941] (New York: Harper, 1942), p. 189.

[70] Labor Day Radio Address, September 1, 1941, ibid., p. 367.

[71] Fireside Chat on National Defense," September 11, 1941, ibid., pp. 388–90. Former Secretary of State George Shultz, incidentally, also used the rattlesnake metaphor in his article calling for action against Iraq: "Act Now," *Washington Post*, September 6, 2002.

I think it is quite clear, in fact, that the president agreed with his top military advisors on the importance of bringing the United States into the European war as quickly as possible. Was his policy toward Japan then framed with an eye toward achieving that goal? George Kennan, for one, seemed to think so, and he was very critical of Roosevelt for pursuing a policy of that sort. "If it really was Roosevelt's feeling," he wrote, "that we ought to enter the European war, then to manoeuvre us first into a war with Japan, or even to permit us to become involved in such a war, was the worst possible way to do it."[72] And Kennan was certainly right in thinking that if America had to enter the European war, it would have been much better to just do it directly and remain at peace with Japan—that maneuvering the country "first into a war with Japan" was the worst possible way to bring America into the war with Germany. The problem was that given both the German policy of avoiding war with America (at least for the time being) and the political situation within the United States, it might have been the *only* way to do it quickly enough.

And if that was in fact the case, I for one would not criticize Roosevelt for managing things the way he did. He had to work with the world as he found it. If this really was "the worst possible way" to get into the war, then it is not Roosevelt but rather the country as a whole that ought to be blamed. Indeed, Kennan himself seemed to recognize that it was America's unwillingness as a nation to use force for purely political purposes, as a deliberate act of policy, that lay at the heart of the problem. "I continue to regret," he said, "that curious quirk in the American political mentality which apparently makes it impossible for us to enter by our own deliberate decision great wars which we later discover, once we are in them, to be of the most apocalyptic importance."[73]

The idea here is that America paid a huge price—namely, having to fight an essentially unnecessary second war with Japan—because it could not bring itself to declare war on Germany as an act of policy. The country paid a huge price because it refused to act "preemptively"— because it refused to go to war, officially at any rate, simply because it felt its security would be imperiled a number of years down the road by a German victory in Europe. That basic attitude virtually forced the administration, which did think in those "preemptive" terms, to stage-manage things so that it would appear the United States was the victim of unprovoked attack.

[72] George Kennan, comment on three papers on Allied leadership in World War II, including one by Robert Dallek on Roosevelt, in *Survey* 21, nos. 1-2 (Winter–Spring 1975): 30.

[73] Ibid. Note also his discussion of this issue in George Kennan, *American Diplomacy, 1900–1950* (Chicago: University of Chicago Press, 1951), pp. 83–84.

This point, of course, has a certain bearing on the way we approach the problem of "preemption" today. What upsets many people about the Bush policy is not so much its acceptance of the idea that the United States might in some cases have to act "preemptively" and deal with threats before the country itself has been attacked, but the way that policy has been presented to the world. They are shocked that this principle of "preemption" has been embraced so overtly and so directly. It is the tone of the policy that they find so offensive. And in fact a strong argument can be made that if that policy is to be pursued at all, the country would be better off if it were packaged differently—if the administration, that is, avoided the sort of rhetoric which it knows people will find provocative. But even if you share that view—even if you feel that issues of this degree of seriousness and complexity need to be discussed in a more restrained and more nuanced way—you still need to recognize that there is another side to this coin. You might think it is unwise to proclaim one's right to take "preemptive" action in too blatant and too vocal a way. But at the same time you need to recognize the possibility that a country like the United States can err in the opposite direction—that it can in fact pay an enormous price for refusing to accept the legitimacy of "preemptive" action and framing its policy accordingly. If the 1941 case teaches us nothing else, it should certainly teach us that.

PREVENTIVE WAR IN HISTORICAL PERSPECTIVE

What do we mean by a "preventive war" policy? When we use the term, we generally have two things in mind. We mean first of all a policy based on the idea that force can be used even if a country has not been attacked. But we also mean a policy rooted in concerns about the future, about what might happen tomorrow if nothing is done today. By that two-part definition, the Bush policy certainly qualifies as a preventive war policy. But does the adoption of that strategy of "preemption" mark a total break with American tradition, or did earlier administrations, to one extent or another, also think in "preemptive" terms?

It turns out that the sort of thinking one finds in the Bush policy documents is not to be viewed as anomalous. Under Roosevelt and Truman, under Eisenhower and Kennedy, and even under Clinton in the 1990s, this kind of thinking came into play in a major way. Concerns about the future—about what might happen if nothing were done—weighed heavily on American policy during the period from 1941 through 1963 and beyond.

That historical finding should not be too surprising, at least not to anyone who has tried to grapple with these issues on a theoretical level and who is familiar with what international relations theorists have had to say on the subject. For one of the main ideas in contemporary American international relations theory is that in a world not governed by supra-national authority, states will do whatever they have to in order to provide for their own security. And if that means taking aggressive action, then they will act aggressively, even for purely defensive purposes.[74] And the pressure to do so, the theorists go on to argue, is particularly strong when states worry about how the strategic balance is shifting and about what might happen if events are allowed to drift.[75] From that general point of view, the sort of thinking I have been talking about here comes across as natural—as a normal response to the pressures you find in a self-help system.

But that kind of approach, at least in its purest form, somewhat overstates the importance of those systemic forces. In reality, a tendency to think in preventive war terms is not quite built into the basic structure of the system. People are instead drawn to this type of thinking only when a certain political judgment is made about the nature and manageability of the conflict at hand. The Germans, for example, began talking about the importance of having it out with the Russians before it was too late only after they had come to the conclusion around 1912 that because of Russia's Balkan policy, war with that country was probably unavoidable.[76]

A preventive war policy is thus based on a judgment about the future. But it is sometimes claimed that because no one can see with any certainty what the future holds, a preventive war policy simply has to be ruled out. Our calculations about the future, the argument runs, are just too fragile to serve as the basis for such a warlike policy.[77] The problem with that argument is that no matter what course of action is chosen, that choice has to rest on a judgment about the future. Various alternative courses of action have to be weighed against each other, and

---

[74] In modern times, this argument goes back to Hobbes, but today it figures prominently in the writings of a number of leading international relations theorists. See especially Robert Jervis, "Cooperation under the Security Dilemma," *World Politics* 30, no. 2 (January 1978); Kenneth Waltz, "The Origins of War in Neorealist Theory," *Journal of Interdisciplinary History* 18, no. 4 (Spring 1988), pp. 619–20; and John Mearsheimer, *The Tragedy of Great Power Politics* (New York: Norton, 2001), esp. pp. 3, 21, 34.

[75] See especially Stephen Van Evera, *Causes of War: Power and the Roots of Conflict* (Ithaca: Cornell University Press, 1999), esp. chap. 4; and Dale Copeland, *The Origins of Major War* (Ithaca: Cornell University Press, 2000).

[76] For the key document, see John C. G. Röhl, "Admiral von Müller and the Approach of War, 1911–1914," *Historical Journal* 12, no. 4 (December 1969): esp. 661.

[77] This, for example, is what Schlesinger seems to argue in "The Immorality of Preemptive War."

the political leadership can make that assessment only by thinking about what is likely to happen if one or another policy is adopted. The issue is not whether policy choices should be made by trying to think about what is likely to happen in the future if the country goes down a particular road. The only real issue here is how good that analysis is—how careful and how well-informed those speculations are.

But to say that these are matters where judgment is called for is to admit that the judgment can go either way, depending on circumstances. This therefore is not an issue that should be dealt with by invoking hard-and-fast principles—by flatly asserting that a preventive war policy is to be dismissed out of hand as "illegal and immoral," or, on the other hand, by flatly asserting that international norms should count for nothing. The problem has to be approached in a more nuanced way. The goal is to strike a balance—to realize that in certain circumstances a very active policy might have to be considered, while recognizing that as a general rule the basic norms of the system need to be treated with respect.

It is important to remember, in this context, that this is the way these issues have been dealt with in the past. No one got upset, during the Second World War, when the United States and Britain attacked French North Africa in November 1942, even though those territories belonged to France, by then a neutral power. The reason no one got upset was that this military operation was so directly related to the larger war, a war in which the most basic interests of America and Britain were on the line. No one got upset about the British attack on the French fleet at Mers-el-Kébir in July 1940. The British were afraid the fleet would fall into German hands, and acted, even though they were not at war with France and even though they could not know with any certainty what would happen if they took no action. But no one got upset, because people understood why it was so important for Britain to take no chances in this matter. And no one was outraged when Churchill, in his book about the origins of the Second World War, basically argued that the western powers should have moved against Hitler early on, while it would have been relatively easy to do so.[78] Churchill was basically making a preventive war argument, but the Nazi threat seemed so obvious in retrospect that what Churchill was saying seemed utterly unproblematic.

And in the case of the Cuban Missile Crisis, there was no hand-wringing at the time about the United States being willing, unilaterally

[78] See Winston Churchill, *The Gathering Storm* (Boston: Houghton Mifflin, 1948), esp. pp. 346–48. Note also the "theme of the volume": "How the English-speaking peoples, through their unwisdom, carelessness, and good nature allowed the wicked to rearm"—the clear implication being that the "wicked" should not have been allowed to do so.

if necessary, to take military action without prior U.N. authorization, even though no one thought a launch of the missiles was imminent. If the Kennedy policy was criticized at all, it was criticized for being too weak, and not just by right-wing Republicans. Senator J. William Fulbright, the Democrat from Arkansas who chaired the Senate Foreign Relations Committee, for example, told Kennedy to his face during the crisis that rather than go the blockade route, "it would be far better to launch an attack on Cuba." Fulbright, in fact, was in favor "of an invasion, and an all-out one, and as quickly as possible."[79] No one was outraged by the fact that Kennedy was willing, in the final analysis, to use force on this issue. The assumption was that the country could have pursued a much tougher policy if it had wanted to—that the country would do whatever it needed to do, and that military action was by no means to be ruled out as "illegal and immoral."

Why is it important to remember these things? Why is it so important to see this whole set of problems in historical perspective? The problems the world now has to deal with are very difficult, and we need to look for guidance wherever we can find it. And we can get some guidance by understanding that these problems are not entirely new, and that people had to face similar problems in the past. By studying and thinking about how they were dealt with, we can develop and refine our own thinking about this whole cluster of issues. Historical study can serve as a sort of laboratory. By studying the past the right way, we can bring important conceptual issues into focus—and we have to do that in order to work out our thinking in this area, so that we can then bring that thinking to bear on questions of policy. But to use history in that way, we have to try to see American policy in the twentieth century for what it actually was. And that, unfortunately, is something that few people in American political life, left or right, seem particularly interested in doing.

[79] Kennedy meeting with Congressional leadership, October 22, 1962, FRUS 1961–63, 11:160–61, and May and Zelikow, *Kennedy Tapes*, pp. 271–72.

CHAPTER NINE

The Iraq Crisis and the Future of the Western Alliance

IN JANUARY 1963, Konrad Adenauer, the chancellor of the Federal Republic of Germany, came to Paris to sign a treaty of friendship with France. This was an event of considerable political importance. The German government, it seemed, had decided to form a kind of bloc with the France of President Charles de Gaulle, a country that for some time had been pursuing a policy with a distinct anti-American edge. Indeed, just one week before Adenauer's visit, de Gaulle had risen up against America. He had announced that France was going to veto Britain's entry into the European Common Market. If the British were allowed in, de Gaulle argued, continental Europe would eventually be absorbed into a "colossal Atlantic Community, dependent on America and under American control," and this France would not permit.[1] The German government seemed to share de Gaulle's sentiments. How else could its willingness to sign a treaty with France at that particular point possibly be interpreted?

The Americans were enraged by what France and Germany had done, and the Kennedy administration, then in power, decided to take a very hard line. The Europeans, President Kennedy felt, could not be expected to pursue a pro-American policy simply because of what the United States had done for them in previous years. "We have been very generous to Europe," he told the National Security Council on January 22, 1963, "and it is now time for us to look out for ourselves, knowing full well that the Europeans will not do anything for us simply because we have in the past helped them."[2] They would come around, in his

---

This article, written in 2004, was originally published in David M. Andrews, ed., *The Atlantic Alliance Under Stress* (Cambridge, England: Cambridge University Press, 2005). In republishing it here I deliberately did not change the text (except for some very minor corrections). A more fully footnoted version of the article, with direct links to many of the sources cited, is available online at http://www.polisci.ucla.edu/faculty/trachtenberg/useur/iraqcrisis.html.

[1] Press conference of January 14, 1963, in Charles de Gaulle, *Discours and Messages*, vol. 4 (Paris: Plon, 1986), p. 69.

[2] Notes on Remarks by President Kennedy before the National Security Council, January 22, 1963, US Department of State, *Foreign Relations of the United States, 1961–1963*, vol. 13, p. 486; henceforth cited in this form: FRUS 1961–63, 13:486.

view, only if the most intense pressure were brought to bear. America would threaten to pull her military forces out of Europe. The Europeans would be forced to make a choice. It would be made clear to them that they could not have it both ways. If they wanted to be fully independent politically, they would also have to be fully independent militarily—that is, they would have to provide for their own defense.

Kennedy had made the same point a few months earlier in a meeting with the famous writer André Malraux, French minister of culture and a de Gaulle confidant. "A Europe beyond our influence—yet counting on us—in which we should have to bear the burden of defense without the power to affect events"—this, the president thought, just could not be.[3] De Gaulle, he warned, "should make no mistake: Americans would be glad to get out of Europe."[4] And this, it should be noted, was no idle threat. America, in Kennedy's view, did not need Europe. As he told his top advisors on January 25, 1963, "we can take care of ourselves and are not dependent upon European support."[5]

West Germany, exposed to Soviet power as it was, was the primary target of this policy. "There is not much we can do about France," Kennedy said, "but we can exert considerable pressure on the Germans."[6] And that pressure could be exerted in one and only one way. "The threat of withdrawing our troops," the president thought, "was about the only sanction we had."[7] It was made abundantly clear to the Germans that if they wanted American military protection, they could not pursue an "independent," Gaullist, anti-American policy. Those warnings had the desired effect. Forced to choose, the Germans in 1963 chose America.[8]

In January 2003, another German chancellor, Gerhard Schröder, met in Paris with another French president, Jacques Chirac. The two men had come together to celebrate the fortieth anniversary of the Franco-German treaty, but they took advantage of the occasion to adopt a common position on the most important foreign policy issue of the day, the question of a possible war on Iraq.

For months, it had been clear that the United States had been heading toward war with that country. U.S. policy had been laid out, for example, in a major speech Vice President Dick Cheney gave on August 26,

---

[3] Kennedy-Malraux meeting, May 11, 1962, FRUS 1961–63, 13:696.

[4] Ibid.

[5] NSC Executive Committee meeting, January 25, 1963, ibid., p. 490.

[6] *Ibid*, p. 489.

[7] NSC Executive Committee meeting, February 5, 1963, ibid., p. 178.

[8] For a fuller account of this story, see Marc Trachtenberg, *A Constructed Peace: The Making of the European Settlement* (Princeton: Princeton University Press, 1999), pp. 303, 369–79.

2002. For Cheney—and there was no doubt that he was speaking for the president—the Iraqi threat was growing, and it was important to deal with it sooner rather than later. The Iraqi dictator, Saddam Hussein, had "systematically broken" all the agreements he had entered into at the end of the Gulf War in 1991. He had promised at that time that Iraq's nuclear, biological, and chemical weapons would be destroyed and an inspection regime had been set up to make sure that those promises were honored. But work on those forbidden weapons had continued. Iraq had "devised an elaborate program" to keep the inspectors in the dark. The inspection regime had thus not been able to guarantee that Iraq's "weapons of mass destruction" (WMD) programs had been shut down permanently. Given the nature of the threat, it was vitally important, Cheney said, to take action before it was too late.[9] And this, one should note, was not just the view of a right-wing clique that had somehow managed to hijack government policy. A number of key senators and respected elder statesmen (including former secretaries of state Henry Kissinger, George Shultz, and James Baker) basically took the same general line.[10]

This was the policy that first Germany and then France came to oppose, and to oppose in a very direct and public way. Chancellor Schröder, in the heat of an electoral campaign, made it clear by the beginning of September 2002 that he was against a war with Iraq no matter what. He would oppose war even if the U.N. Security Council authorized a military operation.[11] German opinion was heavily antiwar and it seemed that Schröder had decided to try to win what was by all accounts a close election "by running against America."[12]

The French position at that time was more ambiguous. In September 2002, it seemed that the French government might be willing eventually to approve the use of force if Iraq were given one last chance to come clean about her weapons programs and to destroy whatever forbidden weapons she still had. The U.S. government had decided, after a serious internal debate, to try to work through the United Nations,

[9] Remarks by the Vice President to the Veterans of Foreign Wars 103rd National Convention, August 26, 2002 (http://www.whitehouse.gov/news/releases/2002/08/20020826.html).

[10] See especially Henry Kissinger, "The Politics of Intervention: Iraq 'Regime Change' is a Revolutionary Strategy," *Los Angeles Times*, August 9, 2002; George Shultz, "Act Now," *Washington Post*, September 6, 2002; James A. Baker, "The Right Way to Change Iraq's Regime," *International Herald Tribune*, August 26, 2002.

[11] Steven Erlanger, "German Leader's Warning: War Plan is a Huge Mistake," *New York Times*, September 5, 2002.

[12] Steven Erlanger, "For Now, Trading Allies for Votes," *New York Times*, September 14, 2002, and Peter Finn, "Ruling Coalition Wins Narrowly in German Vote: Strong Anti-War Stance Helps Schroeder Defeat Conservatives," *Washington Post*, September 23, 2002.

and the French foreign minister, Dominique de Villepin, had proposed a possible course of action. At a lunch with U.S. Secretary of State Colin Powell, Villepin "floated the idea of having two resolutions," one that would demand that Iraq disarm, to be followed by a second authorizing military action if Iraq failed to comply. "Be sure about one thing," Powell told his French colleague. "Don't vote for the first, unless you are prepared to vote for the second." And "Villepin assented, officials who were there said."[13]

A resolution was adopted and the Iraqis allowed the U.N. inspectors, who had left in 1998, to come back in. But as Chirac himself would admit, Iraq was not "sufficiently cooperative."[14] For the French, however, this did not mean that the time for military action had come. Instead, the Chirac government dug in its heels. Its opposition to American policy hardened. In January, when Chirac and Schröder met in Paris, France basically aligned her policy with that of Germany: the two countries had come together to oppose America.[15]

Their efforts focused on the U.N. Security Council. The basic tactic was to insist that the use of force against Iraq would be legal only if the Security Council gave its consent and at the same time to do what they could to make sure the Security Council would not authorize U.S. action, not for quite some time, at any rate. In that way, a U.S. military operation would come across as illegitimate; the hope was that rather than engage in what would be branded an illegal use of force, the Americans would back down and war would be avoided. So for six weeks after the Paris meetings, according to one of the best-informed discussions of this affair, Chirac and Schröder "worked the phones, visited foreign capitals and called in diplomatic chits. Their goal: nothing less than the reining in of what they saw as a rogue superpower. The German ambassador to the UN boasted in one confidential e-mail to colleagues at his foreign ministry that their strategy was to isolate the US and make it 'repentantly come back to the [U.N. Security] Council,' seeking compromise."[16]

---

[13] Steven Weisman, "A Long, Winding Road to a Diplomatic Dead End," *New York Times,* March 17, 2003, and Marc Champion, Charles Fleming, Ian Johnson and Carla Anne Robbins, "Allies at Odds: Behind U.S. Rift With Europeans: Slights and Politics: Schröder and Chirac Discover How Popular Tweaking a Superpower Can Be," *Wall Street Journal,* March 27, 2003. These two articles are the best descriptions of this story that have appeared so far.

[14] Chirac interview with TF1 and France 2, March 10, 2003 (http://www.diplomatie .gouv.fr/actu/bulletin.gb.asp?liste=20030311.gb.html).

[15] Luc de Barochez, "Jacques Chirac and Gerhard Schröder se prononcent pour un rè-glement pacifique: Front franco-allemand sur la crise irakienne," *Le Figaro,* January 23, 2003. See also the text of the joint Chirac-Schröder press conference and joint television interview, both of January 22, 2003.

[16] Champion et al., "Allies at Odds."

It was clear that what was at stake was of absolutely fundamental importance. For the German foreign minister, Joschka Fischer, what was at issue was nothing less than the "question of a new world order after the end of the Cold War."[17] And many Europeans opposed the idea of an American-dominated world order—an order that they saw as based on brute force and on the will of a single extraordinarily powerful country. In their view—and one comes across countless articles in the European, and especially the French, press based on premises of this sort—America was a lawless state, an arrogant, overbearing, presumptuous power, a country that no longer felt any obligation to play by the rules, a country that relied on brute force to get what it wanted. And in this view, Europe, in standing up to America, was championing a very different kind of policy. Europe was standing up for law and for justice, for a "multipolar world," a more balanced world, a world in which there were limits to what any single country could do.

U.S. leaders obviously did not view things the same way. From their point of view, the whole idea of an Iraq armed with weapons of mass destruction, especially nuclear weapons, was intolerable. They took it for granted that the threat of force, or perhaps even the actual use of force, was the one thing that might prevent Iraq from moving ahead with her weapons program. But the German government wanted to rule out the use of force no matter what. "In the 21st century," Foreign Minister Fischer said, "you can't use war to force disarmament."[18] And the French, especially after January, seemed to take much the same line. "War," President Chirac said over and over again, "is always the worst of solutions."[19] For the U.S. government, which was inclined to view a nuclear-armed Iraq as the "worst of solutions," the Germans and even the French had apparently opted for what was in the final analysis a policy of appeasement. And many Americans deeply resented both the sort of anti-U.S. rhetoric coming out of Europe and the sort of policy the French and German governments were pursuing, especially from January 2003 on. The Bush administration was particularly angry with the French for (in its view) having led the United States down the garden path. The French government, it felt, had essentially reneged on the deal Villepin and Powell had worked out in September: a "senior administration official" later told reporters that the diplomatic process "had been going well" until "France stabbed the United States in the back."[20]

---

[17] Quoted in "More Europe," *Der Spiegel*, March 31, 2003.

[18] Fischer interview with *Stern* magazine, March 5, 2003.

[19] See, for example, Chirac and Schröder interview with Olivier Mazerolle and Ulrich Wickert, January 22, 2003, and Chirac-Schröder joint press conference, January 22, 2003.

[20] David Sanger, "Bush Links Europe's Ban on Bio-Crops with Hunger," *New York Times*, May 22, 2003. See also Alexandra Stanley, "Two Disciples Spread Word: The End is

On the surface, the crisis seemed to blow over fairly quickly. U.S. leaders threatened that the French would pay a price for their behavior, but it soon became clear that they had only trivial reprisals in mind. Chirac had warned the eastern Europeans that their support for America during the crisis would "reduce their chances" of entering the European Union.[21] But the Americans at no point warned France and Germany that their actions were putting their alliance with the United States at risk. For Kennedy in 1963, the threat to withdraw the American troops from Europe, and thus effectively to end the alliance, was the only real sanction the Americans had. But forty years later, the Bush administration made no such threat. The Americans, in fact, were soon stressing their continuing commitment to the NATO system, and indeed soon both sides were more or less trying to sweep all the problems that had emerged under the rug.[22]

My basic premise here is that this is not a healthy way of dealing with the issue. I think that some basic questions that emerged during the crisis need to be discussed openly and seriously. So instead of focusing on the question of how U.S. policy in the run-up to the Iraq war is to be assessed, or how the policies of the various allied governments are to be judged, I want to try to analyze some of the fundamental issues that this episode brought to the surface. How much of a problem, first of all, would the development of a mass destruction capability by a regime like that of Iraq in 2002 have actually posed? Aren't nuclear weapons, and their biological and perhaps chemical equivalents, essentially unusable, when both sides in a conflict are armed with them? Wouldn't the development of an Iraqi nuclear capability have led to mutual deterrence and thus to a relatively stable strategic relationship? To the extent that an Iraqi capability of this sort would have posed serious problems, couldn't the Iraqis have been prevented permanently from developing such forces through nonmilitary means? Couldn't an inspection regime have done the trick? And if the control regime wasn't up to the job, would it be legitimate for a country to act essentially on its own, without first getting explicit U.N. Security Council authorization? Was unilateral action impermissible under international law, and

---

Near," *New York Times*, March 17, 2003; Elisabeth Bumiller, "U.S., Angry at French Stance on War, Considers Punishment," *New York Times*, April 24, 2003; Elaine Sciolino, "France Works to Limit Damage from U.S. Anger," *New York Times*, April 25, 2003; and especially Weisman, "Long, Winding Road," and Champion et al., "Allies at Odds."

[21] Chirac's remarks were widely reported in the press. See, for example, Ian Black, "Threat of War: Furious Chirac Hits Out at 'Infantile' Easterners," *The Guardian* (London), February 18, 2003. For the remarks themselves, see Chirac press conference, February 17, 2003.

[22] James Dao, "Powell Says to the French, Yes . . . but Not All Is Forgiven," *New York Times*, May 23, 2003.

is a country that dealt with the problem in that way to be branded a law-breaker? These are not the only important issues that need to be dealt with, but they are important enough, and they are the ones I want to focus on here.

THE QUESTION OF DETERRENCE

There is no question, in my mind at any rate, that the weapons of mass destruction issue—not so much what the Iraqis actually had, but what they were in all probability going to have if no action were taken—lay at the heart of the Iraq crisis.[23] The U.S. government would have been willing to live with the Saddam Hussein regime if it had not thought that that regime had active nuclear, biological, and chemical weapons programs. Even the claim that Iraq had various ties with terrorist groups would not in itself have warranted military action if it had been clear that the regime had honored its commitments and had abandoned all programs for the production of forbidden weapons.[24] And although no such weapons were found in Iraq in the postwar period, and although in all probability none will ever be found, it does not follow that the Bush administration's concern with this issue was artificially trumped up to rationalize a policy of "regime change" that had an entirely different basis. The fear was real; even the German and French authorities believed that Iraq had active programs for the development

[23] To be sure, this view is not universally accepted. In France, for example, a March 2003 poll showed that only 3 percent of those questioned thought the main motivation of the United States for going to war was to "disarm Iraq"; 49 percent thought it was to "take control of Iraq's petroleum resources" (http://www.ifop.com/europe/sondages/opinionf/jgtirak.asp). Indeed, many people have claimed, especially after no such weapons were actually found in Iraq, that the argument about Iraqi weapons of mass destruction was artificially trumped up, to serve as a pretext for a war that the Bush administration wanted to conduct for other reasons. But the fact that an assessment turned out to be mistaken is no proof that it was simply fabricated, and there are many reasons why the argument that the Bush administration was lying on this matter is simply implausible. Henry Kissinger, for example, made one key point in a September 2003 interview: "I attended many closed hearings in Washington, and it is impossible to imagine that representatives of the US administration constantly lied to each other at such hearings when they were talking about Iraqi weapons of mass destruction." Y. Verlin and D. Suslov, "Henry Kissinger: Iraq is an Exception, Not the Rule," *Nexavisimaya Gazeta*, September 17, 2003. For the basic point that the "U.S. intelligence community's belief that Saddam was aggressively pursuing weapons of mass destruction pre-dated Bush's inauguration, and therefore cannot be attributed to political pressure," see Kenneth Pollack's important article, "Spies, Lies, and Weapons: What Went Wrong," *Atlantic Monthly*, January–February 2004.

[24] See, for example, Kenneth Pollack, *The Threatening Storm: The Case for Invading Iraq* (New York: Random House, 2002), pp. xxii, 153–58.

of those prohibited weapons. In early 2002, August Hanning, the head of the German equivalent of the CIA, the BND, said that his agency thought that the Iraqis would "have an atomic bomb in three years."[25] In February 2003, Hanning and other BND officials reportedly told a Bundestag committee that they "believed Iraq had mobile laboratories capable of developing and producing chemical and biological weapons."[26] And in a March 10, 2003, interview, President Chirac himself referred to an "Iraq which obviously possessed weapons of mass destruction, which were in the hands of an indisputably dangerous regime and consequently posed a definite threat to the world."[27] Indeed, the most reasonable inference to be drawn from the story of the U.N. inspection system in the 1990s was that Iraq was determined to move ahead in this area—to do whatever she could get away with. The control regime, of course, had kept Iraq from moving ahead as quickly as she would have liked, but as that regime unraveled, it seemed that nothing would stop her from going ahead with those programs.

But would it have mattered all that much if Iraq had been able to build even a strong nuclear force? Wouldn't the U.S. government have been able to deter the Iraqis from ever actually using those weapons against America or against any of their neighbors? If so, why would an Iraqi nuclear capability have posed a problem? If nuclear weapons are good only for defensive purposes, then why shouldn't countries be allowed to acquire them (or their equivalents)?

In the United States, the most serious criticism of U.S. policy in the crisis turned on this one absolutely fundamental point: that is, on the argument that nuclear weapons cannot be used for coercive purposes—on the idea that in a conflict neither the Iraqis nor their adversaries would have dared to use their nuclear weapons against each other. Indeed, the claim is that they would not even have dared to use non-nuclear forces in a major way. The use of force would have been too risky, given the nature of the weaponry both sides had. If Iraq had acquired nuclear weapons, the prospect of nuclear escalation, this argument runs, would have led to a stable peace, just as it (supposedly) had during the Cold War.

---

[25] Quoted in Jeffrey Goldberg, "The Great Terror," *The New Yorker*, March 25, 2002 (toward the end of the article). Note also the evidence from non-U.S. sources cited in Julian Borger, "Saddam 'will have nuclear weapons material by 2005,'" *The Guardian* (London), August 1, 2002. Richard Butler, the former U.N. chief weapons inspector, was quoted there as saying that "there is now evidence that Saddam has reinvigorated his nuclear weapons programme in the inspection-free years."

[26] Article in the German weekly *Focus* quoted in Agence France Presse report, February 2, 2003. See also "What Now, Mr. President?" cover story in *Der Spiegel*, February 17, 2003.

[27] Chirac interview with TF1 and France 2 (excerpts), March 10, 2003 (http://www.diplomatie.gouv.fr/actu/bulletin.gb.asp?liste=20030311.gb.html).

A number of leading American international relations scholars argue along these lines, but I think they're wrong.[28] If Iraq had developed a nuclear capability, it could, I think, have readily been used for coercive purposes. It could easily have been made clear to the Americans—not by making a direct threat, but (in order to reduce the risk of retaliation) in the guise of a simple prediction—that a continuing American presence in the Gulf, for example, would have led to continuing terrorist attacks against America. It is often assumed, of course, that Iraq could never have implemented such a strategy, because the United States could have made it clear that any such attack would had led to a devastating counterattack: Iraq would essentially have been wiped out if anything of that sort had been attempted. And administration officials have repeatedly warned that the use of massive counter-civilian weapons against America would lead to extremely harsh retaliation. In an article published during the 2000 presidential campaign, for example, Condoleezza Rice, later President Bush's national security advisor, wrote that if countries like Iraq and North Korea acquired weapons of mass destruction, those weapons would be "unusable, because any attempt to use them will bring national obliteration."[29] But if top officials honestly believed that they were truly unusable, the US government could have looked on calmly as such states acquired those kinds of capabilities. The fact that it was willing to go to extraordinary lengths to prevent a country like Iraq from being able to build forces of that sort shows that it understood that a massive counterattack would not be automatic, and that the deterrent effect is therefore far from absolute.

And why is it less than absolute? Suppose the Iraqis developed a nuclear arsenal and adopted a coercive strategy of the sort I just described, and suppose the United States did not accede to whatever demands the Iraqis put forward. And then suppose a bomb or two were exploded on American soil. How then would the U.S. government respond? Would it simply destroy Iraq, even if there were no proof the Iraqi government was behind the attacks? Presumably if America were attacked in this way, the Iraqis would have gone to great lengths to conceal their responsibility. *Direct* threats would not have been issued, and the operation would have been conducted clandestinely, perhaps with a foreign terrorist organization serving as a vehicle of attack. The

[28] The most important example is the argument Kenneth Waltz develops in the chapters he wrote in a book jointly authored with Scott Sagan, *The Spread of Nuclear Weapons: A Debate Renewed* (New York: Norton, 2003). For a critique, see the review I wrote of this book published in *The National Interest* (Fall 2002); a better version of that review is available online (http://www.polisci.ucla.edu/faculty/trachtenberg/cv/prolif.doc).

[29] Quoted in "Serving Notice of a New America that is Poised to Strike First and Alone," *New York Times*, January 27, 2003.

Americans would have their suspicions, but in the absence of evidence it might be very hard to hold the Iraqis accountable—at any rate in a way that would warrant the destruction of their whole country. Even if the preponderance of evidence strongly suggested that the Iraqis were responsible, it is by no means certain that the U.S. government would retaliate by killing millions of Iraqi civilians—innocent by its own reckoning—above all if it believed that such an attack would have led to additional Iraqi counterattacks against the United States or its allies. Would more limited operations—for example, a conventional attack aimed at the overthrow of the Iraqi government—be possible in such a case? If the Iraqis had any nuclear weapons at all, the United States might be very reluctant to launch an attack against a regime whose back was against the wall. Given all these considerations, it would not be absurd or irrational for Iraq to judge that the risks were limited and thus to opt for a coercive strategy. And indeed there is a good chance that such a strategy, if adopted, would have the desired effect. The Americans, anticipating the problems they would face, might give way and allow themselves to be pushed out of the Gulf, or indeed out of the Middle East as a whole. But there would also be a certain probability, in such circumstances, that these devastating weapons would actually have been used, by one or both sides.

All of this may sound somewhat speculative, but it is important to note that the U.S. government was actually concerned with problems of this sort. Indeed, one of the main reasons why nuclear proliferation was thought to be a problem had to do with the fact that it was understood that even small nuclear arsenals could be used to support a coercive policy. Thomas Schelling, for example, in a top-secret report written for the U.S. government in 1962, had considered the possibility of "extortionate use" by countries with small nuclear arsenals. He noted that countries might profitably adopt a policy of exploiting that kind of threat; and he thought in particular that the "strategy of anonymous attack" needed to be examined.[30]

The same sort of concern (but focusing on the threat posed by biological and not nuclear weapons) surfaced during the Gulf Crisis in 1990. The CIA at that time warned that it could not "rule out that Iraq may have contingency plans to use biological weapons covertly." Iraq, it thought, "could attack targets out of range of even its missiles by using special forces, civilian government agents, or foreign terrorists to hand-deliver biological or chemical agents clandestinely."[31] The point

[30] Schelling Study Group Report, "Report on Strategic Developments over the Next Decade for the Inter-Agency Panel," October 12, 1962, pp. 51–55 (pp. 54–55 for the quotations), in National Security Files, box 376, John F. Kennedy Library, Boston.

[31] Avigdor Haselkorn, *The Continuing Storm: Iraq, Poisonous Weapons, and Deterrence* (New Haven: Yale University Press, 1999), p. 68.

about clandestine attack came up again in 2002 as the Iraq problem again began to heat up. Secretary of Defense Donald Rumsfeld, for example, told a congressional committee that the United States needed to be concerned about the threat posed by Iraqi biological weapons (BW). Such weapons, he said, were "simpler to deliver" than nuclear weapons, and could readily be "transferred to terrorist networks, who could allow Iraq to deliver them without Iraq's fingerprints."[32] Charles Duelfer, formerly deputy head of UNSCOM, the U.N. inspection organization for Iraq, and an acknowledged expert in this area, had made the same kind of point in Congressional testimony earlier that year. "BW," he said, "is the most difficult present threat posed by Iraq. They certainly have the capacity to deploy it clandestinely or through surrogates should the regime so decide."[33] In fact, before the Gulf War the Iraqis had themselves suggested that Arab terrorists in the West could serve as instruments of attack.[34]

So the problems an Iraqi nuclear capability would have posed were very real, especially in a world where large-scale terrorism was a fact of life.

INSPECTIONS: A VIABLE SOLUTION?

The prevailing view in the United States during the Iraq crisis was that Saddam Hussein had to be prevented from acquiring a nuclear capability or its equivalent. Many Europeans were also disturbed by the prospect of nuclear or even biological weapons in the hands of the Iraqi dictator. And those attitudes were by no means absurd. But it was one thing to recognize that a serious problem existed and would have to be dealt with, and quite another to say that an invasion of Iraq was the only solution. And indeed those who opposed military action generally argued that a peaceful solution was within reach, and that an inspection regime was a viable alternative to war.

But does that view really stand up to analysis? If the use of force were ruled out (as the Germans, for example, wanted), why would the Iraqis have complied with an effective inspection regime? And how could in-

---

[32] Donald Rumsfeld, Testimony before House Armed Services Committee, September 18, 2002 (http://www.defenselink.mil/speeches/2002/s20020918-secdef2.html).

[33] Charles Duelfer, "Weapons of Mass Destruction Programs in Iraq," testimony before the Subcommittee on Emerging Threats and Capabilities, US Senate Armed Services Committee, February 27, 2002 (http://www.senate.gov/~armed_services/statemnt/2002/Duelfer.pdf).

[34] See Haselkorn, *Continuing Storm*, pp. 67–68, and Lawrence Freedman and Efraim Karsh, *The Gulf Conflict, 1990-1991: Diplomacy and War in the New World Order* (Princeton: Princeton University Press, 1993), pp. 52, 344–45.

spections have provided any effective guarantee that Iraq no longer had any stockpiles of forbidden weapons, nor any programs for the development of such weapons, when the Iraqi government could easily prevent well-informed Iraqis from talking openly with the inspectors? Perhaps on occasion violations would be uncovered, but if those discoveries had no consequences for the regime beyond the destruction of the forbidden material that had been found, how much of a deterrent effect would the inspection regime actually have?[35] In the view of U.S. specialists, and not just people connected with the Bush administration, "an inspection regime that fails to give us high confidence that it is successfully uncovering and blocking any serious WMD development is worse than no regime at all."[36] If nothing were uncovered, people would say that this proves there was nothing to be found and that further action would therefore be unwarranted. If the inspectors, however, did find something, the Iraqis would destroy it, and that would be the end of it. People would in that case say that this again proved that "inspections were working" and that there was therefore no basis for military action. In either case, the effect of the inspection regime would be to shield Iraq and enable it to go ahead with her clandestine weapons programs essentially with impunity.

During the crisis, problems of this sort—the problems related to the forcible disarmament of Iraq—did not receive anything like the attention they deserved. There was not enough attention given on either side of the Atlantic to what might be called the theory of an inspection regime. There was not enough attention given in 2002 to the history of the inspection regime in the 1990s, and to the lessons that might be drawn from that story. Most of the Americans familiar with that story had come to the conclusion that the regime had not worked.[37] It was important at that point to try to understand why it had failed; it was important in that context to try to deal with the question of how a new inspection regime could possibly succeed. But the U.S. government did not push the issue: it did not push the advocates of inspections onto the defensive, by demanding to know how the new regime that was proposed would overcome the problems that had led to the failure of the

[35] See Robert Gallucci's discussion of the inspection regime as it actually functioned during the UNSCOM period. The basic rule was, he points out, "if you find it, you get to destroy it; if you don't destroy it, we get to keep it." Quoted in Jean Krasno and James Sutterlin, *The United Nations and Iraq: Defanging the Viper* (Westport, Conn.: Praeger, 2003), p. 80. Gallucci was deputy executive director of UNSCOM in 1991–92.

[36] Robert Gallucci testimony, 107th Congress, 2nd session, U.S. Senate Foreign Relations Committee, "Hearings to Examine Threats, Consequences and Regional Considerations Surrounding Iraq," July 31, 2002, p. 66.

[37] See, especially, Charles Duelfer, "The Inevitable Failure of Inspections in Iraq," *Arms Control Today* 32, no. 7 (September 2002).

old regime. And in Europe, there was no great interest in examining the issue carefully: if an inspection regime was the alternative to war, what point was there to questioning the viability of such a regime?

So the issue was not dealt with seriously by either side, and the American government, in particular, did not handle this question very skillfully. But the fact that it did not make its case very effectively did not prevent many Americans close to these issues from sensing the problems with the notion that one could deal with the situation by re-establishing an inspection regime. For one thing, they viewed it as odd, to say the least, that the French, who had done their best to weaken the control regime in the 1990s, were now presenting themselves as the champions of inspections.[38] And in Europe, although people rarely went into these issues in great depth, it was widely believed that the Americans were much too quick to give up on inspections. But this is the sort of issue that can be analyzed in a relatively sober way. And to do that, one of the main things we need is a serious political history of the control issue—that is, inspections plus sanctions—from 1991 to 2003, preferably based in large part on captured Iraqi documents. The war may be over, but how Europeans and Americans feel about each other might depend to a certain extent on how issues of this sort are resolved, and one can at least try to think these issues through in the light of the empirical evidence.

THE UNITED STATES AND INTERNATIONAL LAW

One of the most serious charges leveled against the United States in the European press, and indeed by some European governments, was that the American government was not acting in accordance with international law. Those charges were echoed by an important body of American opinion; many international law scholars, in particular, saw things in much the same way. The standard argument was that, largely as a result of America's own efforts, a legal system had come into being at the end of World War II. That system, embodied in the U.N. Charter, and based on the principle of the sovereign equality of all states, had "served as the framework of international relations for the past half century."[39] The U.N. regime had established real limits on the use of

---

[38] For the U.S. view on this point, see especially Fareed Zakaria, "Message to the Foot-Draggers," *Washington Post*, September 24, 2002: "The dust from the Persian Gulf War had not settled when the French government began a quiet but persistent campaign to gut the sanctions against Iraq, turn inspections into a charade and send signals to Saddam Hussein that Paris was ready to do business with him again."

[39] Tom Farer, "Beyond the Charter Frame: Unilateralism or Condominium?" *American Journal of International Law* 96, no. 2 (April 2002): 360.

force; international politics had been "legally domesticated"; instead of a world of unconstrained violence, one had a world based at least to some extent on the rule of law—that is, on respect for basic legal principles.[40]

But now it seemed that the Bush administration was determined to take whatever measures it felt were needed to deal with developments which in its view threatened American security whether those measures were lawful or not. The U.S. government felt free to act "preemptively"—that is, to deal with developing threats through military action well before attacks on America were actually mounted.[41] It would not respect the sovereign rights of countries it viewed as hostile to do whatever they wanted on their own territory—not if those countries shielded terrorists, or were developing weapons that might pose a threat to America, and especially not if those two threats were combined. And it would feel free to take any necessary action, in the final analysis, on its own: it felt it had the "sovereign right" to move ahead without first getting authorization from the U.N. Security Council. The United States, in other words, this argument runs, had broken with tradition and had opted for a "strategy of violence"—for a world in which the strong did whatever they wanted, unconstrained by any legal principle whatsoever. America had thus broken with the rule of law; the claim was that the United States was bringing about a lawless, dangerous, and exceptionally violent world.[42]

American policy toward Iraq after September 11 was interpreted in light of what the Americans were saying about their general strategy. The U.S. government and its supporters had little trouble coming up with a legal justification for America's Iraq policy. The argument was that the use of force against Iraq, a country that everyone agreed had not fully complied with the obligations it had accepted at the end of the Gulf War in 1991, had been legitimated by a whole series of Security Council resolutions, especially by Resolution 687, the famous "mother of all resolutions."[43] But whether valid or not, in a sense this was a

---

[40] The allusion here is to Jürgen Habermas's reference to the "civilizing achievement of legally domesticating the state of nature among belligerent nations" in an interview published in *The Nation*, December 16, 2002.

[41] For an attempt to place this strategy in historical context, see my article "The Bush Strategy in Historical Perspective," to be published in a volume edited by James Wirtz.

[42] See, for example, Charles Lambroschini, "Le droit ne se divise pas," *Le Figaro*, February 21, 2003. Note also Chancellor Schröder's views, as paraphrased in a cover story, "More Europe," published in *Der Spiegel* on March 31, 2003, and especially the reference there to how "the law of the more powerful has replaced the law." For the views of a very eminent French student of international affairs, see Pierre Hassner, "Le retour aux guerres sans règles," *Les Echos*, October 17, 2002: Hassner makes many of these same points.

[43] See, for example, a speech given by the State Department legal advisor, William

purely technical point. The U.S. decision to launch a military operation was bound to be interpreted in the context of the Bush doctrine. Whatever the technical legal justification, the war on Iraq was publicly justified, and is in fact to be understood, as a "preemptive" war.[44] The U.S. government made it clear during the crisis that it felt (as Secretary of State Powell put it) that the United States had the "sovereign right to take military action against Iraq alone."[45] U.N. resolution or no U.N. resolution, the United States felt it had the right to legitimately take action of this sort.

So the real issue here has to do with that basic claim—that is, with the question of the legitimacy under international law of "anticipatory self-defense." And it is important to note that the prevailing, although by no means universal, view among even American students of international law is that the Bush administration view is legally untenable, and that under international law, at least as it has existed since 1945, the right of self-defense is very narrowly circumscribed.[46] According to Article 2, paragraph 4, of the U.N. Charter, all member states are to "refrain in their international relations from the threat or use of force against the territorial integrity or political independence of any state, or in any manner inconsistent with the Purposes of the United Nations." Under the charter, the U.N. Security Council would alone have the right to authorize the use of force. The one exception, provided for in article 51 of the charter, was that states would still have the right, both individually and collectively, to defend themselves against armed attack, pending Security Council action. But that right applied only to the case of actual attack, and not, for example, to a case where attack was merely threatened. The scope for unilateral action was thus evidently very narrow; and with the one exception relating to an actual armed attack, the unilateral use of force, the argument runs, was now legally impermissible, even when what a country honestly saw as its "vital interests"

Howard Taft IV, to the National Association of Attorneys General on March 20, 2003 (http://usinfo.state.gov/regional/nea/iraq/text2003/032129taft.htm).

[44] See especially the text of Vice President Cheney's August 26, 2002, speech (Remarks by the Vice President to the Veterans of Foreign Wars) cited in note 9 of this chapter.

[45] Excerpts from Secretary of State Powell's Davos speech of January 26, 2003, published in the *New York Times*, January 27, 2003.

[46] For a strong dissenting argument, see especially the works of Michael J. Glennon: "The Fog of Law: Self-Defense, Inherence, and Incoherence in Article 51 of the United Nations Charter," *Harvard Journal of Law and Public Policy* 25 (Spring 2002); "Preempting Terrorism: The Case for Anticipatory Self-Defense," *Weekly Standard*, January 28, 2002; and *Limits of Law, Prerogatives of Power: Interventionism after Kosovo* (New York: Oalgrave, 2001). See also Thomas Franck, "Terrorism and the Right of Self-Defense," *American Journal of International Law* 95 (October 2001)—a reply to the charge leveled against the United States by a number of mainly German international lawyers that even the U.S. intervention in Afghanistan against al-Qaeda was unlawful.

were threatened.[47] A "presumption against self-help," it is said, lay at the heart of the U.N. system.[48] According to that interpretation, there was in fact not much that a state could do without Security Council sanction, unless it or one of its allies had actually been attacked. "With the right of self-defence in Art. 51 restricted to the case of armed attack," one scholar writes, "and with no further exception to Art. 2(4) allowing for the use of force by the individual State, the exercise of force for the enforcement of a vested right or for the purpose of ending another State's unlawful behaviour is prohibited."[49] Even reprisals were legally permissible only if they did "not involve the use of armed force."[50]

What is to be made of this whole line of argument? To get at that question, we first have to deal with a more fundamental issue: what gives a certain principle, like the idea that military reprisals are impermissible, the force of law? How do we know that such a principle is legally binding? And those questions in turn are closely related to the general question of how international law is made, since no given principle is legally binding unless it is produced by a process that gives it the force of law. The law, after all, is not just sitting around someplace waiting to be discovered. It has to be created—and created by a process that gives people the sense that the principles that take shape are legally binding. But created by whom? Legal scholars, obviously, do not have the right to actually make the law; the principles they put forward are not legally binding simply because they say they are. And there is no world parliament, no supra-national body with recognized legislative power. Even the U.N. General Assembly does not have the authority under the U.N.'s own charter to actually make law. Nor does the World Court have any law-making power. It does not even have the right under its own statute to issue legally binding interpretations of the law, except when states voluntarily agree to accept its jurisdiction.

How then is international law actually made? The only really plausible answer is that the law is made by the states themselves. "Governments derive their just powers from the consent of the governed," and in this case, it is the states who are the governed, and it is they themselves who in one way or another decide on the principles they are to be governed by. It is not as though the governments of the world have

[47] See, for example, Louis Henkin, *How Nations Behave: Law and Foreign Policy*, 2nd ed. (New York: Columbia University Press, 1979), pp. 137, 141, 155.

[48] Ian Brownlie, *International Law and the Use of Force by States* (New York: Oxford University Press, 1963), p. 268.

[49] Bruno Simma, ed., *The Charter of the United Nations: A Commentary*, 2nd ed. (New York: Oxford University Press, 2002) 1:794.

[50] Ibid.

had the basic principles of international law handed down to them. It is the states themselves who establish international law, by accepting in practice various principles that constrain their behavior, and especially by agreeing to treaties that define what those principles are. "International law," as the famous legal scholar Lasso Oppenheim pointed out long ago, "is a law not above but between states."[51] As a result, the community of states has to accept a given principle as law for that principle to be legally binding. Some scholars go even further. "Each nation," Hans Morgenthau, for example, says, "is bound only by those rules of international law to which it has consented."[52] And this is not just a view that only the most hardened realist theorists hold. Even someone like Louis Henkin, whose thinking was by no means rooted in the realist tradition, made essentially the same point. "In principle," he wrote, "new law, at least, cannot be imposed on any state; even old law cannot survive if enough states, or a few powerful and influential ones, reject it."[53]

It is in this context that the basic texts—above all, the U.N. Charter—that define the international legal order need to be interpreted. If the Charter is to be taken seriously, the governments that drafted it would have had to be serious about bringing a new legal regime into being. It follows that to see what new law was really being created, one has to understand what new obligations governments at the time thought they were taking on. When they agreed to the U.N. Charter, what did the founders of the United Nations think they were doing? What sorts of constraints—that is, new constraints—did they think the U.N. Charter would impose on their future behavior? Did they really believe that the use of force, unless it was explicitly authorized by the Security Council, would no longer be legally permissible, except in the event a state was responding to an actual armed attack on itself or an ally?

The only way to get at the answers is to look at the historical evidence—that is, to look at evidence that throws some real light on the question of what the governments understood the charter to mean when that document was first hammered out. And to understand what they had in mind, it is important not just to look at the record of what was said publicly in the formal discussions at the conferences at which the charter was drafted. If the goal is to understand how people really felt—and not just to understand the line governments were taking in

[51] Lasso Oppenheim, "The Science of International Law: Its Task and Method," *American Journal of International Law* 2, no. 2 (April 1908), 322; see also 332–33.

[52] Hans Morgenthau, *Politics among Nations,* 3rd ed. (New York: Knopf, 1961), p. 279. Morgenthau himself, one should remember, had begun his career as a student of international law.

[53] Henkin, *How Nations Behave,* p. 23.

public—it is obviously essential to look at sources that were secret at the time—the records, for example, of key meetings in which responsible officials expressed their views.[54] And the most important readily available source of this sort—most important, because the U.S. government played the leading role in drafting the U.N. Charter—is the first volume in the U.S. State Department's *Foreign Relations of the United States* series for 1945, the volume dealing with U.N. affairs.

What the evidence in that volume shows is that the U.S. drafters did not believe that they were giving away very much by accepting the charter. According to John Foster Dulles, then a key member of the delegation to the conference drafting that document, the principle that would eventually become article 2(4) of the charter gave the United States pretty much a free hand to use force whenever it liked. Under that principle, he pointed out, the member states "pledged to refrain from the use of force in a manner inconsistent with the purposes of the organization. Since the prevention of aggression was a purpose of the organization, action to prevent aggression in the absence of action by the Security Council would be consistent with the purposes of the organization." That meant that there would be no legal constraint on what the United States could do. As Senator Arthur Vandenberg, the leading Republican on the delegation, noted, Dulles's "point reduced itself to the principle that we have the right to do anything we please in self-defense."[55]

Administration representatives saw things much the same way. Leo Pasvolsky, a key State Department official concerned with U.N. matters, also thought that under the charter as it was being drafted, "if the Security Council fails to agree on an act, then the member state reserves the right to act for the maintenance of peace, justice, etc." "There was certainly no statement in the text" being drafted, he said, "under which we would give up our right of independent action." This was not a trivial point. The British, in fact, as Pasvolsky pointed out, had been "shocked" by how expansive the "American concept of self-defense was."[56]

Indeed, Vandenberg himself had been shocked. He did not dispute the Dulles-Pasvolsky interpretation. But people, he said, "would be disillusioned beyond words" when they came to see what the plan was.

[54] The historian's approach in this regard is somewhat at variance with that of legal scholars, who generally play down the importance of this kind of evidence. See, for example, Simma, ed., *Charter of the United Nations*, 1:27.

[55] Meetings of the U.S. Delegation to the San Francisco Conference, May 4, May 7, and May 8, 1945, FRUS 1945, 1:637, 648; see also p. 593.

[56] Meetings of U.S. Delegation to the San Francisco Conference, May 7 and 12, 1945, FRUS 1945, 1:637, 677.

He had thought that there had been "a general renunciation of the right to use force," but this too, he was told by Senator Connally, the most important Democrat in the delegation, "was not the case."[57] To be sure, the wording was not as explicit as it might have been, but that was only because it was felt that more explicit phrasing might give the Russians too free a hand, not because the Americans were prepared to accept real limitations on their own freedom of action—above all, in the western hemisphere, an area when they claimed "preclusive rights." As Connally put it in this context, "The United States must be able to take care of itself."[58]

The U.N. system, moreover, was built on the assumption that the major powers would be able to act as a bloc. States might be asked to forgo the right of self-help if the larger community was able and willing to come to their aid; but if the system did not provide for their security, and if the system did not protect their rights, they could hardly be expected to abide by the rules against self-help. This rather obvious point has been made by a number of distinguished legal theorists. "It is reasonable to restrict self-help against violations of the law," Hans Kelsen wrote, "only insofar as self-help is replaced by effective collective security." And Julius Stone took it for granted that it did not make sense to rule out forceful self-help by individual states when the Security Council is unable to work as a bloc and no "effective collective measures are available for the remedy of just grievances."[59] But what is important to note here is that this point was recognized even in 1945. The Americans took it for granted that if the U.N. system failed, the right of self-help would revert to the member states.[60] And the official British commentary on the charter noted that "the successful working of the United Nations depends on the preservation of the unanimity of the Great Powers," that "if this unanimity is seriously undermined no provision of the Charter is likely to be of much avail," and that "in such a case the

[57] Ibid., p. 637.

[58] Meetings of the U.S. Delegation to the San Francisco, May 4 and 12, 1945, FRUS 1945, 1:591 ("preclusive rights"), 593, 680. Note also General Embick's reference in the May 4 meeting to the need for America to maintain "preclusive control over this hemisphere" (p. 594).

[59] Hans Kelsen, *Principles of International Law*, 2nd ed. (New York: Holt, Rinehart and Winston, 1966), p. 38; Julius Stone, *Aggression and World Order: A Critique of United Nations Theories of Aggression* (Berkeley and Los Angeles: University of California Press, 1958), pp. 93–98; the quotation is on p. 96. Note also the passage from Judge Sir Robert Jennings's partial dissent in the *Nicaragua* case, quoted in Thomas Franck, *Recourse to Force: State Action Against Threats and Armed Attacks* (New York: Cambridge University Press, 2002), pp. 62–63.

[60] Note Leo Pasvolsky's remarks in the May 12, 1945, meeting of the US delegation to the San Francisco Conference, FRUS 1945, 1:677, and also in the May 7 meeting, FRUS 1945, 1:639.

Members will resume their liberty of action."[61] Such documents show what was in the minds of the governments at the time; they show that they had by no means set out to build the sort of legal structure most international law scholars today assume had been brought into being in 1945. They by no means thought that the use of force without Security Council sanction and for purposes other than defense against actual armed attack would be legally impermissible no matter how divided the great powers were—no matter how poorly, that is, the Security Council regime functioned. The states, in other words, never intended to create a legal regime that would tie their hands too tightly, a regime that would be binding no matter how poorly the U.N. system worked.

But the law is defined not simply by the intent of the drafters. It is also to be interpreted in the light of, and indeed as a product of, subsequent state behavior. And the key point to note here is that not one of the leading powers—not one of the five permanent members of the Security Council—was prepared in practice to limit its use of force in the way the charter seemed to imply. The examples are too well known to need repeating here, but let me talk about two cases, France and post-Soviet Russia. France was particularly vociferous in condemning the U.S. invasion of Iraq as illegal because it was undertaken without explicit Security Council authorization.[62] And yet the French themselves had frequently intervened militarily in what they view as their sphere of influence in "francophone" Africa without first getting U.N. sanction.[63] As for post-Soviet Russia, that country has occasionally intervened (without U.N. authorization) in what the Russians see as their sphere of influence in the "near abroad"—in Moldova, Tajikistan, and Georgia.[64] In September 2002 Russian President Vladimir Putin threat-

---

[61] Great Britain, Foreign Office, *A Commentary on the Charter of the United Nations*, Cmd. 6666 of 1945 (London: HMSO, 1945), p. 17.

[62] Iraq Communiqué issued by the Presidency of the Republic, March 18, 2003.

[63] See, for example, Howard French, "France's Army Keeps Grip in African Ex-Colonies," *New York Times*, May 22, 1996; Louis Balmond (ed.), *Les Interventions militaires françaises en Afrique* (Paris: Pedone, 1998); and Claude Wauthier, *Quatre présidents et l'Afrique: De Gaulle, Pompidou, Giscard d'Estaing, Mitterrand: Quarante ans de politique africaine* (Paris: Seuil, 1995). See also the revealing memoir written by the head of the French intelligence service in the 1970s: Count Alexandre de Marenches (with Christine Ockrent), *Dans le secret des princes* (Paris: Stock, 1986), and translated into English (and with David Andelman as co-author) as *The Fourth World War: Diplomacy and Espionage in the Age of Terrorism* (New York: Morrow, 1992). See especially, in the translated edition, pp. 129–30, for the reference to the many actions involving the use of force, including assassinations of heads of state, undertaken by France in Africa, and pp. 191–96, for a discussion of an important operation in the Central African Empire.

[64] See Andrew Bennett, *Condemned to Repetition? The Rise, Fall, and Reprise of Soviet-Russian Military Interventionism, 1973–1996* (Cambridge, Mass.: MIT Press, 1999), pp. 311–21, and (for the absence of a U.N. mandate), pp. 318, 325–26.

ened to take military action if the Georgians did not prevent their territory from being used as a base for Chechen rebels: "Like America in Iraq, his officials claim, Russia is insisting on its right to take military action, alone if necessary, against a nation which it deems to be in breach of international law."[65] Two years earlier, Putin had made a similar threat to the Taliban authorities in Afghanistan.[66]

I bring these examples up not because I want to point to French or Russian hypocrisy in this area. Hypocrisy of this sort is perfectly normal in international politics and needs to be taken in stride. The real point has to do with the light such examples shed on the question of what international law actually is. The international legal regime is created by states, not by judges or legal scholars. But all the major states were prepared to use force without U.N. sanction for purposes other than self-defense, narrowly defined. It is scarcely conceivable that they would have created and sustained a legal regime that would have made them all into law-breakers.

It follows that the argument that the Americans acted "illegally" because force was used without explicit U.N. Security Council authorization is to be taken with a grain of salt. Indeed, it seems quite clear that this argument has to be interpreted in political terms.[67] A legal framework no one ever took too seriously in the past is now taken very seriously indeed—and from the U.S. point of view, this can only be because it serves the purposes of those hostile to U.S. policy, those who seek to use whatever instrument is at hand for bringing American power under some sort of control. By pushing a particular theory of international law, the goal, it seemed, was to limit U.S. freedom of action, a tactic that

---

[65] "Putin's Folly," *The Economist* [U.S. edition], September 21, 2002. The U.S. government condemned the Russians for "threatening unilateral action against Chechen targets on Georgian territory"—a foolish response, given what the Americans would soon end up doing in Iraq. "Echoing Bush, Putin Asks U.N. to Back Georgia Attack," *New York Times,* September 13, 2002. See also "Putin Warns Georgia to Root Out Chechen Rebels Within Its Borders or Face Attacks," *New York Times,* September 12, 2002, and "Putin Has His Own Candidate for Pre-emption," *New York Times,* October 6, 2002.

[66] Franck, *Recourse to Force,* p. 66.

[67] To capture the idea that juridical arguments are framed with political goals in mind, the French have developed the concept of a "foreign juridical policy." See Guy de Lacharrière, *La politique juridique extérieure* (Paris: Economica, 1983), and Michel Debré et al., eds., *Guy Ladreit de Lacharrière et la politique juridique extérieure de la France* (Paris: Masson, 1989). De Gaulle himself, incidentally, during the Cuban Missile Crisis explicitly supported the idea that American action was legal, even though the United States was not actually being attacked. "President Kennedy wishes to react, and to react now," he told Dean Acheson, who President Kennedy had sent over to brief him on U.S. policy in this affair, "and certainly France can have no objection to that since it is legal for a country to defend itself when it finds itself in danger." Acheson-de Gaulle meeting, October 22, 1962, FRUS 1961–63, 11:166.

was pursued in other areas as well. The aim, as Michael Ignatieff put it, was to tie America down, "like Gulliver with a thousand legal strings."[68]

But perhaps this is going too far. Governments may be cynical, but there is a serious case to be made by those who believe in the sort of legal regime they associate with the U.N. Charter at least as an ideal that we should try to move toward, and that case has to be examined on its own terms.

There are fundamental issues here that we need to try to grapple with. One of the most fundamental is the question of whether we really want a world in which force could be legitimately used only in response to armed attack. And the answer here is not as obvious as one might think. To rule out the use of force except in the case of armed aggression is to allow states to renege on their obligations with relative impunity. Does it make sense, for example, to have a legal system in which states in effect have the right to give shelter and support to terrorists? Does it make sense to set up a legal order that shields law-breakers (as long as their actions do not amount to an "armed attack") and requires law-abiding states "to submit indefinitely to admitted and persistent violations of rights"?[69] Is that what we mean by the "rule of law"?

The U.S. government, for one, never fully accepted the idea that lawless states could legitimately claim the protections of the international legal system. The "rule of law" might govern relations among states that basically accepted the international legal system. But when a country like the United States had to deal with a lawless power, a somewhat different set of rules applied. In 1941, for example, President Roosevelt rejected the German claim that America's policy of helping Britain was not in line with what was expected of a neutral power under international law. Given its own behavior, a state like Nazi Germany, Roosevelt thought, had no right to demand that the United States pursue a policy in accordance with traditional legal standards. It was absurd that one country would be bound by the rule of law, but not the other; it was absurd that international law would in effect privilege the lawless. A "one-way international law," a legal system that lacked "mutuality in its observance"—that, in his view, was utterly unacceptable. Such a system, the president said, would serve only as an "instrument of oppression."[70]

There is a basic problem with the idea that we should try to outlaw

---

[68] Michael Ignatieff, "The American Empire: The Burden," *New York Times Magazine*, January 5, 2003. Josef Joffe has used the same metaphor in many recent speeches and articles.

[69] Stone, *Aggression and World Order*, pp. 97 (for the quotation), 101.

[70] Franklin Roosevelt, Annual Message to the Congress, January 6, 1941, *Public Papers and Addresses of Franklin D. Roosevelt*, 1940 vol. (New York: Macmillan, 1941), p. 669.

the use of force except in response to armed attack. The problem is not just that it is out of touch with political reality. A more fundamental problem arises from the fact that armed conflict does not, as a general rule, result from a simple decision on the part of an aggressor to start a war. It is the outcome, generally speaking, of a political process, one that often takes many years to run its course. It is that process as a whole that needs to be controlled; it is a mistake to focus excessively on just one point in that process, the point at which the decision to use force is made. To concentrate all our legal firepower on that one point is to opt in effect for a rather unsophisticated who-fired-the-first-shot approach to the problem of war causation. It is overall policy, and not just policy at one key moment, that we should seek to influence; it is overall policy that we should therefore seek to judge; the principles we develop, the norms we come up with, should thus relate to policy as a whole. And it is by no means obvious (as the case of the 1930s shows) that policies that rule out the use of force will lead to a more stable international order. For if the goal is to influence the way an international conflict runs its course—that is, to try to make sure that it runs its course in such a way that the conflict is ultimately resolved peacefully—then it may be entirely proper, and indeed necessary, that power be brought to bear. Everything depends on circumstances. This approach, as Michael Walzer points out, "opens a broad path for human judgment—which it is, no doubt, the purpose of the legalist paradigm to narrow or block altogether."[71] But that fact is reason in itself to be wary of the legalist approach to these issues.

If power plays a central role in international politics—and in certain key areas of conflict, power is still clearly of fundamental importance—then the last thing that we should want is to give people the sense that they can ignore power realities with impunity—that they are sheltered by legal norms from retaliation and that they are free to act as irresponsibly as they like. We should want people to face up to realities, to accommodate to basic realities, and in that way to bring about a relatively stable international order.

For the really fundamental point to note here is that a world in which power considerations loom large is not a world of endless violence and destruction. A world based on power, in fact, has a certain stability: as the international relations theorists say, there can be "order without an orderer."[72] If international politics during the Cold War period was relatively stable, especially after 1963, it was not because the international legal system established in 1945 had taken the edge off of interstate vio-

[71] Michael Walzer, *Just and Unjust Wars: A Moral Argument with Historical Illustrations* (New York: Basic Books, 1977), p. 85
[72] This argument is developed in some detail in chapter 1 of this book.

lence. It is simply a mistake to assume that "U.N. Charter norms" actually "served as the framework of international relations for the past half century."[73] The U.N. regime, in fact, counted for very little. Key elements of the international system during that period—for example, the strategy of deterrence based on the threat of retaliation on an absolutely massive scale—were in fact wildly at variance with the international legal framework as the lawyers commonly portray it. "The lawyers," as Walzer says, "have constructed a paper world, which fails at crucial points to correspond to the world the rest of us still live in," and one has to wonder whether that enterprise has done more harm than good.[74]

When people today embrace those legalist conceptions, that position is bound to have major political implications. The prominence of those legal arguments in the political discourse relating to the Iraq crisis is striking, and they played an important role in the politics of the crisis. But those arguments are far more problematic than many people believe, and a more serious analysis of the international law side of the question might lead people to rethink their positions, or at least lead them to look at things in a somewhat different light.

The Crisis in the Alliance

The showdown with Iraq, Henry Kissinger wrote about a month before the war with that country broke out, had "produced the gravest crisis within the Atlantic Alliance since its creation five decades ago," and that view was shared by many observers on both sides of the Atlantic.[75] "It is possible we stand before an epochal break," German Foreign Minister Joschka Fischer declared in early March.[76] In the Iraq crisis, many European governments supported the United States to one degree or another, but European opinion was overwhelmingly opposed to what the U.S. government was doing. The European press, and especially the French press, was full of anti-American abuse, quite unparalleled by anything one saw in the leading American journals.[77] The Iraq crisis had triggered what Josef Joffe, co-editor of *Die Zeit* and an exceptionally well-informed observer of U.S.-European relations, called "an

---

[73] Farer, "Beyond the Charter Frame," 360.

[74] Walzer, *Just and Unjust Wars*, p. xiii.

[75] Henry Kissinger, "NATO's Split: Atlantic Alliance is in its Gravest Crisis," *San Diego Union-Tribune*, February 16, 2003.

[76] "Rumblings of War," *Der Spiegel* [English edition], March 10, 2003.

[77] On April 8, 2003, for example, *Le Monde* carried an article with the title "Bush, obscène mécanicien de l'empire." It is inconceivable that an anti-French article with a similarly inflammatory title would have been published at the time in the *New York Times*.

enormous wave of hatred against the United States."[78] The Americans, it seemed, were lawless, arrogant, and imperialistic—the French had in fact taken to referring to the United States as "the empire." After the war broke out, public opinion polls in France showed about a third of those questioned actually wanted Saddam to win.[79] Anti-American feeling in fact ran high throughout Europe. On April 7, 2003, for example, the *New York Times* carried an article on anti-Americanism in Greece. One well-known Greek critic of the United States was quoted there as calling the Americans "detestable, ruthless cowards and murderers of the people of the world."[80] And all of this had repercussions on the other side of the Atlantic. Many Americans read this sort of thing and thought to themselves: "and these people are supposed to be our *allies*? How can we be *allies* with people who feel that way about us?"

Some people say that what we saw in the run-up to the war with Iraq was just another crisis in the alliance, not fundamentally different from the sort of thing we have seen many times in the past. I have spent many years studying U.S.-European relations during the Cold War period, and my sense is that this view is fundamentally mistaken. This crisis *was* very different from the NATO crises of the Cold War period, even from the most serious of those crises, the crisis of early 1963. During that period, the Europeans and the Americans felt themselves basically to be on the same side. Whatever their differences, the U.S. government and the major European governments did not question each other's basic honesty. But in the case of the Iraq crisis, many Americans who follow these issues had the sense that some key European allies were inclined to take sides *against* the United States—that the goal was to balance *against* the American "hyperpower," to use Hubert Védrine's famous phrase. They were struck by how quick many in Europe were to jump to what were viewed as extreme anti-American conclusions—to assume, for example, that the Americans were lying about Iraq's weapons of mass destruction—and they were struck by the fact that the charge that the U.S. government was playing fast and loose with the truth in this area was itself rooted in a very cavalier use of the evidence.

Let me give a couple of examples of this, each involving Deputy Secretary of Defense Paul Wolfowitz. The first has to do with an interview he gave on May 9, 2003, which served as one of the bases for a story

[78] Quoted in Richard Bernstein, "Foreign Views of U.S. Darken After Sept. 11," *New York Times*, September 11, 2003.

[79] Referred to in Pierre Lellouche et al., "Après la guerre, renouons nos alliances," *Le Figaro*, April 8, 2003.

[80] Anthee Carassava, "Anti-Americanism in Greece is Reinvigorated by War," *New York Times*, April 7, 2003.

called "Bush's Brain Trust" published in the July 2003 issue of *Vanity Fair*; the story itself was released on May 29. According to that article, "Wolfowitz admitted that from the outset, contrary to so many claims from the White House, Iraq's supposed cache of W.M.D. had never been the most compelling casus belli. It was simply one of several: 'For bureaucratic reasons, we settled on one issue, weapons of mass destruction, because it was the one reason everyone could agree on.'"[81] This gave rise to a slew of articles saying, in effect, that Wolfowitz had admitted that the WMD issue was just a "pretext" for a war.[82] But it was quite clear from the transcript of Wolfowitz's taped interview with the *Vanity Fair* writer posted on the Pentagon website that this was a gross distortion of what Wolfowitz had said. His argument was that the WMD issue had been emphasized because it was the one issue that everyone agreed would justify military action against Iraq.[83] The other incident involving Wolfowitz had to do with his supposed admission that "oil was the main reason for military action against Iraq"; again, it turns out that he had said nothing of the sort, a point that again would not have been at all hard to discover.[84] It is not difficult to understand why incidents of this sort were often seen in America as evidence of a deeply ingrained anti-U.S. bias—of an "obsessive" attitude (to use Jean-François Revel's term), one that went far beyond what the evidence actually warranted.[85]

Many Americans, in other words, had the sense that there was a certain tendency in Europe in general, and especially in France, to think the worst of the United States. They were struck, for example, by the reaction in Europe to Secretary Powell's February 5, 2003, speech to the United Nations laying out the U.S. case on Iraq. A good deal of evidence was presented, and although the Iraqis dismissed that evidence as fabricated, the speech impressed most Americans who heard it as a serious and well-thought-out statement. But the mainstream European response was very different. "To Saddam's lies we can probably add

[81] Sam Tanenhaus, "Bush's Brain Trust," *Vanity Fair*, July 2003, p. 169.

[82] For examples of articles using the word "pretext", see "Rounds of Lies," *Der Spiegel*, June 27, 2003; Pierre Marcelle, "Les menteurs," *Libération*, June 4, 2003; and Jeffrey Sachs, "The Real Target of the War in Iraq was Saudi Arabia," *Financial Times* [London], August 13, 2003. There were articles with similar themes in the *Observer* (June 1, 2003), the *Independent* (May 30, 2003), and the *Guardian* (May 31, 2003).

[83] Paul Wolfowitz interview with Sam Tanenhaus, May 9, 2003 (http://www.defenselink.mil/transcripts/2003/tr20030509-depsecdef0223.html).

[84] See, for example, the story in the *Daily Mail* (London), June 5, 2003, p. 7, whose source was the German newspaper *Die Welt*. On this incident, see Sarah Baxter, "If It Makes America Look Bad, It Must Be True, Mustn't It?" *Sunday Times* [London], June 15, 2003.

[85] On this point, see especially Jean-François Revel, *L'obsession anti-américaine: son fonctionnement, ses causes, ses conséquences* (Paris: Plon, 2002).

the administration's own lies"—that was how Yves Thérard reacted in the *Figaro*, and many Europeans reacted that same way.[86] And when no forbidden weapons were found after the war, that suspicion tended to harden into an article of faith, as though a mistaken judgment was the same as a lie. That sort of reaction, as the more historically aware American commentators noted, represented quite a change from the past. In 1962, it was pointed out in this context, when the Americans offered to show de Gaulle the evidence about the Soviet missiles in Cuba, the French president said he did not need to be convinced: "great nations such as yours," he told the American envoy, Dean Acheson, "would not take a serious step if there were any doubt about evidence."[87] But that was obviously not the official French attitude during the Iraq crisis period.

What does all this mean about the future of the western alliance? Many people think that it does not mean all that much—that these problems will blow over as other problems have in the past and that the NATO alliance will remain intact. And it is certainly true that very few people in the United States today openly question the desirability of America's alliance with Europe. Even the expansion of NATO into eastern Europe was generally supported by both political parties—although one has the sense that that support was a mile wide and an inch deep. But NATO itself is still conventionally seen as a "cornerstone" of the international order: it has been around so long that people can scarcely imagine a world without it. If they are pushed on the issue, people will say the United States needs to work with Europe to deal with problems like international terrorism—as though cooperation would be impossible if the alliance were gone, and as though the Europeans would have less of an incentive to cooperate with America if the American security guarantee could no longer be taken for granted.

The U.S. government, moreover, no matter how it feels about France and Germany, is still reluctant (as I write this in June 2004) to even talk about withdrawing from the alliance for fear of embarrassing those European governments who, defying political feeling at home, sided with America in the crisis. The Bush administration does not want to betray the governments who took that position. And beyond that, a whole series of considerations having to do with the unhappy course that events in Iraq have taken in the postwar period now has to be taken into account. There is a certain sense today that the U.S. government has bitten off more than it can chew in Iraq and would like more European help to deal with the situation that has developed there. There is a cer-

---

[86] Yves Thérard, "Powell a dit," *Le Figaro*, February 6, 2003.

[87] See Fareed Zakaria, "A Dangerous Trust Deficit," *Newsweek*, February 10, 2003. De Gaulle's remark is quoted in that piece.

tain sense that the case for war was weaker, in retrospect, than it had seemed at the time the decision to attack Iraq was being made, and that there might be more to be said for the prevailing European view than many Americans had been prepared to admit before the war. And, above all, there is a certain sense that something has to be done about the fact that feeling throughout the world has turned so sharply against the United States, and that the country perhaps needs to start rebuilding its relations with those powers who in the past had been its closest allies. For all these reasons, the U.S. government has tended to take a rather mild line on alliance issues in the post–Iraq war period.

But still one has to wonder about the future of the alliance. If even the Kennedy administration, at the height of the Cold War, was prepared to withdraw from Europe during the 1963 crisis, why would a less cosmopolitan U.S. government remain involved indefinitely—when (from the American point of view) the provocation is far greater than it was in the time of de Gaulle and Adenauer, when the need to stay in Europe has receded with the collapse of the Soviet Union and the end of the Cold War, and when the United States is seen as getting so little benefit from its continuing commitment to the security of Europe? The Kennedy administration felt the Europeans could not have it both ways— they could not pursue an anti-American policy (very mild by today's standards) and still expect to have their security rest ultimately on a system based on American power. It is not hard to imagine that if attitudes remain as they are, the U.S. government, no matter who is running it, will eventually reach much the same conclusion: if the Europeans want to go their own way politically, they have every right to do so, but if they do, they should not expect America to guarantee their security. The feeling would be (as Eisenhower once put it) that the Europeans could not be allowed to make "a sucker out of Uncle Sam."[88]

And one does sense below the surface of political discourse a certain lingering resentment toward the two most important continental allies. One is struck, for example, by Kenneth Pollack's reference, in an important article he published in the *Atlantic Monthly* in early 2004, to the "shameful performance" of France and Germany in the run-up to the war.[89] European views about America—and the prevailing view in the post–Iraq war period is decidedly negative—are even closer to the surface. In such circumstances, it would seem natural, in the long run, for the two sides to drift apart. Alliances, of course, are not ends in them-

[88] Eisenhower-Norstad meeting, November 4, 1959, FRUS 1958–60, vol. 7, no. 1, p. 498.

[89] Pollack, "Spies, Lies, and Weapons." Pollack, one should note, was by no means a blind supporter of the Bush Iraq policy. In the same paragraph that he characterized French and German behavior as shameless, he also referred to the administration's "reckless" rush to war.

selves and they cannot be expected to last forever. They take shape for political reasons, and they end when political interests no longer warrant their continuation.

If it turns out that the Atlantic alliance is no longer viable, then that fact will have to be faced philosophically. Lord Salisbury, perhaps the greatest diplomatist of the late nineteenth century, once said that the "commonest error in politics is sticking to the carcasses of dead policies." The policy of maintaining the NATO alliance may indeed be a dying, if not yet a totally dead, policy, and if it is, it is important to begin thinking about the sort of successor regime that should be established and how the transition to that new regime should be managed. But whether the western alliance is to be saved or replaced by something else, the very fundamental issues the Iraq crisis has brought to the surface need to be analyzed seriously—certainly more seriously than they have been so far.

That analysis has to begin, I think, with the recognition that the core questions here have no easy or obvious answers—with the recognition, as Bernard Brodie put it when he was referring to the complex of problems relating to nuclear weapons, that we are now dealing with issues of "great intellectual difficulty, as well as other kinds of difficulty." I personally have been studying international politics for over forty years now, and the whole set of problems relating to terrorism, nuclear proliferation, biological weapons, and so on, I find extremely difficult—harder to answer, harder even to deal with, than any other set of issues relating to international politics that I have ever encountered, including the nuclear issue as we understood it during the Cold War.

In fact, the main point I am trying to make in this article is that the questions that we now have to deal with are extraordinarily difficult, and the answers are not nearly as obvious as people think. And if we are to get a sense for how difficult these issues are, it seems to me that some historical perspective might be of real value. We often hear people today, for example, talking about American imperialism and about NATO as an "instrument of American domination." But it would help, I think, if people remembered that the U.S. government never wanted to create an American empire in Europe as a kind of end in itself. It would help if people remembered that in the early years of the alliance the U.S. government in fact wanted the Europeans to come together and provide for their own defense—that it wanted Europe to become (to use Eisenhower's phrase) a "third great power bloc" in world affairs—and that it was only when it became clear that a purely European security system was not viable that the Americans reluctantly accepted the idea of a more or less permanent U.S. troop presence in Europe and thus of a security system based, in the final analysis, essentially on

American power.[90] There is a myth that America had imposed itself on Europe—that America from the start sought to dominate Europe, that NATO was a way of enabling America to control Europe, that America was a country whose sheer power had led it to pursue a policy of domination.[91] But the more one understands the real story, the more one is able to see how misleading and indeed how pernicious myths of that sort can be.

The Americans, of course, have a lot of thinking of their own to do—and that applies to Americans on both sides of the Iraq issue. But the Europeans are also going to have to think more deeply about this whole complex of issues. They will have to grapple with them more seriously as they come to see that the American presence in Europe can no longer be taken as an immutable fact of political life. And this is something that may well become clear to them in the not-too-distant future. If basic attitudes do not change dramatically, the two sides are almost bound to drift apart, and an American withdrawal from Europe will become a real possibility. If the Americans reach the conclusion that people in Europe are much too quick to engage in anti-American abuse and that the most important continental governments are more interested in "balancing" against the American "hyperpower" than in dealing seriously with real problems, then it is not hard to imagine the United States disengaging from Europe.

In 1963, President Kennedy said that the United States could "take care" of itself, and the Americans still believe that in the final analysis they do not need Europe. The point is recognized by some of the more serious European commentators. Helga Haftendorn, for example, noted in a recent article that "today the United States can easily do without NATO."[92] But for the Europeans, a U.S. withdrawal would open up a can of worms; a whole series of problems, relating especially to German nuclear weapons and to the relationship between Russia and the rest of Europe, would almost automatically come to the fore. Sooner or later, the Europeans are probably going to have to deal with the issue of whether they would really like the United States to withdraw—and from their point of view, the sooner this issue is addressed, the better. And if, after due consideration, they conclude that they

---

[90] See Trachtenberg, *Constructed Peace*, pp. 147–56.

[91] Note, for example, de Gaulle's reference in passing in his memoirs to America as "un pays que sa puissance sollicite vers la domination." Charles de Gaulle, *Mémoires d'espoir: Le renouveau* (Paris: Plon, 1970), p. 222.

[92] Helga Haftendorn, "One Year after 9/11: A Critical Appraisal of German-American Relations," The Thyssen German American Dialogue Seminar Series, American Institute for Contemporary German Studies, 2002 (http://www.aicgs.org/publications/PDF/haftendorn.pdf).

would like the Americans to stay, then they might want to grapple with the very difficult problems of the new world we now live in, in a more serious way than they have so far.

Looking back on the run-up to the Iraq war, one cannot help but be struck by the shallowness of the discussion—not just in Europe, but in the United States as well. And my assumption here is that this was a big part of the problem—that the reason why the Iraq affair took the course it did, and the reason why U.S.-European relations took the course they did, had a good deal to do with the way the fundamental issues were dealt with. The issues were discussed at much too superficial a level; the core issues were not argued out, with the result that in the end no real meeting of the minds was possible. But that does not mean that we cannot do better in the future. The issues that came up during the Iraq crisis are not going to go away for some time, if ever. My goal here was to show how some of them could be dealt with, but I have done little more than just scratch the surface. There is a lot more scholarly work to be done—and in particular a lot more *historical* work—and it is about time that we started doing it.

Index

Acheson, Dean (U.S. Secretary of State, 1949–53): aims at rollback (1950), 151–52; and Balkan precedents for Japan (1945), 102; complains about Eisenhower's "weakness," 252; dovishness in 1945, 91; and German rearmament (1950), 110–33, 137–40; and international law, 260n33; political personality of, 133–37

Adenauer, Konrad (West German chancellor, 1949–63): and America, 155–56; and Cuban missile crisis, 260n33; and European army (1950), 114–15; and France (1963), 281; and German nuclear weapons, 159; and NPT, 160

Arms control, 174–76, 181. *See also* Mutual and Balanced Force Reduction talks (MBFR); Nuclear Non–Proliferation Treaty (NPT); Nuclear Test Ban Treaty; Preventing Nuclear War, U.S.–Soviet Agreement on; Strategic Arms Limitation Talks (SALT)

Aron, Raymond, 25, 26n56, 61, 198n54

Bahr, Egon (chief advisor to Willy Brandt), 156–57, 167; and ending the bloc system, 173n48, 185n9

Balance of Payments problem. *See* International monetary problem

Balance of Power thinking: attacked by Wilson, 16–17; at the Congress of Vienna, 16, 32; in the eighteenth century, 15, 23–24, 28–30, 33

Balance of Power mechanism: limited effect of, 37–38

Bérard, Armand, 114–15

Berlin issue, 152, 154–57, 260–62

Bevin, Ernest, 87, 105n120, 110

Biological theory, and political behavior, 55–57

Bismarck, Otto von, 9–12

Bradley, General Omar (U.S. JCS Chairman, 1949–53), 112, 124, 130, 133

Brandt, Willy (West German foreign minister, 1967–69, then chancellor, 1969–74),
156–57, 173–74; attitude toward U.S., 167; and nuclear cooperation with France, 159n8, 236; U.S. attitude toward, 184–85, 184n8

Bretton Woods system. *See* International monetary problem

Brezhnev, Leonid (General Secretary of the Communist Party of the Soviet Union, 1964–82), 170–71

Brodie, Bernard, 61, 65, 309

Bulgarian question in 1945, 80–90, 101–106

Bush, George W.: strategy of "preemption," 247–49, 277

Byrnes, James (U.S. Secretary of State, 1945–47): general policy, 91–93, 106–109; and German question, 93–95; and Japan, 101–103; at London Council of Foreign Ministers (September 1945), 84–88; and Moscow agreement (December 1945), 89–91, 100–101, 104–107; and Romania and Bulgaria, 82–87, 101

Byroade, Henry (Director, U.S. State Department Bureau of German Affairs in 1950): plan for German rearmament, 120–24, 128

Carr, E.H., 27n59, 59

Castlereagh, Lord (British foreign secretary, 1812–22), 15n22, 16–17, 32, 269n58

Cheney, Richard (U.S. Vice President, 2001–2009), 282–83

China: and America (Nixon period), 176–80, 217; conflict with USSR, 172–73; as issue in 1941, 271–73; and North Korean nuclear question, 267–68, 269n.58; possible attack on Chinese nuclear facilities, by U.S., 255–56; possible attack on Chinese nuclear facilities, by USSR, 256n23

Chirac, Jacques (French president, 1995–2007), 282–86, 288

Churchill, Winston: and Agadir crisis, 21n45; and Polish question, 80n37; and preventive war, 250, 279

Clausewitz, Carl von, 28
Clinton, Bill (U.S. president, 1993–2001), 263–67
Cold War, viii, 25–26, 32–34, 39–40; interpretation of origins of, 69–72
Connally, John (U.S. Treasury Secretary, 1971–72), 193–97
Connally, Tom (Chair, Senate Foreign Relations Committee, 1941–49), 299
Cooperation, problem of, 19, 21–22, 50–51
Couve de Murville, Maurice (French foreign minister, 1958–68), 151, 188n22, 237n209
Cuban missile crisis (1962), 155–56, 255–62, 279–80: and international law, 255–60, 257n24, 260n33; and United Nations, 60–61

de Gaulle, Charles (French president, 1958–69): and America, 237, 281, 282, 310n91; and Cuban missile crisis, 260, 307; and German nuclear weapons, 161; and German reunification, 156; and international monetary problem, 190, 196, 199n59; Nixon's and Kissinger's admiration for, 183, 187, 209; nuclear strategy of, 224n151, 236n208; and preventive war (1954), 250
Debré, Michel (French defense minister, 1969–73), 188n22, 222, 223, 225n154, 234
Dulles, John Foster (U.S. Secretary of State, 1953–59): at London conference (1947), 84–86; and nuclear sharing, 150–52; and Turkish Straits, 91; and U.N. Charter, 298

Eisenhower, Dwight (U.S. president, 1953–61), 98, 308, 309; and MC 48, 143–46; and nuclear sharing, 150–53; and preemption, 145; and preventive war, 252–54
English School of international relations theory, 45n4
Erhard, Ludwig (West German chancellor, 1963–66), 159
Europe, unification of: and France, 113–15, 199, 204, 211, 213–14, 235–37; and U.S., 113–14, 140–41, 200–203, 233

Fénelon, François de Salignac de la Mothe, 15, 19n35, 33, 41, 42, 54, 63
France: and America, Bush period, 282–

86; and America, Kennedy period, 155, 281–82; and America, Nixon period, 183–243; and "building Europe," 113–15, 199, 204, 211, 213–14, 235–37; and the "condominium"problem, 214–15, 219, 223, 241; and defense of Europe, 223–25, 235–36; and German question, 156, 173n48, 186, 235–37; and German rearmament (1950, 1954), 111–15, 148; and international monetary problem, 196–99, 204–205; and Iraq crisis (2003), 282–88, 304–305; and NATO strategy (1954), 146–49; nuclear relationship of, with U.S., 187–88, 209–11, 220–25, 236
Freedman, Lawrence, 166
Friedman, Milton, 191, 192
Fulbright, J. William (chair, U.S. Senate Foreign Relations Committee, 1959–74): on illegality of blockade, 260n33; urges invasion of Cuba, 280

Galley, Robert (French armed forces minister, 1973–74), 210, 220–25; on U.S. nuclear alert (1973), 226n157
German Empire, foreign policy of: under Bismarck, 9–12; before World War I, 13
Germany, Federal Republic of: and nuclear weapons, 154–61, 159n8, 235–36; policy toward USSR (Ostpolitik), 157–58, 167, 173–74; rearmament of (1950), 110–41; and U.S., 154–57, 161, 167, 282–85
Giscard d'Estaing, Valéry (French finance minister, 1962–66, 1969–74; French president, 1974–81), 199n59, 220, 222n143
Gladstone, William, 139–40
Gomulka, Wladyslaw (First Secretary of Polish communist party, 1943–48, 1956–70), 77–78
Great Britain, foreign policy of: in 1943–45, 72, 74n16, 80, 99; before World War I, 13, 62–63
Gruenther, General Alfred (NATO commander, 1953–56), 143–46

Habermas, Jürgen, 45n3, 294n40
Haftendorn, Helga, 310
Harriman, Averell (U.S. ambassador to USSR, 1943–46), 78, 101–106
Heath, Edward (British prime minister, 1970–74), 208n93

Henkin, Louis, 297
Hitler, Adolf, 38, 82, 275, 279
Hobbes, Thomas, 3–4n1, 47, 51, 53–55, 278n74
Hopkins, Harry, mission to Moscow (1945), 73, 74, 77, 79, 80, 85, 86, 87, 89
Hume, David, 29

Ignatieff, Michael, 302
International law: and Cuban missile crisis, 255–60, 257n24, 260n33; permissibility of the use of force under, 293–304
International monetary problem (1969–73), 188–205
Iraq crisis (2003), 281–311; impact on NATO alliance, 304–11; inspections issue, 291–93; and nuclear weapons, 283, 287–91; question of permissibility of use of force, 293–304
Italy, question of occupation regime in (1943), 98–99

Japan, question of control of, in 1945, 91–92, 101–6
Jervis, Robert, 7n9, 23n47, 31, 32n75, 34n80, 50, 100n108
Jobert, Michel (French foreign minister, 1973–74), 207–11, 213–16, 219n135, 233, 237n209, 240n215
Joffe, Josef, 167, 169, 302n68, 304
Johnson, Lyndon (U.S. president, 1963–69), 161, 166, 174–77

Kennan, George, 6, 42, 79, 92, 106–7, 250, 276
Kennedy, John (U.S. president, 1961–63): and Acheson, 135; basic policy, 154–56, 281–82, 310; and Kissinger, 183n3; and preventive war question, 255–57, 260–62
Kennedy, Robert, 255, 257–58
Kiesinger, Kurt Georg (West German chancellor, 1966–69), 160
Kissinger, Henry: and "absolute security," 15; and Brezhnev, 170–71; and China, 176–77, 179–80, 217, 218n130; "directorate" plan, 239–40; and European unity, 201–3; and France (general), 183–87, 206, 211, 213, 216–20, 234, 238; and France (nuclear relations), 187–88, 209–11, 220–25, 235–36; general policy, 176–82; and Germany, 160, 168n32, 181–82;

184; and Middle East, 180, 226–33, 240–41; and Mutual and Balanced Force Reduction talks, 218–19; and NATO integration, 187–88n22; and nuclear defense of Europe, 166, 241, 242n222; and Preventing Nuclear War agreement, 216–18; and "Year of Europe," 205–13, 215
Korean War, effect of, on German rearmament, 116, 119, 127
Kosciusko-Morizet, Jacques (French ambassador to U.S., 1972–77), 206–9, 216n128, 226n157, 233, 242

London Conference of Foreign Ministers (September 1945), 84–89
Lundestad, Geir, 83–84

MacArthur, General Douglas (Supreme allied commander in Japan, 1945–51), 102–3
McAllister, James, 93
McCloy, John (U.S. High Commissioner in Germany, 1949–52): and German rearmament, 112, 127, 132
McNamara, Robert: and nuclear defense of Europe, 166
MC 48. See NATO strategy (1954)
Mearsheimer, John, 4, 18–20, 36, 39, 50
Mélandri, Pierre, 234
Mendès France, Pierre (French prime minister, 1954–55), 148–49
Metternich, Prince Klemens von (Austrian foreign minister, 1809–48), 16–17, 32, 269n58
Middle East conflict, 179–80, 226–33, 240–41
Mikolajczyk, Stanislaw, 73, 77–79
Molotov, Vyacheslav (Soviet foreign minister, 1939–49): and Byrnes reparation plan, 94, 96n88; and Japan, 102; at London conference (1947), 84–88, 91; meeting with Truman (1945), 73; and spheres of influence, 81–82, 98, 100
Morgenthau, Hans, 25, 39n89, 297
Moscow foreign ministers' meeting (December 1945), 100–101, 104–7
Mutual and Balanced Force Reduction talks (MBFR), 215–19

Nitze, Paul, 130–32, 134, 135n75, 136–37, 251–52

Nixon, Richard (U.S. president, 1969–74): and Acheson, 133n68; and economic issues, 193–96, 200–202; and France, 183–85, 187; general policy, 176–80; and nuclear defense of Europe, 166–67

North Atlantic Treaty Organization (NATO): German ideas about possible end of, 173–74, 184, 185n9; Kissinger and "theological" discussions about, 187–88n22; plan for strengthening (1950), 110–11, 116–33; post–Cold War expansion of, 40, 307. *See also* NATO strategy (1954); NATO nuclear problem (1963–89)

NATO strategy (1954), 142–53; and preemption, 144–45; and predelegation, 145–46; and nuclear sharing, 150–52

NATO nuclear problem (1963–89), 158–68, 181, 241–42, 242n222

North Korean nuclear problem, 262–70

NSC 68, 133–34, 251–52

Nuclear Non-Proliferation Treaty (NPT), 157–58, 160–61; German dislike for, 160, 215n125; North Korea and, 262, 267n54

Nuclear Test Ban Treaty (1963), 156, 256

Nuclear weapons. *See* Arms control; Iraq crisis (2003); NATO strategy; NATO nuclear problem; North Korean nuclear problem; Preventive war thinking

Oppenheim, Lasso, 297

Order, problem of, in international politics, 44–65

Pechatnov, Vladimir, 89

Perry, William (U.S. Secretary of Defense, 1994–97), 263–67

Philosophy of science, implications of, for international relations theory, 49–50

Pierre-Brossolette, Claude, 197–98

Poland, imposition of Communist rule in, 75–78, 107n128; U.S. and British reaction to, 73–75, 78–80, 85–89

Pollack, Kenneth, 308

Pompidou, Georges (French president, 1969–74): and Arab–Israeli war (1974), 226n157, 228; and "building Europe," 199, 213–14, 235–37; "condominium" fears, 215, 219, 219n137, 235; and European defense system, 235–36, 235n204; interest in wheat and oil consumers' cartels, 230n179; and international monetary problem, 196–99, 204–5; and Soviet threat, 223; "strategic testament," 233–34; and U.S., 186–87, 214n120, 218, 235–37; and "Year of Europe," 206–11

Potsdam Conference (1945): and Bulgaria and Romania, 80–82; and German question, 93–96; and Polish question, 79–80

Powell, Colin, 284–85, 295, 306

Preventing Nuclear War (PNW), U.S.-Soviet agreement on (1973), 215–18, 219n135

Preventive war thinking: under Brezhnev, 256n23; under Bush, George W., 247–49, 277, 283; and Churchill, 250, 279; under Clinton, 262–70; under Eisenhower, 252–54; in Germany before 1914, 253–54; in international relations theory, 23–24, 35, 278; under Kennedy, 254–62; under Roosevelt, 269n58, 270–77; under Truman, 250–52

Putin, Vladimir, 300–301

Raimond, Jean-Bernard, 215n125, 219n136

Realism: and the causes of war, 3–8, 18–20, 278; in international relations theory, 3–43, 50–51; "offensive" vs. "defensive" realism, 4–5, 18–20; traditional realism, 6

Ridgway, Matthew, 146

Romanian question in 1945, 80–90, 101–6

Roosevelt, Franklin, 38, 72–73, 99n99; and "enforced disarmament," 269n58; policy of, in 1941, 270–76, 302

Rousseau, Jean-Jacques, 22–24, 35

Rumsfeld, Donald, 248, 291

Russia, foreign policy of: before World War I, 13–14, 254, 278. *See also* Soviet Union

SACEUR (Supreme Allied Commander, Europe), 143–49; predelegation of war-making power to, 31n72, 145–46, 149

Saddam Hussein, 283, 287, 291

Salisbury, Lord, 10, 13, 30–31, 140, 309

Scheel, Walter (West German foreign minister, 1969–74), 231–33

Schelling, Thomas, 164, 181, 290

Schlesinger, Arthur, 248n4, 255, 257, 259n32

Schlesinger, James (U.S. Secretary of Defense, 1973–75), 163n18, 165n22, 220–21, 224

Schmidt, Helmut (West German defense minister, then finance minister, then chancellor, 1969–82), 201, 212

Schröder, Gerhard (German chancellor, 1998–2005), 282–85, 294n42

Schroeder, Paul, 16n25, 31, 36, 248n2, 254n15

Schuman, Robert, 110–12; Schuman Plan, 115, 121

Scowcroft, Brent, 263–64

Security dilemma, 19, 28, 33, 34, 50–51; Cold War as, 32–34

Shultz, George, 192–96, 200–204, 220, 275n71, 283

Slocombe, Walter, 267

Sorensen, Theodore, 255

Soutou, Georges-Henri, 186, 210, 223, 234

Soviet Union: conflict with China, 172; and division of Germany (1945), 95–97, 95n87, 99; foreign policy of, in 1945, 69–71, 88–89, 95–100, 108–9; and German nuclear weapons, 160–61, 172; and German rearmament (1950), 112–13; policy toward West under Brezhnev, 168–76, 178–79; and possibility of a Europe–only war, 162

Soviet Union, military buildup under Brezhnev, 169–70; political and economic change within, 170–72

Stalin, Josif: policy in 1945, 69–71, 95–109; and power politics, 26; and spheres of influence, 95–98

Stark, Admiral Harold, 271, 273, 273–74n66

Strategic Arms Limitation Talks (SALT), 180–81, 215

Strauss, Franz-Josef, 160, 206, 215n125

Truman, Harry: and eastern Europe (1945), 26–27, 73–74, 80–82, 89; and German rearmament (1950), 119n27, 124, 128–29; and preventive war, 251, 251n7

Ulbricht, Walter, 96

United Nations: Charter of, and its meaning, 257n24, 293–304; and Cuban missile crisis, 60–61, 257n24, 259; and Iraq crisis (2003), 283–85

United States, foreign policy of: under Bush, 247–49, 282–86; and China, 176–80, 217, 255–56; and defense of Europe, 142–53, 158–67, 181–82, 242n222; under Eisenhower, 252–54, 309; and European integration, 113–14, 140–41, 200–203, 233; and German nuclear weapons, 154, 156, 161; and German Ostpolitik, 184–85; and German rearmament (1950), 110–41; and Iraq crisis (2003), 282–86; under Johnson, 174–76; under Kennedy, 60, 152, 154–56, 238, 254–62, 281–82, 310; and Middle East, 179–80, 226–33, 240–41; under Nixon, 176–243; preventive war thinking in, 247–80, 283; under Roosevelt, 14, 38, 72–73, 269n58, 270–76, 302; and spheres of influence, 93–95, 103–8, 154; under Truman, 26–27, 71–74, 79–95, 98–99, 101–41, 249–52; and Vietnam War, 63–64; under Wilson, 16–17

Védrine, Hubert, 305

Versailles, Treaty of, 17

Vienna, Congress of, 15–17, 32, 269n58

Vietnam War, 63–64, 162, 178

Villepin, Dominique de, 284–85

Waltz, Kenneth: and America's post–Cold War policy, 40–41; and causes of war, 5, 18, 30, 36; and the Cold War, 25, 39–40; and cooperation, 22, 31; and issues of method, 48–49; and nature of theory, 48–49; and nuclear proliferation, 289; and the problem of order, 44–45

Walzer, Michael, 303, 304

Welles, Sumner, 272–73

Wendt, Alexander, 3

Wight, Martin, 19n34, 30, 45n4, 47–48, 64–65

Wilson, Woodrow, 3, 16–17, 42

Wolfowitz, Paul, 305–6

Yalta Conference (1945), 72–73, 86, 87; Stalin's "joke" at, about free elections in Poland, 107n128

Year of Europe affair (1973), 205–13, 242